THE EMPIRE OF RUSSIA.

THE MONARCHIES

OF

CONTINENTAL EUROPE.

THE

EMPIRE OF RUSSIA;

FROM THE

REMOTEST PERIODS TO THE PRESENT TIME.

BY

JOHN S. C. ABBOTT.

BOSTON:

GRAVES AND YOUNG,

24 CORNHILL.

STEREOTYPED BY
T. B. SMITH & SON
82 & 84 BEEKMAN-ST

PREFACE.

THE world is now too busy to read voluminous history. The interminable details of battles, and the petty intrigues of courtiers and mistresses, have lost their interest. In this volume it has been our object to trace perspicuously the path which Russia has trod from earliest infancy to the present hour. The career of this empire has been so wild and wonderful that the historian can have no occasion to call in the aid of fancy for the embellishment of his narrative.

The author has not deemed it necessary to incumber his pages with notes to substantiate his statements. The renowned Russian historian, Karamsin, who wrote under the patronage of Alexander I., gives ample authentication to all the facts which are stated up to the reign of that emperor. His voluminous history, in classic beauty, is unsurpassed by any of the annals of Greece or Rome. It has been admirably translated into French by Messrs. St. Thomas and Jauffret in eleven imperial quarto volumes. In the critical citations of this author, the reader, curious in such researches, will find every fact in the early history of Russia, here stated, confirmed.

There are but few valuable works upon Russia in the English language. Nearly all, which can be relied upon as authorities, are written either in French or German. The writer would refer those who seek a more minute acquaintance with this empire, now rising so rapidly in importance, first of all to Karamsin. The "Histoire Philosophique et Politique de Russie Depuis les Temps les Plus Reculés Jusqu'au Nos Jours, par J. Esneaux,"

Paris, five volumes, is a valuable work. The "Histoire de Russie par Pierre Charles Levesque," eight volumes, is discriminating and reliable. The various volumes of William Tooke upon Russian history in general, and upon the reign of Catharine, contain much information.

It is only since the reign of Peter the Great that Russia has begun to attract much attention among the enlightened nations of Europe. Voltaire's life of this most renowned of the Russian sovereigns, at its first publication, attracted much notice. Since then, many books have been written upon fragments of Russian history and individual reigns. From most of these the author has selected such events as have appeared to him most instructive and best adapted to give the reader a clear conception of the present condition and future prospects of this gigantic empire. The path she has trod, since her first emergence into civilization from the chaos of barbarism, can be very distinctly traced, and one can easily count the concentric accretions of her growth. This narrative reveals the mistakes which have overwhelmed her with woe, and the wisdom which has, at times, secured for Russia peace and prosperity.

In writing these histories of the monarchies of Continental Europe, the author has no wish to conceal his abhorrence of aristocratic usurpation. Believing in the universal brotherhood of man, his sympathies are most cordially with the oppressed masses. If the people are weak and debased, the claim is only the more urgent upon the powerful and the wise to act the part of elder brothers, holding out the helping hand to those who have fallen. The author feels grateful for the reception which the first number of this series, the Empire of Austria, has received from the American public. He hopes that this volume will not prove less interesting or instructive. In the course of a few months it will be followed by the History of Italy.

CONTENTS.

CHAPTER I.

PARENTAGE AND BIRTH OF RUSSIA.

FROM 500 B. C. TO A. D. 910.

PAGE

CHAPTER II.

GROWTH AND CONSOLIDATION OF RUSSIA.

FROM 910 TO 973.

CHAPTER III.

REIGNS OF VLADIMIR, YAROSLAF, YSIASLAF AND VSEVOLOD.

FROM 973 TO 1092.

CHAPTER IV.

YEARS OF WAR AND WOE.

From 1092 to 1167.

CHAPTER V.

MSTISLAF AND ANDRE.

From 1167 to 1212.

CHAPTER VI.

THE GRAND PRINCES OF VLADIMIR, AND THE INVASION OF GHENGHIS KAHN.

From 1212 to 1238.

CHAPTER VII.

THE SWAY OF THE TARTAR PRINCES.

From 1238 to 1304.

CHAPTER VIII.

RESURRECTION OF THE RUSSIAN MONARCHY.

FROM 1304 TO 1380.

CHAPTER IX.

DMITRI, VASSALI, AND THE MOGOL TAMERLANE

FROM 1380 TO 1462.

CHAPTER X.

THE ILLUSTRIOUS IVAN III.

FROM 1462 TO 1480.

CHAPTER XI.

THE REIGN OF VASSILI.

From 1480 to 1533.

CHAPTER XII.

IVAN IV.—HIS MINORITY.

From 1533 to 1546.

CHAPTER XIII.

THE REIGN OF IVAN IV.

From 1546 to 1552.

CHAPTER XIV.

THE REIGN OF IVAN IV.—CONTINUED.

From 1552 to 1557.

CHAPTER XV.

THE ABDICATION OF IVAN IV.

FROM 1557 TO 1582.

CHAPTER XVI.

THE STORMS OF HEREDITARY SUCCESSION.

FROM 1582 TO 1608.

CHAPTER XVII.

A CHANGE OF DYNASTY.

FROM 1608 TO 1680.

CHAPTER XVIII.

THE REGENCY OF SOPHIA.

From 1680 to 1697.

CHAPTER XIX.

PETER THE GREAT.

From 1697 to 1702.

CHAPTER XX.

CONQUESTS AND ACHIEVEMENTS OF PETER THE GREAT.

From 1702 to 1718.

CHAPTER XXI.

THE TRIAL AND CONDEMNATION OF ALEXIS, AND DEATH OF THE TZAR.

From 1718 to 1725.

CHAPTER XXII.

THE REIGNS OF CATHARINE I., ANNE, THE INFANT IVAN AND ELIZABETH.

FROM 1725 TO 1762.

CHAPTER XXIII.

PETER III. AND HIS BRIDE.

FROM 1728 TO 1762.

CHAPTER XXIV.

THE CONSPIRACY; AND ACCESSION OF CATHARINE II.

FROM 1762 TO 1765.

CHAPTER XXV.

REIGN OF CATHARINE II.

FROM 1765 TO 1774.

CHAPTER XXVI.

REIGN OF CATHARINE II.

FROM 1774 TO 1781.

CHAPTER XXVII.

TERMINATION OF THE REIGN OF CATHARINE II.

FROM 1781 TO 1786.

CHAPTER XXVIII.

THE REIGN OF PAUL I.

FROM 1796 TO 1801.

CHAPTER XXIX.

ASSASSINATION OF PAUL AND ACCESSION OF ALEXANDER.

From 1801 to 1807.

CHAPTER XXX.

REIGN OF ALEXANDER I.

From 1807 to 1825.

CHAPTER XXXI.

NICHOLAS.

From 1825 to 1855.

CHAPTER I.

PARENTAGE AND BIRTH OF RUSSIA.

FROM 500 B. C. TO A. D. 910.

PRIMEVAL RUSSIA.—EXPLORATIONS OF THE GREEKS.—SCYTHIAN INVASION.—CHARACTER OF THE SCYTHIANS.—SARMATIA.—ASSAULTS UPON THE ROMAN EMPIRE.—IRRUPTION OF THE ALAINS.—CONQUESTS OF TRAJAN.—THE GOTHIC INVASION.—THE HUNS.—THEIR CHARACTER AND ASPECT.—THE DEVASTATIONS OF ATTILA.—THE AVARS.—RESULTS OF COMMINGLINGS OF THESE TRIBES.—NORMANS.—BIRTH OF THE RUSSIAN EMPIRE.—THE THREE SOVEREIGNS RURIK, SINEOUS AND TRUVOR.—ADVENTURES OF ASCOLOD AND DIR.—INTRODUCTION OF CHRISTIANITY.—USURPATION OF OLEG.—HIS CONQUESTS.—EXPEDITION AGAINST CONSTANTINOPLE.

THOSE vast realms of northern Europe, now called Russia, have been inhabited for a period beyond the records of history, by wandering tribes of savages. These barbaric hordes have left no monuments of their existence. The annals of Greece and of Rome simply inform us that they were there. Generations came and departed, passing through life's tragic drama, and no one has told their story.

About five hundred years before the birth of our Saviour, the Greeks, sailing up the Bosphorus and braving the storms of the Black Sea, began to plant their colonies along its shores. Instructed by these colonists, Herodotus, who wrote about four hundred and forty years before Christ, gives some information respecting the then condition of interior Russia. The first great irruption into the wastes of Russia, of which history gives us any record, was about one hundred years before our Saviour. An immense multitude of conglomerated tribes, taking the general name of Scythians, with their wives and their children, their flocks and their herds, and their warriors, fiercer than wolves, crossed the Volga, and took possession of the whole country between the Don and the Danube. These barbarians did not molest the Greek colonies, but, on the contrary, were glad to learn of them many of the rudiments of civilization. Some of these tribes retained their ancestral habits of wandering herdsmen, and, with their flocks, traversed the vast and treeless plains, where they found ample pasture. Others selecting sunny and fertile valleys, scattered their seed and cultivated the soil. Thus the Scythians were divided into two quite distinct classes, the herdsmen and the laborers.

The tribes who then peopled the vast wilds of northern Europe and Asia, though almost innumerable, and of different languages and customs, were all called, by the Greeks, Scythians, as we have given the general name of Indians to all the tribes who formerly ranged the forests of North America. The Scythians were as ferocious a race as earth has ever known. They drank the blood of their enemies; tanned their skins for garments; used their skulls for drinking cups; and worshiped a sword as the image or emblem of their favorite deity, the God of War. Philip of Macedon was the first who put any check upon their proud spirit. He conquered them in a decisive battle, and thus taught them that they were not invincible. Alexander the Great assailed them and spread the terror of his arms throughout all the region between the Danube and the Dnieper. Subsequently the Roman legions advanced to the Euxine, and planted their eagles upon the heights of the Caucasus.

The Roman historians seem to have dropped the Scythian name, and they called the whole northern expanse of Europe and Asia, Sarmatia, and the barbarous inhabitants Sarmatians. About the time of our Saviour, some of these fierce tribes from the banks of the Theiss and the Danube, commenced their assaults upon the frontiers of the Roman empire. This was the signal for that war of centuries, which terminated in the overthrow of the throne of the Cæsars. The Roman

Senate, enervated by luxury, condescended to purchase peace of these barbarians, and nations of savages, whose names are now forgotten, exacted tribute, under guise of payment for alliance, from the proud empire. But neither bribes, nor alliances, nor the sword in the hands of enervated Rome, could effectually check the incursions of these bands, who were ever emerging, like wolves, from the mysterious depths of the North.

In the haze of those distant times and remote realms, we catch dim glimpses of locust legions, emerging from the plains and the ravines between the Black Sea and the Caspian, and sweeping like a storm cloud over nearly all of what is now called Russia. These people, to whom the name of Alains was given, had no fixed habitations; they conveyed their women and children in rude carts. Their devastations were alike extended over Europe and Asia, and in the ferocity of their assaults they were as insensible to death as wild beasts could be.

In the second century, the emperor Trajan conquered and took possession of the province of Dacia, which included all of lower Hungary, Transylvania, Moldavia, Wallachia and Bessarabia. The country was divided into Roman provinces, over each of which a prefect was established. In the third century, the Goths, from the shores of the Baltic, came rushing over the wide arena, with the howling of wolves and their gnashing of teeth. They trampled down all opposition, with their war knives drove out the Romans, crossed the Black Sea in their rude vessels, and spread conflagration and death throughout the most flourishing cities and villages of Bythinia, Gallacia and Cappadocia. The famous temple of Diana at Ephesus, these barbarians committed to the flames. They overran all Greece and took Athens by storm. As they were about to destroy the precious libraries of Athens, one of their chieftains said,

"Let us leave to the Greeks their books, that they, in

reading them may forget the arts of war; and that we thus may more easily be able to hold them in subjection."

These Goths established an empire, extending from the Black Sea to the Baltic, and which embraced nearly all of what is now European Russia. Towards the close of the fourth century, another of these appalling waves of barbaric inundation rolled over northern Europe. The Huns, emerging from the northern frontiers of China, traversed the immense intervening deserts, and swept over European Russia, spreading everywhere flames and desolation. The historians of that day seem to find no language sufficiently forcible to describe the hideousness and the ferocity of these savages. They pressed down on the Roman empire as merciless as wolves, and the Cæsars turned pale at the recital of their deeds of blood.

It is indeed a revolting picture. which contemporaneous history gives us of these barbarians. In their faces was concentrated the ugliness of the hyena and the baboon. They tattooed their cheeks, to prevent the growth of their beards. They were short, thick-set, and with back bones curved almost into a semicircle. Herbs, roots and raw meat they devoured, tearing their food with their teeth or hewing it with their swords. To warm and soften their meat, they placed it under their saddles when riding. Nearly all their lives they passed on horseback. Wandering incessantly over the vast plains, they had no fixed habitations, but warmly clad in the untanned skins of beasts, like the beasts they slept wherever the night found them. They had no religion nor laws, no conception of ideas of honor; their langnage was a wretched jargon, and in their nature there seemed to be no moral sense to which compassion or mercy could plead.

Such were the Huns as described by the ancient historians. The Goths struggled against them in vain. They were crushed and subjugated. The king of the Goths, Hermanric, in chagrin and despair, committed suicide, that he might escape slavery. Thousands of the Goths, in their terror, crowded down into the Roman province of Thrace, now the Turkish province of Romania. The empire, then in its decadence, could not drive them back, and they obtained a permanent foothold there. The Huns thus attained the supremacy throughout all of northern Europe. There were then very many tribes of diverse names peopling these vast realms, and incessant wars were waged between them. The domination which the Huns attained was precarious, and not distinctly defined.

The terrible Attila ere long appears as the king of these Huns, about the middle of the fifth century. This wonderful barbarian extended his sway from the Volga to the Rhine, and from the Bosphorus to the shores of the Baltic. Whereever he appeared, blood flowed in torrents. He swept the valley of the Danube with flame and sword, destroying cities, fortresses and villages, and converting the whole region into a desert. At the head of an army of seven hundred thousand men, he plunged all Europe into dismay. Both the Eastern and Western empire were compelled to pay him tribute. He even invaded Gaul, and upon the plains of Chalons was defeated in one of the most bloody battles ever fought in Europe. Contemporary historians record that one hundred and six thousand dead were left upon the field. With the death of Attila, the supremacy of the Huns vanished. The irruption of the Huns was a devastating scourge, which terrified the world. Whole nations were exterminated in their march, until at last the horrible apparition disappeared, almost as suddenly as it arose.

With the disappearance of the Huns, central Russia presents to us the aspect of a vast waste, thinly peopled, with the wrecks of nations and tribes, debased and feeble, living upon the cattle they herded, and occasionally cultivating the soil. And now there comes forward upon this theater of violence and of blood another people, called the Sclavonians, more energetic and more intelligent than any who had preceded them. The origin of the Sclavonians is quite lost in the haze of distance, and in the savage wilds where they first appeared. The few traditions which have been gleaned respecting them are of very little authority.

From about the close of the fifth century the inhabitants of the whole region now embraced by European Russia, were called Sclavonians; and yet it appears that these Sclavonians consisted of many nations, rude and warlike, with various distinctive names. They soon began to crowd upon the Roman empire, and became more formidable than the Goths or the Huns had been. Wading through blood they seized province after province of the empire, destroying and massacring often in mere wantonness. The emperor Justinian was frequently compelled to purchase peace with them and to bribe them to alliance.

And now came another wave of invasion, bloody and overwhelming. The Avars, from the north of China, swept over Asia, seized all the provinces on the Black Sea, overran Greece, and took possession of most of the country between the Volga and the Elbe. The Sclavonians of the Danube, however, successfully resisted them, and maintained their independence. Generations came and went as these hordes, wild, degraded and wretched, swept these northern wilds, in debasement and cruelty rivaling the wolves which howled in their forests. They have left no traces behind them, and the few records of their joyless lives which history has preserved, are merely the gleanings of uncertain tradition. The thinking mind pauses in sadness to contemplate the spectacle of these weary ages, when his brother man was the most ferocious of beasts, and when all the discipline of life tended only to sink him into deeper abysses of brutality and misery. There is here a problem in the divine government which no human wisdom can solve. There is consolation only in the announcement that what we know not now, we shall know hereafter. All these diverse nations blending have formed the present Russians.

Along the shores of the Baltic, these people assumed the name of Scandinavians, and subsequently Normans. Toward the close of the eighth century, the Normans filled Europe with the renown of their exploits, and their banners bade defiance even to the armies of Charlemagne. Early in the ninth century they ravaged France, Italy, Scotland, England, and passed over to Ireland, where they built cities which remain to the present day. "There is no manner of doubt," writes M. Karamsin in his history of Russia, "that five hundred years before Christopher Columbus, they had discovered North America, and instituted commerce with the natives."

It is not until the middle of the ninth century, that we obtain any really reliable information respecting the inhabitants of central Russia. They are described as a light-complexioned, flaxen-haired race, robust, and capable of great endurance. Their huts were cheerless, affording but little shelter, and they lived upon the coarsest food, often devouring their meat raw. The Greeks expressed astonishment at their agility in climbing precipitous cliffs, and admired the hardihood with which they plunged through bogs, and swam the most rapid and swollen streams. He who had the most athletic vigor was the greatest man, and all the ambition and energy of the nation were expended in the acquisition of strength and agility.

They are ever described as strangers to fear, rushing unthinkingly upon certain death. They were always ready to accept combat with the Roman legions. Entire strangers to military strategy, they made no attacks in drilled lines or columns, but the whole tumultuous mass, in wild disorder rushed upon the foe, with the most desperate daring, having no guide but their own ferocity and the chieftains who led small bands. Their weapons consisted of swords, javelins and poisoned arrows, and each man carried a heavy shield. At they crossed the Danube in their bloody forays, incited by love of plunder, the inhabitants of the Roman villages fled before them. When pursued by an invincible force they would relinquish life rather than their booty, even when the plunder was of a kind totally valueless in their savage homes. The ancient annals depict in appalling colors the cruelties they exercised upon their captives. They were, however, as patient in endurance as they were merciless in infliction. No keenness of torture could force from them a cry of pain.

Yet these people, so ferocious, are described as remarkably amiable among themselves, seldom quarreling, honest and truthful, and practicing hospitality with truly patriarchal grace. Whenever they left home, the door was unfastened and food was left for any chance wayfarer. A guest was treated as a heavenly messenger, and was guided on his way with the kindest expressions for his welfare.

The females, as in all barbaric countries, were exposed to every indignity. All the hard labor of life was thrown upon them. When the husband died, the widow was compelled to cast herself upon the funeral pile which consumed his remains. It is said that this barbarous custom, which Christianity abolished, was introduced to prevent the wife from secretly killing her husband. The wife was also regarded as the slave of the husband, and they imagined that if she died at the same time with her husband, she would serve him in another world. The wives often followed their husbands to the wars. From infancy the boys were trained to fight, and were taught that nothing was more disgraceful than to forgive an injury.

A mother was permitted, if she wished, to destroy her female children; but the boys were all preserved to add to the military strength of the nation. It was lawful, also, for the children to put their parents to death when they had become infirm and useless. "Behold," exclaims a Russian historian, "how a people naturally kind, when deprived of the light of revelation can remorselessly outrage nature, and surpass in cruelty the most ferocious animals."

In different sections of this vast region there were different degrees of debasement, influenced by causes no longer known. A tribe called Drevliens, Nestor states, lived in the most gloomy forests with the beasts and like the beasts. They ate any food which a pig would devour, and had as little idea of marriage as have sheep or goats. Among the Sclavonians generally there appears to have been no aristocracy. Each family was an independent republic. Different tribes occasionally met to consult upon questions of common interest, when the men of age, and who had acquired reputation for wisdom, guided in counsel.

Gradually during the progress of their wars an aristocracy arose. Warriors of renown became chiefs, and created for themselves posts of authority and honor. By prowess and plunder they acquired wealth. In their incursions into the empire, they saw the architecture of Greece and Rome, and thus incited, they began to rear castles and fortresses. He who was recognized as the leading warrior in time of battle, retained his authority in the days of peace, which were very few. The castle became necessary for the defense of the tribe or clan, and the chieftain became the feudal noble, invested with unlimited power. At one time every man who was rich enough to own a horse was deemed a noble. The first power recognized was only military authority. But the progress of civilization developed the absolute necessity of other powers to protect the weak, to repress crime, and to guide in the essential steps of nations emerging from darkness into light. With all nations advancing from barbarism, the process has ever been slow by which the civil authority has been separated from the military. It is impossible to educe from the chaos of those times any established principles. Often the duke or leader was chosen with imposing ceremonies. Some men of commanding abilities would gather into their hands the reins of almost unlimited power, and would transmit that power to their sons. Others were chiefs but in name.

We have but dim glimpses of the early religion of this people. In the sixth century they are represented as regarding with awe the deity whom they designated as the creator of thunder. The spectacle of the majestic storms which swept their plains and the lightning bolts hurled from an invisible hand, deeply impressed these untutored people. They endeavored to appease the anger of the supreme being by the sacrifice of bulls and other animals. They also peopled the groves, the fountains, the rivers with deities; statues were rudely chiseled, into which they supposed the spirits of their gods entered, and which they worshiped. They deemed the supreme being himself too elevated for direct human adoration, and only ventured to approach him through gods of a secondary order. They believed in a fallen spirit, a god of evil, who was the author of all the calamities which afflict the human race.

The polished Greeks chiseled their idols, from snow-white marble, into the most exquisite proportions of the human form. Many they invested with all the charms of loveliness, and endowed them with the most amiable attributes. The voluptuous Venus and the laurel-crowned Bacchus were their gods. But the Sclavonians, regarding their deities only as possessors of power and objects of terror, carved their idols gigantic in stature, and hideous in aspect.

From these rude, scattered and discordant populations, the empire of Russia quite suddenly sprang into being. Its birth was one of the most extraordinary events history has transmitted to us. We have seen that the Normans, dwelling along the southern and eastern shores of the Baltic, and visiting the most distant coasts with their commercial and predatory fleets, had attained a degree of power, intelligence and culture, which gave them a decided preëminence over the tribes who were scattered over the wilds of central Russia.

A Sclavonian, whose name tradition says was Gostomysle, a man far superior to his countrymen in intelligence and sagacity, deploring the anarchy which reigned everywhere around him, and admiring the superior civilization of the Normans, persuaded several tribes unitedly to send an embassy to the Normans to solicit of them a king. The embassy was accompanied by a strong force of these fierce warriors, who knew well how to fight, but who had become conscious that they did not know how to govern themselves. Their message was laconic but explicit:

"Our country," said they, "is grand and fertile, but under the reign of disorder. Come and govern us and reign over us."

Three brothers, named Rurik, Sineous and Truvor, illustrious both by birth and achievements, consented to assume the sovereignty, each over a third part of the united applicants; each engaging to coöperate with and uphold the others. Escorted by the armed retinue which had come to receive them, they left their native shores, and entered the wilds of Scandinavia. Rurik established himself at Novgorod, on lake Ilmen. Sineous, advancing some three hundred miles further, north-east, took his station at Bielo Ozero, on the shores of lake Bielo. Truvor went some hundred miles further south to Truvor, in the vicinity of Smolensk.

Thus there were three sovereigns established in Russia, united by the ties of interest and consanguinity. It was then that this region acquired the name of Russia, from the Norman tribe who furnished these three sovereigns. The Russia which thus emerged into being was indeed an infant, compared with the gigantic empire in this day of its growing and vigorous manhood. It embraced then but a few thousand square miles, being all included in the present provinces of St. Petersburg, Novgorod and Pskov. But two years passed away ere Sineous and Truvor died, and Rurik united their territories with his own, and thus established the Russian monarchy. The realms of Rurik grew rapidly by annexation, and soon extended east some two hundred miles beyond where Moscow now stands, to the head waters of the Volga. They were bounded on the south-west by the Dwina. On the north they reached to the wild wastes of arctic snows. Over these distant provinces, Rurik established governors selected from his own nation, the Normans. These provincial governors became feudal lords; and thus, with the monarchy, the feudal system was implanted.

Feudality was the natural first step of a people emerging from barbarism. The sovereign rewarded his favorites, or compensated his servants, civil and military, by ceding to them provinces of greater or less extent, with unlimited authority over the people subject to their control. These lords acknowledged fealty to the sovereign, paid a stipulated amount of tribute, and, in case of war, were bound to enter the field with a given number of men in defense of the crown. It was a system essential, perhaps, to those barbarous times when there was no easy communication between distant regions, no codes of laws, and no authority, before which savage men would bow, but that of the sword.

At this time two young Norman nobles, inspired with that love of war and spirit of adventure which characterized their countrymen, left the court of Rurik at Novgorod, where they had been making a visit, and with well-armed retainers, commenced a journey to Constantinople to offer their services to the emperor. It was twelve hundred miles, directly south, from Novgorod to the imperial city. The adventurers had advanced about half way, when they arrived at a little village, called Kief, upon the banks of the Dnieper. The location of the city was so beautiful, upon a commanding bluff, at the head of the navigation of this majestic stream, and the region around seemed so attractive, that the Norman adventurers,

Ascolod and Dir by name, decided to remain there. They were soon joined by others of their warlike countrymen. The natives appear to have made no opposition to their rule, and thus Kief became the center of a new and independent Russian kingdom. These energetic men rapidly extended their territories, raised a large army, which was thoroughly drilled in all the science of Norman warfare, and then audaciously declared war against Greece and attempted its subjugation. The Dnieper, navigable for boats most of the distance from Kief to the Euxine, favored their enterprise. They launched upon the stream two hundred barges, which they filled with their choicest troops. Rapidly they floated down the stream, spread their sails upon the bosom of the Euxine, entered the Bosporus, and anchoring their fleet at the mouth of the Golden Horn, laid siege to the city. The Emperor Michael III. then reigned at Constantinople. This Northmen invasion was entirely unexpected, and the emperor was absent, engaged in war with the Arabs. A courier was immediately dispatched to inform him of the peril of the city. He hastily returned to his capital which he finally reached, after eluding, with much difficulty, the vigilance of the besiegers. Just as the inhabitants of the city were yielding to despair, there arose a tempest, which swept the Bosporus with resistless fury. The crowded barges were dashed against each other, shattered, wrecked and sunk. The Christians of Constantinople justly attributed their salvation to the interposition of God. Ascolod and Dir, with the wrecks of their army, returned in chagrin to Kief.

The historians of that period relate that the idolatrous Russians were so terrified by this display of the divine displeasure that they immediately sent embassadors to Constantinople, professing their readiness to embrace Christianity, and asking that they might receive the rite of baptism. In attestation of the fact that Christianity at this period entered Russia, we are referred to a well authenticated letter, of the patriarch Photius, written at the close of the year 866.

"The Russians," he says, "so celebrated for their cruelty, conquerors of their neighbors, and who, in their pride, dared to attack the Roman empire, have already renounced their superstitions, and have embraced the religion of Jesus Christ. Lately our most formidable enemies, they have now become our most faithful friends. We have recently sent them a bishop and a priest, and they testify the greatest zeal for Christianity."

It was in this way, it seems, that the religion of our Saviour first entered barbaric Russia. The gospel, thus welcomed, soon became firmly established at Kief, and rapidly extended its conquests in all directions. The two Russian kingdoms, that of Rurik in the north, and that of Ascolod and Dir on the Dnieper, rapidly extended as these enterprising kings, by arms, subjected adjacent nations to their sway. Rurik remained upon the throne fifteen years, and then died, surrendering his crown to his son Igor, still a child. A relative, Oleg, was intrusted with the regency, during the minority of the boy king. Such was the state of Russia in the year 879.

In that dark and cruel age, war was apparently the only thought, military conquest the only glory. The regent, Oleg, taking with him the young prince Igor, immediately set out with a large army on a career of conquest. Marching directly south some hundred miles, and taking possession of all the country by the way, he arrived at last at the head waters of the Dnieper. The renown of the kingdom of Ascolod and Dir had reached his ears; and aware of their military skill and that the ranks of their army were filled with Norman warriors, Oleg decided to seize the two sovereigns by stratagem. As he cautiously approached Kief, he left his army in a secluded encampment, and with a few chosen troops floated down the stream in barges, disguised as merchant boats.

Landing in the night beneath the high and precipitous banks near the town, he placed a number of his soldiers in ambuscade, and then calling upon the princes of Kief, informed them that he had been sent by the king of Novgorod, with a commercial adventure down the Dnieper, and invited them to visit his barges.

The two sovereigns, suspecting no guile, hastened to the banks of the river. Suddenly the men in ambush rose, and piercing them with arrows and javelins, they both fell dead at the feet of Oleg. The two victims of this perfidy were immediately buried upon the spot where they fell. In commemoration of this atrocity, the church of St. Nicholas has been erected near the place, and even to the present day the inhabitants of Kief conduct the traveler to the tomb of Ascolod and Dir. Oleg, now marshaling his army, marched triumphantly into the town, and, without experiencing any formidable opposition, annexed the conquered realm to the northern kingdom.

Oleg was charmed with his conquest. The beautiful site of the town, the broad expanse of the river, the facilities which the stream presented for maritime and military adventures so delighted him that he exclaimed,

"Let Kief be the mother of all the Russian cities."

Oleg established his army in cantonments, strengthened it with fresh recruits, commenced predatory excursions on every side, and soon brought the whole region, for many leagues around, under his subjection. All the subjugated nations were compelled to pay him tribute, though, with the sagacity which marked his whole course, he made the tax so light as not to be burdensome. The territories of Oleg were now vast, widely scattered, and with but the frailest bond of union between them. Between the two capitals of Novgorod and Kief, which were separated by a distance of seven or eight hundred miles, there were many powerful tribes still claiming independence.

Olég directed his energies against them, and his march of conquest was resistless. In the course of two years he established his undisputed sway over the whole region, and thus opened unobstructed communication between his northern and southern provinces. He established a chain of military posts along the line, and placed his renowned warriors in feudal authority over numerous provinces. Each lord, in his castle, was supreme in authority over the vassals subject to his sway. Life and death were in his hands. The fealty he owed his sovereign was paid in a small tribute, and in military service with an appointed number of soldiers whom he led into the field and supported.

Having thus secured safety in the north, Oleg turned his attention to the south. With a well-disciplined army, he marched down the left bank of the river, sweeping the country for an hundred miles in width, everywhere planting his banners and establishing his simple and effective government of baronial lords. It was easy to weaken any formidable or suspected tribe, by the slaughter of the warriors. There were two safeguards against insurrection. The burdens imposed upon the vassals were so light as to induce no murmurings; and all the feudal lords were united to sustain each other. The first movement towards rebellion was drowned in blood.

Igor, the legitimate sovereign, had now attained his majority; but, accustomed as he had long been, to entire obedience, he did not dare to claim the crown from a regent flushed with the brilliancy of his achievements, who had all power in his hands, and who, by a nod, could remove him for ever out of his way.

Igor was one day engaged in the chase, when at the door of a cottage, in a small village near Kief, he saw a young peasant girl, of marvelous grace and beauty. She was a Norman girl of humble parentage. Young Igor, inflamed by her beauty, immediately rode to the door and addressed her. Her voice was melody, her smile ravishing, and in her replies to his questionings, she developed pride of character, quickness of intelligence and invincible modesty, which charmed him and instantly won his most passionate admiration. The young prince rode home sorely wounded. Cupid had shot one of his most fiery arrows into the very center of his heart. Though many high-born ladies had been urged upon Igor, he renounced them all, and allowing beauty to triumph over birth, honorably demanded and received the hand of the lowly-born yet princely-minded and lovely Olga. They were married at Kief in the year 903.

The revolution at Kief had not interrupted the friendly relations existing between Kief and Constantinople. The Christians of the imperial city made great efforts, by sending missionaries to Kief, to multiply the number of Christians there. Oleg, though a pagan, granted free toleration to Christianity, and reciprocated the presents and friendly messages he received from the emperor. But at length Oleg, having consolidated his realms, and ambitions of still greater renown, wealth and power, resolved boldly to declare war against the empire itself, and to march upon Constantinople. The warriors from a hundred tribes, each under their feudal lord, were ranged around his banners. For miles along the banks of the Dnieper at Kief, the river was covered with barges, two thousand in number. An immense body of cavalry accompanied the expedition, following along the shore.

The navigation of the river, which poured its flood through a channel nearly a thousand miles in length from Kief to the Euxine, was difficult and perilous. It required the blind, unthinking courage of semi-barbarians to undertake such an enterprise. There were many cataracts, down which the flotilla would be swept over foaming billows and amidst jagged rocks. In many places the stream was quite impassable by boats, and it was necessary to take all the barges, with their contents, on shore, and drag them for miles through the forest, again to launch them upon smoother water; and all this time they were exposed to attacks from numerous and ferocious foes. Having arrived at the mouth of the Dnieper, they had still six or eight hundred miles of navigation over the waves of that storm-swept sea. And then, at the close, they had to encounter, in deadly fight, all the power of the Roman empire. But unintimidated by these perils, Oleg, leaving Igor with his bride at Kief, launched his boats upon the current, and commenced his desperate enterprise.

CHAPTER II.

GROWTH AND CONSOLIDATION OF RUSSIA

FROM 910 TO 973.

EXPEDITION TO CONSTANTINOPLE.—TREATY WITH THE EMPEROR.—LAST DAYS OF OLEG.—HIS DEATH.—IGOR ASSUMES THE SCEPTER.—HIS EXPEDITION TO THE DON.—DESCENT UPON CONSTANTINOPLE.—HIS DEFEAT.—SECOND EXPEDITION.—PUSILLANIMITY OF THE GREEKS.—DEATH OF IGOR.—REGENCY OF OLGA.—HER CHARACTER.—SUCCESSION OF SVIATOSLAF.—HIS IMPIETY AND AMBITION.—CONQUEST OF BULGARIA.—DIVISION OF THE EMPIRE.—DEFEAT, RUIN AND DEATH OF SVIATOSLAF.—CIVIL WAR.—DEATH OF OLEG.—FLIGHT OF VLADIMER.—SUPREMACY OF YAROPOLK.

THE fleet of Oleg successfully accomplished the navigation of the Dnieper, followed by the horse along the shores. Each barge carried forty warriors. Entering the Black Sea, they spread their sails and ran along the western coast to the mouth of the Bosporus. The enormous armament approaching the imperial city of Constantine by sea and by land, completely invested it. The superstitious Leon, surnamed the Philosopher, sat then upon the throne. He was a feeble man engrossed with the follies of astrology, and without making preparations for any vigorous defense, he contented himself with stretching a chain across the Golden Horn to prevent the hostile fleet from entering the harbor. The cavalry of Oleg, encountering no serious opposition, burnt and plundered all the neighboring regions. The beautiful villas of the wealthy Greeks, their churches and villages all alike fell a prey to the flames. Every species of cruelty and barbarity was practiced by the ruthless invaders.

The effeminate Greeks from the walls of the city gazed upon this sweep of desolation, but ventured not to march from behind their ramparts to assail the foe. Oleg draw his barges upon the shore and dragged them on wheels towards the city, that he might from them construct instruments and engines for scaling the walls. The Greeks were so terrified at this spectacle of energy, that they sent an embassage to Oleg, imploring peace, and offering to pay tribute. To conciliate the invader they sent him large presents of food and wine. Oleg, apprehensive that the viands were poisoned, refused to accept them. He however demanded enormous tribute of the emperor, to which terms the Greeks consented, on condition that Oleg would cease hostilities, and return peaceably to his country. Upon this basis of a treaty, the Russian army retired to some distance from the city, and Oleg sent four commissioners to arrange with the emperor the details of peace. The humiliating treaty exacted was as follows:

I. The Greeks engage to give twelve *grivnas* to each man of the Russian army, and the same sum to each of the warriors in the cities governed by the dependent princes of Oleg.

II. The embassadors, sent by Russia to Constantinople, shall have all their expenses defrayed by the emperor. And, moreover, the emperor engages to give to every Russian merchant in Greece, bread, wine, meat, fish and fruits, for the space of six months; to grant him free access to the public baths, and to furnish him, on his return to his country, with food, anchors, sails, and, in a word, with every thing he needs.

On the other hand the Greeks propose that the Russians, who visit Constantinople for any other purposes than those of commerce, shall not be entitled to this supply of their tables. The Russian prince shall forbid his embassadors from giving any offense to the inhabitants of the Grecian cities or provinces. The quarter of Saint Meme shall be especially appropriated to the Russians, who, upon their arrival, shall give information to the city council. Their names shall be inscribed, and there shall be paid to them every month the sums necessary for their support, no matter from what part of Russia they may have come. A particular gate shall be designated by which they may enter the city, accompanied by an imperial commissary. They shall enter without arms, and never more than fifty at a time; and they shall be permitted, freely, to engage in trade in Constantinople without the payment of any tax.

This treaty, by which the emperor placed his neck beneath the feet of Oleg, was ratified by the most imposing ceremonies of religion. The emperor took the oath upon the evangelists. Oleg swore by his sword and the gods of Russia. In token of his triumph Oleg proudly raised his shield, as a banner, over the battlements of Constantinople, and returned, laden with riches, to Kief, where he was received with the most extravagant demonstrations of adulation and joy.

The treaty thus made with the emperor, and which is preserved in full in the Russian annals, shows that the Russians were no longer savages, but that they had so far emerged from that gloomy state as to be able to appreciate the sacredness of law, the claims of honor and the authority of treaties. It is observable that no signatures are attached to this treaty but those of the Norman princes, which indicates that the original Sclavonic race were in subjection as the vassals of the Normans. Oleg appears to have placed in posts of authority only his own countrymen.

Oleg now, as old age was advancing, passed many years in quietude. Surrounded by an invincible army, and with renown which pervaded the most distant regions, no tribes ventured to disturb his repose. His distance from southern Europe protected him from annoyance from the powerful nations which were forming there. His latter years seem to have been devoted to the arts of peace, for he secured to an unusual degree the love, as well as the admiration, of his subjects. Ancient annalists record that all Russia moaned and wept when he died. He is regarded, as more prominently than any other man, the founder of the Russian empire. He united, though by treachery and blood, the northern and southern kingdoms under one monarch. He then, by conquest, extended his empire over vast realms of barbarians, bringing them all under the simple yet effective government of feudal lords. He consolidated this empire, and by sagacious measures, encouraging arts and commerce, he led his barbarous people onward in the paths of civilization. He gave Russia a name and renown, so that it assumed a position among the nations of the globe, notwithstanding its remote position amidst the wilds of the North. His usurpation, history can not condemn. In those days any man had the right to govern who had the genius of command. Genius was the only legitimacy. But he was an assassin, and can never be washed clean from that crime. He died after a reign of thirty-three years, and was buried, with all the displays of pomp which that dark age could furnish, upon one of the mountains in the vicinity of Kief, which mountain for many generations was called the Tomb of Oleg.

Igor now assumed the reins of government. He had lived in Kief a quiet, almost an effeminate life, with his beautiful bride Olga. A very powerful tribe, the Drevolians, which had been rather restive, even under the rigorous sway of Oleg, thought this a favorable opportunity to regain their independence. They raised the standard of revolt. Igor crushed the insurrection with energy which astonished all who knew him, and which spread his fame far and wide through all the wilds of Russia, as a monarch thoroughly capable of maintaining his command.

Far away in unknown realms, beyond the eastern boundary of Russia, where the gloomy waves of the Irtish, the Tobol, the Oural and the Volga flow through vast deserts, washing the base of fir-clad mountains, and murmuring through wildernesses, the native domain of wolves and bears, there were wandering innumerable tribes, fierce, cruel and barbarous, who held the frontiers of Russia in continual terror. They were called by the generel name of Petchénègues. Igor was compelled to be constantly on the alert to defend his vast frontier from the irruptions of these merciless savages. This incessant warfare led to the organization of a very efficient military power, but there was no glory to be acquired in merely driving back to their dens these wild assailants. Weary of the conflict, he at last consented to purchase a peace with them; and then, seeking the military renown which Oleg had so signally acquired, he resolved to imitate his example and make a descent upon Constantinople. The annals of those days, which seem to be credible, state that he floated down the Dnieper with ten thousand barges, and spread his sails upon the waves of the Euxine. Entering the Bosporus, he landed on both shores of that beautiful strait, and, with the most wanton barbarity, ravaged the country far and near, massacring the inhabitants, pillaging the towns and committing all the buildings to the flames.

There chanced to be at Constantinople, a very energetic Roman general, who was dispatched against them with a Greek fleet and a numerous land force. The Greeks in civilization were far in advance of the Russians. The land force drove the Russians to their boats, and then the Grecian fleet bore down upon them. A new instrument of destruction had been invented, the terrible Greek fire. Attached to arrows and javelins, and in great balls glowing with intensity of flame which water would not quench, it was thrown into the boats of the Russians, enkindling conflagration and exciting terror indescribable. It seemed to the superstitious followers of Igor, that they were assailed by foes hurling the lightnings of Jove. In this fierce conflict Igor, having lost a large number of barges, and many of his men, drew off his remaining forces in disorder, and they slowly returned to their country in disgrace, emaciate and starving. Many of the Russians taken captive by the Greeks were put to death with the most horrible barbarities.

Igor, exasperated rather than intimidated by this terrible disaster, resolved upon another expedition, that he might recover his lost renown by inflicting the most terrible vengeance upon the Greeks. He spent two years in making preparations for the enterprise; called to his aid warriors from the most distant tribes of the empire, and purchased the alliance of the Petchénègues. With an immense array of barges, which for leagues covered the surface of the Dnieper, and with an immense squadron of cavalry following along the banks, he commenced the descent of the river. The emperor was informed that the whole river was filled with barges, descending for the siege and sack of Constantinople. In terror he sent embassadors to Igor to endeavor to avert the storm.

The imperial embassadors met the flotilla near the mouth of the Dnieper, and offered, in the name of the emperor, to pay the same tribute to Igor which had been paid to Oleg, and even to increase that tribute. At the same time they endeavored to disarm the cupidity of the foe by the most magnificent presents. Igor halted his troops, and collecting his chieftains in counsel, communicated to them the message of the emperor. They replied,

"If the emperor will give us the treasure we demand, without our exposing ourselves to the perils of battle, what more can we ask? Who can tell on which side will be the victory?"

Thus influenced, Igor consented to a treaty. The opening words of this curious treaty are worthy of being recorded. They were as follows:

"We, the embassadors of Igor, solemnly declare that this treaty shall continue so long as the sun shall shine, in defiance of the machinations of that evil spirit who is the enemy of peace and the fomenter of discord. The Russians promise never to break this alliance with the horde; those who have been baptized, under penalty of temporal and eternal punishment from God; others, under the penalty of being for ever deprived of the protection of Péroune ;* of never being able to protect themselves with their shields; of being doomed to lacerate themselves with their own swords, arrows and other arms, and of being slaves in this world and that which is to come."

This important treaty consisted of fourteen articles, drawn up with great precision, and in fact making the Greek emperor as it were but a vassal of the Russian monarch. One of the articles of the treaty is quite illustrative of the times. It reads,

"If a Christian kills a Russian, or if a Russian kills a Christian, the friends of the dead have a right to seize the murderer and kill him."

This treaty was concluded at Constantinople, between the emperor and the embassadors of Igor. Imperial embassadors were sent with the written treaty to Kief. Igor, with imposing ceremonies, ascended the sacred hill where was erected the Russian idol of Péroune, and with his chieftains took a solemn oath of friendship to the emperor, and then as a gage of their sincerity deposited at the feet of the idol their arms and shields of gold. The Christian nobles repaired to the cathedral of St. Elias, the most ancient church of Kief, and there took the same oath at the altar of the Christian's God. The renowned Russian historian, Nestor, who was a monk in the monastery at Kief, records that at that time there were numerous Christians in Kief.

Igor sent the imperial embassadors back to Constantinople laden with rich presents. Elated by wealth and success, the Russian king began to impose heavier burdens of taxation upon subjugated nations. The Drevliens resisted. With an insufficient force Igor entered their territories. The Drevliens, with the fury of desperation, fell upon him and he was slain, and his soldiers put to rout. During his reign he held together the vast empire Oleg had placed in his hands,

* One of the Gods of the Russians.

though he had not been able to extend the boundaries of his country. It is worthy of notice, and of the highest praise, that Igor, though a pagan, imitating the example of Oleg, permitted perfect toleration throughout his realms. The gospel of Christ was freely preached, and the Christians enjoyed entire freedom of faith and worship. His reign continued thirty-two years.

Sviatoslaf, the son of Igor, at the time of his father's unhappy death was in his minority. The empire was then in great peril. The Drevliens, one of the most numerous and warlike tribes, were in open and successful revolt. The army accustomed to activity, and now in idleness, was very restive. The old Norman generals, ambitious and haughty, were disposed to pay but little respect to the claims of a prince who was yet in his boyhood. But Providence had provided for this exigence. Olga, the mother of Sviatoslaf, assumed the regency, and developed traits of character which place her in the ranks of the most extraordinary and noble of women. Calling to her aid two of the most influential of the nobles, one of whom was the tutor of her son and the other commander-in-chief of the army, she took the helm of state, and developed powers of wisdom and energy which have rarely been equaled and perhaps never surpassed.

She immediately sent an army into the country of the Drevliens, and punished with terrible severity the murderers of her husband. The powerful tribe was soon brought again into subjection to the Russian crown. As a sort of defiant parade of her power, and to overawe the turbulent Drevliens, she traversed their whole country, with her son, accompanied by a very imposing retinue of her best warriors. Having thus brought them to subjection, she instituted over them a just and benevolent system of government, that they might have no occasion again to rise in revolt. They soon became so warmly attached to her that they ever were foremost in support of her power.

One year had not passed ere Olga was seated as firmly upon the throne as Oleg or Igor had ever been. She then, leaving her son Sviatoslaf at Kief, set out on a tour through her northern provinces. Everywhere, by her wise measures and her deep interest in the welfare of her subjects, she won admiration and love. The annals of those times are full of her praises. The impression produced by this visit was not effaced from the popular mind for five hundred years, being handed down from father to son. The sledge in which she traveled was for many generations preserved as a sacred relic.

She returned to Kief, and there resided with her son, for many years, in peace and happiness. The whole empire was tranquil, and in the lowly cabins of the Russians there was plenty, and no sounds of war or violence disturbed the quiet of their lives. This seems to have been one of the most serene and pleasant periods of Russian history. This noble woman was born a pagan. But the gospel of Christ was preached in the churches of Kief, and she heard it and was deeply impressed with its sublimity and beauty. Her life was drawing to a close. The grandeur of empire she was soon to lay aside for the darkness and the silence of the tomb. These thoughts oppressed her mind, which was, by nature, elevated, sensitive and refined. She sent for the Christian pastors and conversed with them about the immortality of the soul, and salvation through faith in the atonement of our Lord and Saviour Jesus Christ. The good seed of Christian truth fell into good soil. Cordially she embraced the gospel.

That her renunciation of paganism, and her confession of the Saviour might be more impressive, she decided to go to Constantinople to be baptized by the venerable Christian patriarch, who resided there. The Christian emperor, Constantine Porphyrogenete, informed of her approach, prepared to receive her with all the pomp worthy of so illustrious a princess of so powerful a people. He has himself left a record of these most interesting ceremonies. Olga approached the imperial palace, with a very splendid suite composed of nobles of her court, of ladies of distinction, and of the Russian embassadors and merchants residing at Constantinople. The emperor, with a corresponding suite of splendor, met the Russian queen at a short distance from the palace, and conducted her, with her retinue, to the apartments arranged for their entertainment. It was the 9th of September, 955. In the great banqueting hall of the palace there was a magnificent feast prepared. The guests were regaled with richest music. After such an entertainment as even the opulence of the East had seldom furnished, there was an exchange of presents. The emperor and the queen strove to outvie each other in the richness and elegance of their gifts. Every individual in the two retinues, received presents of great value.

The queen at her baptism received the Christian name of Helen. We do not find any record of the ceremonies performed at her baptism. It is simply stated that the emperor himself stood as her sponsor. Olga, as she returned to Kief, with her baptismal vows upon her, and in the freshness of her Christian hopes, manifested great solicitude for her son, who still continued a pagan. But Sviatoslaf was a wild, pleasure-seeking young man, who turned a deaf ear to all his mother's counsels. The unbridled license which paganism granted, was much more congenial to his unrenewed heart than the salutary restraints of the gospel of Christ. The human heart was then and there, as now and here. The Russian historian Karamsin says,

"In vain this pious mother spoke to her son of the happiness of being a Christian; of the peaceful spirit he would find in the worship of the true God. 'How can I,' replied Sviatoslaf, 'make a profession of this new religion, which will expose me to the ridicule of all my companions in arms?' In vain Olga urged upon him that his example might induce others to embrace the gospel of Christ. The young prince was inflexible. He made no effort to prevent others from becoming Christians, but did not disguise his contempt for the Christian faith, and so persistently rejected all the exhortations of his mother, whom he still tenderly loved, that she was at last forced to silence, and could only pray, in sadness, that God would open the eyes and touch the heart of her child."

The young prince having attained his majority in the year 964, assumed the crown. His soul was fired with the ambition of signalizing himself by great military exploits. The blood of Igor, of Oleg and of Rurik coursed through his veins, and he resolved to lead the Russian arms to victories which should eclipse all their exploits. He gathered an immense army, and looked eagerly around to find some arena worthy of the display of his genius.

His character was an extraordinary one, combining all the virtues of ancient chivalry; virtues which guided by Christian faith, constitute the noblest men, but which without piety constitute a man the scourge of his race. *Fame* was the God of Sviatoslaf. To acquire the reputation of a great warrior, he was willing to whelm provinces in blood. But he was too magnanimous to take any mean advantage of their weakness. He would give them fair warning, that no blow should be struck, assassin-like, stealthily and in the dark.

He accustomed his body, Spartan-like, to all the fatigues and exposures of war. He indulged in no luxury of tents or carriages, and ate the flesh of horses and wild beasts, which he roasted himself, over the coals. In his campaigns the ground was his bed, the sky his curtain, his horse blanket his covering, and the saddle his pillow; and he seemed equally regardless of both heat and cold. His soldiers looked to him as their model and emulated his hardihood. Turning his attention first to the vast and almost unknown realms spreading out towards the East, he sent word to the tribes on the Don and the Volga, that he was coming to fight them. As soon as they had time to prepare for their defense he followed his word. Here was chivalric crime and chivalric magnanimity. Marching nine hundred miles directly east from Kief, over the Russian plains, he came to the banks of the Don. The region was inhabited by a very powerful nation called the Khozars. They were arrayed under their sovereign, on the banks of the river to meet the foe. The Khozars had even sent for Greek engineers to aid them in throwing up their fortifications; and they were in an intrenched camp constructed with much military skill. A bloody battle ensued, in which thousands were slain. But Sviatoslaf was victor, and the territory was annexed to Russia, and Russian nobles were placed in feudal possession of its provinces. The conqueror then followed down the Don to the Sea of Azof, fighting sanguinary battles all the way, but everywhere victorious. The terror of his arms inspired wide-spread consternation, and many tribes, throwing aside their weapons, bowed the neck to the Russian king, and implored his clemency.

Sviatoslaf returned to Kief with waving banners, exulting in his renown. He was stimulated, not satiated, by this success; and now planned another expedition still more perilous and grand. On the south of the Danube, near its mouth, was Bulgaria, a vast realm, populous and powerful, which had long bid defiance to all the forces of the Roman empire. The conquest of Bulgaria was an achievement worthy of the chivalry even of Sviatoslaf. With an immense fleet of barges, containing sixty thousand men, he descended the Dnieper to the Euxine. Coasting along the western shore his fleet entered the mouth of the Danube. The Bulgarians fought like heroes to repel the invaders. All their efforts were in vain. The Russians sprang from their barges on the shore, and, protected by their immense bucklers, sword in hand, routed the Bulgarians with great slaughter. Cities and villages rapidly submitted to the conqueror. The king of Bulgaria in his despair rushed upon death. Sviatoslaf, laden with the spoils of the vanquished and crowned with the laurels of victory, surrendered himself to rejoicing and to all the pleasures of voluptuous indulgence.

From these dissipations Sviatoslaf was suddenly recalled by the tidings that his own capital was in danger; that a neighboring tribe, of great military power, taking advantage of his absence with his army, had invested Kief and were hourly expected to take it by assault. In dismay he hastened his return, and found, to his inexpressible relief, that the besiegers had been routed by the stratagem and valor of a Russian general, and that the city and its inhabitants were thus rescued from destruction.

But the Russian king, having tasted the pleasures of a more sunny clime, and having rioted in the excitements of sensual indulgence, soon became weary of tranquil life in Kief. He was also anxious to escape from the reproof which he always felt from the pious life of his mother. He therefore resolved to return to his conquered kingdom of Bulgaria. He said to his mother:

"I had rather live in Bulgaria than at Kief. Bulgaria is the center of wealth, nature and art. The Greeks send there gold and cloths; the Hungarians silver and horses; the Russians furs, wax, honey and slaves."

"Wait, my son, at least till after my death," exclaimed Olga. "I am aged and infirm, and very soon shall be conveyed to my tomb."

This interview hastened the death of Olga. In four days she slept in Jesus. She earnestly entreated her son not to admit of any pagan rites at her funeral. She pointed out the place of her burial, and was interred with Christian prayers, accompanied by the lamentations and tears of all the people. Sviatoslaf, in his foreign wars, which his mother greatly disapproved, had left with her the administration of internal affairs. Nestor speaks of this pious princess in beautiful phrase as *the morning star of salvation for Russia.*

Sviatoslaf, having committed his mother to the tomb, made immediate preparations to transfer his capital from Kief to the more genial clime of Bulgaria. Had he been influenced by statesmanlike considerations it would have been an admirable move. The climate was far preferable to that of Kief, the soil more fertile, and the openings for commerce, through the Danube and the Euxine, immeasurably superior. But Sviatoslaf thought mainly of pleasure.

It was now the year 970. Sviatoslaf had three sons, whom he established, though all in their minority, in administration of affairs in the realms from which he was departing. Yaropolk received the government of Kief. His second son, Oleg, was placed over the powerful nation of Drevliens. A third son, Vlademer, the child of dishonor, not born in wedlock, was intrusted with the command at Novgorod. Having thus arranged these affairs, Sviatoslaf, with a well-appointed army, eagerly set out for his conquered province of Bulgaria. But in the meantime the Bulgarians had organized a strong force to resist the invader. The Russians conquered in a bloody battle, and, by storm, retook Péregeslavetz, the beautiful capital of Bulgaria, where Sviatoslaf established his throne.

The Greeks at Constantinople were alarmed by this near approach of the ever-encroaching and warlike Russians, and trembled lest they should next fall a prey to the rapacity of Sviatoslaf. The emperor, Jean Zimisces, immediately entered into an alliance with the Bulgarians, offering his daughter in marriage to Boris, son of their former king. A bloody war ensued. The Greeks and Bulgarians were victors, and Sviatoslaf, almost gnashing his teeth with rage, was driven back again to the cold regions of the North. The Greek historians give the following description of the personal appearance of Sviatoslaf. He was of medium height and well formed. His physiognomy was severe and stern. His breast was broad, his neck thick, his eyes blue, with heavy eyebrows. He had a broad nose, heavy moustaches, but a slight beard. The large mass of hair which covered his head indicated his nobility. From one of his ears there was suspended a ring of gold, decorated with two pearls and a ruby.

As Sviatoslaf, with his shattered army, ascended the Dnieper in their boats, the Petchénègues, fierce tribes of barbarians, whom Sviatoslaf had subdued, rose in revolt against him. They gathered, in immense numbers, at one of the cataracts of the Dnieper, where it would be necessary for the Russians to transport their boats for some distance by land. They hoped to cut off his retreat and thus secure the entire destruction of their formidable foe. The situation of Sviatoslaf was now desperate. Nothing remained for him but death. With the abandonment of despair he rushed into the thickest of the foe, and soon fell a mangled corpse. How much more happy would have been his life, how much more happy his death, had he followed the counsels of his pious mother. Kouria, chief of the Petchénègues, cut off the head of Sviatoslaf, and ever after used his skull for a drinking cup. The annalist Strikofski, states that he had engraved upon the skull the words, "In seeking the destruction of others you met with your own."

A few fugitives from the army of Sviatoslaf succeeded in reaching Kief, where they communicated the tidings of the death of the king. The empire now found itself divided into three portions, each with its sovereign. Yaropolk was supreme at Kief. Oleg reigned in the spacious country of the Drevliens. Vladimir was established at Novgorod. No one of these princes was disposed to yield the supremacy to either of the others. They were soon in arms. Yaropolk marched against his brother Oleg. The two armies met about one hundred and fifty miles north-west of Kief, near the present town of Obroutch. Oleg and his force were utterly routed. As the whole army, in confusion and dismay, were in pell-mell flight, hotly pursued, the horse of Oleg fell. Nothing could resist, even for an instant, the onswelling flood. He was trampled into the mire, beneath the iron hoofs of squadrons of horse and the tramp of thousands of mailed men. After the battle, his body was found, so mutilated that it was with difficulty recognized. As it was spread upon a mat before the eyes of Yaropolk, he wept bitterly, and caused the remains to be interred with funeral honors. The monument raised to his memory has long since perished; but even to the present day the inhabitants of Obroutch point out the spot where Oleg fell.

Vladimir, prince of Novgorod, terrified by the fate of his brother Oleg, and apprehensive that a similar doom awaited him, sought safety in flight. Forsaking his realm he retired to the Baltic, and took refuge with the powerful Normans from whom his ancestors had come. Yaropolk immediately dispatched lieutenants to take possession of the government, and thus all Russia, as a united kingdom, was again brought under the sway of a single sovereign.

CHAPTER III.

REIGNS OF VLADEMER, YAROSLAF, YSIASLAF AND VSEVOLOD

FROM 973 TO 1092.

FLIGHT OF VALDEMER.—HIS STOLEN BRIDE.—THE MARCH UPON KIEF.—DEBAUCHERY OF VALDEMER.—ZEALOUS PAGANISM.—INTRODUCTION OF CHRISTIANITY.—BAPTISM IN THE DNIEPER.—ENTIRE CHANGE IN THE CHARACTER OF VALDEMER.—HIS GREAT REFORMS.—HIS DEATH.—USURPATION OF SVIATOPOLK THE MISERABLE.—ACCESSION OF YAROSLAF.—HIS ADMINISTRATION AND DEATH.—ACCESSION OF YSIASLAF.—HIS STRANGE REVERSES.—HIS DEATH.—VSEVOLOD ASCENDS THE THRONE.—HIS TWO FLIGHTS TO POLAND.—APPEALS TO THE POPE.—WARS, FAMINE AND PESTILENCE. CHARACTER OF VSEVOLOD.

THOUGH Vlademer had fled from Russia, it was by no means with the intention of making a peaceful surrender of his realms to his ambitious brother. For two years he was incessantly employed, upon the shores of the Baltic, the home of his ancestors, in gathering adventurers around his flag, to march upon Novgorod, and chase from thence the lieutenants of Yaropolk. He at length, at the head of a strong army, triumphantly entered the city. Half way between Novgorod and Kief, was the city and province of Polotsk. The governor was a Norman named Rovgolod. His beautiful daughter Rogneda was affianced to Yaropolk, and they were soon to be married. Vlademer sent embassadors to Rovgolod soliciting an alliance, and asking for the hand of his daughter.

The proud princess, faithful to Yaropolk, returned the stinging reply, that *she would never marry the son of a slave.* We have before mentioned that the mother of Valdemer was not the wife of his father. She was one of the maids of honor of Olga. . This insult roused the indignation of Valdemer to the highest pitch. Burning with rage he marched suddenly upon Polotsk, took the city by storm, killed Rovgolod and his two sons, and compelled Rogneda, his captive, to marry him, paying but little attention to the marriage ceremony. Having thus satiated his vengeance, he marched upon Kief, with a numerous army, composed of chosen warriors from various tribes. Yaropolk, alarmed at the strength with which his brother was approaching, did not dare to give him battle, but accumulated all his force behind the ramparts of Kief. The city soon fell into the hands of Valdemer, and Yaropolk, basely betrayed by one of his generals, was assassinated by two officers of Vlademer, acting under his authority.

Vlademer was now in possession of the sovereign power, and he displayed as much energy in the administration of affairs as he had shown in the acquisition of the crown. He immediately imposed a heavy tax upon the Russians, to raise money to pay his troops. Having consolidated his power he became a very zealous supporter of the old pagan worship, rearing several new idols upon the sacred hill, and placing in his palace a silver statue of Péroune. His soul seems to have been harrowed by the consciousness of crime, and he sought, by the cruel rites of a debasing superstition, to appease the wrath of the Gods.

Still remorse did not prevent him from plunging into the most revolting excesses of debauchery. The chronicles of those times state that he had three hundred concubines in one of his palaces, three hundred in another at Kief, and two hundred at one of his country seats. It is by no means certain that these are exaggerations, for every beautiful maiden in the empire was sought out, to be transferred to his harems. Paganism had no word of remonstrance to utter against such excesses. But Vlademer, devoted as he was to sensual indulgence, was equally fond of war. His armies were ever on the move, and the cry of battle was never intermitted. On the south-east he extended his conquests to the Carpathian mountains, where they skirt the plains of Hungary. In the north-west he extended his sway, by all the energies of fire and blood, even to the shores of the Baltic, and to the Gulf of Finland.

Elated beyond measure by his victories, he attributed his success to the favor of his idol gods, and resolved to express his homage by offerings of human blood. He collected a number of handsome boys and beautiful girls, and drew lots to see which of them should be offered in sacrifice. The lot fell upon a fine boy from one of the Christian families. The frantic father interposed to save his child. But the agents of Vlademer fell fiercely upon them, and they both were slain and offered in sacrifice. Their names, Ivan and Theodore, are still preserved in the Russian church as the first Christian martyrs of Kief.

A few more years of violence and crime passed away, when Vlademer became the subject of that marvelous change which, nine hundred years before, had converted the persecuting Saul into the devoted apostle. The circumstances of his conversion are very peculiar, and are very minutely related by Nestor. Other recitals seem to give authenticity to the narrative. For some time Vlademer had evidently been in much anxiety respecting the doom which awaited him beyond the grave. He sent for the teachers of the different systems of religion, to explain to him the peculiarities of their faith. First came the Mohammedans from Bulgaria; then the Jews from Jerusalem; then the Christians from the papal church at Rome, and then Christians from the Greek church at Constantinople. The Mohammedans and the Jews he rejected promptly, but was undecided respecting the claims of Rome and Constantinople. He then selected ten of the wisest men in his kingdom and sent them to visit Rome and Constantinople and report in which country divine worship was conducted in the manner most worthy of the Supreme Being. The embassadors returning to Kief, reported warmly in favor of the Greek church. Still the mind of Vlademer was oppressed with doubts. He assembled a number of the most virtuous nobles and asked their advice. The question was settled by the remark of one who said, "Had not the religion of the Greek church been the best, the sainted Olga would not have accepted it."

This wonderful event is well authenticated; Nestor gives a recital of it in its minute details; and an old Greek manuscript, preserved in the royal library at Paris, records the visit of these ambassadors to Rome and Constantinople. Vlademer's conversion, however, seems, at this time, to have been intellectual rather than spiritual, a change in his policy of administration rather than a change of heart. Though this external change was a boundless blessing to Russia, there is but little evidence that Vlademer then comprehended that moral renovation which the gospel of Christ effects as its crowning glory. He saw the absurdity of paganism; he felt tortured by remorse; perhaps he felt in some degree the influence of the gospel which was even then faithfully preached in a few churches in idolatrous Kief; and he wished to elevate Russia above the degradation of brutal idolatry.

He deemed it necessary that his renunciation of idolatry and adoption of Christianity should be accompanied with pomp which should produce a wide-spread impression upon Russia. He accordingly collected an immense army, descended the Dnieper in boats, sailed across the Black Sea, and entering the Gulf of Cherson, near Sevastopol, after several bloody battles took military possession of the Crimea. Thus victorious, he sent an embassage to the emperors Basil and Constantine at Constantinople, that he wished the young Christian princess Anne for his bride, and that if they did not promptly grant his request, he would march his army to attack the city.

The emperors, trembling before the approach of such a power, replied that they would not withhold from him the hand of the princess if he would first embrace Christianity. Vlademer of course assented to this, which was the great object he had in view; but demanded that the princess, who was a sister of the emperors, should first be sent to him. The unhappy maiden was overwhelmed with anguish at the reception of these tidings. She regarded the pagan Russians as ferocious savages; and to be compelled to marry their chief was to her a doom more dreadful than death.

But policy, which is the religion of cabinets, demanded the sacrifice. The princess, weeping in despair, was conducted, accompanied by the most distinguished ecclesiastics and nobles of the empire, to the camp of Vlademer, where she was received with the most gorgeous demonstrations of rejoicing. The whole army expressed their gratification by all the utterances of triumph. The ceremony of baptism was immediately performed in the church of St. Basil, in the city of Cherson, and then, at the same hour, the marriage rites with the princess were solemnized. Vlademer ordered a large church to be built at Cherson in memory of his visit. He then returned to Kief, taking with him some preachers of distinction; a communion service wrought in the most graceful proportions of Grecian art, and several exquisite specimens of statuary and sculpture, to inspire his subjects with a love for the beautiful.

He accepted the Christian teachers as his guides, and devoted himself with extraordinary zeal to the work of persuading all his subjects to renounce their idol-worship and accept Christianity. Every measure was adopted to throw contempt upon paganism. The idols were collected and burned in huge bonfires. The sacred statue of Péroune, the most illustrious of the pagan Gods, was dragged ignominiously through the streets, pelted with mud and scourged with whips, until at last, battered and defaced, it was dragged to the top of a precipice and tumbled headlong into the river, amidst the derision and hootings of the multitude.

Our zealous new convert now issued a decree to all the people of Russia, rich and poor, lords and slaves, to repair to the river in the vicinity of Kief to be baptized. At an appointed day the people assembled by thousands on the banks of the Dnieper. Vlademer at length appeared, accompanied by a great number of Greek priests. The signal being given, the whole multitude, men, women and children, waded slowly into the stream. Some boldly advanced out up to their necks in the water; others, more timid, ventured only waist deep. Fathers and mothers led their children by the hand. The priests, standing upon the shore, read the baptismal prayers, and chaunted the praises of God, and then conferred the name of Christians upon these barbarians. The multitude then came up from the water.

Vlademer was in a transport of joy. His strange soul was not insensible to the sublimity of the hour and of the scene. Raising his eyes to heaven he uttered the following prayer:

"Creator of heaven and earth, extend thy blessing to these thy new children. May they know thee as the true God, and be strengthened by thee in the true religion. Come to my help against the temptations of the evil spirit, and I will praise thy name."

Thus, in the year 988, paganism was, by a blow, demolished in Russia, and nominal Christianity introduced throughout the whole realm. A Christian church was erected upon the spot where the statue of Péroune had stood. Architects were brought from Constantinople to build churches of stone in the highest artistic style. Missionaries were sent throughout the whole kingdom, to instruct the people in the doctrines of Christianity, and to administer the rite of baptism. Nearly all the people readily received the new faith. Some, however, attached to the ancient idolatry, refused to abandon it. Vlademer, nobly recognizing the rights of conscience, resorted to no measures of violence. The idolaters were left undisturbed save by the teachings of the missionaries. Thus for several generations idolatry held a lingering life in the remote sections of the empire. Schools were established for the instruction of the young, learned teachers from Greece secured, and books of Christian biography translated into the Russian tongue.

Vlademer had then ten sons. Three others were afterwards born to him. He divided his kingdom into ten provinces or states, over each of which he placed one of these sons as governor. On the frontiers of the empire he caused cities, strongly fortified, to be erected as safeguards against the invasion of remote barbarians. For several years Russia enjoyed peace with but trivial interruptions. The character of Vlademer every year wonderfully improved. Under his Christian teachers he acquired more and more of the Christian spirit, and that spirit was infused into all his public acts. He became the father of his people, and especially the friend and helper of the poor. The king was deeply impressed with the words of our Saviour, "Blessed are the merciful, for they shall obtain mercy," and with the declaration of Solomon, "He who giveth to the poor lendeth to the Lord."

In the excess of his zeal of benevolence he was disposed to forgive all criminals. Thus crime was greatly multiplied, and the very existence of the state became endangered. The clergy, in a body, remonstrated with him, assuring him that God had placed him upon the throne expressly that he might punish the wicked and thus protect the good. He felt the force of this reasoning, and instituted, though with much reluctance, a more rigorous government. War had been his passion. In this respect also his whole nature seemed to be changed, and nothing but the most dire necessity could lead him to an appeal to arms. The princess Anne appears to have been a sincere Christian, and to have exerted the most salutary influence upon the mind of her husband. In the midst of these great measures of reform, sudden sickness seized Vlademer in his palace, and he died, in the year 1015, so unexpectedly that he appointed no successor. His death caused universal lamentations, and thousands crowded to the church of Notre Dame, to take a last look of their beloved sovereign, whose body reposed there for a time in state, in a marble coffin. The remains were then deposited by the side of his last wife, the Christian princess Anne, who had died a few years before. The Russian historian, Karamsin, says:

"This prince, whom the church has recognized as equal to the apostles, merits from history the title of Great. It is God alone who can know whether Vlademer was a true Christian at heart, or if he were influenced simply by political considerations. It is sufficient for us to state that, after having embraced that divine religion, Vlademer appears to have been sanctified by it, and he developed a totally different character from that which he exhibited when involved in the darkness of paganism."

One of the sons of Vlademer, whose name was Sviatopolk, chanced to be at Kief at the time of his father's death. He resolved to usurp the throne and to cause the assassination of all the brothers from whom he could fear any opposition. Three of his brothers speedily fell victims to his bloody perfidy. Yaroslaf, who had been entrusted with the feudal government of Novgorod, being informed of the death of his father, of the usurpation of Sviatopolk and of the assassination of three of his brothers, raised an army of forty thousand men and marched upon Kief. Sviatopolk, informed of his approach, hastened, with all his troops to meet him. The two armies encountered each other upon the banks of the Dnieper about one hundred and fifty miles above Kief. The river separated them, and neither dared to attempt to cross in the presence of the other. Several weeks passed, the two camps thus facing each other, without any collision.

At length Yaroslaf, with the Novgorodians, crossed the stream stealthily and silently in a dark night, and fell fiercely upon the sleeping camp of Sviatopolk. His troops, thus taken by surprise, fought for a short time desperately. They were however soon cut to pieces or dispersed, and Sviatopolk, himself, saved his life only by precipitate flight. Yaroslaf, thus signally victorious, continued his march, without further opposition, to Kief, and entered the capital in triumph. Sviatopolk fled to Poland, secured the coöperation of the Polish king, whose daughter he had married, returned with a numerous army, defeated his brother in a sanguinary battle, drove him back to Novgorod, and again, with flying banners, took possession of Kief. The path of history now leads us through the deepest sloughs of perfidy and crime. Two of the sisters of Yaroslaf were found in Kief. One of them had previously refused the hand of the king of Poland. The barbarian in revenge seized her as his concubine. Sviatopolk, jealous of the authority which his father-in-law claimed, and which he could enforce by means of the Polish army, administered poison in the food of the troops. A terrible and unknown disease broke out in the camp, and thousands perished. The wretch even attempted to poison his father-in-law, but the crime was suspected, and the Polish king, Boleslas, fled to his own realms.

Sviatopolk was thus again left so helpless as to invite attack. Yaroslaf with eagerness availed himself of the opportunity. Raising a new army, he marched upon Kief, retook the city and drove his brother again into exile. The energetic yet miserable man fled to the banks of the Volga, where he formed a large army of the ferocious Petchénègues, exciting their cupidity with promises of boundless pillage. With these wolfish legions, he commenced his march back again upon his own country. The terrible encounter took place on the banks of the Alta. Russian historians describe the conflict as one of the most fierce in which men have ever engaged. The two armies precipitated themselves upon each other with the utmost fury, breast to breast, swords, javelins and clubs clashing against brazen shields. The Novgorodians had taken a solemn oath that they would conquer or die. Three times the combatants from sheer exhaustion ceased the strife. Three times the deadly combat was renewed with redoubled ardor. The sky was illumined with the first rays of the morning when the battle commenced. The evening twilight was already darkening the field before the victory was decided. The hordes of the wretched Sviatopolk were then driven in rabble rout from the field, leaving the ground covered with the slain. The defeat was so awful that Sviatopolk was plunged into utter despair. Half dead with terror, tortured by remorse, and pursued by the frown of Heaven, he fled into the deserts of Bohemia, where he miserably perished, an object of universal execration. In the annals of Russia the surname of *miserable* is ever affixed to this infamous prince.

Yaroslaf, thus crowned by victory, received the undisputed title of sovereign of Russia. It was now the year 1020. For several years Yaroslaf reigned in prosperity. There were occasional risings of barbaric tribes, which, by force of arms, he speedily quelled. Much time and treasure were devoted to the embellishment of the capital; churches were erected; the city was surrounded by brick walls; institutions of learning were encouraged, and, most important of all, the Bible was translated into the Russian language. It is recorded that the king devoutly read the Scriptures himself, both morning and evening, and took great interest in copying the sacred books with his own hands.

The closing years of life this illustrious prince passed in repose and in the exercises of piety, while he still continued, with unintermitted zeal, to watch over the welfare of the state. Nearly all the pastors of the churches were Greeks from Constantinople, and Yaroslaf, apprehensive that the Greeks might acquire too much influence in the empire, made great efforts to raise up Russian ecclesiastics, and to place them in the most important posts. At length the last hours of the monarch arrived, and it was evident that death was near. He assembled his children around his bed, four sons and five daughters, and thus affectingly addressed them:

"I am about to leave the world. I trust that you, my dear children, will not only remember that you are brothers and sisters, but that you will cherish for each other the most tender affection. Ever bear in mind that discord among you will be attended with the most funereal results, and that it will be destructive of the prosperity of the state. By peace and tranquillity alone can its power be consolidated.

"Ysiaslaf will be my successor to ascend the throne of Kief. Obey him as you have obeyed your father. I give Tchernigof to Sviatoslaf; Pereaslavle to Vsevolod; and Smolensk to Viatcheslaf. I hope that each of you will be satisfied with his inheritance. Your oldest brother, in his quality of sovereign prince, will be your natural judge. He will protect the oppressed and punish the guilty."

On the 19th of February, 1054, Yaroslaf died, in the seventy-first year of his age. His subjects followed his remains in tears to the tomb, in the church of St. Sophia, where his marble monument, carved by Grecian artists, is still shown. Influenced by a superstition common in those days, he caused the bones of Oleg and Yaropolk, the two murdered brothers of Vlademer, who had perished in the errors of paganism, to be disinterred, baptized, and then consigned to Christian burial in the church of Kief. He established the first public school in Russia, where three hundred young men, sons of the priests and nobles, received instruction in all those branches which would prepare them for civil or ecclesiastical life. Ambitious of making Kief the rival of Constantinople, he expended large sums in its decoration. Grecian artists were munificently patronized, and paintings and mosaics of exquisite workmanship added attraction to churches reared in the highest style of existing art. He even sent to Greece for singers, that the church choirs might be instructed in the richest utterances of music.

He drew up a code of laws, called Russian Justice, which, for that dark age, is a marvelous monument of sagacity, comprehensive views and equity.

The death of Yaroslaf proved an irreparable calamity; for his successor was incapable of leading on in the march of civilization, and the realm was soon distracted by civil war. It is a gloomy period, of three hundred years, upon which we now must enter, while violence, crime, and consequently misery, desolated the land. It is worthy of record that Nestor attributes the woes which ensued, to the general forgetfulness of God, and the impiety which commenced the reign immediately after the death of Yaroslaf.

"God is just," writes the historian. "He punishes the Russians for their sins. We dare to call ourselves Christians, and yet we live like idolaters. Although multitudes throng every place of entertainment, although the sound of trumpets and harps resounds in our houses, and mountebanks exhibit their tricks and dances, the temples of God are empty, surrendered to solitude and silence."

Bands of barbarians invaded Russia from the distant regions of the Caspian Sea, plundering, killing and burning. They came suddenly, like the thunder-cloud in a summer's day, and as suddenly disappeared where no pursuit could find them. Ambitious nobles, descendants of former kings, plied all the arts of perfidy and of assassination to get possession of different provinces of the empire, each hoping to make his province central and to extend his sway over all the rest of Russia. The brothers of Ysiaslaf became embroiled, and drew the sword against each other. An insurrection was excited in Kief, the populace besieged the palace, and the king saved his life only by a precipitate abandonment of his capital. The military mob pillaged the palace and proclaimed their chieftain, Vseslaf, king.

Ysiaslaf fled to Poland. The Polish king, Boleslas II., who was a grandson of Vlademer, and who had married a

Russian princess, received the fugitive king with the utmost kindness. With a strong Polish army, accompanied by the King of Poland, Ysiaslaf returned to Kief, to recover his capital by the sword. The insurgent chief who had usurped the throne, in cowardly terror fled. Ysiaslaf entered the city with the stern strides of a conqueror and wreaked horrible vengeance upon the inhabitants, making but little discrimination between the innocent and the guilty. Seventy were put to death. A large number had their eyes plucked out; and for a long time the city resounded with the cries of the victims, suffering under all kinds of punishments from the hands of this implacable monarch. Thus the citizens were speedily brought into abject submission. The Polish king, with his army, remained a long time at Kief, luxuriating in every indulgence at the expense of the inhabitants. He then returned to his own country laden with riches.

Ysiaslaf re-ascended the throne, having been absent ten months. Disturbances of a similar character agitated the provinces which were under the government of the brothers of Ysiaslaf, and which had assumed the authority and dignity of independent kingdoms. Thus all Russia was but an arena of war, a volcanic crater of flame and blood. Three years of conflict and woe passed away, when two of the brothers of Ysiaslaf united their armies and marched against him; and again he was compelled to seek a refuge in Poland. He carried with him immense treasure, hoping thus again to engage the services of the Polish army. But Boleslas infamously robbed him of his treasure, and then, to use an expression of Nestor, "*showed him the way out of his kingdom.*"

The woe-stricken exile fled to Germany, and entreated the interposition of the emperor, Henry IV., promising to reward him with immense treasure, and to hold the crown of Russia as tributary to the German empire. The emperor was excited by the alluring offer, and sent embassadors to Sviatoslaf, now enthroned at Kief, ostensibly to propose reconciliation, but in reality to ascertain what the probability was of success in a warlike expedition to so remote a kingdom. The embassadors returned with a very discouraging report.

The banished prince thus disappointed, turned his steps to Rome, and implored the aid of Gregory VII., that renowned pontiff, who was ambitious of universal sovereignty, and who had assumed the title of King of kings. Ysiaslaf, in his humiliation, was ready to renounce his fidelity to the Greek church, and also the dignity of an independent prince. He promised, in consideraiton of the support of the pope, to recognize not only the spiritual power of Rome, but also the temporal authority of the pontiff. He also entered bitter complaints against the King of Poland. Ysiaslaf did not visit Rome in person, but sent his son to confer with the pope. Gregory, rejoiced to acquire spiritual dominion over Russia, received the application in the most friendly manner, and sent embassadors to the fugitive prince with the following letter:

"Gregory, bishop, servant of the servants of God, to Ysiaslaf, prince of the Russians, safety, health and the apostolic benediction.

"Your son, after having visited the sacred places at Rome, has humbly implored that he might be reëstablished in his possessions by the authority of Saint Peter, and has given his solemn vow to be faithful to the chief of the apostles. We have consented to grant his request, which we understand is in accordance with your wishes; and we, in the name of the chief of the apostles, confer upon him the government of the Russian kingdom.

"We pray that Sain Peter may preserve your health, that he will protect your reign and your estates, even to the end of your life, and that you may then enjoy a day of eternal glory.

"Wishing also to give a proof of our desire to be useful to you hereafter, we have charged our embassadors, one of whom is your faithful friend, to treat with you verbally upon all those subjects alluded to in your communication to us. Receive them with kindness as the embassadors of Saint Peter, and receive without restriction all the propositions they may make in our name.

"May God, the all-powerful, illumine your heart with divine light and with temporal blessings, and conduct you to eternal glory. Given at Rome the 15th of May, in the year 1075."

Thus adroitly the pope assumed the sovereignty of Russia, and the right, and the power, by the mere utterance of a word, to confer it upon whom he would. The all-grasping pontiff thus annexed Russia to the domains of Saint Peter. Another short letter Gregory wrote to the King of Poland. It was as follows:

"In appropriating to yourself illegally the treasures of the Russian prince, you have violated the Christian virtues. I conjure you, in the name of God, to restore to him all the property of which you and your subjects have deprived him; for robbers can never enter the kingdom of heaven unless they first restore the plunder they have taken."

Fortunately for the fugitive prince, his usurping brother Sviatoslaf just at this time died, in consequence of a severe surgical operation. The Polish king appears to have refunded the treasure of which he had robbed the exiled monarch, and Ysiaslaf, hiring an army of Polish mercenaries, returned a second time in triumph to his capital. It does not appear that he subsequently paid any regard to the interposition of the pope.

We have now but a long succession of conspiracies, insurrections and battles. In one of these civil conflicts, Ysiaslaf, at the head of a formidable force, met another powerful army, but a few leagues from Kief. In the hottest hour of the battle a reckless cavalier, in the hostile ranks, perceiving Ysiaslaf in the midst of his infantry, precipitated himself on him, pierced him with his lance and threw him dead upon the ground. His body was conveyed in a canoe to Kief, and buried with much funeral pomp in the church of Notre Dame, by the side of the beautiful monument which had been erected to the memory of Vlademer.

Ysiaslaf expunged from the Russian code of laws the death penalty, and substituted, in its stead, heavy fines. The Russian historians, however, record that it is impossible to decide whether this measure was the dictate of humanity, or if he wished in this way to replenish his treasury.

Vsevolod succeeded to the throne of his brother Ysiaslaf, in the year 1078. The children of Ysiaslaf had provinces assigned them in appanage. Vsevolod was a lover of peace, and yet devastation and carnage were spread everywhere before his eyes. Every province in the empire was torn by civil strife. Hundreds of nobles and princes were inflamed with the ambition for supremacy, and with the sword alone could the path be cut to renown. The wages offered the soldiers, on all sides, was pillage. Cities were everywhere sacked and burned, and the realm was crimsoned with blood. Civil war is necessarily followed by the woes of famine, which woes are ever followed by the pestilence. The plague swept the kingdom with terrific violence, and whole provinces were depopulated. In the city of Kief alone, seven thousand perished in the course of ten weeks. Universal terror, and superstitious fear spread through the nation. An earthquake indicated that the world itself was trembling in alarm; an enormous serpent was reported to have been seen falling from heaven; invisible and malignant spirits were riding by day and by night through the streets of the cities, wounding the citizens with blows which, though unseen, were heavy and murderous, and by which blows many were slain. All hearts sank in gloom and fear. Barbarian hordes ravaged both banks of the Dnieper, committing towns and villages to the flames, and killing such of the inhabitants as they did not wish to carry away as captives.

Vsevolod, an amiable man of but very little force of character, was crushed by the calamities which were overwhelming his country. Not an hour of tranquillity could he enjoy. It was the ambition of his nephews, ambitious, energetic, unprincipled princes, struggling for the supremacy, which was mainly the cause of all these disasters

CHAPTER IV.

YEARS OF WAR AND WOE.

FROM 1092 TO 1167.

CHARACTER OF VSEVOLOD.—SUCCESSION OF SVIATOPOLK.—HIS DISCOMFITURE.—DEPLORABLE CONDITION OF RUSSIA.—DEATH OF SVIATOPOLK.—HIS CHARACTER.—ACCESSION OF MONOMAQUE.—CURIOUS FESTIVAL AT KIEF.—ENERGY OF MONOMAQUE.—ALARM OF THE EMPEROR AT CONSTANTINOPLE.—HORRORS OF WAR.—DEATH OF MONOMAQUE.—HIS REMARKABLE CHARACTER.—PIOUS LETTER TO HIS CHILDREN.—ACCESSION OF MSTISLAF.—HIS SHORT BUT STORMY REIGN.—STRUGGLES FOR THE THRONE.—FINAL VICTORY OF YSIASLAF.—MOSCOW IN THE PROVINCE OF SOUZDAL.—DEATH OF YSIASLAF.—WONDERFUL CAREER OF ROSTISLAF.—RISING POWER OF MOSCOW.—GEORGIEVITCH, PRINCE OF MOSCOW.

VSEVOLOD has the reputation of having been a man of piety. But he was quite destitute of that force of character which one required to hold the helm in such stormy times. He was a man of great humanity and of unblemished morals. The woes which desolated his realms, and which he was utterly unable to avert, crushed his spirit and hastened his death. Perceiving that his dying hour was at hand, he sent for his two sons, Vlademer and Rostislaf, and the sorrowing old man breathed his last in their arms.

Vsevolod was the favorite son of Yaroslaf the Great, and his father, with his dying breath, had expressed the wish that Vsevolod, when death should come to him, might be placed in the tomb by his side. These affectionate wishes of the dying father were gratified, and the remains of Vsevolod were deposited, with the most imposing ceremonies of those days, in the church of Saint Sophia, by the side of those of his father. The people, forgetting his weakness and remembering only his amiability, wept at his burial.

Vlademer, the eldest son of Vsevolod, with great magnanimity surrendered the crown to his cousin Sviatopolk, saying, "His father was older than mine, and reigned at Kief before my father. I wish to avoid dissension and the horrors of civil war."

He then proclaimed Sviatopolk sovereign of Russia. The new sovereign had been feudal lord of the province of Novgorod; he, however, soon left his northern capital to take up his residence in the more imperial palaces of Kief. But disaster seemed to be the doom of Russia, and the sounds of rejoicing which attended his accession to the throne had hardly died away ere a new scene of woe burst upon the devoted land.

The young king was rash and headstrong. He provoked the ire of one of the strong neighboring provinces, which was under the sway of an energetic feudal prince, ostensibly a vassal of the crown, but who, in his pride and power, arrogated independence. The banners of a hostile army were soon approaching Kief. Sviatopolk marched heroically to meet them. A battle was fought, in which he and his army were awfully defeated. Thousands were driven by the conquerors into a stream, swollen by the rains, where they miserably perished. The fugitives, led by Sviatopolk, in dismay fled back to Kief and took refuge behind the walls of the city. The enemy pressed on, ravaging, with the most cruel desolation, the whole region around Kief, and in a second battle conquered the king and drove him out of his realms. The whole of southern Russia was abandoned to barbaric destruction. Nestor gives a graphic sketch of the misery which prevailed:

"One saw everywhere," he writes, "villages in flames; churches, houses, granaries were reduced to heaps of ashes; and the unfortunate citizens were either expiring beneath the blows of their enemies, or were awaiting death with terror. Prisoners, half naked, were dragged in chains to the most distant and savage regions. As they toiled along, they said, weeping, one to another, '*I am from such a village, and I from such a village.*' No horses or cattle were to be seen upon our plains. The fields were abandoned to weeds, and ferocious beasts ranged the places but recently occupied by Christians."

The whole reign of Sviatopolk, which continued until the year 1113, was one continued storm of war. It would only weary the reader to endeavor to disentangle the labyrinth of confusion, and to describe the ebbings and floodings of battle. Every man's hand was against his neighbor; and friends to-day were foes to-morrow. Sviatopolk himself was one of the most imperfect of men. He was perfidious, ungrateful and suspicious; haughty in prosperity, mean and cringing in adversity. His religion was the inspiration of superstition and cowardice, not of intelligence and love. Whenever he embarked upon any important expedition, he took an ecclesiastic to the tomb of Saint Theodosius, there to implore the blessing of Heaven. If successful in the enterprise, he returned to the tomb to give thanks. This was the beginning and the end of his piety. Without any scruple he violated the most sacred laws of morality. The marriage vow was entirely disregarded, and he was ever ready to commit any crime which would afford gratification to his passions, or which would advance his interests.

The death of Sviatopolk occurred in a season of general anarchy, and it was uncertain who would seize the throne. The citizens of Kief met in solemn and anxious assembly, and offered the crown to an illustrious noble, Monomaque, a brother of Sviatopolk, and a man who had acquired renown in many enterprises of most desperate daring. In truth it required energy and courage of no ordinary character for a man at that time to accept the crown. Innumerable assailants would immediately fall upon him, putting to the most imminent peril not only the crown, but the head which wore it. By the Russian custom of descent, the crown incontestably belonged to the oldest son of Sviatoslaf, and Monomaque, out of regard to his rights, declined the proffered gift. This refusal was accompanied by the most melancholy results. A terrible tumult broke out in the city. There was no arm of law sufficiently powerful to restrain the mob, and anarchy, with all its desolation, reigned for a time triumphant. A deputation of the most influential citizens of Kief was immediately sent to Monomaque, with the most earnest entreaty that he would hasten to rescue them and their city from the impending ruin. The heroic prince could not turn a deaf ear to this appeal. He hastened to the city, where his presence, combined with the knowledge which all had of his energy and courage, at once appeased the tumult. He ascended the throne, greeted by the acclamations of the whole city. No opposition ventured to manifest itself, and Monomaque was soon in the undisputed possession of power.

Nothing can give one a more vivid idea of the state of the times than the festivals appointed in honor of the new reign as described by the ancient annalists. The bones of two saints were transferred from one church to another in the city. A magnificent coffin of silver, embellished with gold, precious stones, and *bas reliefs*, so exquisitely carved as to excite the admiration even of the Grecian artists, contained the sacred relics, and excited the wonder and veneration of the whole multitude. The imposing ceremony drew to Kief the princes, the clergy, the lords, the warriors, even, from the most distant parts of the empire. The gates of the city and the streets were encumbered with such multitudes that, in order to open a passage for the clergy with the sarcophagus, the monarch caused cloths, garments, precious furs and pieces of silver to be scattered to draw away the throng. A luxurious feast was given to the princes, and, for three days, all the poor of the city were entertained at the expense of the public treasure.

Monomaque now fitted out sundry expeditions under his enterprising son to extend the territories of Russia and to bring tumultuous tribes and nations into subjection and order. His son Mstislaf was sent into the country of the Tchoudes, now Livonia, on the shores of the Baltic. He overran the territory, seized the capital and established order. His son Vsevolod, who was stationed at Novgorod, made an expedition into Finland. His army experienced inconceivable sufferings in that cold, inhospitable clime. Still they overawed the inhabitants and secured tranquillity. Another son, Georges, marched to the Volga, embarked his army in a fleet of barges, and floated along the stream to eastern Bulgaria, conquered an army raised to oppose him, and returned to his principality laden with booty. Another son, Yaropolk, assailed the tumultuous tribes upon the Don. Brilliant success accompanied his enterprise. Among his captives he found one maiden of such rare beauty that he made her his wife. At the same time the kingdom of Russia was invaded by barbarous hordes from the shores of the Caspian. Monomaque himself headed an army and assailed the invaders with such impetuosity that they were driven, with much loss, back again to their wilds.

The military renown Monomaque thus attained made his name a terror even to the most distant tribes, and, for a time, held in awe those turbulent spirits who had been filling the world with violence. Elated by his conquests, Monomaque fitted out an expedition to Greece. A large army descended the Dnieper, took possession of Thrace, and threatened Adrianople. The emperor, in great alarm, sent embassadors to Monomaque with the most precious presents. There was a cornelian exquisitely cut and set, a golden chain and necklace, a crown of gold, and, most precious of all, a crucifix made of wood of the true cross! The metropolitan bishop of Ephesus, who was sent with these presents, was authorized, in the name of the church and of the empire, to place the crown upon the brow of Monomaque in gorgeous coronation in the cathedral church of Kief, and to proclaim Monomaque Emperor of Russia. This crown, called the *golden bonnet of*

Monomaque, is still preserved in the Museum of Antiquities at Moscow.

These were dark and awful days. Horrible as war now is, it was then attended with woes now unknown. Gleb, prince of Minsk, with a ferocious band, attacked the city of Sloutsk; after a terrible scene of carnage, in which most of those capable of bearing arms were slain, the city was burned to ashes, and all the survivors, men, women and children, were driven off as captives to the banks of the Dwina, where they were incorporated with the tribe of their savage conqueror. In revenge, Monomaque sent his son Yaropolk to Droutsk, one of the cities of Gléb. No pen can depict the horrors of the assault. After a few hours of dismay, shriekings and blood, the city was in ashes, and the wretched victims of man's pride and revenge were conducted to the vicinity of Kief, where they reared their huts, and in widowhood, orphanage and penury, commenced life anew. Gleb himself in this foray was taken prisoner, conducted to Kief, and detained there a captive until he died.

Monomaque reigned thirteen years, during which time he was incessantly engaged in wars with the audacious nobles of the provinces who refused to recognize his supremacy, and many of whom were equal to him in power. He died May 19, 1126, in the seventy-third year of his age, renowned, say the ancient annalists, for the splendor of his victories and the purity of his morals. He was fully conscious of the approach of death, and seems to have been sustained, in that trying hour, by the consolations of religion. He lived in an age of darkness and of tumult; but he was a man of prayer, and, according to the light he had, he walked humbly with God. Commending his soul to the Saviour he fell asleep. It is recorded that he was a man of such lively emotions that his voice often trembled, and his eyes were filled with tears as he implored God's blessing upon his distracted country. He wrote, just before his death, a long letter to his children, conceived in the most lovely spirit of piety. We have space but for a few extracts from these Christian counsels of a dying father. The whole letter, written on parchment, is still preserved in the archives of the monarchy.

"The foundation of all virtue," he wrote, "is the fear of God and the love of man. O my dear children, praise God and love your fellow-men. It is not fasting, it is not solitude, it is not a monastic life which will secure for you the divine approval—it is doing good to your fellow-creatures alone. Never forget the poor. Take care of them, and ever remember that your wealth comes from God, and that it is only intrusted to you for a short time. Do not hoard up your riches; that is contrary to the precepts of the Saviour. Be a father to the orphans, the protectors of widows, and never permit the powerful to oppress the weak. Never take the name of God in vain, and never violate your oath. Do not envy the triumph of the wicked, or the success of the impious; but abstain from every thing that is wrong. Banish from your hearts all the suggestions of pride, and remember that we are all perishable—to-day full of life, to-morrow in the tomb. Regard with horror, falsehood, intemperance and impurity—vices equally dangerous to the body and to the soul. Treat aged men with the same respect with which you would treat your parents, and love all men as your brothers.

"When you make a journey in your provinces, do not suffer the members of your suite to inflict the least injury upon the inhabitants. Treat with particular respect strangers, of whatever quality, and if you can not confer upon them favors, treat them with a spirit of benevolence, since, upon the manner with which they are treated, depends the evil or good report which they will take back with them to their own land. Salute every one whom you meet. Love your wives, but do not permit them to govern you. When you have learned any thing useful, endeavor to imprint it upon your memory, and be always seeking to acquire information.

My father spoke five languages, a fact which excited the admiration of strangers.

"Guard against idleness, which is the mother of all vices. Man ought always to be occupied. When you are traveling on horseback, instead of allowing your mind to wander upon vain thoughts, recite your prayers, or, at least, repeat the shortest and best of them all: '*Oh, Lord, have mercy upon us.*' Never retire at night without falling upon your knees before God in prayer, and never let the sun find you in your bed. Always go to church at an early hour in the morning to offer to God the homage of your first and freshest thoughts. This was the custom of my father and of all the pious people who surrounded him. With the first rays of the sun they praised the Lord, and exclaimed, with fervor, 'Condescend, O Lord, with thy divine light to illumine my soul.'"

The faults of Monomaque were those of his age, *non vitia hominis, sed vitia sæculi;* but his virtues were truly Christian, and it can hardly be doubted that, as his earthly crown dropped from his brow, he received a brighter crown in heaven. The devastations of the barbarians in that day were so awful, burning cities and churches, and massacring women and children, that they were regarded as enemies of the human race, and were pursued with exterminating vengeance.

Monomaque left several children and a third wife. One of his wives, Gyda, was a daughter of Harold, King of England. His oldest son, Mstislaf, succeeded to the crown. His brothers received, as their inheritance, the government of extensive provinces. The new monarch, inheriting the energies and the virtues of his illustrious sire, had long been renowned. The barbarians, east of the Volga, as soon as they heard of the death of Monomaque, thought that Russia would fall an easy prey to their arms. In immense numbers they crossed the river, spreading far and wide the most awful devastation. But Mstislaf fell upon them with such impetuosity that they were routed with great slaughter and driven back to their wilds. Their chastisement was so severe that, for a long time, they were intimidated from any further incursions. With wonderful energy, Mstislaf attacked many of the tributary nations, who had claimed a sort of independence, and who were ever rising in insurrection. He speedily brought them into subjection to his sway, and placed over them rulers devoted to his interests. In the dead of winter an expedition was marched against the Tchoudes, who inhabited the southern shores of the bay of Finland. The men were put to death, the cities and villages burned; the women and children were brought away as captives and incorporated with the Russian people.

Mstislaf reigned but about four years, when he suddenly died in the sixtieth year of his age. His whole reign was an incessant warfare with insurgent chiefs and barbarian invaders. There is an awful record, at this time, of the scourge of famine added to the miseries of war. All the northern provinces suffered terribly from this frown of God. Immense quantities of snow covered the ground even to the month of May. The snow then melted suddenly with heavy rains, deluging the fields with water, which slowly retired, converting the country into a wide-spread marsh. It was very late before any seed could be sown. The grain had but just begun to sprout when myriads of locusts appeared, devouring every green thing. A heavy frost early in the autumn destroyed the few fields the locusts had spared, and then commenced the horrors of a universal famine. Men, women and children, wasted and haggard, wandered over the fields seeking green leaves and roots, and dropped dead in their wanderings. The fields and the public places were covered with putrefying corpses which the living had not strength to bury. A fetid miasma, ascending from this cause, added pestilence to famine, and woes ensued too awful to be described.

Immediately after the death of Mstislaf, the inhabitants of Kief assembled and invited his brother Vladimirovitch to assume the crown. This prince then resided at Novgorod, which city he at once left for the capital. He proved to be a feeble prince, and the lords of the remote principalities, assuming independence, bade defiance to his authority. There was no longer any central power, and Russia, instead of being a united kingdom, became a conglomeration of antagonistic states; every feudal lord marshaling his serfs in warfare against his neighbor. In the midst of this state of universal anarchy, caused by the weakness of a virtuous prince who had not sufficient energy to reign, Vladimirovitch died in 1139.

The death of the king was a signal for a general outbreak—a multitude of princes rushing to seize the crown. Viatcheslaf, prince of a large province called Pereiaslavle, was the first to reach Kief with his army. The inhabitants of the city, to avoid the horrors of war, marched in procession to meet him, and conducted him in triumph to the throne. Viatcheslaf had hardly grasped the scepter and stationed his army within the walls, when from the steeples of the city the banners of another advancing host were seen gleaming in the distance, and soon the tramp of their horsemen, and the defiant tones of the trumpet were heard, as another and far more mighty host encircled the city. This new army was led by Vsevolod, prince of a province called Vouychegorod. Viatcheslaf, convinced of the impossibility of resisting such a power as Vsevolod had brought against Kief, immediately consented to retire, and to surrender the throne to his more powerful rival. Vsevolod entered the city in triumph and established himself firmly in power.

There is nothing of interest to be recorded during his reign of seven years, save that Russia was swept by incessant billows of flame and blood. The princes of the provinces were ever rising against his authority. Combinations were formed to dethrone the king, and the king formed combinations to crush his enemies. The Hungarians, the Swedes, the Danes, the Poles, all made war against this energetic prince; but with an iron hand he smote them down. Toil and care soon exhausted his frame, and he was prostrate on his dying bed. Bequeathing his throne to his brother Igor, he died, leaving behind him the reputation of having been one of the most energetic of the kings of this blood-deluged land.

Igor was fully conscious of the perils he thus inherited. He was very unpopular with the inhabitants of Kief, and loud murmurs greeted his accession to power. A conspiracy was formed among the most influential inhabitants of Kief, and a secret embassage was sent to the grand prince, Ysiaslaf, a descendant of Monomaque, inviting him to come, and with their aid, take possession of the throne. The prince attended the summons with alacrity, and marched with a powerful army to Kief. Igor was vanquished in a sanguinary battle, taken captive, imprisoned in a convent, and Ysiaslaf became the nominal monarch of Russia.

Sviatoslaf, the brother of Igor, overwhelmed with anguish in view of his brother's fall and captivity, traversed the expanse of Russia to enlist the sympathies of the distant princes, to march for the rescue of the captive. He was quite successful. An allied army was soon raised, and, under determined leaders, was on the march for Kief. The king, Ysiaslaf, with his troops, advanced to meet them. In the meantime Igor, crushed by misfortune, and hopeless of deliverance, sought solace for his woes in religion. "For a long time," said he, "I have desired to consecrate my heart to God. Even in the height of prosperity this was my strongest wish. What can be more proper for me now that I am at the very gates of the tomb?" For eight days he laid in his cell, expecting every moment to breathe his last. He then, reviving a little, received the tonsure from the hands of the bishop, and renouncing the world, and all its cares and ambitions, devoted himself to the prayers and devotions of the monk.

The king pressed Sviatoslaf with superior forces, conquered him in several battles, and drove him, a fugitive, into dense forests, and into distant wilds. Sviatoslaf, like his brother, weary of the storms of life, also sought the solace which religion affords to the weary and the heart-stricken. Pursued by his relentless foe, he came to a little village called Moscow, far back in the interior. This is the first intimation history gives of this now renowned capital of the most extensive monarchy upon the globe. A prince named Georges reigned here, over the extensive province then called Souzdal, who received the fugitive with heartfelt sympathy. Aided by Georges and several of the surrounding princes, another army was raised, and Sviatoslaf commenced a triumphal march, sweeping all opposition before him, until he arrived a conqueror before the walls of Novgorod.

The people of Kief, enraged by this success of the foe of their popular king, rose in a general tumult, burst into a convent where Igor was found at his devotions, tied a rope about his neck, and dragged him, a mutilated corpse, through the streets.

The king, Ysiaslaf, called for a *levy en masse*, of the inhabitants of Kief, summoned distant feudal barons with their armies to his banner, and marched impetuously to meet the conquering foe. Fierce battles ensued, in which Sviatoslaf was repeatedly vanquished, and retreated to Souzdal again to appeal to Georges for aid. Ysiaslaf summoned the Novgorodians before him, and in the following energetic terms addressed them:

"My brethren," said he, "Georges, the prince of Souzdal, has insulted Novgorod. I have left the capital of Russia to defend you. Do you wish to prosecute the war? The sword is in my hands. Do you desire peace? I will open negotiations."

"War, war," the multitude shouted. "You are our monarch, and we will all follow you, from the youngest to the oldest."

A vast army was immediately assembled on the shores of

the lake of Ilmen, near the city of Novgorod, which commenced its march of three hundred miles, to the remote realms of Souzdal. Georges was unprepared to meet them. He fled, surrendering his country to be ravaged by the foe. His cities and villages were burned, and seven thousand of his subjects were carried captive to Kief. But Georges was not a man to bear such a calamity meekly. He speedily succeeded in forming an alliance with the barbarian nations around him, and burning with rage, followed the army of the retiring foe. He overtook them near the city of Periaslavle. It was the evening of the 23d of August. The unclouded sun was just sinking at the close of a sultry day, and the vesper chants were floating through the temples of the city. The storm of war burst as suddenly as the thunder peals of an autumnal tempest. The result was most awful and fatal to the king. His troops were dispersed and cut to pieces. Ysiaslaf himself with difficulty escaped and reached the ramparts of Kief. The terrified inhabitants entreated him not to remain, as his presence would only expose the city to the horror of being taken by storm.

"Our fathers, our brothers, our sons," they said, "are dead upon the field of battle, or are in chains. We have no arms. Generous prince, do not expose the capital of Russia to pillage. Flee for a time to your remote principalities, there to gather a new army. You know that we will never rest contented under the government of Georges. We will rise in revolt against him, as soon as we shall see your standards approaching."

Ysiaslaf fled, first to Smolensk, some three hundred miles distant, and thence traversed his principalities seeking aid. Georges entered Kief in triumph. Calling his warriors around him, he assigned to them the provinces which he had wrested from the feudal lords of the king.

Hungary, Bohemia and Poland then consisted of barbaric peoples just emerging into national existence. The King of

Hungary had married Euphrosine, the youngest sister of Ysiaslaf. He immediately sent to his brother-in-law ten thousand cavaliers. The Kings of Bohemia and of Poland also entered into an alliance with the exiled prince, and in person led the armies which they contributed to his aid. A war of desperation ensued. It was as a conflict between the tiger and the lion.

The annals of those dark days contained but a weary recital of deeds of violence, blood and woe, which for ten years desolated the land. All Russia was roused. Every feudal lord was leading his vassals to the field. There were combinations and counter-combinations innumerable. Cities were taken and retaken; to-day, the banners of Ysiaslaf float upon the battlements of Kief; to-morrow, those banners are hewn down and the standards of Georges are unfurled to the breeze. Now, we see Ysiaslaf a fugitive, hopeless, in despair. Again, the rolling wheel of fortune raises him from his depression, and, with the strides of a conqueror, he pursues his foe, in his turn vanquished and woe-stricken. But

> "The pomp of heraldry, the pride of power,
> And all that beauty, all that wealth e'er gave,
> Alike await the inevitable hour;
> The paths of glory lead but to the grave."

Death, which Ysiaslaf had braved in a hundred battles, approached him by the slow but resistless march of disease. For a few days the monarch tossed in fevered restlessness on his bed at Kief, and then, from his life of incessant storms on earth, his spirit ascended to the God who gave it. Georges was, at that time, in the lowest state of humiliation. His armies had all perished, and he was wandering in exile, seeking new forces with which to renew the strife.

Rostislaf, grand prince of Novgorod, succeeded to the throne. But Georges, animated by the death of Ysiaslaf, soon found enthusiastic adventurers rallying around his banners.

He marched vigorously to Kief, drove Rostislaf from the capital and seized the scepter. But there was no lull in the tempest of human ambition. Georges had attained the throne by the energies of his sword, and, acting upon the principle that "to the victors belong the spoils," he had driven from their castles all the lords who had been supporters of the past administration. He had conferred their mansions and their territories upon his followers. Human nature has not materially changed. Those in office were fighting to retain their honors and emoluments. Those out of office were struggling to attain the posts which brought wealth and renown. The progress of civilization has, in our country, transferred this fierce battle from the field to the ballot-box. It is, indeed, a glorious change. The battle can be fought thus just as effectually, and infinitely more humanely. It has required the misery of nearly six thousand years to teach, even a few millions of mankind, that the ballot-box is a better instrument for political conflicts than the cartridge-box.

Armies were gathering in all directions to march upon Georges. He was now an old man, weary of war, and endeavored to bribe his foes to peace. He was, however, unsuccessful, and found it to be necessary again to lead his armies into the field. It was the 20th of March, 1157, when Georges, entering Kief in triumph, ascended the throne. On the 1st of May he dined with some of his lords. Immediately after dinner he was taken sick, and, after languishing a fortnight in ever-increasing debility, on the 15th he died.

The inhabitants of Kief, regarding him as an usurper, rejoiced at his death, and immediately sent an embassage to Davidovitch, prince of Tchernigof, a province about one hundred and fifty miles north of Kief, inviting him to hasten to the capital and seize the scepter of Russia.

Kief, and all occidental Russia, thus ravaged by interminable wars, desolated by famine and by flame, was rapidly on the decline, and was fast lapsing into barbarism. Davidovitch had hardly ascended the throne ere he was driven from it by Rostislaf, whom Georges had dethroned. But the remote province of Souzdal, of which Moscow was the capital, situated some seven hundred miles north-east of Kief, was now emerging from barbaric darkness into wealth and civilization. The missionaries of Christ had penetrated those remote realms. Churches were reared, the gospel was preached, peace reigned, industry was encouraged, and, under their influence, Moscow was attaining that supremacy which subsequently made it the heart of the Russian empire.

The inhabitants of Kief received Rostislaf with demonstrations of joy, as they received every prince whom the fortunes of war imposed upon them, hoping that each one would secure for their unhappy city the blessings of tranquillity. Davidovitch fled to Moldavia. There was then in Moldavia, between the rivers Pruth and Sereth, a piratic city called Berlad. It was the resort of vagabonds of all nations and creeds, who pillaged the shores of the Black Sea and plundered the boats ascending and descending the Danube and the Dnieper. These brigands, enriched by plunder and strengthened by accessions of desperadoes from every nation and every tribe, had bidden defiance both to the grand princes of Russia and the powers of the empire.

Eagerly these robber hordes engaged as auxiliaries of Davidovitch. In a tumultuous band they commenced their march to Kief. They were, however, repulsed by the energetic Rostislaf, and Davidovitch, with difficulty escaping from the sanguinary field, fled to Moscow and implored the aid of its independent prince, Georgievitch. The prince listened with interest to his representations, and, following the example of the more illustrious nations of modern times, thought it a good opportunity to enlarge his territories.

The city of Novgorod, capital of the extensive and powerful province of the same name, was some seven hundred miles north of Kief. It was not more than half that distance west of Moscow. The inhabitants were weary of anarchy and blood, and anxious to throw themselves into the arms of any prince who could secure for them tranquillity. The fruit was ripe and was ready to drop into the hands of Georgievitch. He sent word to the Novgorodians that he had decided to take their country under his protection—that he had no wish for war, but that if they manifested any resistance, he should subdue them by force of arms. The Novgorodians received the message with delight, rose in insurrection, and seized their prince, who was the oldest son of Rostislaf, imprisoned nim, his wife and children, in a convent, and with tumultuous joy received as their prince the nephew of Georgievitch. Rostislaf was so powerless that he made no attempt to avenge this insult. Davidovitch made one more desperate effort to obtain the throne. But he fell upon the field of battle, his head being cleft with a saber stroke.

CHAPTER V.

MSTISLAF AND ANDRÉ.

FROM 1167 TO 1212.

CENTRALIZATION OF POWER AT KIEF.—DEATH OF ROSTISLAF.—HIS RELIGIOUS CHARACTER.—MSTISLAF YSIASLAVITCH ASCENDS THE THRONE.—PROCLAMATION OF THE KING.—ITS EFFECT.—PLANS OF ANDRE.—SCENES AT KIEF.—RETURN AND DEATH OF MSTISLAF.—WAR IN NOVGOROD.—PEACE CONCLUDED THROUGHOUT RUSSIA.—INSULT OF ANDRE AND ITS CONSEQUENCES.—GREATNESS OF SOUL DISPLAYED BY ANDRE.—ASSASSINATION OF ANDRE.—RENEWAL OF ANARCHY.—EMIGRATION FROM NOVGOROD.—REIGN OF MICHEL.—VSEVOLOD III.—EVANGELIZATION OF BULGARIA.—DEATH OF VSEVOLOD III.—HIS QUEEN MARIA.

THE prince of Souzdal watched the progress of events in occidental Russia with great interest. He saw clearly that war was impoverishing and ruining the country, and this led him to adopt the most wise and vigorous measures to secure peace within his own flourishing territories. He adopted the system of centralized power, keeping the reins of government firmly in his own hands, and appointing governors over remote provinces, who were merely the executors of his will, and who were responsible to him for all their acts. At Kief the system of independent apanages prevailed. The lord placed at the head of a principality was an unlimited despot, accountable to no one but God for his administration. His fealty to the king consisted merely in an understanding that he was to follow the banner of the sovereign in case of war. But in fact, these feudal lords were more frequently found claiming entire independence, and struggling against their nominal sovereign to wrest from his hands the scepter.

Rostislaf was now far advanced in years. Conscious that death could not be far distant, he took a journey, though in very feeble health, to some of the adjacent provinces, hoping to induce them to receive his son as his successor. On this journey he died at Smolensk, the 14th of March, 1167. Religious thoughts had in his latter years greatly engrossed his attention. He breathed his last, praying with a trembling voice, and fixing his eyes devoutly on an image of the Saviour which he held devoutly in his hand. He exhibited many Christian virtues, and for many years manifested much solicitude that he might be prepared to meet God in judgment. The earnest remonstrances, alone, of his spiritual advisers, dissuaded him from abdicating the throne, and adopting the austerities of a monastic life. He was not a man of commanding character, but it is pleasant to believe that he was, though groping in much darkness, a sincere disciple of the Saviour, and that he passed from earth to join the spirits of the just made perfect in Heaven.

Mstislaf Ysiaslavitch, a nephew of the deceased king, ascended the throne. He had however uncles, nephews and brothers, who were quite disposed to dispute with him the possession of power, and soon civil war was raging all over the kingdom with renewed virulence. Several years of destruction and misery thus passed away, during which thousands of the helpless people perished in their blood, to decide questions of not the slightest moment to them. The doom of the peasants was alike poverty and toil, whether one lord or another lord occupied the castle which overshadowed their huts.

The Dnieper was then the only channel through which commerce could be conducted between Russia and the Greek empire. Barbaric nations inhabited the shores of this stream, and they had long been held in check by the Russian armies. But now the kingdom had become so enfeebled by war and anarchy, all the energies of the Russian princes being exhausted in civil strife, that the barbarians plundered with impunity the boats ascending and descending the stream, and eventually rendered the navigation so perilous, that commercial communication with the empire was at an end. The Russian princes thus debarred from the necessaries and luxuries which they had been accustomed to receive from the more highly civilized and polished Greeks, were impelled to measures of union for mutual protection. The king, in this emergence, issued a proclamation which met with a general response.

"Russia, our beloved country," exclaimed Mstislaf, "groans beneath the stripes which the barbarians are laying upon her, and which we are unable to avenge. They have taken solemn oaths of friendship, they have received our presents, and now, regardless of the faith of treaties, they capture our Christian subjects and drag them as slaves into their desert wilds. There is no longer any safety for our merchant boats navigating the Dnieper. The barbarians have taken possession of that only route through which we can pass into Greece. It is time for us to resort to new measures of energy. My friends and my brothers, let us terminate our unnatural war; let us look to God for help, and, drawing the sword of vengeance, let us fall in united strength upon our savage foes. It is glorious to ascend to Heaven from the field of honor, thus to follow in the footsteps of our father."

This spirited appeal was effective. The princes rallied each at the head of a numerous band of vassals, and thus a large army was soon congregated. The desire to punish the insulting barbarians inspired universal enthusiasm. The masses of the people were aroused to avenge their friends who had been carried into captivity. The priests, with prayers and anthems, blessed the banners of the faithful, and, on the 2d of March, 1168, the army, elate with hope and nerved with vengeance, commenced their descent of the river. The barbarians, terrified by the storm which they had raised, and from whose fury they could attain no shelter, fled so precipitately that they left their wives and their children behind them. The Russians, abandoning the incumbrance of their baggage, pursued them in the hottest haste. Over the hills, and through the valleys, and across the streams pursuers and pursued rushed on, until, at last, the fugitives were overtaken upon the banks of a deep and rapid stream, which they were unable to cross. Mercilessly they were massacred, many Russian prisoners were rescued, and booty to an immense amount was taken, for these river pirates were rich, having for years been plundering the commerce of Greece and Russia. According to the custom of those days the booty was divided between the princes and the soldiers—each man receiving according to his rank.

As the army returned in triumph to the Dniester, to their boundless satisfaction they saw the pennants of a merchant fleet ascending the river from Constantinople, laden with the riches of the empire. The army crowded the shores and greeted the barges with all the demonstrations of exultation and joy.

The punishment of the barbarians being thus effectually accomplished, the princes immediately commenced anew their strife. All their old feuds were revived. Every lord wished to increase his own power and to diminish that of his natural rival. André, of Souzdal, to whom we have before referred, whose capital was the little village of Moscow far away in the interior, deemed the moment favorable for dethroning Mstislaf and extending the area of such freedom as his subjects enjoyed over the realms of Novgorod and Kief. He succeeded in uniting eleven princes with him in his enterprise. His measures were adopted with great secresy. Assembling his armies, curtained by leagues of forests, he, unobserved, commenced his march toward the Dnieper. The banners of the numerous army were already visible from the steeples of Kief before the sovereign was apprised of his danger. For two days the storms of war beat against the walls and roared around the battlements of the city, when the besiegers, bursting over the walls, swept the streets in horrid carnage.

This mother of the Russian cities had often been besieged and often capitulated, but never before had it been taken by storm, and never before, and never since, have the horrors of war been more sternly exhibited. For three days and three nights the city and its inhabitants were surrendered to the brutal soldiery. The imagination shrinks from contemplating the awful scene. The world of woe may be challenged to exhibit any thing worse. Fearful, indeed, must be the corruption when man can be capable of such inhumanity to his fellow man. War unchains the tiger and shows his nature.

Mstislaf, the sovereign, in the midst of the confusion, the uproar and the blood, succeeded almost as by miracle in escaping from the wretched city, basely, however, abandoning his wife and his children to the enemy. Thus fell Kief. For some centuries it had been the capital of Russia. It was such no more. The victorious André, of Moscow, was now, by the energies of his sword, sovereign of the empire. Kief became but a provincial and a tributary city, which the sovereign placed under the governorship of his brother Gleb.

Nearly all the provinces of known Russia were now more or less tributary to André. Three princes only preserved their independence. As the army of André retired, Gleb was left in possession of the throne of Kief. In those days there were always many petty princes, ready to embark with their followers in any enterprise which promised either glory or booty. Mstislaf, the fugitive sovereign, soon gathered around him semi-savage bands, entered the province of Kief, plundering and burning the homes of his former subjects. As he approached Kief, Gleb, unprepared for efficient resistance, was compelled to seek safety in flight. The inhabitants of the city, to escape the horrors of another siege and sack, threw open their gates, and crowded out to meet their former monarch as a returning friend. Mstislaf entered the city in triumph and quietly reseated himself upon the throne. He however ascended it but to die. A sudden disease seized him, and the songs of triumph which greeted his entrance, died away in requiems and wailings, as he was borne to the silent tomb. With dying breath he surrendered his throne to his younger brother Yaroslaf.

André, at Moscow, had other formidable engagements on hand, which prevented his interposition in the affairs of Kief. The Novgorodians had bidden defiance to his authority, and their subjugation was essential, before any troops could be spared to chastise the heir of Mstislaf. The Novgorodian army had even penetrated the realms of André, and were exacting tribute from his provinces. The grand prince, André himself, was far advanced in years, opposed to war, and had probably been pushed on in his enterprises by the ambition of his son, who was also named Mstislaf. This young prince was impetuous and fiery, greedy for military glory, and restless in his graspings for power. The Novgorodians were also warlike and indomitable. The conflict between two such powers arrested the attention of all Russia. Mstislaf made the most extensive preparations for the attack upon the Novgorodians, and they, in their turn, were equally energetic in preparations for the defense. The army marched from Moscow, and following the valley of the Masta, entered the spacious province of Novgorod. They entered the region, not like wolves, not like men, but like demons. The torch was applied to every hut, to every village, to every town. They amused themselves with tossing men, women and children upon their camp-fires, glowing like furnaces. The sword and the spear were too merciful instruments of death. The flames of the burning towns blazed along the horizon night after night, and the cry of the victims roused the Novgorodians to the intensest thirst for vengeance.

With the sweep of utter desolation, Mstislaf approached the city, and when his army stood before the walls, there was behind him a path, leagues in width, and two hundred miles in length, covered with ruins, ashes and the bodies of the dead. It was the 25th of February, 1170. The city was immediately summoned to surrender. The Novgorodians appalled by the fate of Kief, and by the horrors which had accompanied the march of Mstislaf, took a solemn oath that they would struggle to the last drop of blood in defense of their liberties. The clergy in procession, bearing the image of the Virgin in their arms, traversed the fortifications of the city, and with prayers, hymns and the most imposing Christian rites, inspired the soldiers with religious enthusiasm. The Novgorodians threw themselves upon their knees, and in simultaneous prayer cried out, with the blending of ten thousand voices, "O God! come and help us, come and help us." Thus roused to frenzy, with the clergy chanting hymns of battle and pleading with Heaven for success, with the image of the Virgin contemplating their deeds, the soldiers rushed from behind their ramparts upon the foe. Death was no longer dreaded. The only thought of every man was to sell his life as dearly as possible.

Such an onset of maniacal energy no mortal force could stand. The soldiers of Mstislaf fell as the waving grain bows before the tornado. Their defeat was utter and awful. Mercy was not thought of. Sword and javelin cried only for blood, blood. The wretched Mstislaf in dismay fled, leaving two thirds of his army in gory death; and, in his flight, he met that chastisement which his cruelties merited. He had to traverse a path two hundred miles in length, along which not one field of grain had been left undestroyed; where every dwelling was in ashes, and no animal life whatever had escaped his ravages. Starvation was his doom. Every rod of the way his emaciated soldiers dropped dead in their steps. Famine also with all its woes reigned in Novgorod. Under these circumstances, the two parties consented to peace, the Novgorodians retaining their independence, but accepting a brother of the grand prince André to succeed their own prince, who was then at the point of death.

André, having thus terminated the strife with Novgorod by the peace which he loved, turned his attention to Kief, and with characteristic humanity, gratified the wishes of the inhabitants by allowing them to accept Roman, prince of Smolensk, as their chieftain. Roman entered the city, greeted by the most flattering testimonials of the joy of the inhabitants, while they united with him in the oath of allegiance to André as the sovereign of Russia. André, who was ever disposed to establish his sovereign power, not by armies but by equity and moderation, and who seems truly to have felt that the welfare of Russia required that all its provinces should be united under common laws and a common sovereign, turned his attention again to Novgorod, hoping to persuade its inhabitants to relinquish their independence and ally themselves with the general empire.

Rurik, the brother of André, who had been appointed prince of Novgorod, proved unpopular, and was driven from his command. André, instead of endeavoring to force him back upon them by the energies of his armies, with a wise spirit of conciliation acquiesced in their movement, and sent to them his young son, George, as a prince, offering to assist them with his counsel and to aid them with his military force whenever they should desire it. Thus internal peace was established throughout the empire. By gradual advances, and with great sagacity, André, from his humble palace in Moscow, extended his influence over the remote provinces, and established his power.

The princes of Kief and its adjacent provinces became jealous of the encroachments of André, and hostile feelings were excited. The king at length sent an embassador to them with very imperious commands. The embassador was seized at Kief, his hair and beard shaven, and was then sent back to Moscow with the defiant message,

"Until now we have wished to respect you as a father; but since you do not blush to treat us as vassals and as peasants—since you have forgotten that you speak to princes, we spurn your menaces. Execute them. We appeal to the judgment of God."

This grievous insult of word and deed roused the indignation of the aged monarch as it had never been roused before. He assembled an army of fifty thousand men, who were rendezvoused at Novgorod, and placed under the command of the king's son, Georges. Another army, nearly equal in number, was assembled at Tchernigof, collected from the principalities of Polotsk, Tourof, Grodno, Pinsk and Smolensk. The bands of this army were under the several princes of the provinces. Sviatoslaf, grandson of the renowned Oleg, was entrusted with the supreme command. These two majestic forces were soon combined upon the banks of the Dnieper. All resistance fled before them, and with strides of triumph they marched down the valley to Kief. The princes who had aroused this storm of war fled to Vouoychegorod, an important fortress further down the river, where they strongly entrenched themselves, and sternly awaited the advance of the foe. The royalist forces, having taken possession of Kief, pursued the fugitives. The march of armies so vast, conducting war upon so grand a scale, excited the astonishment of all the inhabitants upon the river's banks. A little fortress, defended by a mere handful of men, appeared to them an object unworthy of an army sufficiently powerful to crush an empire.

But in the fortress there was perfect unity, and its commander had the soul of a lion. In the camp of the besiegers there was neither harmony nor zeal. Many of the princes were inimical to the king, and were jealous of his growing power. Others were envious of Sviatoslaf, the commander-in-chief, and were willing to sacrifice their own fame that he might be humbled. Not a few even were in sympathy with the insurgents, and were almost disposed to unite under their banners.

It was the 8th of September, 1173, when the royalist

forces encircled the fortress. Gunpowder was then unknown, and contending armies could only meet hand to hand. For two months the siege was continued, with bloody conflicts every day. Wintry winds swept the plains, and storms of snow whitened the fields, when, from the battlements of the fortress, the besieged saw the banners of another army approaching the arena. They knew not whether the distant battalions were friends or foes; but it was certain that their approach would decide the strife, for each party was so exhausted as to be unable to resist any new assailants. Soon the signals of war proclaimed that an army was approaching for the rescue of the fortress. Shouts of exultation rose from the garrison, which fell like the knell of death upon the ears of the besiegers, freezing on the plains. The alarm which spread through the camp was instantaneous and terrible. The darkness of a November night soon settled down over city and plain. With the first rays of the morning the garrison were upon the walls, when, to their surprise, they saw the whole vast army in rapid and disordered flight. The plains around the fortress were utterly deserted and covered with the wrecks of war. The garrison immediately rushed from behind their ramparts united with their approaching friends and pursued the fugitives.

The royalists, in their dismay, attempted to cross the river on the fragile ice. It broke beneath the enormous weight, and thousands perished in the cold stream. The remainder of this great host were almost to a man either slain or taken captive. Their whole camp and baggage fell into the hands of the conquerors. This wonderful victory, achieved by the energies of Mstislaf, has given him a name in Russian annals as one of the most renowned and brave of the princes of the empire.

George, prince of Novgorod, son of André, escaped from the carnage of that ensanguined field, and overwhelmed with shame, returned to his father in Moscow. The king, in this extremity, developed true greatness of soul. He exhibited neither dejection nor anger, but bowed to the calamity as to a chastisement he needed from God. The victory of the insurgents, if they may be so called, who occupied the provinces in the valley of the Dnieper, was not promotive either of prosperity or peace. Mindful of the former grandeur of Kief, as the ancient capital of the Russian empire, ambitious princes were immediately contending for the possession of that throne. After several months of confusion and blood, André succeeded, by skillful diplomacy, in again inducing them, for the sake of general tranquillity, to come under the general government of the empire. The nobles could not but respect him as the most aged of their princes; as a man of imperial energy and ability, and as the one most worthy to be their chief. He alone had the power to preserve tranquillity in extended Russia. They therefore applied to him to take Kief, under certain restrictions, again into his protection, and to nominate for that city a prince who should be in his alliance. This homage was acceptable to André.

But while he was engaged in this negotiation, a conspiracy was formed against the monarch, and he was cruelly assasinated. It was the night of the 29th of June, 1174. The king was sleeping in a chateau, two miles from Moscow. At midnight the conspirators, twenty in number, having inflamed themselves with brandy, burst into the house and rushed towards the chamber where the aged monarch was reposing. The clamor awoke the king, and he sprang from the bed just as two of the conspirators entered his chamber. Aged as the monarch was, with one blow of his vigorous arm he felled the foremost to the floor. The comrade of the assassin, in the confusion, thinking it was the king who had fallen, plunged his poignard to the hilt in his companion's breast. Other assassins rushed in and fell upon the monarch. He was a man of gigantic powers, and struggled against his foes with almost supernatural energy, filling the chateau with his shrieks for help. At last, pierced with innumerable wounds, he fell in his blood, apparently silent in death. The assassins, terrified by the horrible scene, and apprehensive that the guard might come to the rescue of the king, caught up their dead comrade and fled.

The monarch had, however, but fainted. He almost instantly revived, and with impetuosity and bravery, seized his sword and gave chase to the murderers, shouting with all his strength to his attendants to hasten to his aid. The assassins turned upon him. They had lanterns in their hands, and were twenty to one. The first blow struck off the right arm of the king; a saber thrust pierced his heart, passed through his body, and the monarch fell dead. His last words were, "Lord, into thy hands I commit my spirit." There is, to this day, preserved a cimeter of Grecian workmanship, which tradition says was the sword of André. Upon the blade is incribed in Greek letters, "Holy mother of God, assist thy servant."

The death of the monarch was the signal for the universal outbreak of violence and crime. Where the sovereign is the only law, the death of the monarch is the destruction of the government. The anarchy which sometimes succeeded his death was awful. The Russian annalists cherish the memory of André affectionately. They say that he was courageous, sagacious and a true Christian, and that he merited the title he has received of a second Solomon. Had he established his throne in the more central city of Kief instead of the remote village of Moscow, he could more efficiently have governed the empire; but, blinded by his love for his own northern realms, he was ambitious of elevating his own native village, unfavorable as was its location, into the capital of the empire. During his whole reign he manifested great zeal in extending Christianity through the empire, and evinced great interest in efforts for the conversion of the Jews.

Just before the death of the king, a number of the inhabitants of Novgorod, fatigued with civil strife and crowded out by the density of the population, formed a party to emigrate to the uninhabited lands far away in the East. Traversing a region of about three hundred miles on the parallel of fifty-seven degrees of latitude, they reached the head waters of the Volga. Here they embarked in boats and drifted down the wild stream for a thousand miles to the mouth of the river Kama, where they established a colony. At this point they were twelve hundred miles north of the point where the Volga empties into the Caspian. Other adventurers soon followed, and flourishing colonies sprang up all along the banks of the Kama and the Viatha. This region was the Missouri valley of Russia. By this emigration the Russian name, its manners, its institutions, were extended through a sweep of a thousand miles.

The colonists had many conflicts with the aboriginal inhabitants, but Russian civilization steadily advanced over barbaric force.

Soon after the death of André, the nobles of that region met in a public assembly to organize some form of confederate government. One of the speakers rose and said, "No one is ignorant of the manner in which we have lost our king. He has left but one son, who reigns at Novgorod. The brothers of André are in southern Russia. Who then shall we choose for our sovereign? Let us elect Michel, of Tchernigof. He is the oldest son of Monomaque and the most ancient of the princes of his family."

Embassadors were immediately sent to Michel, offering him the throne and promising him the support of the confederate princes. Michel hastened to Moscow with a strong army, supported by several princes, and took possession of Moscow and the adjacent provinces. A little opposition was manifested, which he speedily quelled with the sword. Great rejoicings welcomed the enthronement of a new prince and the restoration of order. Michel proved worthy of his elevation. He immediately traversed the different provinces in that region, and devoted himself to the tranquillity and prosperity of his people. The popularity of the new sovereign was at its height. All lips praised him, all hearts loved him. He was declared to be a special gift which Heaven, in its boundless mercy, had conferred. Unfortunately, this virtuous prince reigned but one year, leaving, however, in that short time, upon the Russian annals many memorials of his valor and of his virtue. It was a barbaric age, rife with perfidy and crime, yet not one act of treachery or cruelty has sullied his name. It was his ambition to be the father of his people, and the glory he sought was the happiness and the greatness of his country.

Southern Russia was still the theater of interminable civil war. The provinces were impoverished, and Kief was fast sinking to decay. Michel had a brother, Vsevelod, who had accompanied him to Moscow. The nobles and the leading citizens, their eyes still dim with the tears which they had shed over the tomb of their sovereign, urged him to accept the crown. He was not reluctant to accede to their request, and received their oaths of fidelity to him under the title of Vsevelod III. His title, however, was disputed by distant princes, and an armed band, approaching Moscow by surprise, seized the town and reduced it to ashes, ravaged the surrounding region, and carried off the women and children as captives. Vsevelod was, at the time, absent in the extreme northern portion of his territory, but he turned upon his enemies with the heart and with the strength of a lion. It was midwinter. Regardless of storms, and snow and cold, he pursued the foe like the north wind, and crushed them as with an iron hand. With a large number of prisoners he returned to the ruins of Moscow.

Two of the most illustrious of the hostile princes were among the prisoners. The people, enraged at the destruction of their city, fell upon the captives, and, seizing the two princes, tore out their eyes.

Vsevelod was a young man who had not acquired renown. Many of the warlike princes of the spacious provinces regarded his elevation with envy. Sviatoslaf, prince of Tchernigof, was roused to intense hostility, and gathering around him the nobles of his province, resolved with a vigorous arm to seize for himself the throne. Enlisting in his interests several other princes, he commenced his march against his sovereign. Vsevelod prepared with vigor to repulse his assailants. After long and weary marchings the two armies met in the defiles of the mountains. A swift mountain-stream rushing along its rocky bed, between deep and precipitous banks, separated the combatants. For a fortnight they vainly assailed each other, hurling clouds of arrows and javelins across the stream, which generally fell harmless upon brazen helmet and buckler. But few were wounded, and still fewer slain. Yet neither party dared venture the passage of the stream in the presence of the other. At length, weary of the unavailing conflict, Sviatoslaf, the insurgent chief, sent a challenge to Vsevelod, the sovereign.

"Let God," said he, "decide the dispute between us. Let us enter into the open field with our two armies, and submit the question to the arbitrament of battle. You may choose either side of the river which you please."

Vsevelod did not condescend to make any reply to the rebellious prince. Seizing his embassadors, he sent them as captives to Vlademer, a fortress some hundred miles east of Moscow. He hoped thus to provoke Sviatoslaf to attempt the passage of the stream. But Sviatoslaf was not to be thus entrapped. Breaking up his camp, he retired to Novgorod, where he was received with rejoicings by the inhabitants. Here he established himself as a monarch, accumulated his forces, and began, by diplomacy and by arms, to extend his conquests over the adjacent principalities. He sent a powerful army to descend the banks of the Dnieper, capturing all the cities on the right hand and on the left, and binding the inhabitants by oaths of allegiance. The army advancing with resistless strides arrived before the walls of Kief, took possession of the deserted palaces of this ancient capital, and Sviatoslaf proclaimed himself monarch of southern Russia.

But while Sviatoslaf was thus prosecuting his conquests, at the distance of four hundred miles south of Novgorod, Vsevelod advanced with an army to this city, and was in his turn received by the Novgorodians with the ringing of bells, bonfires and shouts of welcome. All the surrounding princes and nobles promptly gave in their adhesion to the victorious sovereign, and Sviatoslaf found that all his conquests had vanished as by magic from beneath his hand.

Under these circumstances, Vsevelod and Sviatoslaf were both inclined to negotiation. As the result, it was agreed that Vsevelod should be recognized as the monarch of Russia, and that Sviatoslaf should reign as tributary prince of Kief. To bind anew the ties of friendship, Vsevelod gave in marriage his beautiful sister to the youngest son of Sviatoslaf. Thus this civil strife was terminated.

But the gates of the temple of Janus were not yet to be closed. Foreign war now commenced, and raged with unusual ferocity. Six hundred miles east of Moscow, was the country of Bulgaria. It comprehended the present Russian province of Orenburg, and was bounded on the east by the Ural mountains, and on the west by the Volga. A population of nearly a million and a half inhabited this mountainous realm. Commerce and arts flourished, and the people were enriched by their commerce with the Grecian empire. They were, however, barbarians, and as even in the nineteenth century the slave trade is urged as a means of evangelizing the heathen of Africa, war was urged with all its carnage and woe, as the agent of disseminating Christianity through pagan

Bulgaria. The motive assigned for the war, was to serve Christ, by the conversion of the infidel. The motives which influenced, were ambition, love of conquest and the desire to add to the opulence and the power of Russia.

Vsevelod made grand preparations for this enterprise. Conferring with the warlike Sviatoslaf and other ambitious princes, a large army was collected at the head waters of the Volga. They floated down the wild stream, in capacious flat-bottomed barges, till they came to the mouth of the Kama. Thus far their expedition had been like the jaunt of a gala day. Summer warmth and sunny skies had cheered them as they floated down the romantic stream, through forests, between mountains and along flowery savannas, with pennants floating gayly in the air, and music swelling from their martial bands. War has always its commencement of pomp and pageantry, followed by its terminations of woe and despair.

Vsevelod in person led the army. Near the mouth of the Kama they abandoned their flotilla, which could not be employed in ascending the rapid stream. Continuing their march by land, they pushed boldly into the country of the Bulgarians, and laid siege to their capital, which was called "The Great City." For six days the battle raged, and the city was taken. It proved, however, to be but a barren conquest. An arrow from the walls pierced the side of a beloved nephew of Vsevelod. The young man, in excruciating agony, died in the arms of the monarch. Vsevelod was so much affected by the sufferings which he was thus called to witness, that, dejected and disheartened, he made the best terms he could, soothing his pride by extorting from the vanquished a vague acknowledgment of subjection to the empire. He then commenced his long march of toil and suffering back again to Moscow, over vast plains and through dense forests, having really accomplished nothing of any moment.

The reign of Vsevelod continued for thirty-seven years. It was a scene of incessant conflict with insurgent princes disputing his power and struggling for the supremacy. Often his imperial title was merely nominal. Again a successful battle would humble his foes and bring them in subjection to the foot of his throne. But, on the whole, during his reign the fragmentary empire gained solidity, the monarchical arm gained strength, and the sovereign obtained a more marked supremacy above the rival princes who had so long disputed the power of the throne. Vsevelod died, generally regretted, on the 12th of April, 1212. In the Russian annals, he has received the surname of Great. His reign, compared with that of most of his predecessors, was happy. He left, in churches and in fortresses, many monuments of his devotion and of his military skill.

His wife, Maria, seems to have been a woman of sincere piety. Her brief pilgrimage on earth, passed six hundred years ago, led her through the same joys and griefs which in the ninteenth century oppress human hearts. The last seven years of her life she passed on a bed of sickness and extreme suffering. The patience she displayed caused her to be compared with the patriarch Job. Just before she died, she assembled her six surviving children around her bed. As with tears they gazed upon the emaciated cheeks of their beloved and dying mother, she urged them to love God, to study the Bible, to give their hearts to the Saviour and to live for heaven. She died universally regretted and revered.

The reign of Vsevelod was cotemporaneous with the conquest of Constantinople by the crusaders. The Latin or Roman church thus for a season extended its dominion over the Greek or Eastern church. The French and Venetians robbed the rich churches of Constantine of their paintings, statuary, relics and all their treasures of art. The Greek emperor himself fled in disguise to Thrace.

The Roman pontiff, Innocent III., deeming this a favorable moment to supplant the Greek religion in Russia, sent letters to the Russian clergy, in which he said:

"The religion of Rome is becoming universally triumphant. The whole Grecian empire has recognized the spiritual power of the pope. Will you be the only people who refuse to enter into the fold of Christ, and to recognize the Roman church as the ark of salvation, out of which no one can be saved? I have sent to you a cardinal; a man noble, well-instructed, and legate of the successors of the Apostles. He has received full power to enlighten the minds of the Russians, and to rescue them from all their errors."

This pastoral exhortation was entirely unavailing. The bishops and clergy of the Russian church still pertinaciously adhered to the faith of their fathers. The crusaders were ere long driven from the imperial city, and the Greek church again attained its supremacy in the East, a supremacy which it has maintained to the present day.

CHAPTER VI.

THE GRAND PRINCES OF VLADIMIR, AND THE INVASION OF GENGHIS KHAN.

From 1212 to 1238.

Accession of Georges.—Famine.—Battle of Lipetsk.—Defeat of Georges.—His Surrender.—Constantin Seizes the Scepter.—Exploits of Mstislaf.—Imbecility of Constantin.—Death of Constantin.—Georges III.—Invasion of Bulgaria.—Progress of the Monarchy.—Right of Succession.—Commerce of the Dnieper.—Genghis Khan.—His Rise and Conquests.—Invasion of Southern Russia.—Death of Genghis Khan.—Succession of his Son Ougadai.—March of Bati.—Entrance into Russia.—Utter Defeat of the Russians.

MOSCOW was the capital of a province then called Souzdal. North-west of this province there was another large principality called Vladimir, with a capital of the same name. North of these provinces there was an extensive territory named Yaroslave. Immediately after the death of Vsevolod, a brother of the deceased monarch, named Georges, ascended the throne with the assent of all the nobles of Souzdal and Vladimir. At the same time his brother Constantin, prince of Yaroslavle, claimed the crown. Eager partizans rallied around the two aspirants. Constantin made the first move by burning the town of Kostroma and carrying off the inhabitants as captives. Georges replied by an equally sanguinary assault upon Rostof. Such, war has ever been.. When princes quarrel, being unable to strike each other, they wreak their vengeance upon innocent and helpless villages, burning their houses, slaying sons and brothers, and either dragging widows and orphans into captivity or leaving them to perish of exposure and starvation.

In this conflict Georges was victor, and he assigned to his

brothers and cousins the administration of the provinces of southern Russia. Still the ancient annals give us nothing but a dreary record of war. A very energetic prince arose, by the name of Mstislaf, who, for years, strode over subjugated provinces, desolating them with fire and sword. Another horrible famine commenced its ravages at this time, caused principally by the desolations of war, throughout all northern and eastern Russia. The starving inhabitants ate the bark of trees, leaves and the most disgusting reptiles. The streets were covered with the bodies of the dead, abandoned to the dogs. Crowds of skeleton men and women wandered through the fields, in vain seeking food, and ever dropping in the convulsions of death. Christian faith is stunned in the contemplation of such woes, and yet it sees in them but the fruits of man's depravity. The enigma of life can find no solution but in divine revelation—and even that revelation does but show in what direction the solution lies.

Mstislaf of Novgorod, encouraged by his military success, and regardless of the woes of the populace, entered into an alliance with Constantin, promising, with his aid, to drive Georges from the throne, and to place the scepter in the hands of Constantin. The king sent an army of ten thousand men against the insurgents. All over Russia there was the choosing of sides, as prince after prince ranged his followers under the banners of one or of the other of the combatants. At last the two armies met upon the banks of the river Kza. The Russian annalists say that the sovereign was surrounded with the banners of thirty regiments, accompanied by a military band of one hundred and forty trumpets and drums.

The insurgent princes, either alarmed by the power of the sovereign, or anxious to spare the effusion of blood, proposed terms of accommodation.

"It is too late to talk of peace," said Georges. "You are now as fishes on the land. You have advanced too far, and your destruction is inevitable."

The embassadors retired in sadness. Georges then assembled his captains, and gave orders to form the troops in line of battle. Addressing the troops, he said:

"Let no soldier's life be spared. Aim particularly at the officers. The helmets, the clothes and the horses of the dead shall belong to you. Let us not be troubled with any prisoners. The princes alone may be taken captive, and reserved for public execution."

Both parties now prepared, with soundings of the trumpet and shoutings of the soldiers, for combat. It was in the early dawn of the morning that the celebrated battle of Lipetsk commenced. The arena of strife was a valley, broken by rugged hills, on the head waters of the Don, about two hundred miles south of Moscow. It was a gloomy day of wind, and clouds and rain; and while the cruel tempest of man's passion swept the earth, an elemental tempest wrecked the skies. From the morning till the evening twilight the battle raged, inspired by the antagonistic forces of haughty confidence and of despair. Darkness separated the combatants, neither party having gained any decisive advantage.

The night was freezing cold, a chill April wind sweeping the mists over the heights, upon which the two hosts, exhausted and bleeding, slept upon their arms, each fearing a midnight surprise. With the earliest dawn of the next morning the battle was renewed; both armies defiantly and simultaneously moving down from the hills to meet on the plains. Mstislaf rode along the ranks of his troops, exclaiming:

"Let no man turn his head. Retreat now is destruction. Let us forget our wives and children, and fight for our lives."

His soldiers, with shouts of enthusiasm, threw aside all encumbering clothes, and uttering those loud outcries with which semi-barbarians ever rush into battle, impetuously fell upon the advancing foe. Mstislaf was a prince of herculean stature and strength. With a battle-ax in his hands, he advanced before the troops, and it is recorded that, striking on the right hand and the left, he cut a path through the ranks of the enemy as a strong man would trample down the grain. A wake of the dead marked his path. It was one of the most deplorable of Russian battles, for the dispute had arrayed the son against the father, brother against brother, friend against friend.

The victory, however, was now not for a moment doubtful. The royal forces were entirely routed, and were pursued with enormous slaughter by the victorious Mstislaf. Nearly ten thousand of the followers of Georges were slain upon the field of battle. Georges having had three horses killed beneath him, escaped, and on the fourth day reached Vladimir, where he found only old men, women, children and ecclesiastics, so entirely had he drained the country for the war. The king himself was the first to announce to the citizens of Vladimir the terrible defeat. Wan from fatigue and suffering, he rode in at the gates, his hair disheveled, and his clothing torn. As he traversed the streets, he called earnestly upon all who remained to rally upon the walls for their defense. It was late in the afternoon when the king reached the metropolis. During the night a throng of fugitives was continually entering the city, wounded and bleeding. In the early morning, the king assembled the citizens in the public square, and urged them to a desperate resistance. But they, disheartened by the awful reverse, exclaimed:

"Prince, courage can no longer save us. Our brethren have perished on the field of battle. Those who have escaped are wounded, exhausted and unarmed. We are unable to oppose the enemy."

Georges entreated them to make at least a show of resistance, that he might open negotiations with the foe. Soon Mstislaf appeared, leading his troops in solid phalanx, with waving banners and trumpet blasts, and surrounded the city. In the night, a terrible conflagration burst forth within the city, and his soldiers entreated him to take advantage of the confusion for an immediate assault. The magnanimous conqueror refused to avail himself of the calamity, and restrained the ardor of his troops. The next morning, Georges despairing of any further defense, rode from the gates into the camp of Mstislaf.

"You are victorious," said he. "Dispose of me and my fortunes as you will. My brother Constantin will be obedient to your wishes."

The unhappy prince was sent into exile. Embarking, with his wife and children, and a few faithful followers, in barges, at the head waters of the Volga, he floated down the stream towards the Caspian Sea, and disappeared for ever from the observation of history.

Constantin was now raised to the imperial throne through the energies of Mstislaf. This latter prince returned to his domains in Novgorod, and under the protection of the throne he rivaled the monarch in splendor and power. Constantin established his capital at Vladimir, about one hundred and fifty miles west of Moscow. The warlike Mstislaf, greedy of renown, with the chivalry of a knight-errant, sought to have a hand in every quarrel then raging far or near. Southern Russia continued in a state of incessant embroilments; and the princes of the provinces, but nominally in subjection to the crown, lived in a state of interminable war. Occasionally they would sheath the sword of civil strife and combine in some important expedition against the Hungarians or the Poles.

But tranquillity reigned in the principality of Vladimir; and the adjacent provinces, influenced by the pacific policy of the sovereign, or overawed by his power, cultivated the arts of peace. Constantin, however, was effeminate as well as peaceful. The tremendous energy of Mstislaf had shed some luster upon him, and thus, for a time, it was supposed that he possessed a share, no one knew how great, of that extraordinary vigor which had placed him on the throne. But now,

Mstislaf was far away on bloody fields in Hungary, and the princes in the vicinity of Vladimir soon found that Constantin had no spirit to resent any of their encroachments. Enormous crimes were perpetrated with impunity. Princes were assassinated, and the murderers seized their castles and their scepters, while the imbecile Constantin, instead of avenging such outrages, contented himself with shedding tears, building churches, distributing alms, and kissing the relics of the saints, which had been sent to him from Constantinople. Thus he lived for several years, a superstitious, perhaps a pious man; but, so utterly devoid of energy, of enlightened views respecting his duty as a ruler, that the helpless were unprotected, and the wicked rioted unpunished in crime. He died in the year 1219 at the early age of thirty-three. Finding death approaching, he called his two sons to his bedside, and exhorted them to live in brotherly affection, to be the benefactors of widows and orphans, and especially to be the supporters of religion. The wife of Constantin, imbibing his spirit, immediately upon his death renounced the world, and retiring to the cloisters of a convent, immured herself in its glooms until she also rejoined her husband in the spirit land.

Georges II., son of Vsevelod, now ascended the throne. He signalized the commencement of his reign by a military excursion to oriental Bulgaria. Descending the Volga in barges to the mouth of the Kama, he invaded, with a well-disciplined army, the realm he wished to subjugate. The Russians approached the city of Ochel. It was strongly fortified with palisades and a double wall of wood. The assailants approached, led by a strong party with hatchets and torches. They were closely followed by archers and lancers to drive the defenders from the ramparts. The palisades were promptly cut down and set on fire. The flames spread to the wooden walls; and over the burning ruins the assailants rushed into the city. A high wind arose, and the whole city, whose buildings were constructed of wood only, soon blazed like a volcano. The wretched citizens had but to choose between the swords of the Russians and the fire. Many, in their despair, plunged their poignards into the bosoms of their wives and children, and then buried the dripping blade in their own hearts. Multitudes of the Russians, even, encircled by the flames in the narrow streets, miserably perished. In a few hours the city and nearly all of its male inhabitants were destroyed. Extensive regions of the country were then ravaged, and Bulgaria, as a conquered province, was considered as annexed to the Russian empire. Georges enriched with plunder and having extorted oaths of allegiance from most of the Bulgarian princes, reascended the Volga to Vladimir. As he was on his return he laid the foundations of a new city, Nijni Novgorod, at the confluence of two important streams about two hundred miles west of Moscow. The city remains to the present day.

It will be perceived through what slow and vacillating steps the Russian monarchy was established. In the earliest dawn of the kingdom, Yaroslaf divided Russia into five principalities. To his eldest son he gave the title of Grand Prince, constituting him, by his will, chief or monarch of the whole kingdom. His younger brothers were placed over the principalities, holding them as vassals of the grand prince at Kief, and transmitting the right of succession to their children. Ysiaslaf, and some of his descendants, men of great energy, succeeded in holding under more or less of restraint the turbulent princes, who were simply entitled *princes*, to distinguish them from the *Grand Prince* or monarch. These princes had under them innumerable vassal lords, who, differing in wealth and extent of dominions, governed, with despotic sway, the serfs or peasants subject to their power. No government could be more simple than this; and it was the necessary resultant of those stormy times.

But in process of time feeble grand princes reigned at Kief. The vassal princes, strengthening themselves in alliances with one another, or seeking aid from foreign semi-civilized nations, such as the Poles, the Danes, the Hungarians, often imposed laws upon their nominal sovereign, and not unfrequently drove him from the throne, and placed upon it a monarch of their own choice. Sviatopolk II. was driven to the humiliation of appearing to defend himself from accusation before the tribunal of his vassal princes. Monomaque and Mstislaf I., with imperial energy, brought all the vassal princes in subjection to their scepter, and reigned as monarchs. But their successors, not possessing like qualities, were unable to maintain the regal dignity; and gradually Kief sank into a provincial town, and the scepter was transferred to the principality of Souzdal.

André, of Souzdal, abolished the system of *appanages*, as it was called, in which the principalities were in entire subjection to the princes who reigned over them, these princes only rendering vassal service to the sovereign. He, in their stead, appointed governors over the distant provinces, who were his agents to execute his commands. This measure gave new energy and consolidation to the monarchy, and added incalculable strength to the regal arm. But the grand princes, who immediately succeeded André, had not efficiency to maintain this system, and the princes again regained their position of comparative independence. Indeed, they were undisputed sovereigns of their principalities, bound only to recognize the superior rank of the grand prince, and to aid him, when called upon, as allies.

In process of time the princes of the five great principalities, Pereiaslavle, Tchernigof, Kief, Novgorod and Smolensk, were subdivided, through the energies of warlike nobles, into minor appanages, or independent provinces, independent in every thing save feudal service, a service often feebly recognized and dimly defined. The sovereigns of the great provinces assumed the title of Grand Princes. The smaller sovereigns were simply called Princes. Under these princes were the petty lords or nobles. The spirit of all evil could not have devised a system better calculated to keep a nation incessantly embroiled in war. The princes of Novgorod claimed the right of choosing their grand prince. In all the other provinces the scepter was nominally hereditary. In point of fact, it was only hereditary when the one who ascended the throne had sufficient vigor of arm to beat back his assailing foes. For two hundred years, during nearly all of the eleventh and twelfth centuries, it is with difficulty we can discern any traces of the monarchy. The history of Russia during this period is but a history of interminable battles between the grand princes, and petty, yet most cruel and bloody, conflicts between the minor princes.

The doctrine of the hereditary descent of the governing power was the cause of nearly all these conflicts. A semi-idiot or a brutal ruffian was thus often found the ruler of millions of energetic men. War and bloodshed were, of course, the inevitable result. This absurdity was, perhaps, a necessary consequence of the ignorance and brutality of the times. But happy is that nation which is sufficiently enlightened to choose its own magistrates and to appreciate the sanctity of the ballot-box. The history of the United States thus far, with its elective administrations, is a marvel of tranquillity, prosperity and joy, as it is recorded amidst the bloody pages of this world's annals.

According to the ancient custom of Russia, the right of succession transferred the crown, not to the oldest son, but to the brother or the most aged member belonging to the family connections of the deceased prince. The energetic Monomaque violated this law by transferring the crown to his son, when, by custom, it should have passed to the prince of Tchernigof. Hence, for ages, there was implacable hatred between these two houses, and Russia was crimsoned with the blood of a hundred battle-fields.

Nearly all the commerce of Russia, at this time, was carried on between Kief and Constantinople by barges traversing the Dnieper and the Black Sea. These barges went strongly armed as a protection against the barbarians who crowded the banks of the river. The stream, being thus the great thoroughfare of commerce, received the popular name of *The Road to Greece.* The Russians exported rich furs in exchange for the cloths and spices of the East. As the Russian power extended toward the rising sun, the Volga and the Caspian Sea became the highways of a prosperous, though an interrupted, commerce. It makes the soul melancholy to reflect upon these long, long ages of rapine, destruction and woe. But for this, had man been true to himself, the whole of Russia might now have been almost a garden of Eden, with every marsh drained, every stream bridged, every field waving with luxuriance, every deformity changed into an object of beauty, with roads and canals intersecting every mile of its territory, with gorgeous cities embellishing the rivers' banks and the mountain sides, and cottages smiling upon every plain. Man has no foe to his happiness so virulent and deadly as his brother man. The heaviest curse is human depravity.

We now approach, in the early part of the thirteenth century, one of the most extraordinary events which has occurred in the history of man : the sweep of Tartar hordes over all of northern Asia and Europe, under their indomitable leader, Genghis Khan.

In the extreme north of the Chinese empire, just south of Irkoutsk, in the midst of desert wilds, unknown to Greek or Roman, there were wandering tribes called Mogols. They were a savage, vagabond race, without any fixed habitations, living by the chase and by herding cattle. The chief of one of these tribes, greedy of renown and power, conquered several of the adjacent tribes, and brought them into very willing subjection to his sway. War was a pastime for their fierce spirits, and their bold chief led them to victory and abundant booty. This barbarian conqueror, Bayadour by name, died in the prime of life, surrendering his wealth and power to his son, Temoutchin, then but thirteen years of age. This boy thus found himself lord of forty thousand families. Still he was but a subordinate prince or khan, owing allegiance to the Tartar sovereign of northern China. Brought up by his mother in the savage simplicity of a wandering shepherd's hut, he developed a character which made him the scourge of the world, and one of its most appalling wonders. The most illustrious monarchies were overturned by the force of his arms, and millions of men were brought into subjection to his power.

At the death of his father, Bayadour, many of the subjugated clans endeavored to break the yoke of the boy prince. Temoutchin, with the vigor and military sagacity of a veteran warrior, assembled an army of thirty thousand men, defeated the rebels, and plunged their leaders, seventy in number, each into a caldron of boiling water. Elated by such brilliant success, the young prince renounced allegiance to the Tartar sovereign and assumed independence. Terrifying his enemies by severity, rewarding his friends with rich gifts, and overawing the populace by claims of supernatural powers, this extraordinary young man commenced a career of conquest which the world has never seen surpassed.

Assembling his ferocious hordes, now enthusiastically devoted to his service, upon the banks of a rapid river, he took a solemn oath to share with them all the bitter and the sweet which he should encounter in the course of his life. The neighboring prince of Kerait ventured to draw the sword against him. He forfeited his head for his audacity, and his skull, trimmed with silver, was converted into a drinking cup. At the close of this expedition, his vast army were disposed in nine different camps, upon the head waters of the river Amour. Each division had tents of a particular color. On a festival day, as all were gazing with admiration upon their youthful leader, a hermit, by previous secret appointment, appeared as a prophet from heaven. Approaching the prince, the pretended embassador from the celestial court, declared, in a loud voice,

"God has given the whole earth to Temoutchin. As the sovereign of the world, he is entitled to the name of Genghis Khan (*the great prince*)."

No one was disposed to question the divine authority of this envoy from the skies. Shouts of applause rent the air, and chiefs and warriors, with unanimous voice, expressed their eagerness to follow their leader wherever he might guide them. Admiration of his prowess and the terror of his arms spread far and wide, and embassadors thronged his tent from adjacent nations, wishing to range themselves beneath his banners. Even the monarch of Thibet, overawed, sent messengers to offer his service as a vassal prince to Genghis Khan.

The conqueror now made an irruption into China proper, and with his wolfish legions, clambering the world-renowned wall, routed all the armies raised to oppose him, and speedily was master of ninety cities. Finding himself encumbered with a crowd of prisoners, he selected a large number of the aged and choked them to death. The sovereign, thoroughly humiliated, purchased peace by a gift of five hundred young men, five hundred beautiful girls, three thousand horses and an immense quantity of silks and gold. Genghis Khan retired to the north with his treasures; but soon again returned, and laid siege to Pekin, the capital of the empire. With the energies of despair, though all unavailingly, the inhabitants attempted their defense. It was the year 1215 when Pekin fell before the arms of the Mogol conqueror. The whole city was immediately committed to flames, and the wasting conflagration raged for a whole month, when nothing was left of the once beautiful and populous city but a heap of ashes.

Leaving troops in garrison throughout the subjugated country, the conqueror commenced his march towards the west, laden with the spoils of plundered cities. Like the rush of a torrent, his armies swept along until they entered the vast wilds of Turkomania. Here the "great and the mighty Saladin" had reigned, extending his sway from the Caspian Sea to the Ganges, dictating laws even to the Caliph at Bagdad, who was the Pope of the Mohammedans. Mahomet II. now held the throne, a prince so haughty and warlike, that he arrogated the name of the second Alexander the Great. With two such spirits heading their armies, a horrible war ensued. The capital of this region, Bokhara, had attained a very considerable degree of civilization, and was renowned for its university, where the Mohammedan youth, of noble families, were educated. The city, after an unavailing attempt at defense, was compelled to capitulate. The elders of the metropolis brought the keys and laid them at the feet of the conqueror. Genghis Khan rode contemptuously on horseback into the sacred mosque, and seizing the Alcoran from the altar, threw it upon the floor and trampled it beneath the hoofs of his steed. The whole city was inhumanly reduced to ashes.

From Bokhara he advanced to Samarcande. This city was strongly fortified, and contained a hundred thousand soldiers within its walls, besides an immense number of elephants trained to fight. The city was soon taken. Thirty thousand were slain, and thirty thousand carried into perpetual slavery. All the adjacent cities soon shared a similar fate. For three years the armies of Genghis Khan ravaged the whole country between the Aral lake and the Indus, with such fearful devastation that for six hundred years the region did not recover from the calamity. Mahomet II., pursued by his indefatigable foe, fled to one of the islands of the Caspian Sea, where he perished in paroxysms of rage and despair.

Genghis Khan having thoroughly subdued this whole region, now sent a division of his army, under two of his most distinguished generals, across the Caspian Sea to subjugate the regions on the western shore. Here, as before, victory accompanied their standards, and, with merciless severity, they swept the whole country to the sea of Azof. The tidings of their advance, so bloody, so resistless, spread into Russia, exciting universal terror. The conquerors, elated with success, rushed on over the plains of Russia, and were already pouring down into the valley of the Dnieper. Mstislaf, prince of Galitch, already so renowned for his warlike exploits, was eager to measure arms with those soldiers, the terror of whose ravages now filled the world. He hurriedly assembled all the neighboring princes at Kief, and urged immediate and vigorous coöperation to repel the common foe. The Russian army was promptly rendezvoused on the banks of the Dnieper, preparatory to its march. Another large army was collected by the Russian princes who inhabited the valley of the Dniester. In a thousand barges they descended the river to the Black Sea. Then entering the Dnieper they ascended the stream to unite with the main army waiting impatiently their arrival.

On the 21st of May, the whole force was put in motion, and after a march of nine days, met the Tartar army on the banks of the river Kalets. The waving banners and the steeds of the Tartar host, covering the plains as far as the eye could extend, in numbers apparently countless, presented an appalling spectacle. Many of the Russian leaders were quite in despair; others, young, ardent, inexperienced, were eager for the fight. The battle immediately commenced, and the combatants fought with all the ferocity which human energies could engender. But the Russians were, in the end, routed entirely. The Tartars drove the bleeding fugitives in wild confusion before them back to the Dnieper. Never before had Russia encountered so frightful a disaster. The whole army was destroyed. Not one tenth of their number escaped that field of massacre. Seven princes, and seventy of the most illustrious nobles were among the slain. The Tartars followed up their victory with their accustomed inhumanity, and, as if it were their intention to depopulate the country, swept it in all directions, putting the inhabitants indiscriminately to the sword. They acted upon the maxim which they ever proclaimed, "The conquered can never be the friends of the conquerors; and the death of the one is essential to the safety of the other."

The whole of southern Russia trembled with terror; and men, women and children, in utter helplessness, with groans and cries fled to the churches, imploring the protection of God. That divine power which alone could aid them, interposed in their behalf. For some unknown reason, Genghis Khan recalled his troops to the shores of the Caspian, where this blood-stained conqueror, in the midst of his invincible armies, dictated laws to the vast regions he had subjected to his will. This frightful storm having left utter desolation behind it, passed away as rapidly as it had approached. Scathed as by the lightnings of heaven, the whole of southern Russia east of the Dnieper was left smoking like a furnace.

The nominal king, Georges II., far distant in the northern realms of Souzdal and Vladimir, listened appalled to the reports of the tempest raging over the southern portion of the kingdom; and when the dark cloud disappeared and its thunders ceased, he congratulated himself in having escaped its fury. After the terrible battle of Kalka, six years passed before the locust legions of the Tartars again made their appearance; and Russia hoped that the scourge had disappeared for ever. In the year 1227, Genghis Khan died. It has been estimated that the ambition of this one man cost the lives of between five and six millions of the human family. He nominated as his successor his oldest son Octai, and enjoined it upon him never to make peace but with vanquished nations. Ambitious of being the conqueror of the world, Octai ravaged with his armies the whole of northern China.

In the heart of Tartary he reared his palace, embellished with the highest attainments of Chinese art.

Raising an army of three hundred thousand men, the Tartar sovereign placed his nephew Bati in command, and ordered him to bring into subjection all the nations on the northern shores of the Caspian Sea, and then to continue his conquests throughout all the expanse of northern Russia. A bloody strife of three years planted his banners upon every cliff and through all the defiles of the Ural mountains, and then the victor plunging down the western declivities of this great natural barrier between Europe and Asia, established his troops, for winter quarters, in the valley of the Volga. To strike the region with terror, he burned the capital city of Bulgaria and put all the inhabitants to the sword. Early in the spring of the year 1238, with an army, say the ancient annalists, "as innumerable as locusts," he crossed the Volga, and threading many almost impenetrable forests, after a march, in a north-west direction, of about four hundred miles, entered the province of Rezdan just south of Souzdal. He then sent an embassage to the king and his confederate princes, saying:

"If you wish for peace with the Tartars you must pay us an annual tribute of one tenth of your possessions."

The heroic reply was returned,

"When you have slain us all, you can then take all that we have."

Bati, at the head of his terrible army, continued his march through the populous province of Rezdan, burning every dwelling and endeavoring, with indiscriminate massacre, to exterminate the inhabitants. City after city fell before them until they approached the capital. This they besieged, first surrounding it with palisades that it might not be possible for any of the inhabitants to escape. The innumerable host pressed the siege day and night, not allowing the defenders one moment for repose. On the sixteenth day, after many had been slain and all the citizens were in utter exhaustion from toil and sleeplessness, they commenced the final assault with ladders and battering rams. The walls of wood were soon set on fire, and, through flame and smoke, the demoniac assailants rushed into the city. Indiscriminate massacre ensued of men, women and children, accompanied with the most revolting cruelty. The carnage continued for many hours, and, when it ceased, the city was reduced to ashes, and not one of its inhabitants was left alive.

The conquerors then rushed on to Moscow. Here the tempest of battle raged for a few days, and then Moscow followed in the footsteps of Rezdan.

CHAPTER VII.

THE SWAY OF THE TARTAR PRINCES.

From 1238 to 1304.

Retreat of Georges II.—Desolating March of the Tartars.—Capture of Vladimir.—Fall of Moscow.—Utter Defeat of Georges.—Conflict at Torjek.—March of the Tartars toward the South.—Subjugation of the Polovtsi.—Capture of Kief.—Humiliation of Yaroslaf.—Overthrow of the Russian Kingdom.—Haughtiness of the Tartars.—Reign of Alexander.—Succession of Yaroslaf.—The Reign of Vassuli.—State of Christianity.—Infamy of Andre.—Struggles with Dmitri.—Independence of the Principalities.—Death of Andre.

THE king, Georges, fled from Moscow before it was invested by the enemy, leaving its defense to two of his sons. Retiring, in a panic, to the remote northern province of Yaroslaf, he encamped, with a small force, upon one of the tributaries of the Mologa, and sent earnest entreaties to numerous princes to hasten, with all the forces they could raise, and join his army.

The Tartars from Moscow marched north-west some one hundred and fifty miles to the imperial city of Vladimir. They appeared before its walls on the 2d of February. On the evening of the 6th the battering rams and ladders were prepared, and it was evident that the storming of the city was soon to begin. The citizens, conscious that nothing awaited them but death or endless slavery, with one accord resolved to sell their lives as dearly as possible. Accompanied by their wives and their children, they assembled in the churches, partook of the sacrament of the Lord's Supper, implored Heaven's blessing upon them, and then husbands, brothers, fathers, took affecting leave of their families and repaired to the walls for the deadly strife.

Early on the morning of the 7th the assault commenced. The impetuosity of the onset was irresistible. In a few moments the walls were scaled, the streets flooded with the foe, the pavements covered with the dead, and the city on fire in an hundred places. The conquerors did not wish to encumber themselves with captives. All were slain. Laden with booty and crimsoned with the blood of their foes, the victors dispersed in every direction, burning and destroying, but encountering no resistance. During the month they took fourteen cities, slaying all the inhabitants but such as they reserved for slaves.

The monarch, Georges, was still upon the banks of the Sité, near where it empties into the Mologa, when he heard the tidings of the destruction of Moscow and Vladimir, and of the massacre of his wife and his children. His eyes filled with tears, and in the anguish of his spirit he prayed that God would enable him to exemplify the patience of Job. Adversity develops the energies of noble spirits. Georges rallied his troops and made a desperate onset upon the foe as they approached his camp. It was the morning of the 4th of March. But again the battle was disastrous to Russia. Mogol numbers triumphed over Russian valor, and the king and nearly all his army were slain. Some days after the battle the bishop of Rostof traversed the field, covered with the bodies of the dead. There he discovered the corpse of the monarch, which he recognized by the clothes. The head had been severed from the body. The bishop removed the gory trunk of the prince and gave it respectful burial in the church of Notre Dame at Rostof. The head was subsequently found and deposited in the coffin with the body.

The conquerors, continuing their march westerly one hundred and fifty miles, burning and destroying as they went, reached the populous city of Torjek. The despairing inhabitants for fifteen days beat off the assailants. The city then fell; its ruin was entire. The dwellings became but the funeral pyres for the bodies of the slain. The army of Bati then continued its march to lake Seliger, the source of the Volga, within one hundred miles of the great city of Novgorod.

"Villages disappeared," write the ancient annalists, "and the heads of the Russians fell under the swords of the Tartars as the grass falls before the scythe."

Instead of pressing on to Novgorod, for some unknown reason Bati turned south, and, marching two hundred miles, laid siege to the strong fortress of Kozelsk, in the principality of Kalouga. The garrison, warned of the advance of the foe, made the most heroic resistance. For four weeks they held their assailants at bay, baffling every effort of the vast numbers who encompassed them. A more determined and heroic defense was never made. At last the fortress fell, and not one soul escaped the exterminating sword. Bati, now satiated with carnage, retired, with his army, to the banks of the Don. Yaroslaf, prince of Kief, and brother of Georges II., hoping that the dreadful storm had passed away, hastened to the smouldering ruins of Vladimir to take the title and the shadowy authority of Grand Prince. Never before were more conspicuously seen the energies of a noble soul. At first it seemed that his reign could be extended only over gory corpses and smouldering ruins. Undismayed by the magnitude of the disaster, he consecrated all the activity of his genius and the loftiness of his spirit to the regeneration of the desolated land.

In the spacious valleys of the Don and its tributaries lived the powerful nation of the Polovtsi, who had often bid defiance to the whole strength of Russia. Kothian, their prince, for a short time made vigorous opposition to the march of the conquerors. But, overwhelmed by numbers, he was at length compelled to retreat, and, with his army of forty thousand men, to seek a refuge in Hungary. The country of the Polovtsi was then abandoned to the Tartars. Having ravaged the central valleys of the Don and the Volga, these demoniac warriors turned their steps again into southern Russia. The inhabitants, frantic with terror, fled from their line of march as lambs fly from wolves. The blasts of their trumpets and the clatter of their horses' hoofs were speedily resounding in the valley of the Dnieper. Soon from the steeples of Kief the banners of the terrible army were seen approaching from the east. They crossed the Dnieper and surrounded the imperial city, which, for some time anticipating the storm, had been making preparation for the most desperate resistance. The ancient annalists say that the noise of their innumerable chariots, the lowing of camels and of the vast herds of cattle which accompanied their march, the neighing of horses and the ferocious cries of the barbarians, created such a clamor that no ordinary voice could be heard in the heart of the city.

The attack was speedily commenced, and the walls were assailed with all the then-known instruments of war. Day and night, without a moment's intermission, the besiegers, like incarnate fiends, plied their works. The Tartars, as ever, were victorious, and Kief, with all its thronging population and all its treasures of wealth, architecture and art, sank in an abyss of flame and blood. It sank to rise no more. Though it has since been partially rebuilt, this ancient capital of the grand princes of Russia, even now presents but the shadow of its pristine splendor.

Onward, still onward, was the cry of the barbarians.

Leaving smoking brands and half-burnt corpses where the imperial city once stood, the insatiable Bati pressed on hundreds of miles further west, assailing, storming, destroying the provinces of Gallicia as far as southern Vladimir within a few leagues of the frontiers of Poland. Russia being thus entirely devastated and at the feet of the conquerors, Bati wheeled his army around toward the south and descended into Hungary. Novgorod was almost the only important city in Russia which escaped the ravages of this terrible foe.

Bati continued his career of conquest, and, in 1245, was almost undisputed master of Russia, of many of the Polish provinces, of Hungary, Croatia, Servia, Bulgaria on the Danube, Moldavia and Wallachia. He then returned to the Volga and established himself there as permanent monarch over all these subjugated realms. No one dared to resist him. Bati sent a haughty message to the Grand Prince Yaroslaf at northern Vladimir, ordering him to come to his camp on the distant Volga. Yaroslaf, in the position in which he found himself—Russia being exhausted, depopulated, covered with ruins and with graves—did not dare disobey. Accompanied by several of his nobles, he took the weary journey, and humbly presented himself in the tent of the conqueror. Bati compelled the humiliated prince to send his young son, Constantin, to Tartary, to the palace of the grand khan Octai, who was about to celebrate, with his chiefs, the brilliant conquests his army had made in China and Europe. If the statements of the annalists of those days may be credited, so sumptuous a fete the world had never seen before. The guests, assembled in the metropolis of the khan, were innumerable. Yaroslaf was compelled to promise allegiance to the Tartar chieftain, and all the other Russian princes, who had survived the general slaughter, were also forced to pay homage and tribute to Bati.

After two years, the young prince, Constantin, returned from Tartary, and then Yaroslaf himself was ordered, with all his relatives, to go to the capital of this barbaric empire on the banks of the Amour, where the Tartar chiefs were to meet to choose a successor to Octai, who had recently died. With tears the unhappy prince bade adieu to his country, and, traversing vast deserts and immense regions of hills and valleys, he at length reached the metropolis of his cruel masters. Here he successfully defended himself against some accusations which had been brought against him, and, after a detention of several months, he was permitted to set out on his return. He had proceeded but a few hundred miles on the weary journey when he was taken sick, and died the 20th of September, 1246. The faithful nobles who accompanied him bore his remains to Vladimir, where they were interred.

There was no longer a Russian kingdom. The country had lost its independence; and the Tartar sway, rude, vacillating and awfully cruel, extended from remote China to the shores of the Baltic. The Roman, Grecian and Russian empires thus crumbling, the world was threatened with an universal inundation of barbarism. Russian princes, with more or less power ruled over the serfs who tilled their lands, but there was no recognized head of the once powerful kingdom, and no Russian prince ventured to disobey the commands even of the humblest captain of the Tartar hordes.

While affairs were in this deplorable state, a Russian prince, Daniel, of Gallicia, engaged secretly, but with great vigor, in the attempt to secure the coöperation of the rest of Europe to emancipate Russia from the Tartar yoke. Greece, overawed by the barbarians, did not dare to make any hostile movement against them. Daniel turned to Rome, and promised the pope, Innocent IV., that Russia should return to the Roman church, and would march under the papal flag if the pope would rouse Christian Europe against the Tartars.

The pope eagerly embraced these offers, pronounced Daniel to be King of Russia, and sent the papal legate to appoint Roman bishops over the Greek church. At the same time he wished to crown Daniel with regal splendor.

"I have need," exclaimed the prince, "of an army, not of a crown. A crown is but a childish ornament when the yoke of the barbarian is galling our necks."

Daniel at length consented, for the sake of its moral influence, to be crowned king, and the pope issued his letters calling upon the faithful to unite under the banners of the cross, to drive the barbarians from Europe. This union, however, accomplished but little, as the pope was only anxious to bring the Greek church under the sway of Rome, and Daniel sought only military aid to expel the Tartars; each endeavoring to surrender as little and to gain as much as possible.

One of the Christian nobles endeavored to persuade Mangou, a Tartar chieftain, of the superiority of the Christian religion. The pagan replied;

"We are not ignorant that there is a God; and we love him with all our heart. There are more ways of salvation than there are fingers on your hands. If God has given you the Bible, he has given us our *wise men* (Magi). But *you* do not obey the precepts of your Bible, while *we* are perfectly obedient to the instructions of our Magi, and never think of disputing their authority."

The pride of these Tartar conquerors may be inferred from the following letter, sent by the great khan to Louis, King of France:

"In the name of God, the all powerful, I command you, King Louis, to be obedient to me. When the will of Heaven shall be accomplished—when the universe shall have recognized me as its sovereign, tranquillity will then be seen restored to earth. But if you dare to despise the decrees of God, and to say that your country is remote, your mountains inaccessible, and your seas deep and wide, and that you fear not my displeasure, then the Almighty will speedily show you how terrible is my power."

After the death of Yaroslaf, his uncle Alexander assumed the sovereignty of the grand principality. He was a prince of much military renown. Bati, who was still encamped upon the banks of the Volga, sent to him a message as follows:

"Prince of Novgorod: it is well known by you that God has subjected to our sway innumerable peoples. If you wish to live in tranquillity, immediately come to me, in my tent, that you may witness the glory and the grandeur of the Mogols."

Alexander obeyed with the promptness of a slave. Bati received the prince with great condescension, but commanded him to continue his journey some hundreds of leagues further to the east, that he might pay homage to the grand khan in Tartary. It was a terrible journey, beneath a blazing sun, over burning plains, whitened by the bones of those who had perished by the way. Those dreary solitudes had for ages been traversed by caravans, and instead of cities and villages, and the hum of busy life, the eye met only the tombs in which the dead mouldered; and the silence of the grave oppressed the soul.

In the year 1249, Alexander returned from his humiliating journey to Tartary. The khan was so well satisfied with his conduct, that he appointed him king of all the realms of southern Russia. The pope, now thoroughly alienated from Daniel, corresponded with Alexander, entreating him to bring the Greek church under the supremacy of Rome, and thus secure for himself the protection and the blessing of the father of all the faithful. Alexander returned the peremptory reply,

"We wish to follow the true doctrines of the church. As for your doctrines, we have no desire either to adopt them or to know them."

Alexander administered the government so much in accordance with the will of his haughty masters, that the khan gradually increased his dominion. Bati, the Tartar chieftain, who was encamped with his army on the banks of the Volga and the Don, died in the year 1257, and his bloody sword, the only scepter of his power, passed into the hands of his brother Berki. Alexander felt compelled to hasten to the Tartar camp, with expressions of homage to the new captain, and with rich presents to conciliate his favor. Many of the Tartars had by this time embraced Christianity, and there were frequent intermarriages between the Russian nobles and princesses of the Tartar race. It is a curious fact, that even then the Tartars were so conscious of the power of the clergy over the popular mind, that they employed all the arts of courtesy and bribes to secure their influence to hold the Russians in subjection.

The Tartars exacted enormous tribute from the subjugated country. An insurrection, headed by a son of Alexander, broke out at Novgorod. The grand prince, terrified in view of the Mogol wrath which might be expected to overwhelm him, arrested and imprisoned his son, who had countenanced the enterprise, and punished the nobles implicated in the movement with terrible severity. Some were hung; others had their eyes plucked out and their noses cut off. But, unappeased by this fearful retribution, the Tartars were immediately on the march to avenge, with their own hands, the crime of rebellion. Their footsteps were marked with such desolation and cruelty that the Russians, goaded to despair, again ventured, like the crushed worm, an impotent resistance. Alexander himself was compelled to join the Tartars, and aid in cutting down his wretched countrymen.

The Tartars haughtily entered Novgorod. Silence and desolation reigned through its streets. They went from house to house, extorting, as they well knew how, treasure which beggared families and ruined the city. Throughout all Russia the princes were compelled to break down the walls of their cities and to demolish their fortifications. In the year 1262, Alexander was alarmed by some indications of displeasure on the part of the grand khan, and he decided to take an immediate journey to the Mogol capital with rich presents, there to attempt to explain away any suspicions which might be entertained. His health was feeble, and suffered much from the exposures of the journey. He was detained in the Mogol court in captivity, though treated with much consideration, for a year. He then returned home, so crushed in health and spirits, that he died on the 14th of November, 1263. The prince was buried at Vladimir, and was borne to the grave surrounded by the tears and lamentations of his subjects. He seems to have died the death of the righteous, breathing most fervent prayers of penitence and of love. In the distressing situation in which his country was placed, he could do nothing but seek to alleviate its woe; and to this object he devoted all the energies of his life. The name of Alexander Nevsky is still pronounced in Russia with love and admiration. His remains, after reposing in the church of Notre Dame, at Vladimir, until the eighteenth century, were transported, by Peter the Great, to the banks of the Neva, to give renown to the capital which that illustrious monarch was rearing there.

Yaroslaf, of Tiver, succeeded almost immediately his father in the nominal sway of Russia. The new sovereign promised fealty to the Tartars, and feared no rival while sustained by their swords. His oppression becoming intolerable, the tocsin was sounded in the streets of Novgorod, and the whole populace rose in insurrection. The movement was successful. The favorites and advisers of Yaroslaf were put to death, and the prince himself was exiled. There is something quite refreshing in the energetic spirit with which the populace transmitted their sentence of repudiation to the discomfited prince, blockaded in his palace. The citizens met in a vast gathering in the church of St. Nicholas, and sent to him the following act of accusation:

"Why have you seized the mansion of one of our nobles? Why have you robbed others of their money? Why have you driven from Novgorod strangers who were living peaceably in the midst of us? Why do your game-keepers exclude us from the chase, and drive us from our own fields? It is time to put an end to such violence. Leave us. Go where you please, but leave us, for we shall choose another prince."

Yaroslaf, terrified and humiliated, sent his son to the public assembly with the assurance that he was ready to conform to all their wishes, if they would return to their allegiance.

"It is too late," was the reply. "Leave us immediately, or we shall be exposed to the inconvenience of driving you away."

Yaroslaf immediately left the city and sought safety in exile. The Novgorodians then offered the soiled and battered crown to Dmitry, a nephew of the deposed prince. But Dmitry, fearing the vengeance of the Tartars, replied, "I am not willing to ascend a throne from which you have expelled my uncle."

Yaroslaf immediately sent an embassador to the encampment of the Tartars, where they were ever eagerly waiting for any enterprise which promised carnage and plunder. The embassador, imploring their aid, said,

"The Novgorodians are your enemies. They have shamefully expelled Yaroslaf, and thus treated your authority with insolence. They have deposed Yaroslaf, merely because he was faithful in collecting tribute for you."

By such a crisis, republicanism was necessarily introduced in Novgorod. The people, destitute of a prince, and threatened by an approaching army, made vigorous efforts for resistance. The two armies soon met face to face, and they were on the eve of a terrible battle, when the worthy metropolitan bishop, Cyrille, interposed and succeeded in effecting a treaty which arrested the flow of torrents of blood. The Novgorodians again accepted Yaroslaf, he making the most solemn promises of amendment. The embassadors of the Tartar khan conducted Yarsolaf again to the throne.

The Tartars now embraced, almost simultaneously and universally, the Mohammedan religion, and were inspired with the most fanatic zeal for its extension. Yaroslaf retained his throne only by employing all possible means to conciliate the Tartars. He died in the year 1272, as he was also on his return journey from a visit to the Tartar court.

Vassali, a younger brother of Yaroslaf, now ascended the throne, establishing himself at Vladimir. The grand duchy of Lithuania, extending over a region of sixty thousand square miles, was situated just north of Poland. The Tartars, dissatisfied with the Lithuanians, prepared an expedition against them, and marching with a great army, compelled many of the Russian princes to follow their banners. The Tartars spread desolation over the whole tract of country they traversed, and on their return took a careful census of the population of all the principalities of Russia, that they might decide upon the tribute to be imposed. The Russians were so broken in spirit that they submitted to all these indignities without a murmur. Still there were to be seen here and there indications of discontent. An ecclesiastical council was held at Vladimir, in the year 1274. All the bishops of the north of Russia were assembled to rectify certain abuses which had crept into the church. A copy of the canons then adopted, written upon parchment, is still preserved in the Russian archives.

"What a chastisement," exclaim the bishops, "have we received for our neglect of the true principles of Christianity! God has scattered us over the whole surface of the globe. Our cities have fallen into the hands of the enemy. Our princes have perished on the field of battle. Our families have been dragged into slavery. Our temples have become the prey of destruction; and every day we groan more and more heavily beneath the yoke which is imposed upon us."

It was decreed in this council of truly Christian men, that, as a public expression of the importance of a holy life, none should be introduced into the ranks of the clergy but those whose morals had been irreproachable from their earliest infancy. "A single pastor," said the decree of this council, "faithfully devoted to his Master's service, is more precious than a thousand worldly priests."

Vassali died in the year 1276, and was succeeded by a

prince of Vladimir, named Dmitri. He immediately left his native principality and took up his residence in Novgorod, which city at this time seems to have been regarded as the capital of the subjugated and dishonored kingdom. The indomitable tribes inhabiting the fastnesses of the Caucasian mountains had, thus far, maintained their independence. The Tartars called upon Russia for troops to aid in their subjugation; and four of the princes, one of whom, André of Gorodetz, was a brother of Dmitri the king, submissively led the required army into the Mogol encampment.

André, by his flattery, his presents and his servile devotion to the interests of the khan, secured a decree of dethronement against his brother and his own appointment as grand prince. Then, with a combined army of Tartars and Russians, he marched upon Novgorod to take possession of the crown. Resistance was not to be thought of, and Dmitri precipitately fled. Karamsin thus describes the sweep of this Tartar wave of woe:

"The Mogols pillaged and burned the houses, the monasteries, the churches, from which they took the images, the precious vases and the books richly bound. Large troops of the inhabitants were dragged into slavery, or fell beneath the sabers of the ferocious soldiers of the khan. The young sisters in the convents were exposed to the brutality of these monsters. The unhappy laborers, who, to escape death or captivity, had fled into the deserts, perished of exposure and starvation. Not an inhabitant was left who did not weep over the death of a father, a son, a brother or a friend."

Thus André ascended the throne, and then returned the soldiers of the khan laden with the booty which they had so cruelly and iniquitously obtained. The barbarians, always greedy of rapine and blood, were ever delighted to find occasion to ravage the principalities of Russia. The Tartars, having withdrawn, Dmitri secured the coöperation of some powerful princes, drove his brother from Novgorod, and again grasped the scepter which his brother had wrested from him. The two brothers continued bitterly hostile to each other, and years passed of petty intrigues and with occasional scenes of violence and blood as Dmitri struggled to hold the crown which André as perseveringly strove to seize. Again André obtained another Mogol army, which swept Russia with fearful destruction, and, taking possession of Vladimir and Moscow, and every city and village on their way, plundering, burning and destroying, marched resistlessly to Novgorod, and placed again the traitorous, blood-stained monster on the throne.

Dmitri, abandoning his palaces and his treasures, fled to a remote principality, where he soon died, in the year 1294, an old man battered and wrecked by the storms of a life of woe. He is celebrated in the Russian annals only by the disasters which accompanied his reign. According to the Russian historians, the infamous André, his elder brother being now dead, found himself *legitimately* the sovereign of Russia. As no one dared to dispute his authority, the ill-fated kingdom passed a few years in tranquillity.

At length Daniel, prince of Moscow, claimed independence of the nominal king, or grand prince, as he was called. In fact, most of the principalities were, at this time, entirely independent of the grand prince of Novgorod, whose supremacy was, in general, but an empty and powerless title. As Daniel was one of the nearest neighbors of André, and reigned over a desolate and impoverished realm, the grand prince was disposed to bring him into subjection. But neither of the princes dared to march their armies without first appealing to their Mogol masters. Daniel sent an embassador to the Mogol camp, but André went in person with his young and beautiful wife. The khan sent his embassador to Vladimir, there to summon before him the two princes and their friends and to adjudge their cause.

In the heat and bitterness of the debate, the two princes

drew their swords and fell upon each other. Their followers joined in the melee, and a scene of tumult and blood ensued characteristic of those barbaric times. The Tartar guard rushed in and separated the combatants. The Tartar judge extorted rich presents from both of the appellants and *settled* the question by leaving it *entirely unsettled*, ordering them both to go home. They separated like two boys who have been found quarreling, and who have both been soundly whipped for their pugnacity. In the autumn of the year 1303 an assembly of the Russian princes was convened at Pereiaslavle, to which congress the imperious khan sent his commands.

"It is my will," said the Tartar chief, "that the principalities of Russia should henceforth enjoy tranquillity. I therefore command all the princes to put an end to their dissensions and each one to content himself with the possessions and the power he now has."

Russia thus ceased to be even nominally a monarchy, unless we regard the Khan of Tartary as its sovereign. It was a conglomeration of principalities, ruled by princes, with irresponsible power, but all paying tribute to a foreign despot, and obliged to obey his will whenever he saw fit to make that will known. Still there continued incessant tempests of civil war, violent but of brief duration, to which the khan paid no attention, he deeming it beneath his dignity to intermeddle with such petty conflicts.

André died on the 27th July, 1304, execrated by his cotemporaries, and he has been consigned to infamy by posterity. As he approached the spirit land he was tortured with the dread of the scenes which he might encounter there. His crimes had condemned thousands to death and other thousands to live-long woe. He sought by priestcraft, and penances, and monastic vows, and garments of sackcloth, to efface the stains of a soul crimsoned with crime. He died, and his guilty spirit passed away to meet God in judgment.

CHAPTER VIII.

RESURRECTION OF THE RUSSIAN MONARCHY.

FROM 1304 TO 1380.

DEFEAT OF GEORGES AND THE TARTARS —INDIGNATION OF THE KHAN.—MICHEL SUMMONED TO THE HORDE.—HIS TRIAL AND EXECUTION.—ASSASSINATION OF GEORGES.—EXECUTION OF DMITRI.—REPULSE AND DEATH OF THE EMBASSADOR OF THE KHAN.—VENGEANCE OF THE KHAN.—INCREASING PROSPERITY OF RUSSIA.—THE GREAT PLAGUE.—SUPREMACY OF SIMON.—ANARCHY IN THE HORDE.—PLAGUE AND CONFLAGRATION.—THE TARTARS REPULSED.—RECONQUEST OF BULGARIA.—THE GREAT BATTLE OF KOULIKOF.—UTTER ROUT OF THE TARTARS.

THE Tartars, now fierce Mohammedans, began to oppress severely, particularly in Kief, the Christians. The metropolitan bishop of this ancient city, with the whole body of the clergy, pursued by persecution, fled to Vladimir; and others of the Christians of Kief were scattered over the kingdom.

The death of André was as fatal to Russia as had been his reign. Two rival princes, Michel of Tver, and Georges of Moscow, grasped at the shadow of a scepter which had fallen from his hands. In consequence, war and anarchy for a long time prevailed. At length, Michel, having appealed to the Tartars and gained their support, ascended the frail throne. But a fierce war now raged between Novgorod and Moscow. In the prosecution of this war, Georges obtained some advantage which led Michel to appeal to the khan. The prince of Moscow was immediately summoned to appear in the presence of the Tartar chieftain. By the most ignoble fawning and promises of plunder, Georges obtained the support of the khan, and returning with a Tartar horde, cruelly devastated the principality of his foe. Michel and all his subjects, roused to the highest pitch of indignation, marched to meet the enemy. The two armies encountered each other a few leagues from Moscow. The followers of Michel, fighting with the energies of despair, were unexpectedly successful, and Georges, with his Russian and Tartar troops, was thoroughly defeated.

Kavgadi, the leader of the Tartar allies of Georges, was taken prisoner. Michel, appalled by the thought of the vengeance he might anticipate from the great khan, whose power he had thus ventured to defy, treated his captive, Kavgadi, with the highest consideration, and immediately set him at liberty loaded with presents. Georges, accompanied by Kavgadi, repaired promptly to the court of the khan, Usbeck, who was then encamped, with a numerous army, upon the shores of the Caspian Sea. Soon an embassador of the khan arrived at Vladimir, and informed Michel that Usbeck was exasperated against him to the highest degree.

"Hasten," said he, "to the court of the great khan, or within a month you will see your provinces inundated by his troops. Think of your peril, when Kavgadi has informed Usbeck that you have dared to resist his authority."

Terrified by these words, the nobles of Michel entreated him not to place himself in the power of the khan, but to allow some one of them to visit the *horde*, as it was then called, in his stead, and endeavor to appease the wrath of the monarch.

"No," replied the high-minded prince; "Usbeck demands my presence not yours. Far be it from me, by my disobedience, to expose my country to ruin. If I resist the commands of the khan, my country will be doomed to new woes; thousands of Christians will perish, the victims of his fury. It is impossible for us to repel the forces of the Tartars. What other asylum is there then for me but death? Is it not better for me to die, if I may thus save the lives of my faithful subjects?"

He made his will, divided his estates among his sons, and entreating them ever to be faithful to the dictates of virtue, bade them an eternal adieu. Michel encountered the khan near the mouth of the Don, as it enters the Sea of Azof. Usbeck was on a magnificent hunting excursion, accompanied by his chieftains and his army. For six weeks he did not deign to pay any attention to the Russian prince, not even condescending to order him to be guarded. The rich presents Michel had brought, in token of homage, were neither received nor rejected, but were merely disregarded as of no moment whatever.

At length, one morning, suddenly, as if recollecting something which had been forgotten, Usbeck ordered his lords to summon Michel before them and adjudge his cause. A tent was spread as a tribunal of justice, near the tent of the khan; and the unhappy prince, bound with cords, was led before his judges. He was accused of the unpardonable crime of having drawn his sword against the soldiers of the khan. No justification could be offered. Michel was cruelly fettered with chains and thrown into a dungeon. An enormous collar of iron was riveted around his neck.

Usbeck then set out for the chase, on an expedition which was to last for one or two months. The annals of the time describe this expedition with great particularity, presenting a scene of pomp almost surpassing credence. Some allowance must doubtless be made for exaggeration; and yet there is a minuteness of detail which, accompanied by corroborative evidence of the populousness and the power of these Tartar tribes, invests the narrative with a good degree of authenticity. We are informed that several hundreds of thousands of men were in movement; that each soldier was clothed in rich uniform and mounted upon a beautiful horse; that merchants transported, in innumerable chariots, the most precious fabrics of Greece and of the Indies, and that luxury and gayety reigned throughout the immense camp, which, in the midst of savage deserts, presented the aspect of brilliant and populous cities. Michel, who was awaiting his sentence from Usbeck, was dragged, loaded with chains, in the train of the horde. Georges was in high favor with the khan, and was importunately urging the condemnation of his rival.

With wonderful fortitude the prince endured his humiliation and tortures. The nobles who had accompanied him were plunged into inconsolable grief. Michel endeavored to solace them. He manifested, through the whole of this terrible trial, the spirit of the Christian, passing whole nights in prayer and in chanting the Psalms of David. As his hands were bound, one of his pages held the sacred book before him. His faithful followers urged him to take advantage of the confusion and tumult of the camp to effect his escape. "Never," exclaimed Michel, "will I degrade myself by flight. Moreover, should I escape, that would save *me* only, not my country. God's will be done."

The horde was now encamped among the mountains of Circassia. It was the 22d of November, 1319, when, just after morning prayers, which were conducted by an abbé and two priests, who accompanied the Russian prince, Michel was informed that Usbeck had sentenced him to death. He immediately called his young son Constantin, a lad twelve years of age, into his presence, and gave his last directions to his wife and children.

"Say to them," enjoined this Christian prince, "that I go down into the tomb cherishing for them the most ardent affection. I recommend to their care the generous nobles, the faithful servants who have manifested so much zeal for their sovereign, both when he was upon the throne and when in chains."

These thoughts of home overwhelmed him, and, for a moment losing his fortitude, he burst into tears. Causing the Bible to be opened to the Psalms of David, which, in all ages, have been the great fountain of consolation to the afflicted, he read from the fifty-sixth Psalm, fifth verse, "Fearfulness and trembling are come upon me, and horror hath overwhelmed me."

"Prince," said the abbé, "in the same Psalm with which you are so familiar, are the words, 'Cast thy burden upon the Lord, and he shall sustain thee. He shall never suffer the righteous to be moved.'"

Michel simply replied by quoting again from the same inspired page: "Oh that I had wings like a dove; for then would I fly away and be at rest."

At that moment one of the pages entered the tent, pale and trembling, and informed that a great crowd of people were approaching. "I know why they are coming," said the prince, and he immediately sent his young son away on a message, that the child might not witness the cruel execution of his father. Two brawny barbarians entered the tent. As the prince was fervently praying, they smote him down with clubs, trampled him beneath their feet, and then plunged a poignard into his heart. The crowd which had followed the executioners, according to their custom rushed into the royal tent for pillage. The gory body was left in the hands of the Russian nobles. They enveloped the remains in precious clothes, and bore them with affectionate care back to Moscow.

Georges, now confirmed in the dignity of grand prince by the khan, returned to Vladimir, where he established his government, sending his brother to Novgorod to reign over that principality in his name. Dmitri, and others of the sons of Michel, for several years waged implacable warfare against Georges, with but little success. The khan, however, did not deign to interfere in a strife which caused him no trouble. But in the year 1325 Georges again went to the horde on the eastern banks of the Caspian. At the same time, Dmitri appeared in the encampment. Meeting Georges accidentally, whom he justly regarded as the murderer of his father, he drew his sword, and plunged it to the hilt in the heart of the grand prince. The khan, accustomed to such deeds of violence, was not disposed to punish the son who had thus avenged the death of his father. But the friends of Georges so importunately urged that to pardon such a crime would be an ineffaceable stain upon his honor, would be an indication of weakness, and would encourage the Russian princes in the commission of other outrages, that after the lapse of ten months, during which time Dmitri had been detained a captive, Usbeck ordered his execution, and the unfortunate prince was beheaded. Dmitri was then but twenty-seven years of age.

And yet Usbeck seems to have had some regard for the cause of the young prince, for he immediately appointed Alexander, a brother of Dmitri, and son of Michel, to succeed Georges in the grand principality. The Novgorodians promptly received him as their ruler. Affairs were in this state when, at the close of the summer of 1327, an embassador of Usbeck appeared, with a band of Tartars, and entered the royal city of Tver, which was the residence of Alexander. The principality of the Tver was spread along the head waters of the Volga, just north of the principality of Moscow. The report spread through the city that the Mogol embassador, Schevkal, who was a zealous Mohammedan, had come to convert the Russians to Mohammedanism, that he intended the death of Alexander, to ascend the throne himself, and to distribute the cities of the principality to his followers.

The Tverians, in a paroxysm of terror and despair, rallied for the support of their prince and their religion. In a terrible tumult all the inhabitants rose and precipated themselves upon the embassador and his valiant body guard. From morning until night the battle raged in the streets of Tver. The Tartars, overpowered by numbers, and greatly weakened by losses during the day, took refuge in a palace. The citizens set the palace on fire, and every Tartar perished, either consumed by the flames or cut down by the Russians.

When Usbeck heard of this event, he was, at first, stupefied by the audacity of the deed. He imagined that all Russia was in the conspiracy, and that there was to be a general rising to throw off the Tartar yoke. Still Usbeck, with his characteristic sagacity, decided to employ the Russians to subdue the Russians. He at once deposed and outlawed Alexander, and declared Jean Danielovitch, of Moscow, to be grand prince, who promised the most obsequious obedience to his wishes. At the same time he sent an army of fifty thousand Tartars to coöperate with the Russian army, which Jean Danielovitch was commanded to put in motion for the invasion of the principality of Tver. It was in vain to think of resistance, and Alexander fled. The invading army, with awful devastation, ravaged the principality. Multitudes were slain. Others were dragged into captivity. The smoking ruins of the cities and villages of Tver became the monument of the wrath of the khan. Alexander, pursued by the implacable wrath of Usbeck, was finally taken and beheaded.

But few particulars are known respecting the condition of southern Russia at this time. The principalities were under the government of princes who were all tributary to the Tartars, and yet these princes were incessantly quarreling with one another, and the whole country was the scene of violence and blood.

The energies of the Tartar horde were now engrossed by internal dissensions and oriental wars, and for many years, the conquerors still drawing their annual tribute from the country, but in no other way interfering with its concerns, devoted all their energies to conspiracies and bloody battles among themselves. Moscow now became the capital of the country, and under the peaceful reign of Jean, increased rapidly in wealth and splendor. Jean, acting professedly as the agent of Usbeck, extorted from many of the principalities double tribute, one half of which he furtively appropriated to the increase of the wealth, splendor and power of his own dominions. His reign was on the whole one of the most prosperous Russia had enjoyed for ages. Agriculture and commerce flourished. The Volga was covered with boats, conveying to the Caspian the furs and manufactures of the North, and laden, on their return, with the spices and fabrics of the Indies. On the 31st of March, 1340, Jean died. As he felt the approach of death his spirit was overawed by the realities of the eternal world. Laying aside his regal robes he assumed the dress of a monk, and entering a monastery, devoted his last days zealously to prayer. His end was peace.

Immediately after his death there were several princes who were ambitious of grasping the scepter which he had dropped, and, as Usbeck alone could settle that question, there was a general rush to the horde. Simeon, the eldest son of Jean, and his brothers, were among the foremost who presented themselves in the tent of the all-powerful khan. Simeon eloquently urged the fidelity with which his father had always served the Mogol prince, and he promised, in his turn, to do every thing in his power to merit the favor of the khan. So successfully did he prosecute his suit that the khan declared him to be grand prince, and commanded all his rivals to obey him as their chief.

The manners of the barbarian Mogols had, for some time, been assuming a marked change. They emerged from their native wilds as fierce and untamed as wolves. The herds of cattle they drove along with them supplied them with food, and the skins of these animals supplied them with clothing and with tents. Their home was wherever they happened to be encamped, but, having reached the banks of the Black Sea and the fertile valleys of the Volga and the Don, they became acquainted with the luxuries of Europe and of the more civilized portions of Asia. Commerce enriched them. Large cities were erected, embellished by the genius of Grecian and Italian architects. Life became more desirable, and the wealthy chieftains, indulging in luxury, were less eager to encounter the exposure and perils of battle. The love of wealth now became with them a ruling passion. For gold they would grant any favors. The golden promises of Simeon completely won the heart of Usbeck, and the young prince returned to Moscow flushed with success. He assumed such airs of superiority and of power as secured for him the title of *The Superb.* He caused himself to be crowned king, with much religious pomp, in the cathedral of Vladimir. Novgorod manifested some resistance to his assumptions. He instantly invaded the principality, hewed down all opposition, and punished his opponents with such severity that there was a simultaneous cry for mercy. Rapidly he extended his power, and the fragmentary principalities of Russia began again to assume the aspect of concentration and adhesion.

Ere two years had elapsed, Usbeck, the khan, died. This remarkable man had been, for some time, the friend and the ally of Pope Beniot XII., who had hoped to convert him to the Christian religion. The khan had even allowed the pope to introduce Christianity to the Tartar territories bordering on the Black Sea. Tchanibek, the oldest son of Usbeck, upon the death of his father, assassinated his brothers, and thus attained the supreme authority. He was a zealous Mohammedan, and commenced his reign by commanding all the princes of the principalities of Russia to hasten to the horde and prostrate themselves, in token of homage, before his throne. The least delay would subject the offender to confiscation and death. Simeon was one of the first to do homage to the new khan. He was received with great favor, and dismissed confirmed in all his privileges.

In the year 1346, one of the most desolating plagues recorded in history, commenced its ravages in China, and swept over all Asia and nearly all Europe. The disease is recorded in the ancient annals under the name of Black Death. Thirteen millions of the population were, in the course of a few months, swept into the grave. Entire cities were depopulated, and the dead by thousands lay unburied. The pestilence swept with terrible fury the encampments of the Tartars, and weakened that despotic power beyond all recovery. But one third of the population of the principalities of Pskof and of Novgorod were left living. At London fifty thousand were interred in a single cemetery. The disease commenced with swellings on the fleshy parts of the body, a violent spitting of blood ensued, which was followed by death the second or third day.

It is impossible, according to the ancient annalists, to imagine a spectacle so terrible. Young and old, fathers and children, were buried in the same grave. Entire families disappeared in a day. Each curate found, every morning, thirty dead bodies, often more, in his church. Greedy men at first offered their services to the dying, hoping to obtain their estates, but when it was found that the disease was communicated by touch, even the most wealthy could obtain no aid. The son fled from the father. The brother avoided the brother. Still there were not a few examples of the most generous and self-sacrificing devotion. Medical skill was of no avail whatever, and the churches were thronged with the multitudes who, in the midst of the dying and the dead, were crying to God for aid. Multitudes in their terror bequeathed all their property to the church, and sought refuge in the monasteries. It truth, it appeared as if Heaven had pronounced the sentence of immediate death upon the whole human family.

Five times, during his short reign, Simeon was compelled to repair to the horde, to remove suspicions and appease displeasure. He at length so far ingratiated himself into favor with the khan, that the Tartar sovereign conferred upon him the title of Grand Prince of *all the Russias.* The death of Simeon in the year 1353, caused a general rush of the princes of the several principalities to the Tartar horde, each emulous of being appointed his successor. Tchanibek, the khan, after suitable deliberation, conferred the dignity upon Jean Ivanovitch of Moscow. His reign of six years was disturbed by a multiplicity of intestine feuds, but no events occurred worthy of record. He died in 1359.

Again the Russian princes crowded to the horde, as, in every age, office seekers have thronged the court. The khan, after due deliberation, conferred the investiture of the grand principality upon Dmitri of Souzdal, though the appointment was received with great dissatisfaction by the other princes. But now the power of the Tartars was rapidly on the decline. Assassination succeeded assassination, one chieftain after another securing the assassination of his rival and with bloody hands ascending the Mogol throne. The swords of the Mogol warriors were turned against each other, as rival chieftains rallied their followers for attack or defense. Civil war raged among these fierce bands with most terrible ferocity. Famine and pestilence followed the ravages of the sword.

While the horde was in this state of distraction, antagonistic khans began to court the aid of the Russian princes, and a successful Tartar chieftain, who had poignarded his rival, and thus attained the throne, deposed Dmitri of Souzdal, and declared a young prince, Dmitri of Moscow, to be sovereign of Russia. But as the khan, whose whole energies were required to retain his disputed throne, could send no army into Russia to enforce this decree, Dmitri of Souzdal paid but little attention to the paper edict. Immediately the Russian princes arrayed themselves on different sides. The conflict was short, but decisive, and the victorious prince of Moscow was crowned as sovereign. The light of a resurrection morning was now dawning upon the Russian monarchy. There were, fortunately, at this time, two rival khans beyond the waves of the Caspian opposing each other with bloody cimeters. The energetic young prince, by fortunate marriage, and by the success of his arms, rapidly extended his authority. But again the awful plague swept Russia. The annalists of those days thus describe the symptoms and the character of the malady:

"One felt himself suddenly struck as by a knife plunged into the heart through the shoulder blades or between the two shoulders. An intense fire seemed to burn the entrails; blood flowed freely from the throat; a violent perspiration ensued, followed by severe chills; tumors gathered upon the neck, the hip, under the arms or behind the shoulder blades. The end was invariably the same—death, inevitable, speedy, but terrible."

Out of a hundred persons, frequently not more than ten would be left alive. Moscow was almost depopulated. In Smolensk but five individuals escaped, and they were compelled to abandon the city, the houses and the streets being encumbered with the putrefying bodies of the dead.* Just before this disaster, Moscow suffered severely from a conflagration. The imperial palace and a large portion of the city were laid in ashes. The prince then resolved to construct a Kremlin of stone, and he laid the foundations of a gorgeous palace in the year 1367.

Dmitri now began to bid defiance to the Tartars, doubly weakened by the sweep of the pestilence and by internal discord. There were a few minor conflicts, in which the Russians were victorious, and, elated by success, they began to rally for a united effort to shake off the degrading Mogol yoke. Three bands of the Tartars were encamped at the mouth of the Dnieper. The Russians descended the river in barges, assailed them with the valor which their fathers had displayed, and drove the pagans, in wild rout, to the shores of the Sea of Azof.

The Tartars, astounded at such unprecedented audacity, forgetting, for the time, their personal animosities, collected a large army, and commenced a march upon Moscow. The

* See Histoire de l'Empire de Russie, par M. Karamsin. Traduite par MM. St. Thomas et Jauffret. Tome cinquieme, p. 10.

grand prince dispatched his couriers in every direction to assemble the princes of the empire with all the soldiers they could bring into the field. Again the Tartars were repulsed. For many years the Tartars had been in possession of Bulgaria, an extensive region east of the Volga. In the year 1376, the grand prince, Dmitri, fitted out an expedition for the reconquest of that country. The Russian arms were signally successful. The Tartars, beaten on all hands, their cities burned, their boats destroyed, were compelled to submit to the conqueror. A large sum of money was extorted from them to be distributed among the troops. They were forced to acknowledge themselves, in their turn, tributary to Russia, and to accept Russian magistrates for the government of their cities.

Encouraged by this success, the grand prince made arrangements for other exploits. A border warfare ensued, which was continued for several years with alternating success and with great ferocity. Neither party spared age or sex, and cities and villages were indiscriminately committed to the flames. Russia was soon alarmed by the rumor that Mamai, a Tartar chieftain, was approaching the frontiers of Russia with one of the largest armies the Mogols had ever raised. This intelligence roused the Russians to the highest pitch of energy to meet their foes in a decisive battle. An immense force was soon assembled at Moscow from all parts of the kingdom. After having completed all his arrangements, Dmitri, with his chief captains, repaired to the church of the Trinity to receive the benediction of the metropolitan bishop.

"You will triumph," said the venerable ecclesiastic, "but only after terrible carnage. You will vanquish the enemy, but your laurels will be sprinkled with the blood of a vast number of Christian heroes."

The troops, accompanied by ecclesiastics who bore the banners of the cross, passed out at the gate of the Kremlin.

As the majestic host defiled from the city, the grand prince passed the hours in the church of Saint Michael, kneeling upon the tomb of his ancestors, fervently imploring the blessing of Heaven. Animated by the strength which prayer ever gives, he embraced his wife, saying, "God will be our defender," and then, mounting his horse, placed himself at the head of his army. It was a beautiful summer's day, calm, serene and cloudless, and the whole army were sanguine in the hope that God would smile upon their enterprise. Marching nearly south, along the valley of the Moskwa, they reached, in a few days, the large city of Kolomna, a hundred miles distant, on the banks of the Oka. Here they were joined by several confederate princes, with their contingents of troops, swelling the army to one hundred and fifty thousand men. Seventy-five thousand of these were cavalry, superbly mounted. Never had Russia, even in her days of greatest splendor, witnessed a more magnificent array.

Mamai, the Tartar khan, had assembled the horde, in numbers which he deemed overwhelming, on the waters of the Don. Resolved not to await the irruption of the foe, on the 20th of August, Dmitri, with his army, crossed the Oka, and pressed forward towards the valley of the Don. They reached this stream on the 6th of September. Soon detachments of the advanced guards of the two armies met, and several skirmishes ensued. Dmitri assembled his generals in solemn conclave, and saying to them, "The hour of God's judgment has sounded," gave minute directions for the conflict. Aided by a dense fog, which concealed their operations from the view of the enemy, the army crossed the Don, the cavalry fording the stream, while the infantry passed over by a hastily-constructed bridge. Dmitri deployed his columns in battle array upon the vast plain of Koulikof. A mound of earth was thrown up, that Dmitri, upon its summit, might overlook the whole plain.

As the Russian prince stood upon this pyramid and contemplated his army, there was spread before him such a spectacle as mortal eyes have seldom seen. A hundred and fifty thousand men were marshaled on the plain. It was the morning of the 8th of September, 1380. Thousands of banners fluttered in the breeze. The polished armor of the cavaliers, cuirass, spear and helmet, glittered in the rays of the sun. Seventy-five thousand steeds, gorgeously caparisoned, were neighing and prancing over the verdant savanna. The soldiers, according to their custom, shouted the prayer, which rose like the roar of many waters, "Great God, grant to our sovereign the victory." The whole sublime scene moved the soul of Dmitry to its profoundest depths; and as he reflected that in a few hours perhaps the greater portion of that multitude might lie dead upon the field, tears gushed from his eyes, and kneeling upon the summit of the mound, in the presence of the whole army, he extended his hands towards heaven in a fervent prayer that God would protect Russia and Christianity from the heel of the infidel. Then, mounting his horse, he rode along the ranks, exclaiming,

"My brothers dearly beloved; my faithful companions in arms: by your exploits this day you will live for ever in the memory of men; and those of you who fall will find, beyond the tomb, the crown of martyrs."

The Tartar host approached upon the boundless plain slowly and cautiously, but in numbers even exceeding those of the Russians. Notwithstanding the most earnest remonstrances of his generals, Dmitri led the charge, exposing himself to every peril which the humblest soldier was called to meet.

"It is not in me," said he, "to seek a place of safety while crying out to you, '*My brothers, let us die for our country!*' My actions shall correspond with my words. I am your chief. I will be your guide. I will go in advance, and, if I die, it is for you to avenge me."

Again ascending the mound, the king, with a loud voice, read the forty-sixth Psalm: "God is our refuge and strength, a very present help in trouble. Therefore will not we fear though the earth be removed, and though the mountains be carried into the midst of the sea." The battle was immediately commenced, with ferocity on both sides which has probably never been surpassed. For three hours the two armies were blended in a hand to hand fight, spreading over a space seven miles in length. Blood flowed in torrents, and the sod was covered with the slain. Here the Russians were victorious and the Tartars fled before them. There the Tartars, with frenzied shouts, chased the Russians in awful rout over the plain. Dmitri had stationed a strong reserve behind a forest. When both parties were utterly exhausted, suddenly this reserve emerged from their retreat and rushed upon the foe. Vladimir, the brother of Dmitri, led the charge. The Mogols, surprised, confounded, overwhelmed and utterly routed, in the wildest confusion, and with outcries which rent the heavens, turned and fled. "The God of the Christians has conquered," exclaimed the Tartar chief, gnashing his teeth in despair. The Tartars were hewed down by saber strokes from unexhausted arms, and trampled beneath the hoofs of the war horse. The entire camp of the horde, with immense booty of tents, chariots, horses, camels, cattle and precious commodities of every kind, fell into the hands of the captors.

The valorous prince Vladimir, the hero of the day, returned to the field of battle, which his cavalry had swept like a tornado, and planting his banner upon a mound, with signal trumpets, summoned the whole victorious host to rally around it. The princes, the nobles, from every part of the extended field, gathered beneath its folds. But to their consternation, the grand prince, Dmitri, was missing. Amidst the surgings of the battle he had disappeared, and was nowhere to be found.

CHAPTER IX

DMITRI, VASSALI, AND THE MOGOL TAMERLANE.

FROM 1380 TO 1462.

RECOVERY OF DMITRI.—NEW TARTAR INVASION.—THE ASSAULT AND CAPTURE OF MOSCOW.—NEW SUBJUGATION OF THE RUSSIANS.—LITHUANIA EMBRACES CHRISTIANITY.—ESCAPE OF VASSALI FROM THE HORDE.—DEATH OF DMITRI.—TAMERLANE.—HIS ORIGIN AND CAREER.—HIS INVASION OF INDIA.—DEFEAT OF BAJAZET.—TAMERLANE INVADES RUSSIA.—PREPARATIONS FOR RESISTANCE.—SUDDEN RETREAT OF THE TARTARS.—DEATH OF VASSALI.—ACCESSION OF VASSALI VASSILIOVITCH.—THE DISPUTED SUCCESSION.—APPEAL TO THE KHAN.—REBELLION OF YOURI.—CRUELTY OF VASSALI.—THE RETRIBUTION.

"WHERE is my brother?" exclaimed Vladimir; "where is he to whom we are indebted for all this glory?" No one could give any information respecting Dmitri. In the tumult he had disappeared. Sadly the chieftains dispersed over the plain to search for him among the dead. After a long exploration, two soldiers found him in the midst of a heap of the slain. Stunned by a blow, he had fallen from his horse, and was apparently lifeless. As with filial love they hung over his remains, bathing his bloody brow, he opened his eyes. Gradually he recovered consciousness; and as he saw the indications of triumph in the faces of his friends, heard the words of assurance that he had gained the victory, and witnessed the Russian banners all over the field, floating above the dead bodies of the Tartars, in a transport of joy he folded his hands upon his breast, closed his eyes and breathed forth a fervent, grateful prayer to God. The princes stood silently and reverently by, as their sovereign thus returned thanks to Heaven.

Joy operated so effectually as a stimulus, that the prince, who had been stunned, but not seriously wounded, mounted his horse and rode over the hard-fought field. Though thousands of the Russians were silent in death, the prince could count more than four times as many dead bodies of the enemy. According to the annals of the time, a hundred thousand Tartars were slain on that day. Couriers were immediately dispatched to all the principalities with the joyful tidings. The anxiety had been so great, that, from the moment the army passed the Don, the churches had been thronged by day and by night, and incessant prayers had ascended to heaven for its success. No language can describe the enthusiasm which the glad tidings inspired. It was felt that henceforth the prosperity, the glory, the independence of Russia was secured for ever; that the supremacy of the horde was annihilated; that the blood of the Christians, shed upon the plain of Koulikof, was the last sacrifice Russia was doomed to make.

But in these anticipations, Russia was destined to be sadly disappointed. Mamai, the discomfited Tartar chieftain, overwhelmed with shame and rage, reached, with the wreck of his army, one of the great encampments of the Tartars on the banks of the Volga. A new khan, the world-renowned Tamerlane, now swayed the scepter of Tartar power. Two years were devoted to immense preparations for the new invasion of Russia. Suddenly and unexpectedly, Dmitri was informed that the Tartars were approaching in strength unprecedented. Russia was unprepared for the attack, and terror congealed all hearts. The invaders, crossing the Volga and the Oka, pressed rapidly towards Moscow.

Dmitri, deeming it in vain to attempt the defense of the capital, fled, with his wife and children, two hundred miles north, to the fortress of Kostroma. A young prince, Ostei, was left in command of the city, with orders to hold it to the last extremity against the Tartars, and with the assurance that the king would return, as speedily as possible, with an army from Kostroma to his relief. The panic in the city was fearful, and the gates were crowded, day and night, by the women and children, the infirm and the timid seeking safety in flight. Ostei made the most vigorous preparations for defense, while the king, with untiring energy, was accumulating an army of relief. The merchants and laborers from the neighboring villages, and even the monks and priests crowded to Moscow, demanding arms for the defense of the metropolis. From the battlements of the city, the advance of the barbarians could be traced by the volumes of smoke which arose, as from a furnace, through the day, and by the flames which flashed along the horizon, from the burning cities and villages, through the night.

On the evening of the 23d of August, 1382, the Tartars appeared before the gates of the city. Some of the chiefs rode slowly around the ramparts, examining the ditch, the walls, the height of the towers, and selected the most favorable spot for commencing the assault. The Tartars did not appear in such overwhelming numbers as report had taught the Russians to expect, and they felt quite sanguine that they should be able to defend the city. But the ensuing morning dispelled all these hopes. It then appeared that these Tartars were but the advance guard of the great army. With the earliest dawn, as far as the eye could reach, the inundation of warriors came rolling on, and terror vanquished all hearts. This army was under the command of a Tartar chieftain called Toktamonish. The assault was instantly commenced, and continued without cessation four days and nights.

At length the city fell, vanquished, it is said, by stratagem rather than by force. The Tartars clambering, by means of ten thousand ladders, over the walls, and rushing through the gates, with no ear for mercy, commenced the slaughter of the inhabitants. The city was set on fire in all directions, and a scene of horror ensued indescribable and unimaginable. The barbarians, laden with booty, and satiated with blood and carnage, encamped on the plain outside of the walls, exulting in the entireness of their vengeance. Moscow, the gorgeous capital, was no more. The dwellings of the city became but the funeral pyre for the bodies of the inhabitants. The Tartars, intoxicated with blood, dispersed over the whole principality; and all its populous cities, Vladimir, Zvenigorod, Yourief, Mojaisk and Dmitrof, experienced the same fate with that of Moscow. The khan then retired, crossing the Oka at Kolomna.

Dmitri arrived with his army at Moscow, only to behold the ruins. The enemy had already disappeared. In profoundest affliction, he gave orders for the interment of the charred and blackened bodies of the dead. Eighty thousand, by count, were interred, which number did not include the many who had been consumed entirely by the conflagration. The walls of the city and the towers of the Kremlin still remained. With great energy, the prince devoted himself to the rebuilding and the repeopling of the capital; many years, however, passed away ere it regained even the shadow of its former splendor.

Thus again Russia, brought under the sway of the Tartars, was compelled to pay tribute, and Dmitri was forced to send his own son to the horde, where he was long detained as a hostage. The grand duchy of Lithuania, bordering on Poland, was spread over a region of sixty thousand square miles. The grand duke, Jaghellon, a burly pagan, had married Hedwige, Queen of Poland, promising, as one of the conditions of this marriage which would unite Lithuania and Poland, to embrace Christianity.* He was married and baptized at Cracow, receiving the Christian name of Ladislaus. He then ordered the adoption of Christianity throughout Lithuania, and the universal baptism of his subjects. In order to facilitate the baptism of over a million at once, the inhabitants were collected at several central points. They were

* For an account of the romantic circumstances attending this marriage, see *Empire of Austria*, pp. 53 and 54.

arranged in vast groups, and were sprinkled with water which had been blessed by the priests. As the formula of baptism was pronounced, to one entire group the name of Peter was given, to another the name of Paul, to another that of John. These converts were received, not into the Greek church, which was dominant in Russia, but to the Romish church, which prevailed in Poland. Jaghellon became immediately the inveterate foe of the Russians, whom he called heretics, for new proselytes are almost invariably inspired with fanatic zeal, and he forbade the marriage of any of his Catholic subjects with members of the Russian church. This event caused great grief to Dmitri, for he had relied upon the coöperation of the warlike Lithuanians to aid him to repel the Mogols.

Affairs were in this condition when Vassali, the son of Dmitri, escaped from the horde after a three years' captivity, and, traversing Poland and Lithuania, arrived safely at Moscow. Dmitri was now forty years of age. He was a man of colossal stature, and of vigorous health. His hair and beard were black as the raven's wing, and his ruddy cheek and piercing eye seemed to give promise of a long life. But suddenly he was seized with a fatal disease, and it was soon evident that death was near. The intellect of the dying prince was unclouded, and, with much fortitude, in a long interview, he bade adieu to his wife and his children. He designated his son Vassali, then but seventeen years of age, as his successor, and then, after offering a touching prayer, folded his hands across his breast, in the form of a cross, and died without a struggle. The grief of the Russians was profound and universal. For ages they had not known a prince so illustrious or so devoted to the welfare of his country.

The young Vassali had been but a few years on the throne when Tamerlane himself advanced with countless hordes from the far Orient, crushing down all opposition, and sweeping over prostrate nations like the pestilence which had preceded him, and whose track he followed. Tamerlane was the son of a petty Mogol prince. He was born in a season of anarchy, and when the whole Tartar horde was distracted with civil dissensions. The impetuous young man had hardly begun to think, ere he had formed the resolve to attain the supremacy over all the Mogol tribes, to conquer the whole known world, and thus to render himself immortal in the annals of glory. Behind a curtain of mountains, and protected by vast deserts, his persuasive genius collected a large band of followers, who with enthusiasm adopted his views and hailed him their chief.

After inuring them to fatigue, and drilling them thoroughly in the exercises of battle, he commenced his career. The most signal victory followed his steps, and he soon acquired the title of hero. Ambitious, war-loving, thousands crowded to his standards, and he had but just attained the age of thirty-five when he was the undisputed monarch of all the Mogol tribes, and the whole Asiatic world trembled at the mention of his name. He took his seat proudly upon the throne of Genghis Khan, a crown of gold was placed upon his brow, a royal girdle encircled his waist, and in accordance with oriental usage his robes glittered with jewels and gold. At his feet were his renowned chieftains, kneeling around his throne in homage. Tamerlane then took an oath, that by his future exploits he would justify the title he had already acquired, and that all the kings of the earth should yet lie prostrate before him.

And now commenced an incessant series of wars, and victory ever crowned the banners of Tamerlane. He was soon in possession of all the countries on the eastern shores of the Caspian Sea. He then entered Persia, and conquered the whole realm between the Oxus and the Tigris. Bagdad, until now the proud capital of the caliphs, submitted to his sway. Soon the whole region of Asia, from the Sea of Aral to the Persian Gulf, and from Teflis to the great Arabian desert, recognized the empire of Tamerlane. The conqueror then assembled his companions in arms, and thus addressed them:

"Friends and fellow-soldiers; fortune, who recognizes me as her child, invites us to new conquests. The universe trembles at my name, and the movement even of one of my fingers causes the earth to quake. The realms of India are open to us. Woe to those who oppose my will. I will annihilate them unless they acknowledge me as their lord."

With flying banners and pealing trumpets he crossed the Indus, and marched upon Delhi, which for three centuries had been governed by the Mohammedan sultans. No opposition could retard the sweep of his locust legions; and the renowned city at once passed into his hands. Indulging in no delay, the order was still *onwards*, and the hosts soon bathed their dusty limbs in the waves of the Ganges. Here he was informed that Bajazet, the Grand Seignior of Turkey, was on a career of conquest which rivaled his own; that he had overrun all of Asia Minor; that, crossing the Hellespont, he had subjugated Servia, Macedonia, Thessaly, and that he was even besieging the imperial city of Constantine. The jealousy of Tamerlane was thoroughly aroused. He instantly turned upon his steps to seek this foe, worthy of his arms, dispatching to him the following defiant message:

"Learn," wrote Tamerlane to Bajazet, "that the earth is covered with my warriors from sea to sea. Kings compose my body guard, and range themselves as servants before my tent. Are you ignorant that the destiny of the universe is in my hands? Who are you? A Turkoman ant. And dare you raise your head against an elephant? If in the forests of Natolia you have obtained some trivial successes; if the timid Europeans have fled like cowards before you, return thanks to Mohammed for your success, for it is not owing to your own valor. Listen to the counsels of wisdom. Be content with the heritage of your fathers, and, however small that heritage may be, beware how you attempt, in the slightest degree, to extend its limits, lest death be the penalty of your temerity."

To this insolent letter, Bajazet responded in terms equally defiant.

"For a long time," he wrote, "Bajazet has burned with the desire to measure himself with Tamerlane, and he returns thanks to the All-powerful that Tamerlane now comes himself, to present his head to the cimeter of Bajazet."

The two conquerors gathered all their resources for the great and decisive battle. Tamerlane speedily reached Aleppo, which city, after a bloody conflict, he entered in triumph. The Tartar chieftain was an impostor and a hypocrite, as well as a merciless butcher of his fellow-men. He assembled the learned men of Aleppo, and assured them in most eloquent terms that he was the devoted friend of God, and that the enemies who resisted his will were responsible to God for all the evils their obstinacy rendered it necessary for him to inflict. Before every conflict he fell upon his knees in the presence of the army in prayer. After every victory, he assembled his troops to return thanks to God. There are some sad accounts to be settled at the judgment day. In marching from Aleppo to Damascus, Tamerlane visited ostentatiously the pretended tomb of Noah, that upon the shrine of that patriarch, so profoundly venerated by the Mohammedans, he might display his devotion.

Damascus was pillaged of all its treasures, which had been accumulating for ages, and was then laid in ashes. The two armies, headed by their respective chieftains, met in Galacia, near Ancyra. It was the 16th of June, 1402. The storm of war raged for a few hours, and the army of Bajazet was cut to pieces by superior numbers, and he himself was taken captive. Tamerlane treated his prisoner with the most condescending kindness, seated him by his side upon the imperial couch, and endeavored to solace him by philosophical disquisitions upon the mutability of all human affairs. The annals of the day do not sustain the rumor that Bajazet was confined in an iron cage.

The empire of Tamerlane now extended from the Caspian and the Mediterranean to the Nile and the Ganges. He established his capital at Samarcand, some six hundred miles east of the Caspian Sea. To this central capital he returned after each of his expeditions, devoting immense treasures to the erection of mosques, the construction of gardens, the excavation of canals and the erection of cities. And now, in the pride and plenitude of his power, he commenced his march upon Russia.

His army, four hundred thousand strong, defiled from the gates of Samarcand, and marching to the north, between the Aral and the Caspian Seas, traversed vast plains, where thousands of wild cattle had long enjoyed undisturbed pasturage. These cattle afforded them abundant food. The chase, in which they engaged on a magnificent scale, offered a very brilliant spectacle. Thousands of horsemen spread out in an immense circle, making the tent of the emperor the central point. With trumpet blasts, the clash of arms and clouds of javelins and arrows, the cattle and wild beasts of every kind were driven in upon the imperial tent, where Tamerlane and his lords amused themselves with their destruction. The soldiers gathered around the food thus abundantly supplied, innumerable fires were built, and feasting and mirth closed the day. Vast herds of cattle were driven along for the ordinary supply of the troops, affording all the nourishment which these rude barbarians required. Pressing forward, in a long march, which occupied several months, Tamerlane crossed the Volga, and entered the south-eastern principalities of Russia. The tidings of the invasion spread rapidly, and all Russia was paralyzed with terror. The grand prince, Vassali, however, strove with all his energies to rouse the Russians to resistance. An army was speedily collected, and veteran leaders placed in command. The Russian troops were rapidly concentrated near Kolomna, on the banks of the Oka, to dispute the passage of the river. All the churches of Moscow and of Russia were thronged with the terrified inhabitants imploring divine aid, the clergy conducting the devotions by day and by night.

Tamerlane, crossing from the Volga to the Don, ascended the valley of the latter stream, spreading the most cruel devastation everywhere around him. It was his design to confound his enemies with terror. He was pressing on resistlessly towards Moscow, and had arrived within a few days' march of the Russian army on the banks of the Oka, when suddenly he stopped, and remained fifteen days without moving from his encampment. Then, for some cause, which history has never satisfactorly explained, he turned, retraced his steps, and his banners soon disappeared beyond the frontiers of the empire. It was early in September when he commenced this retrograde march. Some have surmised that he feared the Russians, strongly posted on the banks of the Oka, others that he dreaded the approaching Russian winter; others that intelligence of some conspiracy in his distant realms arrested his steps, and others that God, in answer to prayer, directly interposed, and rescued Russia from ruin.

The joy of the Russians was almost delirious; and no one thought even of pursuing a foe, who without arriving within sight of the banners of the grand prince, or without hearing the sound of his war trumpets, had fled as in a panic.

The whole of the remaining reign of Vassali was a scene of tumult and strife. Civil war agitated the principalities. The Lithuanians, united with Poland, were incessant in their endeavors to extend the triumph of their arms over the Russian provinces; and the Tartar hordes again swept Russia with the most horrible devastation. In the midst of calamities and lamentations, Vassali approached his grave. He died on the 29th of February, 1425, in the fifty-third year of his age, and the thirty-sixth of his reign.

Vassali Vassalievitch, son of the deceased monarch, was but ten years of age when the scepter of Russia passed into his hands. Youri, the eldest brother of the late king, demanded the throne in accordance with the ancient custom of descent, and denied the right of his brother to bequeath the crown to his son. After much trouble, both of the rival claimants consented to submit the question to the decision of the Tartar khan, to whom it appears that Russia still paid tribute. Vassali was to remain upon the throne until the question was decided. Six years passed away, and yet no answer to the appeal had been obtained from the khan. At length both agreed to visit the horde in person. It was a perilous movement, and Vassali, as yet but a boy sixteen years of age, wept bitterly as he left the church, where he had implored the prayers of the faithful, and set out upon his journey. All the powers of bribery and intrigue were employed by each party to obtain a favorable verdict.

A tribunal was appointed to adjudge the cause, over which Machmet, the khan, presided. Vassali claimed the dominion, on the ground of the new rule of descent adopted by the Russian princes. Youri pleaded the ancient custom of the empire. The power which the Tartar horde still exercised, may be inferred from the humiliating speech which Jean, a noble of Moscow, made on this occasion, in advocacy of the cause of the young Vassali. Approaching Machmet, and bowing profoundly before him, he said,

"Sovereign king, your humble slave conjures you to permit him to speak in behalf of his young prince. Youri founds his claim upon the ancient institutions of Russia. Vassali appeals only to your generous protection, for he knows that Russia is but one of the provinces of your vast domains. You, as its sovereign, can dispose of the throne according to your pleasure. Condescend to reflect that the uncle *demands*, the nephew *supplicates*. What signify ancient or modern customs when all depends upon your royal will? Is it not that august will which has confirmed the testament of Vassali Dmitrievitch, by which his son was nominated as heir of the principality of Moscow? For six years, Vassali Vassilievitch has been upon the throne. Would you have allowed him thus to remain there had you not recognized him as the legitimate prince?"

This base flattery accomplished its object. Vassali was pronounced grand prince, and, in accordance with Tartar custom, the uncle was compelled to hold the bridle while his successful rival, at the door of the tent, mounted his horse. On their return to Moscow, Vassali was crowned, with great pomp, in the church of Notre Dame. Youri, while at the horde, dared not manifest the slightest opposition to the decision, but, having returned to his own country, he murmured loudly, rallied his friends, excited disaffection, and soon kindled the flames of civil war.

Youri soon marched, with an army, upon Moscow, took the city by storm, and Vassali, who had displayed but little energy of character, was made captive. Youri proclaimed himself grand prince, and Vassali in vain endeavored to move the compassion of his captor by tears. The uncle, however, so far had pity for his vanquished nephew as to appoint him to the governorship of the city of Kolomna. This seemed perfectly to satisfy the pusillanimous young man, and, after partaking of a splendid feast with his uncle, he departed, rejoicing, from the capital where he had been enthroned, to the provincial city assigned to him.

A curious result ensued. Youri brought to Moscow his own friends, who were placed in the posts of honor and authority. Such general discontent was excited, that the citizens, in crowds, abandoned Moscow and repaired to Kolomna, and rallied, with the utmost enthusiasm, around their ejected sovereign. The dwellings and the streets of Moscow became silent and deserted. Kolomna, on the contrary, was thronged. To use the expression of a Russian annalist, the people gathered around their prince as bees cluster around their queen. The tidings of the life, activity and thriving business to be found at Kolomna, lured ever-increasing numbers, and, in a few months, grass was growing in the streets of Moscow, while Kolomna had become the thronged metropolis of the principality. The nobles, with their armies, gathered around Vassali, and Youri was so thoroughly abandoned, that, con vinced of the impossibility of maintaining his position, he sent word to his nephew that he yielded to him the capital, and immediately left for his native principality of Galitch.

The journey of Vassali, from Kolomna to Moscow, a dis tance of two hundred miles, was a brilliant triumph. An immense crowd accompanied the grand prince the whole distance, raising incessant shouts of joy. But Youri was by no means prepared to relinquish his claim, and soon the armies of the two rivals were struggling upon the field of battle. While the conflict was raging, Youri suddenly died at the age of sixty years. One of the sons of Youri made an attempt to regain the throne which his father had lost, but he failed in the attempt, and was taken captive. Vassali, as cruel as he was pusillanimous, in vengeance, plucked out the eyes of his cousin. Vassali, now seated peacefully upon his throne, exerted himself to keep on friendly relations with the horde, by being prompt in the payment of the tribute which they exacted.

In June, 1444, the Tartars, having taken some offense, again invaded Russia. Vassali had no force of character to resist them. Under his weak reign the grand principality had lost all its vigor. The Tartars surprised the Russian army near Moscow, and overwhelming them with numbers, two to one, trampled them beneath their horses. Vassali fought fiercely, as sometimes even the most timid will fight when hedged in by despair. An arrow pierced his hand; a saber stroke cut off several of his fingers; a javelin pierced his shoulder; thirteen wounds covered his head and breast, when by the blow of a battle-ax he was struck to the ground and taken prisoner. The Tartars, elated with their signal victory, and fearful that all Russia might rise for the rescue of its prince, retreated rapidly, carrying with them their captive and immense booty. As they retired they plundered and burned every city and village on their way. After a captivity of three months the prince was released, upon paying a moderate ransom, and returned to Moscow.

Still new sorrows awaited the prince. He was doomed to experience that, even in this world, Providence often rewards a man according to his deeds. The brothers of the prince, whose eyes Vassali had caused to be plucked out, formed a conspiracy against him; and they were encouraged in this conspiracy by the detestation with which the grand prince was now generally regarded.

During the night of the 12th of February, 1446, the conspirators entered the Kremlin. Vassali, who attempted to compensate for his neglect of true religion by punctilious and ostentatious observance of ecclesiastical rites, was in the church of the Trinity attending a midnight mass. Silently the conspirators surrounded the church with their troops. Vassali was prostrate upon the tomb of a Russian saint, apparently absorbed in devotion. Soon the alarm was given, and the prince, in a paroxysm of terror, threw himself upon his knees, and for once, at least, in his life, prayed with sincerity and fervor. His pathetic cries to God for help caused many of the nobles around him to weep. The prince was immediately seized, no opposition being offered, and was confined in one of the palaces of Moscow. Four nights after his capture, some agents of the conspirators entered his apartment and tore out his eyes, as he had torn out the eyes of his cousin. He was then sent, with his wife, to a castle in a distant city, and his children were immured in a convent. Dmitri Chemyaka, the prime mover of this conspiracy, now assumed the reins of government. Gradually the grand principality had lost its power over the other principalities of the empire, and Russia was again, virtually, a conglomeration of independent states.

Public opinion now turned so sternly against Chemyaka, and such bitter murmurs rose around his throne for the cruelty he had practiced upon Vassali, that he felt constrained to liberate the prince, and to assign him a residence of splendor upon the shores of lake Kouben. Chemyaka, thus constrained to set the body of his captive free, wished to enchain his soul by the most solemn oaths. With all his court he visited Vassali. The blinded prince, with characteristic duplicity, expressed heartfelt penitence in view of his past course, and took the most solemn oaths never to attempt to disturb the reign of his conqueror.

Vassali received the city of Vologda in appanage, to which he retired, with his family, and with the nobles and bishops who still adhered to him. But a few months had passed ere he, with his friends, had enlisted the coöperation of many princes, and especially of the Tartar horde, and was on the march with a strong army to drive Chemyaka from Moscow. Chemyaka, utterly discomfited, fled, and Moscow fell easily into the hands of Vassali the blind.

Anguish of body and of soul seems now to have changed the nature of Vassali, and with energy, disinterestedness and wisdom undeveloped before, he consecrated himself to the welfare of his country. He associated with himself his young son Ivan, who subsequently attained the title of the Great. "But Chemyaka," writes Karamsin, "still lived, and his heart, ferocious, implacable, sought new means of vengeance. His death seemed necessary for the safety of the state, and some one gave him poison, of which he died the next day. The author, of an action so contrary to religion, to the principles of morality and of honor, remains unknown. A lawyer, named Beda, who conveyed the news of his death to Moscow, was elevated to the rank of secretary by the grand prince, who exhibited on that occasion an indiscreet joy." On the 14th of March, 1462, Vassali terminated his eventful and tumultuous life, at the age of forty-seven. His reign was during one of the darkest periods in the Russian annals. Life to him, and to his cotemporaries, was but a pitiless tempest, through which hardly one ray of sunshine penetrated. It was under his reign that the horrible punishment of the *knout* was introduced into Moscow, a barbaric mode of scourging unknown to the ancient Russians. Fire-arms were also beginning to be introduced, which weapons have diminished rather than increased the carnage of fields of battle.

CHAPTER X.

THE ILLUSTRIOUS IVAN III.

FROM 1462 TO 1480.

IVAN III.—HIS PRECOCITY AND RISING POWER.—THE THREE GREAT HORDES.—RUSSIAN EXPEDITION AGAINST KEZAN.—DEFEAT OF THE TARTARS.—CAPTURE OF CONSTANTINOPLE BY THE TURKS.—THE PRINCESS SOPHIA.—HER JOURNEY TO RUSSIA, AND MARRIAGE WITH IVAN III.—INCREASING RENOWN OF RUSSIA.—NEW DIFFICULTY WITH THE HORDE.—THE TARTARS INVADE RUSSIA.—STRIFE ON THE BANKS OF THE OKA.—LETTER OF THE METROPOLITAN BISHOP.—UNPRECEDENTED PANIC.—LIBERATION OF RUSSIA.

IN the middle of the fifteenth century, Constantinople was to Russia what Paris, in the reign of Louis XIV., was to modern Europe. The imperial city of Constantine was the central point of ecclesiastical magnificence, of courtly splendor, of taste, of all intellectual culture.* To the Greeks the Russians were indebted for their religion, their civilization and their social culture.

Ivan III., who had for some time been associated with his father in the government, was now recognized as the undisputed prince of the grand principality, though his sway over the other provinces of Russia was very feeble, and very obscurely defined. At twelve years of age, Ivan was married to Maria, a princess of Tver. At eighteen years of age he was the father of a son, to whom he gave his own name. When he had attained the age of twenty-two years, his father died, and the reins of government passed entirely into his hands. From his earliest years, he gave indications of a character of much more than ordinary judgment and maturity. Upon his

* Karamsin, vol. ix., p. 436.

accession to the throne, he not only declined making any appeal to the khan for the ratification of his authority, but refused to pay the tribute which the horde had so long extorted. The result was, that the Tartars were speedily rallying their forces, with vows of vengeance. But on the march, fortunately for Russia, they fell into a dispute among themselves, and exhausted their energies in mutual slaughter.

According to the Greek chronology, the world was then approaching the end of the seven thousandth year since the creation, and the impression was universal that the end of the world was at hand. It is worthy of remark that this conviction seemed rather to increase recklessness and crime than to be promotive of virtue. But the years glided on, and gradually the impression faded away. Ivan, with extraordinary energy and sagacity, devoted himself to the consolidation of the Russian empire, and the development of all its sources of wealth. The refractory princes he assailed one by one, and, favored by a peculiar combination of circumstances, succeeded in chastising them into obedience.

The great Mogol power was essentially concentrated in three immense hordes. All these three combined when there was a work of national importance to be achieved. The largest of the hordes, and the most eastern, spread over a region of undefined extent, some hundreds of miles east of the Caspian Sea. The most western occupied a large territory upon the Volga and the Kama, called Kezan. From this, their encampment, where they had already erected many flourishing cities, enriched by commerce with India and Greece, they were continually ravaging the frontiers of Russia, often penetrating the country three or four hundred miles, laying the largest cities in ashes, and then retiring laden with plunder and prisoners. This encampment of the horde was but five hundred miles east of Moscow; but much of the country directly intervening was an uninhabited waste, so great was the terror which the barbarians inspired.

Ivan resolved to take Kezan from the horde. It was the boldest resolve which any Russian prince had conceived for ages. All the mechanics in the great cities which lined the banks of the upper Volga and the Oka, were employed in constructing barges, which were armed with the most approved instruments of war. The enthusiasm of Russia was roused to the highest pitch by this naval expedition, which presented a spectacle as novel as it was magnificent and exciting.

War has its pageantry as well as its woe. The two flotillas, with fluttering pennants and resounding music, and crowded with gayly-dressed and sanguine warriors, floated down the streams until they met, at the confluence of these rivers, near Nizni Novgorod. Here the two fleets, covering the Volga for many leagues, were united. Spreading their sails, they passed rapidly down the river about two hundred miles, until they arrived at Kezan, the capital of the horde. Deeming their enterprise a religious one, in which the cross of Christ was to be planted against the banners of the infidel, they all partook of the sacrament of the Lord's Supper, and engaged in the most earnest exercises of devotion the evening before they reached their place of landing.

In those days intelligence was only transmitted by means of couriers, at vast expense, and either accompanied by an army or by a strong body guard. The Mogols had no suspicion of the tempest which was about to break over their heads. On the 21st of May, 1469, before the dawn of the morning, the Russians leaped upon the shore near Kezan, the capital, and with trumpet blasts and appalling cries, rushed upon the sleeping inhabitants. Without resistance they penetrated the streets. The Russians, in war, were as barbaric as the Tartars. The city was set on fire; indiscriminate slaughter ensued, and awful vengeance was taken for the woes which the horde had for ages inflicted upon Russia. But few escaped. Those who fell not by the sword perished in the flames. Many

Russian prisoners were found in the city who had been in slavery for years.

Thus far, success, exceeding the most sanguine anticipations, had accompanied the enterprise. The victorious Russians, burdened with the plunder of the city, reëmbarked, and, descending the river some distance, landed upon an island which presented every attraction for a party of pleasure, and there they passed a week in rest, in feasting and in all festive joys. Ibrahim, prince of the horde, escaped the general carnage, and, in a few days, rallied such a force of cavalry as to make a fierce assault upon the invaders. The strife continued, from morning until night, without any decisive results, when both parties were glad to seek repose, with the Volga flowing between them. The next morning neither were willing to renew the combat. Ibrahim soon had a flotilla upon the Volga nearly equal to that of the Russians. The war now raged, embittered by every passion which can goad the soul of man to madness.

One of the Russian princes, a man of astonishing nerve and agility, in one of these conflicts sprang into a Tartar boat, smiting, with his war club, upon the right hand and the left, and, leaping from boat to boat of the foe, warded off every blow, striking down multitudes, until he finally returned, in safety, to his own flotilla, cheered by the huzzas of his troops. The Mogols were punished, not subdued; but this punishment, so unexpected and severe, was quite a new experience for them. The Russian troops, elated with their success, returned to Nizni Novgorod. In the autumn, Ivan III. sent another army, under the command of his two brothers, Youri and André, to coöperate with the troops in Nizni Novgorod in a new expedition. This army left Moscow in two divisions, one of which marched across the country, and the other descended the Volga in barges. Ibrahim had made every effort in his power to prepare to repel the invasion. A decisive battle was fought. The Mogols, completely vanquished, were compelled to accept such terms as the conqueror condescended to grant.

This victory attracted the attention of Europe, and the great monarchies of the southern portion of the continent began to regard Russia as an infant power which might yet rise to importance. Another event at this time occurred which brought Russia still more prominently into the view of the nations of the South. In the year 1467, the grand prince, with tears of anguish, buried his young and beautiful spouse. Five years of widowhood had passed away. The Turks had overrun Asia Minor, and, crossing the Hellespont under Mohammed II., with bloody cimeter had taken Constantinople by storm, cutting down sixty thousand of its inhabitants, and bringing all Greece under the Turkish sway. The Mohammedan placed his heel upon the head of the Christian, and Constantinople became the capital of Moslem power. This was in the year 1472.

Constantin Paleologue was the last of the Grecian emperors. One of his brothers, Thomas, escaping from the ruins of his country, fled to Rome, where, in consideration of his illustrious rank and lineage, he received a large monthly stipend from the pope. Thomas had a daughter, Sophia, a princess of rare beauty, and richly endowed with all mental graces and attractions. The pope sought a spouse worthy of this princess, who was the descendant of a long line of emperors. Mohammed II., having overrun all Greece, flushed with victory, was collecting his forces for the invasion of the Italian peninsula, and his vaunt, *that he would feed his horse from the altar of St. Peter's*, had thrilled the ear of Catholic Europe. The pope, Paul II., anxious to rouse all the Christian powers against the Turks, wished to make the marriage of the Grecian princess promotive of his political views. Her beauty, her genius and her exalted birth rendered her a rare prize.

Rumors had reached Rome of the vast population and

extraordinary wealth of Russia; nearly all the great Russian rivers emptied into the Black Sea, and along these channels the Russian flotillas could easily descend upon the conquerors of Constantinople; Russia was united with Greece by the ties of the same religion, and the recent victory over the Tartars had given the grand prince great renown. These considerations influenced the pope to send an embassador to Moscow, proposing to Ivan III. the hand of Sophia. To increase the apparent value of the offer, the embassador was authorized to state that the princess had refused the hand of the King of France, and also of the Duke of Milan, she being unwilling, as a member of the Greek church, to ally herself with a prince of the Latin religion.

Nothing could have been more attractive to Ivan III., and his nobles, than this alliance. "God himself," exclaimed a bishop, "must have conferred the gift. She is a shoot from an imperial tree which formerly overspread all orthodox Christians. This alliance will make Moscow another Constantinople, and will confer upon our sovereign the rights of the Grecian emperors."

The grand prince, not deeming it decorous to appear too eager, and yet solicitous lest he might lose the prize, sent an embassador, with a numerous suite, to Rome, with a letter to the pope, and to report more particularly respecting the princess, not forgetting to bring him her portrait. This embassage was speedily followed by another, authorized to complete the arrangements. The embassadors were received with signal honors by Sextus IV., who had just succeeded Paul II., and at length it was solemnly announced, in a full conclave of cardinals, on the 22d of May, 1472, that the Russian prince wished to espouse Sophia. Some of the cardinals objected to the orthodoxy of Ivan III.; but the pope replied that it was by condescension and kindness alone that they could hope to open the eyes of one spiritually blind; a sentiment which it is to be regretted that the court of Rome and also all other communions have too often ignored.

On the 1st of June the princess was sacredly affianced in the church of St. Peter's to the prince of Moscow, the embassadors of Ivan III. assuring the pope of the zeal of their monarch for the happy reunion of the Greek and Latin churches. The pope conferred a very rich dowry upon Sophia, and sent his legate to accompany her to Russia, attended by a splendid suite of the most illustrious Romans. The affianced princess had a special court or her own, with its functionaries of every grade, and its established etiquette. A large number of Greeks followed her to Moscow, hoping to find in that distant capital a second country. Directions were given by the pope that, in every city through which she should pass, the princess should receive the honors due to her rank, and that, especially throughout Italy and Germany, she should be furnished with entertainment, relays of horses and guides, until she should arrive at the frontiers of Russia.

Sophia left Rome on the 24th of August, and after a rapid journey of six days, arrived, on the 1st of September, at Lubec, on the extreme southern shore of the Baltic. Here she remained ten days, and on the 10th of September embarked in a ship expressly and gorgeously equipped for her accommodation. A sail of eight hundred miles along the Baltic Sea, which occupied twenty days, conveyed the princess to Revel, near the mouth of the Gulf of Finland. Arriving at this city on the 30th of September, she remained there for rest, ten days, during which time she was regaled with the utmost magnificence by the authorities of the place. Couriers had been immediately dispatched, by the way of Novgorod, to Moscow, to inform the prince of her arrival. Her journey from Revel to lake Tchoude presented but a continued triumphal show. On the 11th of October she reached the shores of the lake. A flotilla of barges, decorated with garlands and pennants, here awaited her. A pleasant sail of two days conveyed her across the lake. Immediately upon landing at Pskov, she repaired, with all her retinue, to the church of Notre Dame, to give thanks to Heaven for the prosperity which had thus far attended her journey. From the church she was conducted to the palace of the prince of that province, where she received from the nobles many precious gifts.

After a five days' sojourn at Pskov, she left the city to continue her journey. Upon taking her departure, she aroused the enthusiasm of the citizens by the following words:

"I must hasten to present myself before your prince who is soon to be mine. I thank the magistrates, the nobles and the citizens generally for the reception which they have given me, and I promise never to neglect to plead the cause of Pskov at the court of Moscow."

At Novgorod she was again entertained with all the splendor which Russian opulence and art could display. The Russian winter had already commenced, and the princess entered Moscow, in a sledge, on the 12th of November. An innumerable crowd accompanied her. She was welcomed at the gates of the city by the metropolitan bishop, who conducted her to the church, where she received his benediction. She was then presented to the mother of the grand prince, who introduced her to her future spouse. Immediately the marriage ceremony was performed with the most imposing pomp of the Greek church.

This marriage contributed much in making Russia better known throughout Europe. In that age, far more than now, exalted birth was esteemed the greatest of earthly honors; and Sophia, the daughter of a long line of emperors, was followed by the eyes of every court in Europe to her distant destination. Moreover, many Greeks, of high æsthetic and intellectual culture, exiled from their country by the domination of the Turk, followed their princess to Russia. They, by their knowledge of the arts and sciences, rendered essential service to their adopted kingdom, which was just emerging from barbarism. They enriched the libraries by the books which they had rescued from the barbarism of the Turks, and contributed much to the eclat of the court of Moscow by the introduction of the pompous ceremonies of the Grecian court. Indeed, from this date Moscow was often called a second Constantinople. The capital was rapidly embellished with palaces and churches, constructed in the highest style of Grecian and Italian architecture. From Italy, also, mechanics were introduced, who established foundries for casting cannon, and mints for the coinage of money.

The prominent object in the mind of Ivan III. was the consolidation of all the ancient principalities into one great empire, being firmly resolved to justify the title which he had assumed, of *Sovereign of all the Russias.* He wished to give new vigor to the monarchical power, to abolish the ancient system of almost independent appanages which was leading to incessant wars, and to wrest from the princes those prerogatives which limited the authority of the sovereign. This was a formidable undertaking, requiring great sagacity and firmness, but it would doubtless be promotive of the welfare of Russia to be under the sway of one general sovereign, rather than to be exposed to the despotism of a hundred petty and quarrelsome princes. Ivan III. was anxious to accomplish this result without violating any treaty, without committing any arbitrary or violent act which could rouse opposition.

That he might triumph over the princes, it was necessary for him to secure the affections of the people. The palace was consequently rendered easy of access to them all. Appointed days were consecrated to justice, and, from morning until evening, the grand prince listened to any complaints from his subjects. The old magistrates had generally forfeited all claim to esteem. Regarding only their own interests, they trafficked in offices, favored their relatives, persecuted their enemies and surrounded themselves with crowds of parasites who stifled, in the courts of justice, all the complaints of the oppressed. Novgorod was first brought into entire subjection to the crown; then Pskov.

While affairs were moving thus prosperously in Russia, the horde upon the Volga was also recovering its energies; and a new khan, Akhmet, war-loving and inflated by the success which his sword had already achieved, resolved to bring Russia again into subjection. He accordingly, in the year 1480, sent an embassy, bearing an image of the khan as their credentials, to Moscow, to demand the tribute which of old had been paid to the Tartars. Ivan III. was in no mood to receive the insult patiently. He admitted the embassage into the audience chamber of his palace. His nobles, in imposing array, were gathered around prepared for a scene such as was not unusual in those barbaric times. As soon as the embassadors entered and were presented, the image of the khan was dashed to the floor by the order of Ivan, and trampled under feet; and all the Mogol embassadors, with the exception of one, were slain.

"Go," said Ivan sternly to him, "go to your master and tell him what you have seen; tell him that if he has the insolence again to trouble my repose, I will treat him as I have served his image and his embassadors."

This emphatic declaration of war was followed on both sides by the mustering of armies The horde was soon in motion, passing from the Volga to the Don in numbers which were represented to be as the sands of the sea. They rapidly and resistlessly ascended the valley of this river, marking their path by a swath of ruin many miles in width. The grand prince took the command of the Russian army in person, and rendezvoused his troops at Kalouga, thence stationing them along the northern banks of the Oka, to dispute the passage of that stream. All Russia was in a state of feverish excitement. One decisive battle would settle the question, whether the invaders were to be driven in bloody rout out of the empire, or, whether the whole kingdom was to be surrendered to devastation by savages as fierce and merciless as wolves.

About the middle of October the two armies met upon the opposite banks of the Oka, with only the waters of that narrow stream to separate them. Cannon and muskets were then just coming into use, but they were rude and feeble instruments compared with the power of such weapons at the present day. Swords, arrows, javelins, clubs, axes, battering-rams and catapults, and the tramplings of horse were the engines of destruction which man then wielded most potently against his fellow-man. The quarrel was a very simple one. Some hundreds of thousands of Mogols had marched to the heart of Russia, leaving behind them a path of flame and blood nearly a thousand miles in length, that they might compel the Russians to pay them tribute. Some hundred thousand Russians had met them there, to resist even to death their insolent and oppressive demand.

The Tartars were far superior in numbers to the Russians, but Ivan had made such a skillful disposition of his troops that Akhmet could not cross the stream. For nearly a week the two armies fought from the opposite banks, throwing at each other bullets, balls, stones, arrows and javelins. A few were wounded and some slain in this impotent warfare.

The Russians were, however, very faint-hearted. It was evident that, should the Tartars effect the passage of the river, the Russians, already demoralized by fear, would be speedily overpowered. The grand prince himself was so apprehensive as to the result, that he sent one of his nobles with rich presents to the khan and proposed terms of peace. Akhmet rejected the presents, and sent back the haughty reply:

"I have come thus far to take vengeance upon Ivan; to punish him for neglecting for nine years to appear before me with tribute and in homage. Let him come penitently into my presence and kiss my stirrup, and then perhaps, if my lords intercede for him, I may forgive him."

As soon as it was heard in Moscow that the grand prince was manifesting such timidity, the clergy sent to him a letter urging the vigorous defense of their country and of their religion. The letter was written by Vassian, the archbishop of Moscow, and was signed, on behalf of the clergy, by several of the higher ecclesiastics. We have not space to introduce the whole of this noble epistle, which is worthy of being held in perpetual remembrance. The following extracts will show its spirit. It was in the form of a letter from the archbishop to the king; to which letter others of the clergy gave their assent:

"It is our duty to announce the truth to kings, and that which I have already spoken in the ear of your majesty I now write, to inspire you with new courage and energy. When, influenced by the prayers and the councils of your bishop, you left Moscow for the army, with the firm intention of attacking the enemy of the Christians, we prostrated ourselves day and night before God, pleading with him to grant the victory to our armies. Nevertheless, we learn that at the approach of Akhmet, of that ferocious warrior who has already caused thousands of Christians to perish, and who menaces your throne and your country, you tremble before him—you implore peace of him, and send to him embassadors, while that impious warrior breathes only vengeance and despises your prayer.

"Ah, grand prince, to what counselors have you lent your ear? What men, unworthy of the name of Christian, have given you such advice? Will you throw away your arms and shamefully take to flight? But reflect from what a height of grandeur your majesty will descend; to what a depth of humiliation you will fall! Are you willing, oh prince, to surrender Russia to fire and blood, your churches to pillage, your subjects to the sword of the enemy? What heart is so insensible as not to be overwhelmed by the thought even of such a calamity?

"No; we will trust in the all-powerful God! No; you will not abandon us! You will blush at the name of a fugitive, of being the betrayer of your country. Lay aside all fear. Redouble your confidence in God. Then one shall chase a thousand, and two shall put ten thousand to flight. There is no God like ours. Do you say that the oath, taken by your ancestors, binds you not to raise your arms against the khan? But we, your metropolitan bishop, and all the other bishops, representatives of Jesus Christ, absolve you from that oath, extorted by force; we all give you our benediction, and conjure you to march against Akhmet, who is but a brigand and an enemy of God.

"God is a Father full of tenderness for his children. He knows when to punish and when to pardon. And if formerly he submerged Pharaoh to save the children of Israel, he will, in the same manner, save you and your people, if you purify your heart by penitence, for you are a man and a sinner. The penitence of a monarch is his sacred obligation to obey the laws of justice, to cherish his people, to renounce every act of violence, and grant pardon even to the guilty. It is thus that God will elevate you among us, as formerly he elevated Moses, Joshua and the other liberators of Israel, that Russia, a new Israel, may be delivered by you from the impious Akhmet, that other Pharaoh.

"I pray you, grand prince, do not censure me for my feeble words, for it is written, 'Give instruction to a wise man and he will be yet wiser.'* So may it be. Receive our benediction, you and your children, all the nobles and chieftains, and all your brave warriors, children of Jesus Christ. Amen."

This letter, instead of giving the king offense, inspired him with new zeal and courage. He immediately abandoned

* Proverbs of Solomon, ix. 9.

all idea of peace. A fortnight had now passed in comparative inaction, the Russians and Tartars menacing each other from opposite sides of the stream. The cold month of November had now come, and a thin coating of ice began to spread over the surface of the stream. It was evident that Akhmet was only waiting for the river to be frozen over, and that, in a few days, he would be able to cross at any point. The grand prince, seeing that the decisive battle could not much longer be deferred, ordered his troops, in the night, to make a change of position, that he might occupy the plains of Borosk as a field more favorable for his troops. But the Russian soldiers, still agitated by the fears which their sovereign had not been able to conceal, regarded this order as the signal for retreat. The panic spread from rank to rank, and, favored by the obscurity of the night, soon the whole host, in the wildest confusion, were in rapid flight. No efforts of the officers could arrest the dismay. Before the morning, the Russian camp was entirely deserted, and the fugitives were rushing, like an inundation, up the valley of the Moskwa toward the imperial city.

But God did not desert Russia in this decisive hour. He appears to have heard and answered the prayers which had so incessantly ascended. In the Russian annals, their preservation is wholly attributed to the interposition of that God whose aid the bishops, the clergy and Christian men and women in hundreds of churches had so earnestly implored. The Tartars, seeing, in the earliest dawn of the morning, the banks of the river entirely abandoned by the Russians, imagined that the flight was but a ruse of war, that ambuscades were prepared for them, and, remembering previous scenes of exterminating slaughter, they, also, were seized with a panic, and commenced a retreat. This movement itself increased the alarm. Terror spread rapidly. In an hour, the whole Tartar host, abandoning their tents and their baggage, were in tumultuous flight.

As the sun rose, an unprecedented spectacle was presented. Two immense armies were flying from each other in indescribable confusion and dismay, each actually frightened out of its wits, and no one pursuing either. The Russians did not stop for a long breath until they attained the walls of Moscow. Akhmet, having reached the head waters of the Don, retreated rapidly down that stream, wreaking such vengeance as he could by the way, but not venturing to stop until he had reached his strongholds upon the banks of the Volga. Thus, singularly, *providentially*, terminated this last serious invasion of Russia by the Tartars. A Russian annalist, in attributing the glory of this well-authenticated event all to God, writes: "Shall men, vain and feeble, celebrate the terror of their arms? No! it is not to the might of earth's warriors, it is not to human wisdom that Russia owes her safety, but only to the goodness of God."

Ivan III., in the cathedrals of Moscow, offered long continued praises to God for this victory, obtained without the effusion of blood. An annual festival was established in honor of this great event. Akhmet, with his troops disorganized and scattered, had hardly reached the Volga, ere he was attacked by a rival khan, who drove him some five hundred miles south to the shore of the Sea of Azof. Here his rival overtook him, killed him with his own hand, took his wives and his daughters captives, seized all his riches, and then, seeking friendly relations with Russia, sent word to Moscow that the great enemy of the grand prince was in his grave.

Thus terminated for ever the sway of the Tartars over the Russians. For two hundred years, Russia had been held by the khans in slavery. Though the horde long continued to exist as a band of lawless and uncivilized men, often engaged in predatory excursions, no further attempts were made to exact either tribute or homage.

CHAPTER XI.

THE REIGN OF VASSILI

FROM 1480 TO 1533.

ALLIANCE WITH HUNGARY.—A TRAVELER FROM GERMANY.—TREATY BETWEEN RUSSIA AND GERMANY.—EMBASSAGE TO TURKEY.—COURT ETIQUETTE.—DEATH OF THE PRINCESS SOPHIA.—DEATH OF IVAN.—ADVANCEMENT OF KNOWLEDGE.—SUCCESSION OF VASSALI.—ATTACK UPON THE HORDE.—ROUT OF THE RUSSIANS.—THE GRAND PRINCE TAKES THE TITLE OF EMPEROR.—TURKISH ENVOY TO MOSCOW.—EFFORTS TO ARM EUROPE AGAINST THE TURKS.—DEATH OF THE EMPEROR MAXIMILIAN, AND ACCESSION OF CHARLES V. TO THE EMPIRE OF GERMANY.—DEATH OF VASSILI.

THE retreat of the Tartars did not redound much to the glory of Ivan. The citizens of Moscow, in the midst of their rejoicings, were far from being satisfied with their sovereign. They thought that he had not exhibited that courage which characterizes grand souls, and that he had been signally wanting in that devotion which leads one to sacrifice himself for the good of his country. They lavished, however, their praises upon the clergy, especially upon the Archbishop Vassian, whose letter to the grand prince was read and re-read throughout the kingdom with the greatest enthusiasm. This noble prelate, whose Christian heroism had saved his country, soon after fell sick and died, deplored by all Russia.

Hungary was at this time governed by Matthias, son of the renowned Hunniades,* a prince equally renowned for his valor and his genius. Matthias, threatened by Poland, sent embassadors to Russia to seek alliance with Ivan III. Eagerly Russia accepted the proposition, and entered into friendly connections with Hungary, which kingdom was then, in civilization, quite in advance of the northern empire.

* See Empire of Austria, p. 71.

In the year 1486, an illustrious cavalier, named Nicholas Poppel, visited Russia, taking a letter of introduction to the grand prince from Frederic III., Emperor of Germany. He had no particular mission, and was led only by motives of curiosity. "I have seen," said the traveler, "all the Christian countries and all the kings, and I wished, also, to see Russia and the grand prince."

The lords at Moscow had no faith in these words, and were persuaded that he was a spy sent by their enemy, the King of Poland. Though they watched him narrowly, he was not incommoded, and left the kingdom after having satisfied his desire to see all that was remarkable. His report to the German emperor was such that, two years after, he returned, in the quality of an embassador from Frederic III., with a letter to Ivan III., dated Ulm, December 26th, 1488. The nobles now received Poppel with great cordiality. He said to them:

"After having left Russia, I went to find the emperor and the princes of Germany at Nuremburg. I spent a long time giving them information respecting your country and the grand prince. I corrected the false impression, conceived by them, that Ivan III. was but the vassal of Casimir, King of Poland. 'That is impossible,' I said to them. 'The monarch of Moscow is much more powerful and much richer than the King of Poland. His estates are immense, his people numerous, his wisdom extraordinary.' All the court listened to me with astonishment, and especially the emperor himself, who often invited me to dine, and passed hours with me conversing upon Russia. At length, the emperor, desiring to enter into an alliance with the grand prince, has sent me to the court of your majesty as his embassador."

He then solicited, in the name of Frederic III., the hand of Ivan's daughter, Helen, for the nephew of the emperor, Albert, margrave of Baden. The proposition for the marriage of the daughter of the grand prince with a mere margrave was coldly received. Ivan, however, sent an embassador to Germany with the following instructions:

"Should the emperor ask if the grand prince will consent to the marriage of his daughter with the margrave of Baden, reply that such an alliance is not worthy of the grandeur of the Russian monarch, brother of the ancient emperors of Greece, who, in establishing themselves at Constantinople, ceded the city of Rome to the popes. Leave the emperor, however, to see that there is some hope of success should he desire one of our princesses for his son, the King Maximilian."

The Russian embassador was received in Germany with the most flattering attentions, even being conducted to a seat upon the throne by the side of the emperor. It is said that Maximilian, who was then a widower, wished to marry Helen, the daughter of the grand prince, but he wished, very naturally, first to see her through the eyes of his embassador, and to ascertain the amount of her dowry. To this request a polite refusal was returned.

"How could one suppose," writes the Russian historian Karamsin, "that an illustrious monarch and a princess, his daughter, could consent to the affront of submitting the princess to the judgment of a foreign minister, who might declare her unworthy of his master?"

The pride of the Russian court was touched, and the emperor's embassador was informed, in very plain language, that the grand prince was not at all disposed to make a matter of merchandise of his daughter—that, *after* her marriage, the grand prince would present her with a dowry such as he should deem proportionate to the rank of the united pair, and that, above all, should she marry Maximilian, she should not change her religion, but should always have residing with her chaplains of the Greek church. Thus terminated the question of the marriage. A treaty, however, of alliance was formed between the two nations which was signed at Moscow, August 16th, 1490. In this treaty, Ivan

III. subscribes himself, "by the grace of God, monarch of all the Russias, prince of Vladimir, Moscow, Novgorod, Pskof, Yougra, Viatha, Perme and Bulgaria." We thus see what portion of the country was then deemed subject to his sway.

Ivan III., continually occupied in extending, consolidating and developing the resources of his vast empire, could not but look with jealousy upon the encroachments of the Turks, who had already overrun all Greece, who had taken a large part of Hungary, and who were surging up the Danube in wave after wave of terrible invasion. Still, sound judgment taught him that the hour had not yet come for him to interpose; that it was his present policy to devote all his energies to the increase of Russian wealth and power. It was a matter of the first importance that Russia should enjoy the privileges of commerce with those cities of Greece now occupied by the Turks, to which Russia had access through the Dnieper and the Don, and partially through the vast floods of the Volga. But the Russian merchants were incessantly annoyed by the oppression of the lawless Turks. The following letter from Ivan III. to the Sultan Bajazet II., gives one a very clear idea of the relations existing between the two countries at that time. It is dated Moscow, August 31st, 1492.

"To Bajazet, Sultan, King of the princes of Turkey, Sovereign of the earth and of the sea, we, Ivan III., by the grace of God, only true and hereditary monarch of all the Russias, and of many other countries of the North and of the East; behold! that which we deem it our duty to write to your majesty. We have never sent embassadors to each other with friendly greetings. Nevertheless, the Russian merchants have traversed your estates in the exercise of a traffic advantageous to both of our empires. Often they complain to me of the vexations they encounter from your magistrates, but I have kept silence. The last summer, the pacha of Azof forced them to dig a ditch, and to carry stones for the construction of the edifices of the city; more than this, they have compelled our merchants of Azof and of Caffa to dispose of their merchandise for one half their value. If any one of the merchants happens to fall sick, the magistrates place seals upon the goods of all, and, if he dies, the State seizes all these goods, and restores but half if he recover. No regard is paid to the clauses of a will, the Turkish magistrates recognizing no heirs but themselves to the property of the Russians.

"Such glaring injustice has compelled me to forbid my merchants to engage in traffic in your country. From whence come these acts of violence? Formerly these merchants paid only the legal tax, and they were permitted to trade without annoyance. Are you aware of this, or not? One word more. Mahomet II., your father, was a prince of grandeur and renown. He wished, it is reported, to send to us embassadors, proposing friendly relations. Providence frustrated the execution of this project. But why should we not now see the accomplishment of this plan? We await your response."

The Russian embassador received orders from Ivan III. to present his document to the sultan, standing, and not upon his knees, as was the custom in the Turkish court; he was not to yield precedence to the embassador of any other nation whatever, and was to address himself only to the sultan, and not to the pachas. Plestchief, the Russian envoy, obeyed his instructions to the letter, and by his haughty bearing excited the indignation of the Turkish nobles. The pacha of Constantinople received him with great politeness, loaded him with attentions, invited him to dine, and begged him to accept of a present of some rich dresses, and a purse of ten thousand sequins. The haughty Russian declined the invitation to dine, returning the purse and the robes with the ungracious response,

"I have nothing to say to pachas. I have no need to

wear their clothes, neither have I any need of their money. I wish only to speak to the sultan."

Notwithstanding this arrogance, Bajazet II., the sultan, received Plestchief politely, and returned a conciliatory answer to the grand prince, promising the redress of those grievances of which he complained. The Turk was decidedly more civilized than the Christian. He wrote to Mengli Ghirei, the pacha of the Crimea, where most of these annoyances had occurred:

"The monarch of Russia, with whom I desire to live in friendly relations, has sent to me a clown. I can not consequently allow any of my people to accompany him back to Russia, lest they should find him offensive. Respected as I am from the east to the west, I blush in being exposed to such an affront. It is in consequence my wish that my son, the sultan of Caffa, should correspond directly with the grand prince of Moscow."

With a sense of delicacy as attractive as it is rare, Bajazet II. refrained from complaining of the boorishness of the Russian envoy, but wrote to the grand prince, Ivan III., in the following courteous terms:

"You have sent, in the sincerity of your soul, one of your lords to the threshold of my palace. He has seen me and has handed me your letter, which I have pressed to my heart, since you have expressed a desire to become my friend. Let your embassadors and your merchants no longer fear to frequent our country. They have only to come to certify to the veracity of all which your envoy will report to you from us. May God grant him a prosperous journey and the grace to convey to you our profound salutation—to you and to your friends; for those whom you love are equally dear to us."

In the whole of this transaction the Turkish court appears far superior to the Russian in the refinements and graces of polished life. There seems to be something in a southern clime which ameliorates harshness of manners. The Grecian emperors, perhaps, in abandoning their palaces, left also to their conquerors that suavity which has transmitted even to our day the enviable title of the "polished Greek."

In the year 1503, Ivan III. lost his spouse, the Greek princess Sophia. Her death affected the aged monarch deeply, and seriously impaired his health. Twenty-five years had now elapsed since he received the young and beautiful princess as his bride, and during all these tumultuous years her genius and attractions had been the most brilliant ornament of his court. The infirmities of age pressed heavily upon the king, and it was manifest that his days could not much longer be prolonged. With much ceremony, in the presence of his lords, he dictated his will, declaring his oldest son Vassili to be his successor as monarch, and assigning to all his younger children rich possessions. The passion for the aggrandizement of Russia still glowed strongly in his bosom even in the hour of death. Vassili, though twenty-five years of age, was as yet unmarried. He decided to select his spouse from the daughters of the Russian nobles, and fifteen hundred of the most beautiful belles of the kingdom were brought to the court that the prince, from among them, might make his selection. The choice fell upon a maiden of exquisite beauty, of Tartar descent. Her father was an officer in the army, a son of one of the chiefs of the horde. The marriage was immediately consummated, and all Moscow was in a blaze of illumination, rejoicing over the nuptials of the heir to the crown. The decay of the aged monarch, however, advanced, day by day. His death, at last, was quite sudden, in the night of the 27th of October, 1505, at the age of sixty-six years and nine months, and at the close of a reign of forty three years and a half.

Ivan III. will, through all ages, retain the rank of one of the most illustrious of the sovereigns of Russia. The excellencies of his character and the length of his reign, combined in enabling him to give an abiding direction to the career of his country. He made his appearance on the political stage just in the time when a new system of government, favorable to the power of the sovereigns of Europe, was rising upon the ruins of feudalism. The royal authority was gaining rapidly in England and in France. Spain, freed from the domination of the Moors, had just become a power of the first rank. The fleets of Portugal were whitening the most distant seas, conferring upon the energetic kingdom wonderful wealth and power. Italy, though divided, exulted in her fleet, her maritime wealth, and her elevation above all other nations in the arts, the sciences and the intrigues of politics. Frederic IV., Emperor of Germany, an inefficient, apathetic man, was unable to restore repose to the empire, distracted by civil war. His energetic son, Maximilian, was already meditating that political change which should give new strength to the monarch, and which finally raised the house of Austria to the highest point of earthly grandeur. Hungary, Bohemia and Poland, governed by near relatives, might almost be considered as a single power, and they were, as by instinct, allied with Austria in endeavors to resist the encroachments of the Turks.

Inventions and discoveries of the greatest importance were made in the world during the reign of Ivan III. Guttenburg and Faust in Strasbourg invented the art of printing. Christopher Columbus discovered the New World. Until then the productions of India reached central Europe through Persia, the Caspian Sea and the Sea of Azof. On the 20th of November, 1497, Vasco de Gama doubled the Cape of Good Hope, thus opening a new route to the Indies, and adding immeasurably to the enterprise and wealth of the world. A new epoch seemed to dawn upon mankind, favorable at least to the tranquillity of nations, the progress of civilization and the strength of governments. Thus far Russia, in her remote seclusion, had taken no part in the politics of Europe. It was not until the reign of Ivan III. that this great northern empire emerged from that state of chaos in which she had neither possessed definiteness of form nor assured existence.

Ivan III. found his nation in subjection to the Tartars. He threw off the yoke; became one of the most illustrious monarchs in Europe, commanding respect throughout Christendom; he took his position by the side of emperors and sultans, and by the native energies of his mind, unenlightened by study, he gave the wisest precepts for the internal and the external government of his realms. But he was a rude, stern man, the legitimate growth of those savage times. It is recorded that a single angry look from him would make any woman faint; that at the table the nobles trembled before him, not daring to utter a word.

Vassili now ascended the throne, and with great energy carried out the principles established by his father. The first important measure of the new monarch was to fit out an expedition against the still powerful but vagabond horde at Kezan, on the Volga, to punish them for some acts of insubordination. A powerful armament descended the Volga in barges. The infantry landed near Kezan on the 22d of May, 1506. The Tartars, with a numerous array of cavalry, were ready to receive their assailants, and fell upon them with such impetuosity and courage that the Russians were overpowered, and driven back, with much slaughter, to their boats. They consequently retreated to await the arrival of the cavalry. The Tartars, imagining that the foe, utterly discomfited, had fled back to Moscow, surrendered themselves to excessive joy. A month passed away, and on the 22d of June an immense assemblage of uncounted thousands of Tartars were gathered in festivity on the plains of Arsk, which spread around their capital city. More than a thousand tents were spread upon the field. Merchants from all parts were gathered there displaying their goods, and a scene of festivity and splendor was exhibited, such as modern civilization has never paralleled.

Suddenly the Russian army, horse and infantry, were seen upon the plain, as if they had dropped from the clouds. They rushed upon the encampment, cutting down the terrified multitude, with awful butchery, and trampling them beneath their horses' feet. The fugitives, in dismay, sought to regain the city, crushing each other in their flight and in the desperate endeavor to crowd in at the gates and along the narrow streets. The Russians, exhausted by their victory, and lured by the luxuries which filled the tents, instead of taking the city by storm, as, in the confusion they probably could have done, surrendered themselves to pillage and voluptuous indulgence. They found the tents filled with food, liquors of all kinds and a great quantity of precious commodities, and forgetting they were in the presence of an enemy, they plunged into the wildest excesses of festivity and wassail.

The disgraceful carousal was briefly terminated during the night, but renewed, with additional zest, in the morning. The songs and the shouts of the drunken soldiers were heard in the streets of Kezan, and, from the battlements, the Tartars beheld these orgies, equaling the most frantic revels of pagan bacchanals. The Tartar khan, from the top of a bastion, watched the spectacle, and perceiving the negligence of his enemies, prepared for a surprise and for vengeance. On the 25th of June, just at the dawn of day, the gates were thrown open, and twenty thousand horsemen and thirty thousand infantry precipitated themselves with frightful yells upon the Russians, stupefied with sleep and wine. Though the Russians exceeded the Tartars two to one, yet they fled towards their boats like a flock of sheep, without order and without arms. The plain was speedily strewn with their dead bodies and crimsoned with their blood. Too much terrified to think even of resistance, they clambered into their barges, cut the cables, and pushed out into the stream. But for the valor of the Russian cavalry all would have been destroyed. In the deepest humiliation the fugitives returned to Moscow.

Vassili resolved upon another expedition which should inflict signal vengeance upon the horde. But while he was making his preparations, the khan, terrified in view of the storm which was gathering, sent an embassage to Moscow imploring pardon and peace, offering to deliver up all the prisoners and to take a new oath of homage to the grand prince. Vassili, who was just on the eve of a war with Poland, with alacrity accepted these concessions. The King of Poland had heard, with much joy, of the death of Ivan III., whose energetic arm he had greatly feared, and he now hoped to take advantage of the youth and inexperience of Vassili. A harassing warfare was commenced between Russia and Poland, which raged for several years. Peace was finally made, Russia extorting from Poland several important provinces.

In the year 1514, Vassili, entering into a treaty with Maximilian, the Emperor of Germany, laid aside the title of grand prince and assumed for himself that of emperor, which was *Kayser* in the German language and *Tzar* in the Russian. With great energy Vassili pushed the work of concentrating and extending his empire, every year strengthening his power over the distant principalities. Bajazet II., the Turkish sultan, the victim of a conspiracy, was dethroned by his son Selim. Vassili, wishing, for the sake of commerce, to maintain friendly relations with Turkey, sent an embassador to the new sultan. The embassador, Alexeief, was authorized to make all proper protestations of friendship, but to be very cautious not to compromit the dignity of his sovereign. He was instructed not to prostrate himself before the sultan, as was the oriental custom, but merely to offer his hands. He was to convey rich presents to Selim, with a letter from the Russian court, but was by no means to enquire for the health of the sultan, unless the sultan should first enquire for the health of the emperor.

Notwithstanding these chilling punctilios, Selim received the Russian embassador with much cordiality, and sent back with him a Turkish embassador to the court of Moscow. Nine months, from August to May, were occupied in the weary journey. While traversing the vast deserts of Veronage, their horses, exhausted and starving, sank beneath them, and they were obliged to toil along for weary leagues on foot, suffering from the want both of food and water. They nearly perished before reaching the frontiers of Rezan, but here they found horses and retinue awaiting them, sent by Vassili. Upon their arrival at Moscow, the Turkish embassador was received with great enthusiasm. It was deemed an honor, as yet unparalleled in Russia, that the terrible conquerors of Constantinople, before whose arms all Christendom was trembling, should send an embassador fifteen hundred miles to Moscow to seek the alliance of the emperor.

The Turkish envoy was received with great magnificence by Vassili, seated upon his throne, and surrounded by his nobles clad in robes of the most costly furs. The embassador, Theodoric Kamal, a Greek by birth, with the courtesy of the polished Greek, kneeling, kissed the hand of the emperor, presented him the letter of his master, the sultan, beautifully written upon parchment in Arabic letters, and assured the emperor of the wish of the sultan to live with him in eternal friendship. But the Turk, loud in protestations, was not disposed to alliance. It was evident that the office of a spy constituted the most important part of the mission of Kamal.

This embassador had but just left the court of Moscow when another appeared, from the Emperor Maximilian, of Germany. The message with which the Baron Herberstein was commissioned from the court of Vienna to the court of Moscow is sufficiently important to be recorded.

"Ought not sovereigns," said the embassador, "to seek the glory of religion and the happiness of their subjects? Such are the principles which have ever guided the emperor. If he has waged war, it has never been from the love of false glory, nor to seize the territories of others, but to punish those who have dared to provoke him. Despising danger, he has been seen in battle, exposing himself like the humblest soldier, and gaining victories against superior forces because the Almighty lends his arm to aid the virtuous.

"The Emperor of Germany is now reposing in the bosom of tranquillity. The pope and all the princes of Italy have become his allies. Spain, Naples, Sicily and twenty-six other realms recognize his grandson, Charles V., for their legitimate and hereditary monarch. The King of Portugal is attached to him by the ties of relationship, and the King of England by the bonds of sincere friendship. The sovereigns of Denmark and Hungary have married the grand-daughters of Maximilian, and the King of Poland testifies to unbounded confidence in him. I will not speak of your majesty, for the Emperor of Russia well knows how to appreciate the sentiments of the Emperor of Germany.

"The King of France and the republic of Venice, influenced by selfish interests, and disregarding the prosperity of Christianity, have taken no part in this fraternal alliance of all the rest of Europe; but they are now beginning to manifest a love for peace, and I have just learned that a treaty is about to be concluded with them, also. Let any one now cast a glance over the world and he will see but one Christian prince who is not attached to the Emperor Maximilian either by the ties of friendship or affection. All Christian Europe is in profound peace excepting Russia and Poland.

"Maximilian has sent me to your majesty, illustrious monarch, to entreat you to restore repose to Christianity and to your states. Peace causes empires to flourish; war destroys their resources and hastens their downfall. Who can be sure of victory? Fortune often frustrates the wisest plans.

"Thus far I have spoken in the name of my master. I I wish now to add, that on my journey I have been informed, by the Turkish embassador himself, that the sultan has just captured Damascus, Jerusalem and all Egypt. A traveler, worthy of credence, has confirmed this deplorable intelligence. If, before these events, the power of the sultan inspired us with just fear, ought not this success of his arms to augment our apprehensions?"

Russia and Poland had long been engaged in a bloody frontier war, each endeavoring to wrest provinces from the other; but Russia was steadily on the advance. The embassage of Maximilian was not productive of peace. On the contrary, Vassili immediately sent an embassador to Vienna to endeavor to secure the aid of Austria in his war with Poland. Maximilian received the envoy with very extraordinary marks of favor. He was invited to sit, in the presence of the emperor, with his hat upon his head, and whenever the embassador, during the conference, mentioned the name of the Russian emperor, Maximilian uncovered his head in token of respect. The great object of Maximilian's ambition was to arm all Europe against the Turks; and he was exceedingly anxious to secure the coöperation of a power so energetic as that of Russia had now proved herself to be. Even then with consummate foresight he wrote:

"The integrity of Poland is indispensable to the general interests of Europe. The grandeur of Russia is becoming dangerous."

Maximilian soon sent another embassador to Moscow, who very forcibly described the conquests made by the Turks in Europe, Asia and Africa, from the Thracian Bosporus to the sands of Egypt, and from the mountains of Caucasia to Venice. He spoke of the melancholy captivity of the Greek church, which was the mother of Russian Christianity; of the profanation of the holy sepulcher; of Nazareth, Bethlehem and Sinai, which had fallen under the domination of the Turk. He suggested that the Turks, in possession of the Tauride—as the country upon the north shore of the Black Sea, bounded by the Dnieper and the Sea of Azof was then called—threatened the independence of Russia herself; that Vassili had every thing to fear from the ferocity, the perfidy and the success of Selim, who, stained with the blood of his father and his three brothers, dared to assume the title of master of the world. He entreated Vassili, as one of the most powerful of the Christian princes, to follow the banner of Jesus Christ, and to cease to make war upon Poland, thus exhausting the Christian powers.

Maximilian died before his embassador returned, and thus these negotiations were interrupted. But Russia was then all engrossed with the desire of obtaining provinces from Poland. Turkey was too formidable a foe to think of assailing, and the idea at that time of wresting any territory from Turkey was preposterous. All Europe combined could only hope to check any *further advance* of the Moslem cimeters. Influenced by these considerations, Vassili sent another embassador to Constantinople to propose a treaty with Selim, which might aid Russia in the strife with her hereditary rival. The sultan, glad of any opportunity to weaken the Christian powers, ordered his pachas to harass Poland in every possible way on the south, thus enabling Russia more easily to assail the distracted kingdom on the north. The King of Poland, Sigismond, was in consternation.

Poland was united with Rome in religion. The pope, Leo X., anxious to secure the coöperation of both Poland and Russia against the Turks, who were the great foe Christianity had most to dread, proposed that the King of Poland, a renowned warrior, should be entrusted with the supreme command of the Christian armies, and adroitly suggested to Vassili, that Constantinople was the legitimate heritage of a Russian monarch, who was the descendant of a Grecian princess; that it was sound policy for him to turn his attention to Turkey; for Poland, being a weaker power, and combined of two discordant elements, the original Poland and Lithuania, would of neccessity be gradually absorbed by the growth of Russia.

Vassili hated the pope, because he had ordered *Te Deums* in Rome, in celebration of a victory which the Poles had obtained over the Russians, and had called the Russians *heretics*. But still the bait the pope presented was too alluring not to be caught at. In the labyrinthine mazes of politics, however, there were obstacles to the development of this policy which years only could remove.

Upon the death of Maximilian, Charles V. of Spain ascended the throne of the German empire, and established a power, the most formidable that had been known in Europe for seven hundred years, that is, since the age of Charlemagne. Vassili was in the midst of these plans of aggrandizement when death came with its unexpected summons. He was in the fifty-fourth year of his age, with mental and physical vigor unimpaired. A small pimple appeared on his left thigh, not larger than the head of a pin, but from its commencement attended with excruciating pain. It soon resolved itself into a malignant ulcer, which rapidly exhausted all the vital energies. The dying king was exceedingly anxious to prepare himself to stand before the judgment seat of God. He spent days and nights in prayer, gave most affectionate exhortations to all around him to live for heaven, assumed monastic robes, resolving that, should he recover, he would devote himself exclusively to the service of God. It was midnight the 3d of December, 1533. The king had just partaken of the sacrament of the Lord's Supper. Suddenly his tongue was paralyzed, his eyes fixed, his hands dropped by his side, and the metropolitan bishop, who had been administering the last rites of religion, exclaimed, "It is all over. The king is dead."

CHAPTER XII.

IVAN IV.—HIS MINORITY.

FROM 1533 TO 1546.

VASSILI AT THE CHASE.—ATTENTION TO DISTINGUISHED FOREIGNERS.—THE AUTOCRACY.—SPLENDOR OF THE EDIFICES.—SLAVERY.—ARISTOCRACY.—INFANCY OF IVAN IV.—REGENCY OF HELENE.—CONSPIRACIES AND TUMULTS.—WAR WITH SIGISMOND OF POLAND.—DEATH OF HELENE.—STRUGGLES OF THE NOBLES.—APPALLING SUFFERINGS OF DMITRI.—INCURSION OF THE TARTARS.—SUCCESSFUL CONSPIRACY.—IVAN IV. AT THE CHASE.—CORONATION OF IVAN IV.

UNDER Vassili, the Russian court attained a degree of splendor which had before been unknown. The Baron of Herberstein thus describes the appearance of the monarch when engaging in the pleasures of the chase:

"As soon as we saw the monarch entering the field, we dismounted and advanced to meet him on foot. He was mounted upon a magnificent charger, gorgeously caparisoned. He wore upon his head a tall cap, embroidered with precious stones, and surmounted by gilded plumes which waved in the wind. A poignard and two knives were attached to his girdle. He had upon his right, Aley, tzar of Kazan, armed with a bow and arrows; at his left, two young princes, one of whom held an ax, and the other a number of arms. His suite consisted of more than three hundred cavaliers."

The chase was continued, over the boundless plains, for many days and often weeks. When night approached, the whole party, often consisting of thousands, dismounted and reared their village of tents. The tent of the emperor was ample, gorgeous, and furnished with all the appliances of luxury. Hounds were first introduced into these sports in Russia by Vassili. The evening hours were passed in festivity, with abundance of good cheer, and in narrating the adventures of the day.

Whenever the emperor appeared in public, he was preceded by esquires chosen from among the young nobles distinguished for their beauty, the delicacy of their features and the perfect proportion of their forms. Clothed in robes of white satin and armed with small hatchets of silver, they marched before the emperor, and appeared to strangers, say his cotemporaries, "like angels descended from the skies."

Vassili was especially fond of magnificence in the audiences which he gave to foreign embassadors. To impress them with an idea of the vast population and wealth of Russia, and of the glory and power of the sovereign, Vassili ordered, on the day of presentation, that all the ordinary avocations of life should cease, and the citizens, clothed in their richest dresses, were to crowd around the walls of the Kremlin. All the young nobles in the vicinity, with their retinues, were summoned. The troops were under arms, and the most distinguished officers, glittering in the panoply of war, rode to meet the envoys.* In the hall of audience, crowded to its utmost capacity, there was silence, as of the grave. The king sat upon his throne, his bonnet upon one side of him, his scepter upon the other. His nobles were seated around upon couches draped in purple and embroidered with pearls and gold.

Following the example of Ivan III., Vassili was unwearied in his endeavors to induce foreigners of distinction, particularly artists, physicians and men of science, to take up their residence in Russia. Any stranger, distinguished for genius or capability of any kind, who entered Russia, found it not easy to leave the kingdom. A Greek physician, of much celebrity, from Constantinople, visited Moscow. Vassili could

* Francis da Callo relates that when he was received by the emperor, forty thousand soldiers were under arms, in the richest uniform, extending from the Kremlin to the hotel of the embassadors.

not find it in his heart to relinquish so rich a prize, and detained him with golden bonds, which the unhappy man, mourning for his wife and children, in vain endeavored to break away. At last the sultan was influenced to write in behalf of the Greek.

"Permit," he wrote, "Marc to return to Constantinople to rejoin his family. He went to Russia only for a temporary visit."

The emperor replied:

"For a long time Marc has served me to his and my perfect satisfaction. He is now my lieutenant at Novgorod. Send to him his wife and children."

The power of the sovereign was absolute. His will was the supreme law. The lives, the fortunes of the clergy, the laity, the lords, the citizens were dependent upon his pleasure. The Russians regarded their monarch as the executor of the divine will. Their ordinary language was, *God and the prince decree it.* The Russians generally defend this *autocracy* as the only true principle of government. The philosophic Karamsin writes:

"Ivan III. and Vassili knew how to establish permanently the nature of one government by constituting in *autocracy* the necessary attribute of empire, its sole constitution, and the only basis of safety, force and prosperity. This limitless power of the prince is regarded as *tyranny* in the eye of strangers, because, in their inconsiderate judgment, they forget that *tyranny* is the abuse of autocracy, and that the same tyranny may exist in a republic when citizens or powerful magistrates oppress society. Autocracy does not signify the absence of laws, since law is everywhere where there is any duty to be performed, and the first duty of princes, is it not to watch over the happiness of their people?"

To the traveler, in the age of Vassili, Russia appeared like a vast desert compared with the other countries of Europe. The sparseness of the habitations, the extended plains, dense forests and roads, rough and desolate, attested that Russia was still in the cradle of its civilization. But as one approached Moscow, the signs of animated life rapidly increased. Convoys crowded the grand route, which traversed vast prairies waving with grain and embellished with all the works of industry. In the midst of this plain rose the majestic domes and glittering towers of Moscow. The convents, in massive piles, scattered around, resembled beautiful villages. The palace of the Kremlin alone, was a city in itself. Around this, as the nucleus, but spreading over a wide extent, were the streets of the metropolis, the palaces of the nobles, the mansions of the wealthy citizens and the shops of the artisans. The city in that day was, indeed, one of "magnificent distances," almost every dwelling being surrounded by a garden in luxurious cultivation. In the year 1520, the houses, by count, which was ordered by the grand prince, amounted to forty-one thousand five hundred.

The metropolitan bishop, the grand dignitaries of the court, the princes and lords occupied splendid mansions of wood reared by Grecian and Italian architects in the environs of the Kremlin. On wide and beautiful streets there were a large number of very magnificent churches also built of wood. The bazaars or shops, filled with the rich merchandise of Europe and of Asia, were collected in one quarter of the city, and were surrounded by a high stone wall as a protection against the armies, domestic or foreign, which were ever sweeping over the land.

From the eleventh to the sixteenth century, slavery may be said to have been universal in Russia. Absolutely every man but the monarch was a slave. The highest nobles and princes avowed themselves the slaves of the monarch. There was no law but the will of the sovereign. He could deprive any one of property and of life, and there was no power to call him to account but the poignard of the assassin or the sword of rebellion. In like manner the peasant serfs were slaves of the nobles, with no privileges whatever, except such as the humanity or the selfishness of their lords might grant But gradually custom, controlling public opinion, assumed almost the form of law. The kings established certain rules for the promotion of industry and the regulation of commerce. Merchants and scholars attained a degree of practical independence which was based on indulgence rather than any constitutional right, and, during the reign of Vassili, the law alone could doom the serf to death, and he began to be regarded as a *man*, as a *citizen* protected by the laws.* From this time we begin to see the progress of humanity and of higher conceptions of social life. It is, perhaps, worthy of record that anciently the peasants or serfs were universally designated by the name *smerdi*, which simply means *smelling offensively*. Is the exhalation of an offensive odor the necessary property of a people imbruted by poverty and filth? In America that unpleasant effluvium has generally been considered a peculiarity pertaining to the colored race. Philosophic observation may show that it is a disease, the result of uncleanliness, but, like other diseases, often transmitted from the guilty parent to the unoffending child. We have known white peeple who were exceedingly offensive in this respect, and colored people who were not so at all.

The pride of illustrious birth was carried to the greatest extreme, and a noble would blush to enter into any friendly relations whatever with a plebeian. The nobles considered all business degrading excepting war, and spent the weary months, when not under arms, in indolence in their castles. The young women of the higher families were in a deplorable state of captivity. Etiquette did not allow them to mingle with society, or even to be seen except by their parents, and they had no employment except sewing or knitting, no mental culture and no sources of amusement. It was not the custom for the young men to choose their wives, but the father of

* Karamsin, tome vii., page 265.

the maiden selected some eligible match for his daughter, and made propositions to the family of his contemplated son-in-law, stating the dowry he would confer upon the bride, and the parties were frequently married without ever having previously seen each other.

The death of Vassili transmitted the crown to his only son, Ivan, an infant but three years of age. By the will of the dying monarch, the regency, during the minority of the child, was placed in the hands of the youthful mother, the princess Hélène. The brothers of Vassili and twenty nobles of distinction were appointed as counselors for the queen regent. Two men, however, in concert with Hélène, soon took the reins of government into their own hands. One of these was a sturdy, ambitious old noble, Michel Glinsky, an uncle of Hélène; the other was a young and handsome prince, Ivan Telennef, who was suspected of tender *liaisons* with his royal mistress.

The first act of the new government was to assemble all the higher clergy in the church of the Assumption, where the metropolitan bishop gave his benediction to the child destined to reign over Russia, and who was there declared to be accountable to God only for his actions. At the same time embassadors were sent to all the courts of Europe to announce the death of Vassili and the accession of Ivan IV. to the throne.

But a week passed after these ceremonies ere the prince Youri, one of the brothers of Vassili, was arrested, charged with conspiracy to wrest the crown from his young nephew. He was thrown into prison, where he was left to perish by the slow torture of starvation. This severity excited great terror in Moscow. The Russians, ever strongly attached to their sovereigns, now found themselves under the reign of an oligarchy which they detested. Conspiracies and rumors of conspiracies agitated the court. Many were arrested upon suspicion alone, and, cruelly chained, were thrown into dungeons.

Michel Glinsky, indignant at the shameful intimacy evidently existing between Hélène and Telennef, ventured to remonstrate with the regent boldly and earnestly, assuring her that the eyes of the court were scrutinizing her conduct, and that such vice, disgraceful anywhere, was peculiarly hideous upon a throne, where all looked for examples of virtue. The audacious noble, though president of the council, was immediately arrested under an accusation of treason, and was thrown into a dungeon, where, soon after, he was assassinated. A reign of terror now commenced, and imprisonment and death awaited all those who undertook in any way to thwart the plans of Hélène and Telennef.

André, the youngest of the brothers of Vassili, a man of feeble character, now alone remained of the royal princes at court. He was nominally the tutor of his nephew, the young emperor, Ivan IV., and though a prominent member of the council which Vassili had established, he had no influence in the government which had been grasped so energetically and despotically by Hélène and her paramour Telennef. At length André, trembling for his own life, timidly raised the banners of revolt, and gathered quite an army around him. But he had no energy to conduct a war. He was speedily taken, and, loaded with chains, was thrown into a dungeon, where, after a few weeks of most cruel deprivations, he miserably perished. Thirty of the lords, implicated with him in the rebellion, were hung upon the trees around Novgorod. Many others were put to torture and perished on the rack. Hélène, surrendering herself to the dominion of guilty love, developed the ferocity of a tigress.

Sigismond, King of Poland, taking advantage of the general discontent of the Russians under the sway of Hélène, formed an alliance with the horde upon the lower waters of the Don, and invaded Russia, burning and destroying with mercilessness which demons could not have surpassed. Prince Telennef headed an army to repel them. The pen wearies in describing the horrors of these scenes. One hundred thousand Russians are now flying before one hundred and fifty thousand Polanders. Hundreds of miles of territory are ravaged. Cities and villages are stormed, plundered, burned; women and children are cut down and trampled beneath the feet of cavalry, or escape shrieking into the forests, where they perish of exposure and starvation. But an army of recruits comes to the aid of the Russians. And now one hundred and fifty thousand Polanders are driven before two hundred thousand Russians. They sweep across the frontier like dust driven by the tornado. And now the cities and villages of Poland blaze; her streams run red with blood. The Polish wives and daughters in their turn struggle, shriek and die. From exhaustion the warfare ceases. The two antagonists, moaning and bleeding, wait for a few years but to recover sufficent strength .to renew the strife, and then the brutal, demoniac butchery commences anew. Such is the history of man.

In this brief, but bloody war, the city of Staradoub, in Russia, was besieged by an army of Poles and Tartars. The assault was urged with the most desperate energy and fearlessness. The defense was conducted with equal ferocity. Thousands fell on both sides in every mangled form of death. At last the besiegers undermined the walls, and placing beneath hundreds of barrels of gunpowder, as with the burst of a volcano, uphove the massive bastions to the clouds. They fell in a storm of ruin upon the city, setting it on fire in many places. Through the flames and over the smouldering ruins, Poles and Tartars, blackened with smoke and smeared with blood, rushed into the city, and in a few hours thirteen thousand of the inhabitants were weltering in their gore. None were left alive. And this is but a specimen of the wars which raged for ages. The world now has but the faintest conception of the seas of blood and woe through which humanity has waded to attain even its present feeble recognition of fraternity.

In this, as in every war with Poland, Russia was gaining, ever wresting from her rival the provinces of Lithuania, and attaching them to the gigantic empire. In the year 1534, Hélène commenced the enterprise of surrounding the whole of Moscow with a ditch, and a wall capable of resisting the batterings of artillery. An Italian engineer, named Petrok Maloi, superintended these works. The foundation of the walls was laid with imposing religious ceremonies. The wall was crowned with four towers at the opening of the four gates. Hélène was so conscious of the importance of augmenting the population of Russia, that she offered land and freedom from taxes for a term of years to all who would migrate into her territory from Poland. Perhaps also she had a double object, wishing to weaken a rival power. Much counterfeit coin was found to be in circulation. The regent issued an edict, that any one found guilty of depreciating the current standard of coin, should be punished with death, and this death was to be barbarously inflicted by first cutting off the hands of the culprit, and then pouring melted lead through a tunnel down his throat.

On the 3d of April, 1538, Hélène, in the prime of life, and with all her sins in full vigor and unrepented, retired to her bed at night, suddenly and seriously sick. Some one had succeeded in administering to her a dose of poison. She shrieked for a few hours in mortal agony, and soon after the hour of twelve was tolled, her spirit ascended to meet God in judgment. Being dead, she had no favors to confer and no terrors to execute; and her festering remains were the same day hurried ignominiously to the grave. Her paramour, Telennef, alone wept over her death. Russia rejoiced, and yet with trembling. Whose strong arm would now seize the helm of the tempest-torn ship of State, no one could tell.

The young prince, Ivan IV., was but seven years of age at the death of his mother Hélène. For several days there was ominous silence in Moscow, the stillness which precedes the storm. The death of the regent had come so suddenly, so unexpectedly, that none were prepared for it. A week passed away, during which time parties were forming and conspiracies ripening, while Telennef was desperately endeavoring to retain that power which he had so despotically wielded in conjunction with his royal mistress. The prince Vassili Schouisky, who had occupied the first place in the councils of Vassili, opened the drama. Having secured the coöperation of a large number of nobles, he declared himself the head of the government, arrested all the favorites of Hélène, and threw Telennef, bound with chains, into a dun geon. There he was left to die of starvation—barbarity, which, though in accordance with that brutal age, even all the similar excesses of Telennef could not justify. The beautiful sister of Telennef, Agrippene by name, was torn from the saloons her loveliness had embellished, and was imprisoned for life in a convent. The victims of the cruelty of Hélène, who were still languishing in prison, were set at liberty.

Schouisky was a widower, and in the fiftieth year of his age. He wished to strengthen his power by engaging the coöperation of the still formidable energies of the horde at Kezan, and accordingly married, quite hurriedly, the daughter of the czar of the horde. But the regal diadem proved to him but a crown of thorns. Conspiracy succeeded conspiracy, and Schouisky felt compelled to enlist all the terrors of the dungeon, the scaffold and the block to maintain his place. Six months only passed away, ere he too was writhing upon the royal couch in the agonies of death, whether paralyzed by poison or smitten by the hand of God, the day of judgment alone can reveal.

Ivan Schouisky, the brother of the deceased usurper, now stepped into the dangerous post which death had so suddenly rendered vacant. He was a weak man, assuming the most pompous airs, quite unable to discriminate between imposing grandeur and ridiculous parade. He soon became both despised and detested. This state of things encouraged the two hordes of Kezan and Tauride to unite, and with an army of a hundred thousand men they penetrated Russia almost unopposed, burning and plundering in all directions.

Under these circumstances the metropolitan bishop, Joseph, a man of sincere piety and of very elevated character, and who enjoyed in the highest degree the confidence both of the aristocracy and of the people, presented himself before the council, urged the incapacity of Ivan Schouisky to govern, and proposed that Ivan Belsky, a nobleman of great energy and moral worth, should be chosen regent. The proposal was carried by acclamation. So unanimous was the vote, so cordial was the adoption of the republican principle of election, that Ivan Schouisky was powerless and was merely dismissed.

The new regent, sustained by the clergy and the aristocracy, governed the State with wisdom and moderation. All kinds of persecution ceased, and vigorous measures were adopted for the promotion of the public welfare. Old abuses were repressed; vicious governors deposed, and the rising flames of civil strife were quenched. Even the hitherto unheard-of novelty of trial by jury was introduced. Jurors were chosen from among the most intelligent citizens. Though there was some bitter opposition among the corrupt nobles to these salutary reforms, the clergy, as a body, sustained them, and so did also even a majority of the lords. It was Christianity and the church which introduced these humanizing measures.

Among the innumerable tragedies of those days, let one be mentioned illustrative of the terrific wrongs to which all are exposed under a despotic government. There was a young prince, Dmitri, a child, grandson of Vassili the blind, whose claims to the throne were feared. He was thrown into prison and there forgotton. For forty-nine years he had now remained in a damp and dismal dungeon. He had committed no crime. He was accused of no crime. It was only feared that restive nobles might use him as an instrument for the furtherance of their plans. All the years of youth and of manhood had passed in darkness and misery. No beam of the sun ever penetrated his tomb. All unheeded the tides of life surged in the world above him, while his mind with his body was wasting away in the long agony.

> "O who can tell what days, what nights he spent,
> Of tideless, waveless, sailless, shoreless woe."

Mercy now entered his cell, but it was too late even for that angel visitant to bring a gleam of joy. His friends were all dead. His name was forgotten on earth. He knew nothing of the world or of its ways. His mind was enfeebled, and even the slender stock of knowledge which he had possessed as a child, had vanished away. They broke off his chains and removed him from his dungeon to a comfortable chamber. The poor old man, dazzled by the light and bewildered by the change, lingered joylessly and without a smile for a few weeks and died. Immortality alone offers a solution for these mysteries. "After death cometh the judgment."

The Christian bishop, Joseph, and Ivan Belsky, the regent, in cordial coöperation, endeavored in all things to promote prosperity and happiness. Again there was a coalition of the Tartars for the invasion of Russia. The three hordes, in Kezan, in the Tauride and at the mouth of the Volga, united, and in an army one hundred thousand strong, with numerous cavalry and powerful artillery, commenced their march. The Russian troops were hastily collected upon the banks of the Oka, there to take their stand and dispute the passage of the stream. By order of the clergy, prayers were offered incessantly in the churches by day and by night, that God would avert this terrible invasion. The young prince, Ivan IV., was now ten years of age. The citizens of Moscow were moved to tears and to the deepest enthusiasm on hearing their young prince, in the church of the Assumption, offer aloud and fervently the prayer,

"Oh heavenly Father! thou who didst protect our ancestors against the cruel Tamerlane, take us also under thy holy protection—us in childhood and orphanage. Our mind and our body are still feeble, and yet the nation looks to us for deliverance."

Accompanied by the metropolitan Joseph, he entered the council and said,

"The enemy is approaching. Decide for me whether it be best that I should remain here or go to meet the foe."

With one voice they exclaimed, "Prince, remain at Moscow."

They then took a solemn oath to die, if necessary, for their prince. The citizens came forward in crowds and volunteered for the defense of the walls. The faubourgs were surrounded with pallisades, and batteries of artillery were placed to sweep, in all directions, the approaches to the city. The enthusiasm was so astonishing that the Russian annalists ascribe it to a supernatural cause. On the 30th of July, 1541, the Tartar army appeared upon the southern banks of the Oka, crowning all the heights which bordered the stream. Immediately they made an attempt to force the passage. But the Russians, thoroughly prepared for the assault, repelled them with prodigious slaughter. Night put an end to the contest. The Russians were elated with their success, and waited eagerly for the morning to renew the strife. They even hoped to be able to cross the river and to sweep the camp of their foes. The fires of their bivouacs blazed all the night, reinforcements were continually arriving, and their songs of joy floated across the water, and fell heavily upon the hearts of the dismayed Tartars.

At midnight the khan, and the whole host, conscious of their peril, commenced a precipitate retreat, in their haste abandoning many guns and much of their baggage. The

Russians pursued the foe, but were not able to overtake them, so rapidly did they retrace their steps.

The news of the expulsion of the enemy spread rapidly through Russia. The conduct of the grand prince everywhere excited the most lively enthusiasm. He entered the church, and in an affecting prayer returned thanks to God for the deliverance. The people, with unanimity, exclaimed,

"Grand prince, your angelic prayers and your happy star have caused us to triumph."

Awful, however, were the woes which fell upon those people who were on the line of march of the barbaric Tartars.

Ivan Belsky, the regent, had now attained the highest degree of good fortune, and in his own conscience, and in the general approbation of the people, he found ample recompense for his deeds of humanity, and his patriotic exertions. But envy, that poison of society, raised up against him enemies. Ivan Schouisky, who had been deposed by vote of the council, organized a conspiracy among the disaffected nobles, and on the night of the 3d of January, 1542, three hundred cavaliers surrounded the residences of the regent and of the metropolitan bishop, seized them and hurried them to prison, and in the prison finished their work by the assassination of Ivan Belsky.

Ivan Schouisky, sustained by the sabers of his partisans, reassumed the government. A new metropolitan bishop, Macaire was appointed to take the place of Joseph, who was deposed and imprisoned. The clergy, overawed, were silent. The reign of silence was again commenced, and all the posts of honor and influence were placed in the hands of the partisans of Schouisky. The government, such as it was, was now in the hands of a triumvirate consisting of Ivan, André and Feodor. Not a syllable of opposition would these men endure, and the dungeon and the assassin's poignard silenced all murmurs. The young prince, Ivan IV., was now thirteen years of age. He was endowed by nature with a mind of extraordinary sagacity and force, but his education had been entirely neglected, and the scenes of perfidy and violence he was continually witnessing were developing, a character which menaced Russia with many woes.

The infamous Schiouskies sought to secure the friendship of the young prince by ministering, in every possible way, to his pleasures. They led him to the chase, encouraged whatever disposition he chanced to manifest, and endeavored to train him in a state of feebleness and ignorance which might promote their ambitious plans. The Kremlin became the scene of constant intrigues. Cabal succeeded cabal. The position of the triumvirate became, month after month, more perilous. The young prince gave decisive indications of discontent. It began to be whispered into his ears that it was time for him to assume the reins of government, and he was assured that all Russia was waiting, eager to obey his orders. The metropolitan bishop, either from a sense of justice or of policy, also espoused the cause of the youthful sovereign. It was evident that another party was rising into power.

On the 29th of December, 1534, Ivan IV. went with a large party of his lords to the chase. Instructed beforehand in the measures he was to adopt, he, quite unexpectedly to the triumvirate, summoned all his lords around him, and, assuming an imperious and threatening tone, declared that the triumvirate had abused his extreme youth, had trampled upon justice, and, as culprits, deserved to die. In his great clemency, however, he decided to spare the lives of two, executing only one as an example to the nation. The oldest of the three, André Schouisky, was immediately seized and handed over to the conductors of the hounds. They set the dogs upon him, and he was speedily torn to pieces in the presence of the company, and his mangled remains were scattered over the plain.

The partisans of Schouisky, terrified by this deed, were afraid to utter a murmur. The nobles generally were alarmed, for it was evident that though they had escaped the violence of the triumvirate, they had fallen into hands equally to be dreaded. Confiscations and other acts of rigor rapidly succeeded, and the young prince, still too youthful to govern by the decision of his own mind, was quite under the control of the Glinskys, through whose council he had shaken off the triumvirate of the Schouiskies. Ivan IV. now made the tour of his kingdom, but with no other object than the promotion of his personal gratification. Most of his time was devoted to the excitements of the chase in the savage forests which spread over a large portion of his realms. He was always surrounded by a brilliant staff of nobles, and the sufferings of the people were all concealed from his view. The enormous expenses of his court were exacted from the people he visited, and his steps were followed by lamentations.

In the year 1546, Ivan attained the eighteenth year of his age, and made great preparations for his coronation. The imposing rites were to be performed at Moscow. On the 16th of January, the grand prince entered one of the saloons of his palaces while the nobles, the princes, the officers of the court, all richly dressed, were assembled in the ante-chamber. The confessor of the grand prince, having received from Ivan IV. a crucifix, placed it upon a plate of gold with the crown and other regalia, and conveyed them to the church of the Assumption accompanied by the grand equerry, Glinsky, and other important personages of the court. Soon after, the grand prince also repaired to the church. He was preceded by an ecclesiastic holding in his hand a crucifix, and sprinkling to the right and to the left holy water upon the crowd.

Ivan IV., surrounded by all the splendors of his court, entered the church, where he was encircled by the ecclesiastics, and received the benediction of the metropolitan bishop. A hymn was then sang by the accumulated choirs, which astounded the audience; after which mass was celebrated. In the midst of the cathedral, a platform was erected, which was ascended by twelve steps. Upon this platform there were two thrones of equal splendor, covered with cloth of gold, one for the monarch, the other for the metropolitan bishop. In front of the stage there was a desk, richly decorated, upon which were placed the crown regalia. The monarch and the bishop took their seats. The bishop, rising, pronounced a benediction upon the monarch, placed the crown upon his head, the scepter in his hand, and then, with a loud voice, prayed that God would endow this new David with the influences of the Holy Spirit, establish his throne in righteousness, and render him terrible to evil doers and a benefactor to those who should do well. The ceremonies were closed by an anthem by the choir. The young emperor then returned, with his court, to the Kremlin, through streets carpeted with velvet and damask. As they walked along, the emperor's brother, Youri, scattered among the crowd handsfull of gold coin, which he took from a vase carried at his side by Michel Glinsky. The moment Ivan IV. left the church, the people, till then motionless and silent, precipitated themselves upon the platform, and all the rich cloths which had decorated it were torn to shreds, each individual eager to possess a souvenir of the memorable day.

CHAPTER XIII.

THE REIGN OF IVAN IV.

FROM 1546 TO 1552.

THE TITLE OF TZAR.—MARRIAGE OF IVAN IV.—VIRTUES OF HIS BRIDE.—DEPRAVED CHARACTER OF THE YOUNG EMPEROR.—TERRIBLE CONFLAGRATIONS.—INSURRECTIONS.—THE REBUKE.—WONDERFUL CHANGE IN THE CHARACTER OF IVAN IV.—CONFESSIONS OF SIN AND MEASURES OF REFORM.—SYLVESTRE AND ALEXIS ADACHEF.—THE CODE OF LAWS.—REFORMS IN THE CHURCH.—ENCOURAGEMENT TO MEN OF SCIENCE AND LETTERS.—THE EMBASSAGE OF SCHLIT.—WAR WITH KEZAN.—DISASTERS AND DISGRACE.—IMMENSE PREPARATION FOR THE CHASTISEMENT OF THE HORDE.—THE MARCH.—REPULSE OF THE TAUREDIANS.—SIEGE OF KEZAN.—INCIDENTS OF THE SIEGE.

THOUGH the monarchs of Russia, in all their relations with foreign powers, took the title of Tzar or Emperor, they also retained that of Grand Prince which was consecrated by ancient usage. And now the envoys of Ivan IV. were traversing Russia in all directions to find, among the maidens of noble blood, one whose beauty would render her worthy of the sovereign. The choice at last fell upon Anastasia, the daughter of a lady of illustrious rank, who was a widow. Language is exhausted, by the Russian annalists, in describing the perfections of her person, mind and heart. All conceivable social and moral excellences were in her united with the most brilliant intellectual gifts and the most exquisite loveliness.

The marriage was performed by the bishop in the church of Notre Dame. "You are now," said the metropolitan, in conclusion, "united for ever, by virtue of the mysteries of the gospel. Prostrate yourselves, then, before the Most High, and secure his favor by the practice of every virtue. But those virtues which should especially distinguish you, are the love of truth and of benevolence. Prince, love and honor your spouse. Princess, truly Christian, be submissive to your husband; for as the Redeemer is the head of the church, so is man the head of the woman."

For many days Moscow was surrendered to festivity and rejoicings. The emperor devoted his attention to the rich, the empress to the poor. Anastasia, since the death of her father, had lived remote from the capital, in the most profound rural seclusion. Suddenly, and as by magic, she found herself transported to the scenes of the highest earthly grandeur, but still she maintained the same beautiful simplicity of character which she had developed in the saddened home of her widowed mother. Ivan IV. was a man of ungovernable passions, and accustomed only to idleness, he devoted himself to the most gross and ignoble pleasures. Mercilessly he confiscated the estates of those who displeased him, and with caprice equal to his mercilessness, he conferred their possessions upon his favorites. He seemed to regard this arbitrary conduct as indicative of his independence and grandeur.

The situation of Russia was perhaps never more deplorable than at the commencement of the reign of Ivan IV. The Glinskys were in high favor, and easily persuaded the young emperor to gratify all their desires. Laden with honors and riches, they turned a deaf ear to all the murmurs which despotism, the most atrocious, extorted from every portion of the empire. The inhabitants of Pskof, oppressed beyond endurance by an infamous governor, sent seventy of their most influential citizens to Moscow to present their grievances to the emperor. Ivan IV. raved like a madman at what he called the insolence of his subjects, in complaining of their governor. Almost choking with rage, he ordered the seventy deputies to be put to death by the most cruel tortures.

Anastasia wept in anguish over these scenes, and her prayers were incessantly ascending, that God would change the heart of her husband. Her prayers were heard and answered. The same power which changed Saul of Tarsus into Paul the Apostle, seemed to renew the soul of Ivan IV. History is full of these marvelous transformations—a mental phenomenon only to be explained by the scriptural doctrine of regeneration. In Ivan's case, as in that of thousands of others, afflictions were instruments made available by the Holy Spirit for the heart's renewal.

Moscow was at this time a capital of vast extent and of great magnificence. As timber was abundant and easily worked, most of the buildings, even the churches and the palaces, were constructed of wood. Though almost every house was surrounded by a garden, these enclosures were necessarily not extensive, and the city was peculiarly exposed to the perils of conflagration.

On the 12th of April, 1547, the cry of fire alarmed the inhabitants, and soon the flames were spreading with fury which baffled all human power. The store-houses of commerce, the magazines of the crown, the convent of Epiphany and a large number of dwellings, extending from the gate of Illinsky, to the Kremlin and the Moskwa, were consumed. The river alone arrested the destruction. A powder magazine took fire, and with a terrible explosion its towers were thrown into the air, taking with them a large section of the walls. The ruins fell like an avalanche into the river, completely filling up its channel, adding the destruction of a deluge to that of the fire.

A week had hardly passed ere the cry of fire again was raised, and, in a few hours, the whole section of the city on the other side of the Yaouza was in ashes. This region was mostly occupied by mechanics and manufacturers, and immense suffering ensued. Six weeks elapsed, and the inhabitants were just beginning to recover from their consternation, and were sweeping away the ashes to rebuild, when on the 20th of June, the wind at the time blowing a gale, the fearful cry of fire again rang through the streets. The palaces of the nobles were now in flames. The palace of the Kremlin itself, the gorgeous streets which surrounded it, and the whole of the grand faubourg in a few moments were glowing like a furnace. God had come with flaming fire as his minister of vengeance, and resistance was unavailing. The whole city was now in ashes, and presented the aspect of an immense funeral pile, over which was spread a pall of thick and black smoke. The wooden edifices disappeared entirely. Those of stone and brick presented a still more gloomy aspect, with only portions of their walls standing, crumbling and blackened. The howling of the tempest, the roar of the flames, the crash of falling buildings, and the shrieks of the inhabitants, were all frequently overpowered by the explosions of the powder magazines in the arsenals of the Kremlin.

To many of the people it seemed that the day of judgment had actually arrived, that the trump of the archangel was sounding, and that the final conflagration had arrived. The palace of the emperor, his treasures, his precious things, his arms, his venerated images and the archives of the kingdom, all were devoured. The destruction of the city was almost as entire and as signal a proof of the divine displeasure as that of Sodom and Gomorrah. Even the metropolitan bishop, who was in the church of the Assumption, pleading for divine interposition, was with great difficulty rescued. Smothered, and in a state almost of insensibility, he was conveyed through billows of flame and smoke. Seventeen hundred adults, besides uncounted children, perished in the fire.

For many days the wretched inhabitants were seen wandering about, in the fields and among the ruins, searching for their children, their friends or any articles of furniture which might, by chance, have escaped the flames. Many became maniacs, and their cries arose in all directions like the howlings of wild beasts. The emperor and the nobles, to avoid the spectacle of so much misery, retired to the village of

Vorobeif, a few miles from Moscow. The whole population of Moscow, being in a state of despair, and reckless of consequences, were ripe for any conspiracy against an emperor and his favorites, whose iniquities, in their judgment, had brought down upon them the indignation of Heaven.

Several of the higher clergy, in coöperation with some of the princes and nobles, resolved to arouse the energies of the populace to effect a change in the government. The Glinskys were the advisers and instigators of the king. Against them the fury of the populace was easily directed. These doomed minions of despotism were pursued with fury energized by despair. Ivan IV. was quite unable to protect them. The Glinskys, with their numerous partisans, had returned to Moscow to make arrangements for the rebuilding of the Kremlin when the mob fell upon them, and they were nearly all slain. In the eye of the populace, there was something so sacred in the person of their prince that no one thought of offering him any harm.

Ivan IV., astounded by this outbreak, was trembling in his palace at Vorobeif, and his truly pious wife, Anastasia, was, with tears, pleading with Heaven, when one of the clergy, an extraordinary man named Sylvestre, endowed with the boldness of an ancient prophet, entered the presence of the emperor. He was venerable in years, and his gray locks fell in clusters upon his shoulders. The boy king was overawed by his appearance. One word from that capricious king would cause the head of Sylvestre to fall from the block. But the intrepid Christian, with the solemnity of an embassador from God, with pointed finger and eye sparkling with indignation, thus addressed him:

"God's avenging hand is suspended over the head of a God-forgetting, man-oppressing tzar. Fire from heaven has consumed Moscow. The anger of the Most High has called up the people in revolt, and is spreading over the kingdom anarchy, fury and blood."

Then taking from his bosom a copy of the New Testament, he read to the king those divinely-inspired precepts which are alike applicable to monarchs and peasants, and, in tones subdued by sadness, urged the king to follow these sacred lessons. The warning was heeded, and Ivan became "a new creature." Whatever explanations philosophy may attempt of the sudden and marvelous change of the character of Ivan IV., the fact remains one of the marvels of history. He appears to have been immediately overwhelmed with a sense of his guilt; with tears he extended his hand to the courageous monitor, asked imploringly what he could do to avert the wrath and secure the favor of Heaven, and placed himself at once under the guidance of his new-found friend.

Sylvestre, a humble, world-renouncing Christian, sought nothing for himself, and would accept neither riches nor honors, but he remained near the throne to strengthen the young monarch in his good resolutions. There was a young man, Alexis Adachef, connected with the court who possessed a character of extraordinary nobleness and loveliness. He was of remarkable personal beauty, and his soul. was pure and sensitive. Entirely devoted to the good of others, without the least apparent mixture of sordid motives, he engaged in the service of the tzar, and became to him a friend of priceless value. Alexis, mingling freely with the people, was acquainted with all their wants and griefs, and he coöperating with Sylvestre, inspired the emperor with a heart to conceive and energy to execute all good things.

From this conjunction is to be dated the commencement of the glory of the reign of Ivan IV. The first endeavor of the reformed monarch was to quell the tumult among the people. Three days after the assassination of the Glinskys, a mob from Moscow rushed out to the village of Vorobeif, surrounded the palace and demanded one of the aunts of the emperor and another of the nobles who had become obnoxious to them. The king immediately opened a fire upon the mob and dispersed them. This decisive act restored order. Ivan IV. immediately devoted all his energies to preparing dwellings for the houseless poor and in relieving their necessities. His whole soul seemed aroused to promote the happiness of his subjects, both temporal and spiritual, and all selfish considerations were apparently obliterated from his mind. In order to consolidate, by the aids of religion, the happy change effected in the government and in his own heart, the young sovereign shut himself up for several days in solitude, and, in the exercises of self-examination, fasting and prayer, made the entire consecration of himself to his Maker. He then assembled the bishops in one of the churches, and, in their presence, with touching words and tearful eyes, made confession of his faults, implored divine forgiveness, and then, with the calmness of a soul relieved of the burden of sin, received the sacrament of the Lord's Supper.

With true nobility of soul, he wished his penitence to be as conspicuous as his sins had been. He resolved to humble himself before his Maker in the presence of all Russia, that his subjects universally might understand the new principles which animated his heart, and the new desires which would enlist his energies. Every city in the empire received orders to send deputies to Moscow, chosen from all the ranks of society, to attend to matters of the utmost importance to the country. The Sabbath morning after their arrival, they were all assembled, an immense multitude, in one of the public squares of the city. The czar, accompanied by the clergy and the nobles, left the palace of the Kremlin to meet the deputies. The solemnity of the Sabbath hallowed the scene, and the people received their sovereign in profound silence.

The metropolitan bishop first offered a prayer. Ivan IV. then, standing on a platform, addressed the bishop in the following terms:

"Holy father! Your zeal for religion, your love for our country are well known to me; aid me in my good intentions.

I lost, while an infant, my parents, and the nobles, who sought only their own aggrandizement, neglected entirely my education, and have usurped, in my name, wealth and power. They have enriched themselves by injustice, and have crushed the poor without any one daring to check their ambition. I was, as it were, both deaf and dumb in my deplorable ignorance, for I heard not the lamentations of the poor, and my words solaced them not in their sorrows. Who can tell the tears which have been shed, the blood which has flowed? For all these things the judgment of God is to be feared."

Bowing then on all sides to the people, the monarch continuing, thus addressed them:

"O, you my people, whom the All-powerful has entrusted to my care, I invoke this day, in my behalf, both your religion and the love you have for me. It is impossible to repair past faults, but I will hereafter be your protector from oppression and all wrong. Forget those griefs which shall never be renewed. Lay aside every subject of discord, and let Christian love fraternize your hearts. From this day I will be your judge and your defender."

Religious ceremonies, simple yet imposing, closed this scene. Alexis Adachef was appointed minister of justice, receiving special instructions to watch the empire with a vigilant eye, that the poor especially should be subject to no oppression. From that moment all the actions of the sovereign were guided by the counsels of Sylvestre and Adachef. Ivan IV. assembled around him a council of his wisest and best men, and ever presided in person over their meetings. With great energy he entered upon the work of establishing a code of laws, which should be based upon the love of justice and good order. In the year 1550 this important code was promulgated, which forms almost the basis of Russian civilization.

On the 23d of February, 1551, a large convention of the clergy, of the nobles and of the principal citizens of the empire, was assembled at the Kremlin, and the emperor presented to them, for their own consideration and approval, the code of laws which had been framed. The mind of Ivan IV. expanded rapidly under these noble toils, and in a speech of great eloquence he urged them to examine these laws, to point out any defects and to coöperate with him in every endeavor for the prosperity of Russia.

After having thus settled the affairs of the State, the monarch turned his attention to those of the Church, urging the clergy to devote themselves to the work of ecclesiastical reform; to add simplicity to the ceremonies of religion, to prepare books of piety for the people, to train up a thoroughly instructed clergy for the pulpits, to establish rules for the decorous observance of divine worship, to abolish useless monasteries, to purify the convents of all immorality, and to insist that ecclesiastics, of every grade, should be patterns of piety for their flocks. The clergy eagerly engaged in this plan of reform, and vied with their Christian monarch in their efforts for the public weal.

Among the number of projects truly worthy of the grand prince, we must not neglect particular mention of his attempt to enrich Russia by encouraging the emigration, from other lands, of men distinguished in the arts and sciences. A distinguished German, named Schlit, being in Moscow in 1547, informed the tzar of the rapid progress Germany was making in civilization and enlightenment. Ivan IV. listened attentively, and after many interviews and protracted questionings, proposed that he should return to Germany as an envoy from Russia, and invite, in his name, to Moscow, artists, physicians, apothecaries, printers, mechanics, and also literary men, skilled in the languages, dead or living, and learned theologians.

Schlit accepted the mission and hastened to Augsburg, where the Emperor Charles V. was then presiding over a diet. Schlit presented to him a letter from Ivan IV. relative to this business. Charles was a little doubtful as to the expediency of allowing illustrious men from his empire to émigrate and thus add to the consideration and power of a rival kingdom. Nevertheless, after a long deliberation with the assembled States, he consented to gratify the tzar, on consideration that he would engage, by oath, not to allow any of the artists or the literati to pass from Russia into Turkey, and that he would not employ their talents in any manner hurtful to the German empire. Turkey was at that time assuming an attitude so formidable, that it was deemed expedient to increase the power of Russia, as that kingdom might thus more effectually aid as a barrier against the Turks; while, at the same time, it was deemed a matter of the utmost moment that Turkey should receive no aid whatever from Christian civilization.

Charles V. accordingly gave Schlit a written commission to raise his corps of emigrants. He soon assembled one hundred and twenty illustrious men at Lubeck, where they were to embark for Russia. But, in the mean time, the opposition had gained ground, and even Charles V. himself had become apprehensive that Russia, thus enlightened, might attain to formidable power. He accordingly had Schlit arrested. The corps of emigrants, thus deprived of their leader, and consequently disheartened, soon dispersed. Several months passed away before Ivan IV. received intelligence of the sad fate of his envoy. Though the plan thus failed, nevertheless, quite a number of these German artists, notwithstanding the prohibition of the emperor, effected their escape from Germany, secretly entered Russia, and engaged in the service of the tzar, were they were very efficient in contributing to Russian civilization.

The barbarian horde at Kezan still continued to annoy Russia with very many incursions. Some were mere petty forays, others were extended invasions, but all were alike merciless and bloody. In February, 1550, Ivan IV., then but twenty two years of age, placed himself at the head of a large army to descend the Volga and punish the horde. The monarch was young and totally inexperienced in war. A series of terrible disasters from storms and floods thinned his ranks, and the monarch in great dejection returned to Moscow to replenish his forces. Again, early in December, he hastened to meet his army which had been rendezvoused at Nigni Novgorod, on the Volga, about three hundred miles west of Moscow. In the early spring they descended the river, and in great force encamped before the walls of Kezan. The walls were of wood. The Russians were sixty thousand strong, and were aided with several batteries of artillery. The assault was immediately commenced, and for one whole day the battle raged with equal valor on the part of the assailants and the defendants. The next day a storm arose, the rain falling abundantly and freezing as it touched the ground. The encampment was flooded, and the assailants, unable to make any progress, were again compelled to beat a retreat. These reverses mortified the young tzar, though he succeeded in effecting a treaty with the barbarians, which in some degree covered his disgrace.

But the horde, entirely disorganized, paid no regard to treaties and continued their depredations. Again, in the year 1552, the tzar prepared another expedition to check their ravages. He announced to the council, in a very solemn session, that the time had arrived when it was necessary, at all hazards, to check the pride of the horde.

"God is my witness," said he, "that I do not seek vain glory, but I wish to secure the repose of my people. How shall I be able in the day of judgment to say to the Most High, 'Behold me and the subjects thou hast entrusted to my care,' if I do not shelter them from the eternal enemies of Russia, from these barbarians from whom one can have neither peace nor truce?"

The lords endeavored to persuade the emperor to remain at Moscow, and to entrust the expedition to his experienced generals, but he declared that he would not expose his army to perils and fatigues which he was not also ready and willing to share. Though many were in favor of a winter's campaign, as Kezan was surrounded with streams and lakes which the ice would then bridge, yet Ivan decided upon the summer as more favorable for the transportation of his army down the rivers. By the latter part of May the waters of the Volga and the Oka were covered with bateaux laden with artillery and with military stores, and the banks of those streams were crowded with troops upon the march. Nigni Novgorod, where the Oka empties into the Volga, was as usual the appointed place of rendezvous. The 16th of June Ivan took leave of the Empress Anastasia. Her emotion at parting was so great that she fell fainting into the arms of her husband.

From his palace Ivan proceeded to the church of the Assumption, where the blessing of Heaven was implored, and then issuing orders that the bishops, all over the empire, should offer prayers daily for the success of the expedition, he mounted his horse, and accompanied by the cavalry of his guard, took the route to Kolumna, a city on the Oka, about a hundred miles south of Moscow.

It will be remembered that the Tartar horde existed in several vast encampments. One of these encampments occupied Tauride, as the region north of the Crimea, and including that peninsula, was then called. These barbarians, thinking that the Russian army was now five hundred miles west of Moscow at Kezan, and that the empire was thus defenseless, with a vast army of invasion were on the eager march for Moscow. Ivan at Kolumna heard joyfully of their approach, for he was prepared to meet them and to chastise them with merited severity. On the 22d of July, the horde, unconscious of their danger, surrounded the walls of Toola, a city about a hundred miles south of Kolumna. Ivan himself, heading a division of the army, fell fiercely upon them, and the Tartars were totally routed, losing artillery, camels, banners and a large number of prisoners. They were pursued a long distance as in wild rout they fled back to their own country.

This brilliant success greatly elated the army. Ivan IV., sending his trophies to Moscow, as an encouragement to the capital, again put his army in motion towards Kezan. The relation which existed between the sovereign and his pastor, the faithful metropolitan bishop, may be inferred from the following communications which passed between them, equally worthy of them both.

"May the soul of your majesty," wrote the metropolitan, "remain pure and chaste. Be humble in prosperity and courageous in adversity. The piety of a sovereign saves and blesses his empire." The tzar replied,

"Worthy pastor of the church, we thank you for your Christian instructions. We will engrave them on our heart. Continue to us your wise counsels, and aid us also with your prayers. We advance against the enemy. May the Lord soon enable us to secure peace and repose to the Christians."

On the 13th of August, with his assembled army, he reached Viask on the Volga, about fifty miles above Kezan. Here he encamped to concentrate and rest his troops after so long a march. Barges freighted with provisions, merchandise and munitions of war, were incessantly arriving from the vast regions watered by the Volga and the Oka. As by magic an immense city spread out over the green plain. Tents glistened in the sun, banners waved, and horsemen and footmen, in all the gorgeous panoply of war, extended as far as the eye could reach.

While resting here, Ivan IV. sent an embassy to Kezan, saying that the tzar sought their repentance and amendment, not their destruction; that if they would deliver up to punishment the authors of sedition, and would give satisfactory pledges of future friendliness, they might live in peace under the paternal government of the tzar. To this message a contemptuous and defiant response was returned by the Tartar khan. The answer was closed with these words: "We are anxiously awaiting your arrival, and are all ready to commence our festivities."

That very day, the Russian army, amounting to one hundred and fifty thousand men, arrived within sight of Kezan. A prairie four miles in width, carpeted with flowers, extended from the Volga to the range of mountains at the base of which the city stood. The Tartars, abounding in wealth, by the aid of engineers and architects from all lands, had surrounded the city with massive walls defended with towers, ramparts and bastions in the most formidable strength of military art as then known. Within the walls rose the minarets of innumerable mosques and the turrets of palaces embellished with all the gorgeousness of oriental wealth and taste. The horde, relying upon the strength of their fortification, remained behind their walls, where they prepared for a defense which they doubted not would be successful. Two days were employed in disembarking the artillery and the munitions of war.

While thus engaged, a deserter escaped from the city and announced to the tzar that the fortress was abundantly supplied with artillery, provisions and all means of defense; that the garrison consisted of thirty-two thousand seven hundred veteran soldiers; that a numerous corps of cavalry had been detached to scour the surrounding country and raise an army of cavalry and infantry to assail the besiegers in flank and rear, while the garrisons should be prepared to sally from their entrenchments.

On the 23d of August, at the dawn of day, the army, advancing from the river, approached the city. The moment the sun appeared in the horizon, at the sound of innumerable trumpets, the whole army arrested their steps and the sacred standard was unfurled, presenting the effigy of Jesus Christ, our Saviour, surmounted by a golden cross. Ivan IV. and his staff alighted from their horses, and, beneath the shadow of the banner, with prayers and other exercises of devotion, received the sacrament of the Lord's Supper. The monarch then rode along the ranks, and, in an impassioned harangue, roused the soldiers to the noblest enthusiasm. Exalting the glory of those who might fall in the defense of religion, he assured them in the name of Russia that their wives and their children should never be forgotten, but that they should be the objects of his special care and should ever enjoy protection and abundance. In conclusion, he assured them that he was determined to sacrifice his own life, if necessary, to secure the triumph of the cross. These words were received with shouts of acclaim. The chaplain of Ivan, elevated in the view of the whole army, pronounced a solemn benediction upon the sovereign and upon all the troops, and then bowing to the sacred standard, exclaimed,

"O Lord, it is in thy name we now march against the infidels."

With waving banners and pealing trumpets, the army was now conducted before the walls of the city. Every thing there seemed abandoned and in profound silence and solitude. Not the slightest movement could be perceived. Not an individual appeared upon the walls. Many of the Russians began to rejoice, imagining that the tzar of Kezan, struck with terror, had fled with all his army into the forest. But the generals, more experienced, suspected a snare, and regarded the aspect of affairs as a motive for redoubled prudence. With great caution they made their dispositions for commencing the siege. As a division of seven thousand troops were crossing a bridge which they had thrown over a ditch near the walls, suddenly a violent uproar succeeded the profound silence which had reigned in the city. The air was filled with cries of rage. The massive gates rolled open upon their hinges, and fifteen thousand mounted Tartars, armed to the teeth, rushed upon the little band with a shock utterly resistless, and, in a few moments, the Russians were cut to pieces in the presence of the whole army. The victorious Tartars, having achieved this signal exploit, swept back again into the city and the gates were closed. This event taught the Russians prudence.

Anticipating a long siege, a city of tents was reared, with its streets and squares, beyond the reach of the guns from the walls. Three churches of canvas were constructed, where worship was daily held. Day after day, the siege was conducted with the usual events witnessed around a beleaguered fortress. There were the thunderings of artillery, the explosion of mines, fierce and bloody sorties, the shrieks of the combatants, and the city ever burning by flames enkindled by red hot shot thrown over the walls. The Russian batteries grew every day more and more formidable, and the ramparts crumbled beneath their blows. The Russian army was so numerous that the soldiers relieved themselves at the batteries, and the bombardment was continued day and night. At length a Tartar army was seen descending the distant mountains and hastening to the relief of the garrison. Ivan dispatched one half his army to meet them. The Tartars, after a sanguinary conflict, were cut to pieces. As the division returned covered with dust and blood, and exulting in their great achievement, Ivan displayed the prisoners, the banners, and the spoil he had taken, before the walls of the city. A herald was then sent, to address these words to the besieged:

"Ivan promises you life, liberty and pardon for the past, if you will submit yourselves to him."

The response returned was,

"We had rather die by our own pure hands, than perish by those of miserable Christians."

This answer was followed by a storm of all the missiles of war.

The monarch, wishing as far as possible to save the city from destruction, and to avoid the effusion of blood, directed a German engineer to sink a mine under an important portion of the walls. The miners proceeded until they could hear the footsteps of the Kezanians over their heads. Eleven tons of powder were placed in the vault. On the 5th of September; the match was applied. The explosion was awful. Large portions of the wall, towers, buildings, rocks, the mutilated bodies of men, were thrown hundreds of feet into the air and fell upon the city, crushing the dwellings and the inhabitants. The besieged were seized with mortal terror, not knowing to what to attribute so dire a calamity. The Russians, who were prepared for the explosion, waving their swords, with loud outcries rushed in at the breach. But the Kezanians, soon recovering from their consternation, with their breasts and their artillery presented a new rampart, and beat back the foe. Thus, day after day, the horrible carnage continued. Within the city and without the city, death held high carnival. There were famine and pestilence and misery in all imaginable forms within the walls. In the camp of the besiegers, there were mutilation, and death's agonies and despair. Army after army of Tartars came to the help of the besieged, but they were mown down mercilessly by Russian sabers, and trampled beneath Russian hoofs.

Ivan, morning and evening, with his generals, entered the church to implore the blessing of God upon his enterprise. In no other way could he rescue Russia from the invasion of these barbarians, than by thus appealing to the energies of the sword. In the contemplation of such a tragedy, the mind struggles in bewilderment, and can only say, "Be still and know that I am God."

CHAPTER XIV.

THE REIGN OF IVAN IV.—CONTINUED.

FROM 1552 TO 1557.

SIEGE OF KEZAN.—ARTIFICES OF WAR.—THE EXPLOSION OF MINES.—THE FINAL ASSAULT.—COMPLETE SUBJUGATION OF KEZAN.—GRATITUDE AND LIBERALITY OF THE TZAR.—RETURN TO MOSCOW.—JOY OF THE INHABITANTS.—BIRTH OF AN HEIR TO THE CROWN.—INSURRECTION IN KEZAN.—THE INSURRECTION QUELLED.—CONQUEST OF ASTRUCHAN.—THE ENGLISH EXPEDITION IN SEARCH OF A NORTH-EAST PASSAGE TO INDIA.—THE ESTABLISHMENT AT ARCHANGEL.—COMMERCIAL RELATIONS BETWEEN FRANCE AND RUSSIA.—RUSSIAN EMBASSY TO ENGLAND.—EXTENSION OF COMMERCE.

THE Russians had now been a month before the walls of Kezan. Ten thousand of the defenders had already been slain. The autumnal sun was rapidly declining, and the storms of winter were approaching. Secretly they now constructed, a mile and a half from the camp, an immense tower upon wheels, and rising higher than the walls of the city. Upon the platform of this tower they placed sixteen cannon, of the largest caliber, which were worked by the most skillful gunners. In the night this terrible machine was rolled up to the walls, and with the first dawn of the morning opened its fire upon the dwellings and the streets. The carnage was at first horrible, but the besieged at length took refuge in subterranean walks and covered ways, where they indomitably continued the conflict. The artillery, placed upon the walls of Kezan, were speedily dismounted by the batteries on the tower.

A new series of mines beneath the walls were now constructed by the Russian engineers, which were to operate with destructive power, hitherto unrecorded in the annals of war. On the 1st of October the tzar announced to the army that the mines were ready to be fired, and wished them to prepare for the general assault. While one half of the troops continued the incessant bombardment, the other half were assembled in the churches to purify themselves for the conflict by confession, penitence, prayer and the partaking of the sacrament of the Lord's Supper. The divisions then exchanged that the whole army might prostrate itself before God. Ivan IV. himself retired with his confessor and passed several hours in earnest devotion. The night preceding the assault there was no repose in either camp. The Kezanians, who were anxiously awaiting events, had perceived an extraordinary movement among the Russians, as each battalion was guided to the spot whence it was to rush over the ruins immediately after the explosion. Forty-eight tons (*tonneaux*) of powder had been placed in the mines.

The morning of the 2d of October dawned serene and cloudless. The earliest light revealed the Russians and the Kezanians each at their posts. The moment the sun appeared above the horizon the explosion took place. First the earth trembled and rose and fell for many miles as if shaken by an earthquake. A smothered roar, swelling into pealing thunder ensued, which appalled every mind. Immense volumes of smoke, thick and suffocating, instantaneously rolled over the city and the beleagueing camp, converting day into night. A horrible melange of timbers, rocks, guns and mutilated bodies of men, women and children were hurled into the air through this storm cloud of war, and fell in hideous ruin alike upon the besiegers and the besieged. At the moment when the explosion took place, one of the bishops in the church was reading the words of our Saviour foretelling the peaceful reign of fraternity and of heavenly love, "Henceforth there shall be but one flock and one shepherd." Strange contrast between the spirit of heaven and the woes of a fallen world!

For a moment even the Russians, though all prepared for the explosion, were paralyzed by its direful effects. But instantly recovering, they raised the simultaneous shout, "God is with us," and rushing over the debris of ruin and blood, penetrated the city. The Tartars met them with the fury of despair, appealing, in their turn, to Allah and Mohammed. Soon the Russian banner floated over tottering towers and blackened walls, though for many hours the battle raged with fierceness, which human energies can not exceed.

Prince Vorotinsky, early in the afternoon, soiled with blood and blackened with smoke, rode from the ruins of the city into the presence of Ivan, and bowing, said,

"Sire, rejoice; your bravery and your good fortune have secured the victory. Kezan is ours. The khan is in your power, the people are slain or taken captive. Unspeakable riches have fallen into our hands."

"Let God be glorified," cried Ivan, raising his eyes and his hands to heaven. Then taking the sacred standard in his own hands, he entered the city, planted the banner in one of the principal squares, ordered a *Te Deum* there to be chanted, and then directed that upon that spot the foundation should be laid of the first Christian temple. All the booty Ivan surrendered to the army, saying,

"The only riches I desire, are the repose and the honor of Russia."

Then assembling his troops around him, he thus addressed them:

"Valiant lords, generals, officers, all of you who in this solemn day have suffered for the glory of God, for religion, your country and your emperor, you have acquired immortal glory. Never before did a people develop such bravery; never before was so signal a victory gained. How can I suitably reward your glorious actions?

"And you who repose on the field of honor, noble children of Russia, you are already in the celestial realms, in the midst of Christian martyrs and all resplendent with glory. This is the recompense with which God has rewarded you.

But as for us, it is our duty to transmit your names to future ages, and the sacred list in which they shall be enrolled shall be placed in the temple of the Lord, that they may ever live in the memory of men.

"You, who bathed in your blood, still live to experience the effects of my love and my gratitude; all of you brave warriors now before me, listen attentively to my words, and repose perfect confidence in the promises I make to you this day, that I will cherish you and protect you to the end of my life."

These were not idle words. Ivan personally visited the wounded, cheered them with his sympathy, and ever after watched over them with parental care. His brother-in-law, Daniel, was immediately sent an envoy to the empress and to the metropolitan bishop, to inform them of the victory. The day was closed by a festival, in a gorgeous tent, where all the principal officers and lords were invited to dine with the tzar. A proclamation was addressed to all the tribes and nations of the conquered region.

"Come," said the Russian tzar, "without fear to me. The past is forgotten; for perfidy has received its reward. I shall require of you only the tribute which you have heretofore paid to the tzars of Kezan."

On the 3d of October the dead were buried and the whole city was cleansed. The next day, Ivan, accompanied by his clergy, his council and the chiefs of his army, made his triumphal entrance, and laid, on the designated spot, the corner-stone of the cathedral church of the Visitation. He also made the tour of the city, bearing the sacred banner, and consecrating Kezan to the true God. The clergy sprinkled holy water upon the streets and upon the walls of the houses, imploring the benediction of Heaven upon this new rampart of Christianity. They prayed that the inhabitants might be preserved from all maladies, that they might be strengthened to repel every enemy, and that the city might for ever remain the glorious heritage of Russia. Having traversed the whole city and designated the places for the erection of churches, the tzar gave orders for the immediate rebuilding of the fortifications, and then, accompanied by his court, he took possession of the palace of the khan, over which now floated the banners of the cross.

It was thus that one of the most considerable principalities of the descendants of Ghengis Khan fell into the hands of Russia. Kezan was founded upon the ruins of ancient Bulgaria, and, situated upon the frontiers of Russia, had long filled the empire with terror. Ivan immediately established a new government for the city and the surrounding region, which was occupied by five different nations, powerful in numbers and redoubtable in war. An army of about ten thousand men was left to garrison the fortresses of the city. On the 11th of October the emperor prepared to return to Moscow. Many of the lords counseled that he should remain at Kezan until spring, that the more distant regions might be overawed by the presence of the army. But the monarch, impatient to see his spouse and to present himself in Moscow fresh from these fields of glory, rejected these sage counsels and adopted the advice of those who also wished to repose beneath the laurels they had already acquired. Passing the night of the 11th of October on the banks of the Volga, he embarked on the morning of the 12th in a barge to ascend the stream, while the cavalry followed along upon the banks. The emperor passed one day at Sviazk and then proceeded to Nigni Novgorod. The whole city, men, women and children, flocked to meet him. They could not find words strong enough to express their gratitude for their deliverance from the terrible incursions of the horde. They fell at their monarch's feet, bathed his hands with their tears and implored Heaven's blessing upon him.

From Nigni Novgorod the emperor took the land route through Balakna and Vladimir to Moscow. On the way he met a courier from the Empress Anastasia, announcing to him that she had given birth to a son whom she named Dmitri. The tzar, in the tumult of his joy, leaped from his horse, passionately embraced Trakhaniot, the herald, and then falling upon his knees with tears trickling down his cheeks, rendered thanks to God for the gift. Not knowing how upon the spot to recompense the herald for the blissful tidings, he took the royal cloak from his own shoulders and spread it over Trakhaniot, and passed into his hands the magnificent charger from which the monarch had just alighted. He spent the night of the 28th of October in a small village but a few miles from Moscow, all things being prepared for his triumphant entrance into the capital the next day. With the earliest light of the morning he advanced toward the city. The crowd, even at that early hour, was so great that, for a distance of four miles, there was but a narrow passage left through the dense ranks of the people for the tzar and his guard. The emperor advanced slowly, greeted by the acclaim of more than a million of his people. With uncovered head he bowed to the right and to the left, while the multitude incessantly cried, "May Heaven grant long life to our pious tzar, conqueror of barbarians and saviour of Christians."

At the gate he was met by the metropolitan, the bishops, the lords and the princes ranged in order of procession under the sacred banner. Ivan IV. dismounted and addressed them in touching words of congratulation. The response of the metropolitan was soulfull, flooding the eyes of the monarch and exciting all who heard it to the highest enthusiasm.

"As for us, O tzar," he said, in conclusion, "in testimony of our gratitude for your toils and your glorious exploits, we prostrate ourselves before you."

At these words the metropolitan, the clergy, the dignitaries and the people fell upon their knees before their sovereign, bowing their faces to the ground. There were sobbings and shoutings, cries of benedictions and transports of joy.

The monarch was now conducted to the Kremlin, which had been rebuilt, and attended mass in the church of the Assumption. He then hastened to the palace to greet his spouse. The happy mother was in the chamber of convalescence with her beautiful boy at her side. For once, at least, there was joy in a palace.

The enthusiasm which reigned in the capital and throughout all Russia was such as has never been surpassed. The people, trained to faith and devotion, crowded the churches, which were constantly open, addressing incessant thanksgivings to Heaven. The preachers exhausted the powers of eloquence in describing the grandeur of the actions of their prince—his exertions, fatigues, bravery, the stratagems of war during the siege, the despairing ferocity of the Kezanians and the final and glorious result.

After several days passed in the bosom of his family, Ivan gave a grand festival in his palace, on the 8th of November. The metropolitan, the bishops, the abbés, the princes, and all the lords and warriors who had distinguished themselves during the siege of Kezan, were invited. "Never," say the annalists, "had there before been seen at Moscow a fête so sumptuous, joy so intense, or liberality so princely." The fête continued for three days, during which the emperor did not cease to distribute, with a liberal hand, proofs of his munificence. His bounty was extended from the metropolitan bishop down to the humblest soldier distinguished for his bravery or his wounds. The monarch, thus surrounded with glory, beloved by his people, the conqueror of a foreign empire and the pacificator of his own, distinguished for the nobleness of his personal character and the grandeur of his exploits, alike wise as a legislator and humane as a man, was still but twenty-two years of age. His career thus far presents a phenomenon quite unparalleled in history.

As soon as Anastasia was able to leave her couch she accompanied the tzar to the monastery of Yroitzky, where his infant son Dmitri received the ordinance of baptism. It seems to be the doom of life that every calm should be succeeded by a storm; that days of sunshine should be followed by darkness and tempests. Early in the year 1553 tidings reached Moscow that the barbarians at Kezan were in bloody insurrection. The Russian troops had been worsted in many conflicts; very many of them were slain. The danger was imminent that the insurrection would prove successful, and that the Russians would be entirely exterminated from Kezan. The imprudence of the emperor, in withdrawing before the conquest was consolidated, was now apparent to all. To add to the consternation the monarch himself was suddenly seized with an inflammatory fever; the progress of the malady was so rapid that almost immediately his life was despaired of. The mind of the tzar was unclouded, and being informed of his danger, without any apparent agitation he called for his secretary to draw up his last will and testament. The monarch nominated for his successor his infant son, Dmitri. To render the act more imposing, he requested the lords, who were assembled in an adjoining saloon, to take the oath of allegiance to his son. Immediately the spirit of revolt was manifested. Many of the lords dreaded the long minority of the infant prince, and the government of the regency which would probably ensue. The contest, loud and angry, reached the ears of the king, and he sent for the refractory lords to approach his bedside. Ivan, burning with fever, with hardly strength to speak, and expecting every hour to die, turned his eyes to them reproachfully and said,

"Who then do you wish to choose for your tzar? I am too feeble to speak long. Dmitri, though in his cradle, is none the less your legitimate sovereign. If you are deaf to the voice of conscience you must answer for it before God."

One of the nobles frankly responded,

"Sire, we are all devoted to you and to your son. But we fear the regency of Yourief, who will undoubtedly govern

Russia in the name of an infant who has not yet attained his intellectual faculties. This is the true cause of our solicitude. To how many calamities were we not exposed during the government of the lords, before your majesty had attained the age of reason. It is necessary to avoid the recurrence of such woes."

The monarch was now too feeble to speak, and the nobles withdrew from his chamber. Some took the oath to obey the will of the sovereign, others refused, and the bitter strife extended through the city and the kingdom. The dissentients rallied round prince Vladimir, and the nation was threatened with civil war. The next day the tzar had revived a little, and again assembled the lords in his chamber and entreated them to take the oath of submission to his son and to Anastasia, the guardian of the infant prince. Overcome by the exertion the monarch sank into a state of lethargy, and to all seemed to be dying. But being young, temperate and vigorous, it proved but the crisis of the disease. He awoke from his sleep calm and decidedly convalescent. Deeply wounded by the unexpected opposition which he had encountered, he yet manifested no spirit of revenge, though Anastasia, with woman's more sensitive nature, could never forget the opposition which had been manifested towards herself and her child.

Ivan during his sickness had made a vow that, in case of recovery, he would visit, in homage, the monastery of St. Cyrille, some thousand miles distant beyond the waves of the Volga. It is pleasant to record the remonstrance which Maxime, one of the clergy, made against the fulfillment of his wishes.

"You are about," said he, "to undertake a dangerous journey with your spouse and your infant child. Can the fulfillment of a vow which reason disapproves, be agreeable to God? It is useless to seek in deserts that heavenly Father who fills the universe with his presence. If you desire to testify to Heaven the gratitude you feel, do good upon the throne. The conquest of Kezan, an event so propitious for Russia, has nevertheless caused the death of many Christians. The widows, the mothers, the orphans of warriors who fell upon the field of honor, are overwhelmed with affliction. Endeavor to comfort them and to dry their tears by your beneficence. These are the deeds pleasing to God and worthy of a tzar."

Nevertheless the monarch persisted in his plan, and entered upon the long journey. He buried his child by the way, and returned overwhelmed with grief. But he encountered a greater calamity than the death of the young prince, in bad advice which he received from Vassian, the aged and venerable prince of Kolumna.

"Sire," said this unwise ecclesiastic, "if you wish to become a monarch truly absolute, ask advice of no one, and deem no one wiser than yourself. Establish it as an irrevocable principle never to receive the counsels of others, but, on the contrary, give counsel to them. Command, but never obey. Then you will be a true sovereign, terrible to the lords. Remember that the counselors of the wisest princes always in the end dominate over them."

The subtle poison which this discourse distilled, penetrated the soul of Ivan. He seized the hand of Vassian, pressed it to his lips, and said,

"My father himself could not have given me advice more salutary."

Bitterly was the prince deceived. Experience has proved that, in the counsel of the wise and virtuous, there is safety. There was no sudden change in the character of Ivan. He still continued for some years to manifest the most sincere esteem for the opinions of Sylvestre and Adachef. But the poison of bad principles was gradually diffusing itself through his heart. A year had not passed away, ere Ivan was consoled by the birth of another son. In the meantime he devoted himself with ardor to measures for the restoration of tranquillity in Kezan. A numerous army was assembled at Nigni Novgorod, with orders to commence the campaign for the reconquest of the country as soon as the cold of winter should bridge the lakes and streams. The Tartars had made very vigorous efforts to repel their foes, by summoning every fighting man to the field, and by the construction of fortresses and throwing up of redoubts.

In November of 1553, the storm of battle was recommenced on fields of ice, and amidst smothering tempests of snow. For more than a month there was not a day without a conflict. In these incessant engagements the Tartars lost ten thousand men slain and six thousand prisoners. One thousand six hundred of the most distinguished of these prisoners, princes, nobles and chieftains, who had been the most conspicuous in the rebellion, were put to death. Nevertheless these severities did not stifle the insurrection; the Tartars, in banditti bands, even crossing the Volga, pillaging, massacring and burning with savage cruelty. For five years the war raged in Kezan, with every accompaniment of ferocity and misery. The country was devastated and almost depopulated. Hardly a chief of note was left alive. The horrors of war then ceased. The Russians took possession of the country, filled it with their own emigrants, reared churches, established Christianity, and spread over the community the protection of Russian law. Most of the Kezanians who remained embraced Christianity, and from that time Kezan, the ancient Bulgaria, has remained an integral portion of the Russian empire.

Soon after, a new conquest, more easy, but not less glorious, was added to that of Kezan. The city and province of Astrachan, situated at the mouth of the Volga as it enters the Caspian, had existed from the remotest antiquity, enjoying wealth and renown, even before the foundation of the Russian empire. In the third century of the Christian era, it was celebrated for its commerce, and it became one of the favorite capitals of the all-conquering Tartars. Russia, being now in possession of all the upper waters of the Volga, decided to extend their dominions down the river to the Caspian. It was not difficult to find ample causes of complaint against pagan and barbaric hordes, whose only profession was robbery and war.

Early in the spring of 1554 a numerous and choice army descended the Volga in bateaux to the delta on which Astrachan is built. The low lands, intersected by the branching stream, is composed of innumerable islands. The inhabitants of the city, abandoning the capital entirely, took refuge among these islands, where they enjoyed great advantages in repelling assailants. The Russians took possession of the city, prosecuted the war vigorously through the summer, and the tzar, on the 20th of October, which was his birthday, received the gratifying intelligence that every foe was quelled, and that the Russian government was firmly established on the shores of the Caspian. Well might Russia now be proud of its territorial greatness. The opening of these new realms encouraged commerce, promoted wealth, and developed to an extraordinary degree the resources of the empire.

England was, at that time, far beyond the bounds of the political horizon of Russia. In fact, the Russians hardly knew that there was such a nation. Great Britain was not, at that time, a maritime power of the first order. Spain, Portugal, Venice and Genoa were then the great monarchs of the ocean. England was just beginning to become the dangerous rival of those States whom she has already so infinitely surpassed in maritime greatness. She had then formed the project of opening a shorter route to the Indies through the North Sea, and, in 1553, during the reign of Edward VI., had dispatched an expedition of three vessels, under Hugh Willoughby, in search of a north-east passage. These vessels, separated by a tempest, were unable to reunite, and two of them were wrecked upon the icy coast of Russian Lapland in the extreme latitude of eighty degrees north. Willoughby and his companions perished. Some Lapland fishermen found their remains in the winter of the year 1554. Willoughby was seated in a cabin constructed upon the shore with his journal before him, with which he appeared to have been occupied until the moment of his death. The other ship, commanded by Captain Chanceller, was more fortunate. He penetrated the White Sea, and, on the 24th of August, landed in the Bay of Dwina at the Russian monastery of St. Nicholas, where now stands the city of Archangel. The English informed the inhabitants, who were astonished at the apparition of such a ship in their waters, that they were bearers of a letter to the tzar from the King of England, who desired to establish commercial relations with the great and hitherto almost unknown northern empire. The commandant of the country furnished the mariners with provisions, and immediately dispatched a courier to Ivan at Moscow, which was some six hundred miles south of the Bay of Dwina.

Ivan IV. wisely judged that this circumstance might prove favorable to Russian commerce, and immediately sent a courier to invite Chanceller to come to Moscow, at the same time making arrangements for him to accomplish the journey with speed and comfort. Chanceller, with some of his officers, accepted the invitation. Arriving at Moscow, the English were struck with astonishment in view of the magnificence of the court, the polished address and the dignified manners of the nobles, the rich costume of the courtiers, and, particularly, with the jeweled and golden brilliance of the throne, upon which was seated a young monarch decorated in the most dazzling style of regal splendor, and in whose presence all observed the most respectful silence. Chanceller presented to Ivan IV. the letter of Edward VI. It was a noble letter, worthy of England's monarch, and, being translated into many languages, was addressed generally to all the sovereigns of the East and the North. The letter was dated, "London, in the year 5517 of the creation, and of our reign the 17." The English were honorably received, and were invited to dine with the tzar in the royal palace, which furnished them with a new occasion of astonishment from the sumptuousness which surrounded the sovereign. The guests, more than a hundred in number, were served on plates of gold. The goblets were of the same metal. The servants, one hundred and fifty in number, were also in livery richly decorated wlth gold lace.

The tzar wrote to Edward that he desired to form with him an alliance of friendship conformable to the precepts of the Christian religion and of every wise government; that he was anxious to do any thing in his power which should be agreeable to the King of England, and that the English embassadors and merchants who might come to Russia should be protected, treated as friends and should enjoy perfect security.

When Chanceller returned to England, Edward VI. was already in the tomb, and Mary, *Bloody Mary*, the child of brutal Henry VIII., was on the throne. The letter of Ivan IV. caused intense excitement throughout England. Every one spoke of Russia as of a country newly discovered, and all were eager to obtain information respecting its history and its geography. An association of merchants was immediately formed to open avenues of commerce with this new world. Another expedition of two ships was fitted out, commanded by Chanceller, to conclude a treaty of commerce with the tzar. Mary, and her husband, Philip of Spain, who was son of the Emperor Charles V., wrote a letter to the Russian monarch full of the most gracious expressions.

Chanceller and his companions were received with the same cordial hospitality as before. Ivan gave them a seat at his own table, loaded them with favors and gave to the Queen of England the title of " my dearly beloved sister." A commission of Russian merchants was apppointed to confer with the English to form a commercial treaty. It was decided that the principal place for the exchange of merchandise should be at Kolmogar, on the Bay of Dwina, nearly opposite the convent of St. Nicholas; that each party should be free to name its own prices, but that every kind of fraud should be judged after the criminal code of Russia. Ivan then delivered to the English a diploma, granting them permission to traffic freely in all the cities of Russia without molestation and without paying any tribute or tax. They were free to establish themselves wherever they pleased, to purchase houses and shops, and to engage servants and mechanics in their employ, and to exact from them oaths of fidelity. It was also agreed that a man should be responsible for his own conduct only, and not for that of his agents, and that though the sovereign might punish the criminal with the loss of liberty and even of life, yet, under no circumstances, should he touch his property; that should always pass to his natural heirs.

The port of St. Nicholas, which, for ages, had been silent and solitary in these northern waters where the English had found but a poor and gloomy monastery, the tomb, as it were, of hooded monks, soon became a busy place of traffic. The English constructed there a large and beautiful mansion for the accommodation of their merchants, and streets were formed, lined with spacious storehouses. The principal merchandise which the English then imported into Russia consisted of cloths and sugar. The merchants offered twelve guineas for what was then called a half piece of cloth, and four shillings a pound for sugar.

In 1556, Chanceller embarked for England with four ships richly laden with the gold and the produce of Russia, accompanied by Joseph Nepeia, an embassador to the Queen of England. Fortune, which, until then, had smiled upon this hardy mariner, now turned adverse. Tempests dispersed his ships, and one only reached London. Chanceller himself perished in the waves upon the coast of Scotland. The ships dashed upon the rocks, and the Russian embassador, Nepeia, barely escaped with his life. Arriving at London, he was overwhelmed with caresses and presents. The most distinguished dignitaries of the State and one hundred and forty merchants, accompanied by a great number of attendants, all richly clad and mounted upon superb horses, rode out to meet him. They presented to him a horse magnificently caparisoned, and thus escorted, the first Russian embassador made his entrance into the capital of Great Britain. The inhabitants of London crowded the streets to catch a sight of the illustrious Russian, and thousands of voices greeted him with the heartiest acclaim. A magnificent mansion was assigned for his residence, which was furnished in the highest style of splendor. He was invited to innumerable festivals, and the court were eager to exhibit to him every thing worthy of notice in the city of London. He was conducted to the cathedral of St. Paul, to Westminster Abbey, to the Tower and to all the parks and palaces. The queen received Nepeia with the most marked consideration. At one of the most gorgeous festivals he was seated by her side, the observed of all observers.

The embassador could only regret that the rich presents of furs and Russian fabrics which the tzar had sent by his hand to Mary, were all engulfed upon the coast of Scotland. The queen sent to the tzar the most beautiful fabrics of the English looms, the most exquisitely constructed weapons of war, such as sabers, guns and pistols, and a living lion and lioness, animals which never before had been seen within the bounds of the Russian empire. In September, 1557, Nepeia embarked for Russia, taking with him several English artisans, miners and physicians. Ivan was anxious to lose no opportunity to gain from foreign lands every thing which could contribute to Russian civilization. The letter which Mary and Philip returned to Moscow was flatteringly addressed to the august emperor, Ivan IV. When the tzar learned all the honors and the testimonials of affection with which his embassador had been greeted in London, he considered the English as the most precious of all the friends of Russia. He ordered mansions to be prepared for the accommodation of their merchants in all the commercial cities of the empire, and he treated them in other respects with such marked tokens of regard, that all the letters which they wrote to London were filled with expressions of gratitude towards the Russian sovereign.

In the year 1557 an English commercial fleet entered the Baltic Sea and proceeded to the mouth of the Dwina to establish there an entrepot of English merchandise. The commander-in-chief of the squadron visited Moscow, where he was received with the greatest cordiality, and thence passed down the Volga to Astrachan, that he might there establish commercial relations with Persia. The tzar, reposing entire confidence in the London merchants, entered into their views and promised to grant them every facility for the transportation of English merchandise, even to the remotest sections of the empire. This commercial alliance with Great Britain, founded upon reciprocal advantages, without any commingling of political jealousies, was impressed with a certain character of magnanimity and fraternity which greatly augmented the renown of the reign of Ivan IV., and which was a signal proof of the sagacity of his administration. How beautiful are the records of peace when contrasted with the hideous annals of war!

The merchants of the other nations of southern and western Europe were not slow to profit by the discovery that the English had made. Ships from Holland, freighted with the goods of that ingenious and industrious people, were soon coasting along the bays of the great empire, and penetrating her rivers, engaged in traffic which neither Russia or England seemed disposed to disturb. While the tzar was engaged in those objects which we have thus rapidly traced, other questions of immense magnitude engrossed his mind. The Tartar horde in Tauride terrified by the destruction of the horde in

Kezan, were ravaging southern Russia with continual invasions which the tzar found it difficult to repress. Poland was also hostile, ever watching for an opportunity to strike a deadly blow, and Sweden, under Gustavus Vasa, was in open war with the empire.

CHAPTER XV.

THE ABDICATION OF IVAN IV.

FROM 1557 TO 1582.

TERROR OF THE HORDE IN TAURIDE.—WAR WITH GUSTAVUS VASA OF SWEDEN.—POLITICAL PUNCTILIOS.—THE KINGDOM OF LIVONIA ANNEXED TO SWEDEN.—DEATH OF ANASTASIA.—CONSPIRACY AGAINST IVAN.—HIS ABDICATION.—HIS RESUMPTION OF THE CROWN.—INVASION OF RUSSIA BY THE TARTARS AND TURKS.—HEROISM OF ZEBRINOW.—UTTER DISCOMFITURE OF THE TARTARS.—RELATIONS BETWEEN QUEEN ELIZABETH OF ENGLAND, AND RUSSIA.—INTREPID EMBASSAGE.—NEW WAR WITH POLAND.—DISASTERS OF RUSSIA.—THE EMPEROR KILLS HIS OWN SON.—ANGUISH OF IVAN IV.

THE entire subjugation of the Tartars in Kezan terrified the horde in Tauride, lest their turn to be overwhelmed should next come. Devlet Ghirei, the khan of this horde, was a man of great ability and ferocity. Ivan IV. was urged by his counselors immediately to advance to the conquest of the Crimea. The achievement could then doubtless have been easily accomplished. But it was a journey of nearly a thousand miles from Moscow to Tauride. The route was very imperfectly known; much of the intervening region was an inhospitable wilderness. The Sultan of Turkey was the sovereign master of the horde, and Ivan feared that all the terrible energies of Turkey would be roused against him.

There was, moreover, another enemy nearer at home whom Ivan had greater cause to fear. Gustavus Vasa, the King of Sweden, had, for some time, contemplated with alarm the rapidly increasing power of Russia. He accordingly formed a coalition with the Kings of Poland and Livonia, and with the powerful Dukes of Prussia and of Denmark, for those two States were then but dukedoms, to oppose the ambition of the tzar. An occasion for hostilities was found in a dispute, respecting the boundaries between Russia and Sweden. The terrible tragedy of war was inducted by a prologue of burning villages, trampled harvests and massacred peasants, upon the frontiers. Sieges, bombardments and fierce battles ensued, with the alternations of success. From one triumphal march of invasion into Sweden, the Russians returned so laden with prisoners, that, as their annalists record, a man was sold for one dollar, and a girl for five shillings.

At length, as usual, both parties became weary of toil and blood, and were anxious for a respite. Gustavus proposed terms of reconciliation. Ivan IV. accepted the overtures, though he returned a reproachful and indignant answer.

"Your people," he wrote, "have exhausted their ferocity upon our territories. Not only have they burned our cities and massacred our subjects, but they have even profaned our churches, purloined our images and destroyed our bells. The inhabitants of Novgorod implored the aid of our grand army. My soldiers burned with impatience to carry the war to Stockholm, but I restrained them; so anxious was I to avoid the effusion of human blood. All the misery resulting from this war, is to be attributed to your pride. Admitting that you were ignorant of the grandeur of Novgorod, you might have learned the facts from your own merchants. They could have told you, that even the suburbs of Novgorod are superior to the whole of your capital of Stockholm. Lay aside this pride, and give up your quarrelsome disposition. We are willing to live in peace with you."

Sweden was not in a condition to resent this rebuke. In February, 1557, the embassadors of Gustavus, consisting of four of the most illustrious men in the empire, clergy and nobles, accompanied by a brilliant suite, arrived in Moscow. They were not received as friends, but as distinguished prisoners, who were to be treated with consideration, and whose wants were to be abundantly supplied. The tzar refused to have any direct intercourse with them, and would only treat through the dignitaries of his court. A truce was concluded for forty years. The tzar, to impress the embassadors with his wealth and grandeur, entertained them sumptuously, and they were served from vessels of gold.

Though peace was thus made with Sweden, a foolish quarrel, for some time, prevented the conclusion of a treaty with Poland. Ivan IV. demanded, that Augustus, *King* of Poland, should recognize him as *Emperor* of Russia. Augustus replied, that there were but two emperors in the world, the Emperor of Germany and the Sultan of Turkey. Ivan sent, through his embassadors, to Augustus; the letters of Pope Clement, of the Emperor Maximilian, of the Sultan, of the Kings of Spain, Sweden and Denmark, and the recent dispatch of the King of England, all of whom recognized his title of tzar, or emperor. Still, the Polish king would not allow Ivan a title, which seemed to place the Russian throne on an eminence above that of Poland. Unfriendly relations consequently continued, with jealousies and border strifes, though there was no vigorous outbreak of war.

Ivan IV. now succeeded in attaching Livonia to the great and growing empire. It came in first as tributary, purchasing, by an annual contribution, peace with Russia and protection. Though there were many subsequent conflicts with Livonia, the territory subsequently became an integral portion of the empire. Russia had now become so great, that her growth was yearly manifest as surrounding regions were absorbed by her superior civilization and her armies. The unenlightened States which surrounded her, were ever provoking hostilities, invasion, and becoming absorbed. In the year 1558, the Tartars of Tauride, having assembled an army of one hundred thousand horsemen, a combination of Tartars and Turks, suddenly entered Russia, and sweeping resistlessly on, a war tempest of utter desolation, reached within two hundred miles of Moscow. There they learned that Ivan himself, with an army more numerous than their own, was on the march to meet them. Turning, they retreated more rapidly than they advanced. Notwithstanding their retreat, Ivan resolved to pursue them to their own haunts. A large number of bateaux was constructed and launched upon the Don and also upon the Dnieper. The army, in these two divisions, descended these streams, one to the Sea of Azof, the other to the mouth of the Dnieper. Thence invading Tauride, both by the east and the west, they drove the terrified inhabitants, taken entirely by surprise, like sheep before them. The tents of these nomads they committed to the flames. Their flocks and herds were seized, with a great amount of booty, and many Russian captives were liberated. The Tartars fled to fastnesses whence they could not be pursued. Some Turks being taken with the horde, Ivan sent them with rich presents to the sultan, stating that he did not make war against Turkey, only against the robbers of Tauride. The Russian troops returned from this triumphant expedition, by ascending the waters of the Dnieper. All Russia was filled with rejoicing, while the churches resounded with "Te Deums."

And now domestic griefs came to darken the palace of Ivan. For thirteen years he had enjoyed all the happiness which conjugal love can confer. Anastasia was still in the brilliance of youth and beauty, when she was attacked by dangerous sickness. As she was lying upon her couch, helpless and burning with fever, the cry of fire was heard. The day was excessively hot; the windows of the palace all open, and a drouth of several weeks made every thing dry as tinder. The conflagration commenced in an adjoining street, and, in a moment, volumes of flame and smoke were swept by the wind, enveloping the Kremlin, and showering upon it and into it, innumerable flakes of fire. The queen was thrown into a paroxysm of terror; the attendants hastily placed her upon a litter and bore her, almost suffocated, through the blazing streets out of the city, to the village of Kolomensk. The emperor then returned to assist in arresting the conflagration. He exposed himself like a common laborer, inspiring others with intrepidity by mounting ladders, carrying water and opposing the flames in the most dangerous positions. The conflagration proved awful in its ravages, many of the inhabitants perishing in the flames.

This calamitous event was more than the feeble frame of Anastasia could endure. She rapidly failed, and on the 7th of August, 1560, she expired. The grief of Ivan was heart-rending, and never was national affliction manifested in a more sincere and touching manner. Not only the whole court, but almost the entire city of Moscow, followed the remains of Anastasia to their interment. Many, in the bitterness of their grief, sobbed aloud. The most inconsolable were the poor and friendless, calling Anastasia by the name of mother. The anguish of Ivan for a time quite unmanned him, and he wept like a child. The loss of Anastasia did indeed prove to Ivan the greatest of earthly calamities. She had been his guardian angel, his guide to virtue. Having lost his guide, he fell into many errors from which Anastasia would have preserved him.

In the course of a few months, either the tears of Ivan were dried up, or political considerations seemed to render it necessary for him to seek another wife. Notwithstanding the long hereditary hostility which had existed between Russia and Poland, perhaps *in consequence of it*, Ivan made proposals for a Polish princess, Catharine, sister of Sigismond Augustus, the king. The Poles demanded, as an essential item in the marriage contract, that the children of Catharine should take the precedence of those of Anastasia as heirs to the throne. This iniquitous demand the tzar rejected with the scorn it merited. The revenge in which the Poles indulged was characteristic of the rudeness of the times. The court of Augustus sent a white mare, beautifully caparisoned, to Ivan, with the message, that such a wife he would find to be in accordance with his character and wants. The outrageous insult incensed Ivan to the highest degree, and he vowed that the Poles should feel the weight of his displeasure. Catharine, in the meantime, was married to the Duke of Finland, who was brother to the King of Sweden, and whose sister was married to the King of Denmark. Thus the three kingdoms of Poland, Sweden and Denmark, and the Duchy of Finland were strongly allied by matrimonial ties, and were ready to combine against the Russian emperor.

Ivan IV. nursed his vengeance, waiting for an opportunity to strike a blow which should be felt. Elizabeth was now Queen of England, and her embassador at the court of Russia was in high favor with the emperor. Probably through his influence Ivan showed great favor to the Lutheran clergy, who were gradually gaining followers in the empire. He frequently admitted them to court, and even listened to their arguments in favor of the reformed religion. The higher clergy and the lords were much incensed by this liberality, which, in their view, endangered the ancient usages, both civil and religious, of the realm, and a very formidable conspiracy was organized against the tzar.

Ivan IV. was apprised of the conspiracy, and, with singular boldness and magnanimity, immediately assembled his leading nobles and higher clergy in the great audience-chamber of the Kremlin. He presented himself before them in the glittering robes and with all the insignia of royalty. Divesting himself of them all, he said to his astonished auditors,

"You have deemed me unworthy any longer to occupy the throne. I here and now give in my abdication, and request you to nominate some person whom you may consider worthy to be your sovereign."

Without permitting any reply he dismissed them, and the next day convened all the clergy of Moscow in the church of St. Mary. A high mass was celebrated by the metropolitan, in which the monarch assisted, and he then took an affecting leave of them all, in a solemn renunciation of all claims to the crown. Accompanied by his two sons, he retired to the strong yet secluded castle of Caloujintz, situated about five miles from Moscow. Here he remained several days, waiting, it is generally supposed, for a delegation to call, imploring him again to resume the crown. In this expectation he was not disappointed. The lords were unprepared for such decisive action. In their councils there was nothing but confusion. Anarchy was rapidly commencing its reign, which would be followed inevitably by civil war. The partisans of the emperor in the provinces were very numerous, and could be rallied by a word from him; and no one imagined that the emperor had any idea of retiring so peacefully. It was not doubted that he would soon appear at the head of an army, and punish relentlessly the disaffected, who would all then be revealed. The citizens, the nobles and the clergy met together and appointed a numerous deputation to call upon the emperor and implore him again to resume the reins of power.

"Your faithful subjects, sire," exclaimed the petitioners, "are deeply afflicted. The State is exposed to fearful peril from dissension within and enemies without. We do therefore most earnestly entreat your majesty, as a faithful shepherd, still to watch over his flock; we do entreat you to return to your throne, to continue your favor to the deserving, and not to forsake your faithful subjects in consequence of the errors of a few."

Ivan listened with much apparent indifference to this pathetic address, and either really felt, or affected, great reluctance again to resume the cares of royalty. He requested a day's time to consider their proposal. The next morning the nobles were again convened, and Ivan acquainted them with his decision. Rebuking them with severity for their ingratitude, reproaching them with the danger to which his life had been exposed through their conspiracy, he declared that he could not again assume the cares and the perils of the crown. Still his refusal was not so decisive as to exclude all room for further entreaties. They renewed their supplications with tears, for Russia was, indeed, exposed to all the horrors of civil war, should Ivan persist in his resolve, and it was certain that the empire, thus distracted, would at once be invaded by both Poles and Turks.

Thus importuned, Ivan at last consented to return to the Kremlin. He resolved, however, to make an example of those who had conspired against him, which should warn loudly against the renewal of similar attempts. The principal movers in the plot were executed. Ivan then surrounded himself with a body guard of two hundred men carefully selected from the distant provinces, and who were in no way under the influence of any of the lords. This body guard, composed of low-born, uneducated men, incapable of being roused to any high enthusiasm, subsequently proved quite a nuisance.

Ivan IV. had but just resumed his seat upon the throne when couriers from the southern provinces brought the alarming intelligence that an immense army of combined Tartars and Turks had invaded the empire and were on the rapid march, burning and destroying all before them. Selim, the son and successor of Solyman the Magnificent, entered into an alliance with several oriental princes, who were to send him succors by the way of the Caspian Sea, and raised an army of three hundred thousand men. These troops were embarked at Constantinople, and, crossing the Black Sea and the Sea of Azof, entered Tauride. Here they were joined by a reinforcement of Crimean Tartars, consisting of forty thousand well-armed and veteran fighters. With this force the sultan marched directly across the country to the Russian city and province of Astrachan, at the mouth of the Volga.

But a heroic man, Zerebrinow, was in command of the fortresses in this remote province of the Russian empire. He immediately assembled all his available troops, and, advancing to meet the foe, selected his own ground for the battle in a narrow defile where the vast masses of the enemy would only encumber each other. Falling upon the invaders unexpectedly from ambuscades, he routed the Turks with great carnage. They were compelled to retreat, having lost nearly all their baggage and heavy artillery. The triumphant Russians pursued them all the way back to the city of Azof, cannonading them with the artillery and the ammunition they had wrested from their foes. Here the Turks attempted to make a final stand, but a chance shot from one of the guns penetrated the immense powder magazine, and an explosion so terrific ensued that two thirds of the city were entirely demolished.

The Turks, in consternation, now made a rush for their ships. But Zerebrinow, with coolness and sagacity which no horrors could disturb, had already planted his batteries to sweep them with a storm of bullets and balls. The cannonade was instantly commenced. The missiles of death fell like hail stones into the crowded boats and upon the crowded decks. Many of the ships were sunk, others disabled, and but a few, torn and riddled, succeeded in escaping to sea, where the most of them also perished beneath the waves of the stormy Euxine. Such was the utter desolation of this one brief war tempest which lasted but a few weeks.

Queen Elizabeth, anxious to maintain friendly relations with an empire so vast, and opening before her subjects such a field of profitable commerce, having been informed of the conspiracy against Ivan IV., of his abdication, and of his resumption of the crown, sent to him an embassador with expressions of her kindest wishes, and assured him that should he ever be reduced to the disagreeable necessity of leaving his empire, he would find a safe retreat in England, where he would be received and provided for in a manner suitable to his dignity, where he could enjoy the free exercise of his religion and be permitted to depart whenever he should wish.

The tolerant spirit manifested by Ivan IV. towards the

Lutherans, continued to disturb the ecclesiastics; and the clergy and nobles of the province of Novgorod, headed by the archbishop, formed a plot of dissevering Novgorod from the empire, and attaching it to the kingdom of Poland. This conspiracy assumed a very formidable attitude, and one of the brothers of the tzar was involved in it. Ivan immediately sent an army of fifteen thousand men to quell the revolt. We have no account of this transaction but from the pens of those who were envenomed by their animosity to the religious toleration of Ivan. We must consequently receive their narratives with some allowance.

The army, according to their account, ravaged the whole province; took the city by storm; and cut down in indiscriminate slaughter twenty-five thousand men, women and children. The brother of Ivan IV. was seized and thrown into prison, where he miserably perished. The archbishop was stripped of his canonical robes, clad in the dress of a harlequin, paraded through the streets on a gray mare, an object of derision to the people, and then was imprisoned for life. Such cruelty does not seem at all in accordance with the character of Ivan, while the grossest exaggeration is in accordance with the character of all civil and religious partisans.

War with Poland seems to have been the chronic state of Russia. Whenever either party could get a chance to strike the other a blow, the blow was sure to be given; and they were alike unscrupulous whether it were a saber blow in the face or a dagger thrust in the back. In the year 1571, a Russian army pursued a discomfited band of Livonian insurgents across the frontier into Poland. The Poles eagerly joined the insurgents, and sent envoys to invite the Crimean Tartars to invade Russia from Tauride, while Poland and Livonia should assail the empire from the west. The Tartars were always ready for war at a moment's notice. Seventy thousand men were immediately on the march. They rapidly traversed the southern provinces, trampling down all opposition until they reached the Oka. Here they encountered a few Russian troops who attempted to dispute the passage of the stream. They were, however, speedily overpowered by the Tartars and were compelled to retreat. Pressing on, they arrived within sixty miles of the city, when they found the Russians again concentered, but now in large numbers, to oppose their progress. A fierce battle was fought. Again the Russians were overpowered, and the Tartars, trampling them beneath their horses' hoofs, with yells of triumph, pressed on towards the metropolis. The whole city was in consternation, for it had no means of effectual resistance. Ivan IV. in his terror packed up his most valuable effects, and, with the royal family, fled to a strong fortress far away in the North.

From the battlements of the city, the banners of these terrible barbarians were soon seen on the approach. With bugle blasts and savage shouts they rushed in at the gates, swept the streets with their sabers, pillaged houses and churches, and set the city on fire in all directions. The city was at that time, according to the testimony of the cotemporary annalists, forty miles in circumference. The weltering flames rose and fell as in the crater of a volcano, and in six hours the city was in ashes. Thousands perished in the flames. The fire, communicating with a powder magazine, produced an explosion which uphove the buildings like an earthquake, and prostrated more than a third of a mile of the city walls. According to the most reliable testimony, there perished in Moscow, by fire and sword, from this one raid of the Tartars, more than one hundred and fifty thousand of its inhabitants.

The Tartars, tottering beneath the burden of their spoil, and dragging after them many thousand prisoners of distinction, slowly, proudly, defiantly retired. With barbaric genius they sent to the tzar a naked cimiter, accompanied by the following message:

"This is a token left to your majesty by an enemy, whose

revenge is still unsatiated, and who will soon return again to complete the work which he has but just begun."

Such is war. It is but a succession of miseries. A hundred and fifty thousand Tartars perished but a few months before in the waves of the Euxine. Now, a hundred and fifty thousand Russians perish, in their turn, amidst the flames of Moscow. When we contemplate the wars which have incessantly ravaged this globe, the history of man seems to be but the record of the strifes of demons, with occasional gleams of angel magnanimity.

After the retreat of the Tartars, Ivan IV. convened a council of war, punished with death those officers who had fled before the enemy as he himself had done; and, rendered pliant by accumulated misfortune, he presented such overtures to the King of Poland as to obtain the promise of a truce for three years. Soon after this, Sigismond, King of Poland, died. The crown was elective, and the nobles, who met to choose a new monarch, by a considerable majority invited Maximilian II., Emperor of Germany, to assume the scepter. They assigned as a reason for this choice, which surprised Europe, the religious liberality of the emperor, who, as they justly remarked, had conciliated the contending factions of the Christian world, and had acquired more glory by his pacific policy than other princes had acquired in the exploits of war.

A minority of the nobles were displeased with this choice, and refusing to accede to the vote of the majority, proceeded to another election, and chose Stephen Bathori, a warrior chief of Transylvania, as their sovereign.* The two parties now rallied around their rival candidates and prepared for war. Ivan IV. could not allow so favorable an opportunity to interfere in the politics of Poland to escape him. He immediately sent embassadors to Maximilian, offering to assist him with all the power of the Russian armies against Stephen

* See Empire of Austria, page 181.

Bathori. Maximilian gratefully acknowledged the generosity of the tzar, and promised to return the favor whenever an opportunity should be presented. At the same time, Stephen Bathori, who had already been crowned King of Poland, sent an embassador to Moscow to inform Ivan of his election and coronation, and to propose friendly relations with Russia. Ivan answered frankly that a treaty already existed between him and the Emperor Maximilian, but that, since he wished to live on friendly terms with Poland, whoever her monarch might be, he would send embassadors to examine into the claims of the rival candidates for the crown. Thus adroitly he endeavored to obtain for himself the position of umpire between Maximilian and Stephen Bathori. The death of the Emperor Maximilian on the 12th of October, 1576, settled this strife, and Stephen attained the undisputed sovereignty of Poland.

Almost the first measure of the new sovereign, in accordance with hereditary usage, was war against Russia. His object was to regain those territories which the tzar had heretofore wrested from the Poles. Apparently trivial incidents reveal the rude and fierce character of the times. Stephen chivalrously sent first an embassador, Basil Lapotinsky, to the court of Ivan, to demand the restitution of the provinces. Lapotinsky was accompanied by a numerous train of nobles, magnificently mounted and armed to the teeth. As the glittering cavalcade, protected by its flag of truce, swept along through the cities of Russia towards Moscow, and it became known that they were the bearers of an imperious message, demanding the surrender of portions of the Russian empire, the populace were with difficulty restrained from falling upon them.

Through a thousand dangers they reached Moscow. When there, Lapotinsky declared that he came not as a suppliant, but to present a claim which his master was prepared to enforce, if necessary, with the sword, and that, in accordance with the character of his mission, he was directed, in his audience with Ivan, to present the letter with one hand while he held his unsheathed saber in the other. The officers of the imperial household assured him that such bravado would inevitably cost him his life.

"The tzar," Lapotinsky replied, "can easily take my life, and he may do so if he please, but nothing shall prevent me from performing the duty with which I am intrusted, with the utmost exactitude."

The audience day arrived. Lapotinsky was conducted to the Kremlin. The tzar, in his imperial robes glittering with diamonds and pearls, received him in a magnificent hall. The haughty embassador, with great dignity and in respectful terms, yet bold and decisive, demanded reparation for the injuries which Russia had inflicted upon Poland. His gleaming saber was carelessly held in one hand and the letter to the tzar, from the King of Poland, in the other. Having finished his brief speech, he received a cimeter from one of his suite, and, advancing firmly, yet very respectfully, to the monarch, presented them both, saying,

"Here is peace and here is war. It is for your majesty to choose between them."

Ivan IV. was capable of appreciating the nobility of such a character. The intrepidity of the embassador, which was defiled with no comminglings of insolence, excited his admiration. The emperor, with a smile, took the letter, which was written on parchment in the Russian language and sealed with a seal of gold. Slowly and carefully he read it, and then addressing the embassador, said,

"Such menaces will not induce Russia to surrender her dominions to Poland. We, who have vanquished the Poles on so many fields of battle, who have conquered the Tartars of Kezan and Astrachan, and who have triumphed over the forces of the Ottoman empire, will soon cause the King of Poland to repent his rashness."

He then dismissed the embassador, ordering him to be

treated with the respect due his high station. War being thus formally declared, both parties prepared to prosecute it with the utmost vigor. The tzar immediately commenced raising a large army, reinforced his garrisons, and sent a secret envoy to Tauride, to excite the Crimean Tartars to invade Poland on the south-east while Russia should make an assault from the north.

The Poles opened the campaign by crossing the frontiers with a large army, seizing several minor cities and laying siege to the important fortress of Polotzk. After a long siege, which constituted one of those terrific tragedies of blood and woe with which the pages of history are filled, but which no pen can describe and no imagination can conceive, the city, a pile of gory and smouldering ruins, fell into the hands of the Poles. Battle after battle, siege after siege ensued, in nearly all of which the Poles were successful. They were guided by their monarch in person, a veteran warrior, who possessed extraordinary military skill. The blasts of winter drove both parties from the field. But, in the earliest spring, the campaign was opened again with redoubled energy. Again the Poles, who had obtained strong reinforcements of troops from Germany and Hungary, were signally successful. Though the fighting was constant and arduous, the whole campaign was but a series of conquests on the part of Stephen, and when the snows of another winter whitened the fields, the Polish banners were waving over large portions of the Russian territory. The details of these scenes are revolting. Fire, blood and the brutal passions of demoniac men were combined in deeds of horror, the recital of which makes the ears to tingle.

Before the buds of another spring had opened into leaf, the contending armies were again upon the march. Poland had now succeeded in enlisting Sweden in her cause, and Russia began to be quite seriously imperiled. Riga, on the Dwina, soon fell into the hands of the Poles, and their banners were resistlessly on the advance. Ivan IV., much dejected, proposed terms of peace. Stephen refused to treat unless Russia would surrender the whole of Livonia, a province nearly three times as large as the State of Massachusetts, to Poland. The tzar was compelled essentially to yield to these hard terms.

The treaty of peace was signed on the 15th of January, 1582. Ivan IV. surrendered to Poland all of Livonia which bordered on Poland, which contained thirty-four towns and castles, together with several other important fortresses on the frontiers. A truce was concluded for ten years, should both parties live so long. But should either die, the survivor was at liberty immediately to attack the territory of the deceased. No mention whatever was made of Sweden in this treaty. This neglect gave such offense to the Swedish court, that, in petty revenge, they sent an *Italian cook* to the Polish court as an embassador with the most arrogant demands. Stephen very wisely treated the insult, which he probably deserved, with contempt.

The result of this war, so humiliating to Russia, rendered Ivan very unpopular. Murmurs loud and deep were heard all over the empire. Many of the nobles threw themselves at the feet of the tzar and entreated him not to assent to so disgraceful a treaty, assuring him that the whole nation were ready at his call to rise and drive the invaders from the empire. Ivan was greatly incensed, and petulantly replied that if they were not satisfied with his administration they had better choose another sovereign. Suspecting that his son was inciting this movement, and that he perhaps was aiming at the crown, Ivan assailed him in the bitterest terms of reproach. The young prince replied in a manner which so exasperated his father, that he struck him with a staff which he had in his hand. The staff was tipped with an iron ferule which unfortunately hit the young man on the temple, and he fell senseless at his father's feet.

The anguish of Ivan was unspeakable. His paroxysm of

anger instantly gave place to a more intense paroxysm of grief and remorse. He threw himself upon the body of his son, pressed him fervently to his heart, and addressed him in the most endearing terms of affection and affliction. The prince so far revived as to be able to exchange a few words with his father, but in four days he died. The blow which deprived the son of life, for ever after deprived the father of peace. He was seldom again seen to smile. Any mention of his son would ever throw him into a paroxysm of tears. For a long time he could with difficulty be persuaded to take any nourishment or to change his dress. With the utmost possible demonstrations of grief and respect the remains of the prince were conveyed to the grave. The death of this young man was a calamity to Russia. He was the worthy son of Anastasia, and from his mother he had inherited both genius and moral worth. By a subsequent marriage Ivan had two other sons, Feodor and Dmitri. But they were of different blood; feeble in intellect and possessed no requisites for the exalted station opening before them.

CHAPTER XVI.

THE STORMS OF HEREDITARY SUCCESSION.

FROM 1582 TO 1608.

ANGUISH AND DEATH OF IVAN IV.—HIS CHARACTER.—FEODOR AND DMITRI.—USURPATION OF BORIS GUDENOW.—THE POLISH ELECTION.—CONQUEST OF SIBERIA.—ASSASSINATION OF DMITRI.—DEATH OF FEODOR.—BORIS CROWNED KING.—CONSPIRACIES.—REAPPEARANCE OF DMITRI.—BORIS POISONED.—THE PRETENDER CROWNED.—EMBARRASSMENTS OF DMITRI.—A NEW PRETENDER.—ASSASSINATION OF DMITRI.—CROWNING OF ZUSKI.—INDIGNATION OF POLAND.—HISTORICAL ROMANCE.

THE hasty blow which deprived the son of Ivan of life was also fatal to the father. He never recovered from the effects. After a few months of anguish and remorse, Ivan IV. sank sorrowing to the grave. Penitent, prayerful and assured that his sins were forgiven, he met death with perfect composure. The last days of his life were devoted exclusively to such preparations for his departure that the welfare of his people might be undisturbed. He ordered a general act of amnesty to be proclaimed to all the prisoners throughout all the empire, abolished several onerous taxes, restored several confiscated estates to their original owners, and urged his son, Feodor, who was to be his successor, to make every possible endeavor to live at peace with his neighbors, that Russia might thus be saved from the woes of war. Exhausted by a long interview with his son, he took a bath; on coming out he reclined upon a couch, and suddenly, without a struggle or a groan, was dead.

Ivan IV. has ever been regarded as one of the most illustrious of the Russian monarchs. He was eminently a learned prince for the times in which he lived, entertaining uncommonly just views both of religion and politics. In religion he was tolerant far above his age, allowing no Christians to be persecuted for their belief. We regret that this high praise must be limited by his treatment of the Jews, whom he could not endure. With conscientiousness, unenlightened and bigoted, he declared that those who had betrayed and crucified the Saviour of the world ought not to be tolerated by any Christian prince. He accordingly ordered every Jew either to be baptized into the Christian faith or to depart from the empire.

Ivan was naturally of a very hasty temper, which was nurtured by the cruel and shameful neglect of his early years. Though he struggled against this infirmity, it would occasionally break out in paroxysms which caused bitter repentance. The death of his son, caused by one of these outbreaks, was the great woe of his life. Still he was distinguished for his love of justice. At stated times the aggrieved of every rank were admitted to his presence, where they in person presented their petitions. If any minister or governor was found guilty of oppression, he was sure to meet with condign punishment. This impartiality, from which no noble was exempted, at times exasperated greatly the haughty aristocracy. He was also inflexible in his determination to confer office only upon those who were worthy of the trust. No solicitations or views of self-interest could induce him to swerve from this resolve. Intemperance he especially abominated, and frowned upon the degrading vice alike in prince or peasant. He conferred an inestimable favor upon Russia by causing a compilation, for the use of his subjects, of a body of laws, which was called "The Book of Justice." This code was presented to the judges, and was regarded as authority in all law proceedings.

The historians of those days record that his memory was so remarkable that he could call all the officers of his army by name, and could even remember the name of every prisoner he had taken, numbering many thousands. In those days of dim enlightenment, when the masses were little elevated above the animal, the popular mind was more easily impressed by material than intellectual grandeur. It was then deemed necessary, among the unenlightened nations of Europe, to overawe the multitude by the splendor of the throne—by scepters, robes and diadems glittering with priceless jewels and with gold. The crown regalia of Russia were inestimably rich. The robe of the monarch was of purple, embroidered with precious stones, and even his shoes sparkled with diamonds of dazzling luster.

When he sat upon his throne to receive foreign embassadors, or the members of his own court, he held in his right hand a globe, the emblem of universal monarchy, enriched with all the jeweled splendor which art could entwine around it. In his left hand he held a scepter, which also dazzled the eye by its superb embellishments. His fingers were laden with the most precious gems the Indies could afford. Whenever he appeared in public, the arms of the empire, finely embroidered upon a spread eagle, and magnificently adorned, were borne as a banner before him; and the masses of the people bowed before their monarch, thus arrayed, as though he were a god.

Ivan IV. left two sons, Feodor and Dmitri. Feodor, who succeeded his father, was twenty years of age, weak, characterless, though quite amiable. In his early youth his chief pleasure seemed to consist in ringing the bells of Moscow, which led his father, at one time, to say that he was fitter to be the son of a sexton than of a prince. Dmitri was an infant. He was placed, by his father's will, under the tutelage of an energetic, ambitious noble, by the name of Bogdan Bielski. This aspiring nobleman, conscious of the incapacity of Feodor to govern, laid his plans to obtain the throne for himself.

Feodor was crowned immediately after the death of his father, and proceeded at once to carry out the provisions of his will by liberating the prisoners, abolishing the taxes and restoring confiscated estates. He also abolished the body guard of the tzar, which had become peculiarly obnoxious to the nation. These measures rendered him, for a time, very popular. This popularity thwarted Bielski in the plan of organizing the people and the nobles in a conspiracy against the young monarch, and the nobles even became so much alarmed by the proceedings of the haughty minister, who was so evidently aiming at the usurpation of the throne, that they besieged him in his castle. The fortress was strong, and the powerful feudal lord, rallying his vassals around him, made a valiant and a protracted defense. At length, finding that he would be compelled to surrender, he attempted to escape in disguise. Being taken a captive, he was offered his choice, death, or the renunciation of all political influence and departure into exile. He chose the latter, and retired beyond the Volga to one of the most remote provinces of Kezan.

Feodor had married the daughter of one of the most illustrious of his nobles. His father-in-law, a man of peculiar address and capacity, with ability both to conceive and execute the greatest undertakings, soon attained supremacy over the mind of the feeble monarch. The name of this noble, who became renowned in Russian annals, was Boris Gudenow He had the rare faculty of winning the favor of all whom he approached. With rapid strides he attained the posts of prime minister, commander-in-chief and co-regent of the empire. A Polish embassador at this time visited Moscow, and, witnessing the extreme feebleness of Feodor, sent word to his ambitious master, Stephen Bathori, that nothing would be easier than to invade Russia successfully; that Smolensk could easily be taken, and that thence the Polish army might find an almost unobstructed march to Moscow. But death soon removed the Polish monarch from the labyrinths of war and diplomacy.

Boris was now virtually the monarch of Russia, reigning,

however, in the name of Feodor. We have before mentioned that Poland was an elective monarchy. Immediately upon the death of a sovereign, the nobles, with their bands of retainers, often eighty thousand in number, met upon a large plain, where they spent many days in intrigues and finally in the election of a new chieftain. Boris Gudenow now roused all his energies in the endeavor to unite Poland and Russia under one monarchy by the election of Feodor as sovereign of the latter kingdom. The Polish nobles, proud and self-confident, and apprised of the incapacity of Feodor, were many of them in favor of the plan, as Boris had adroitly intimated to them that they might regard the measure rather as the annexing Russia to Poland than Poland to Russia. All that Boris cared for was the fact accomplished. He was willing that the agents of his schemes should be influenced by any motives which might be most efficacious.

The Polish diet met in a stormy session, and finally, a majority of its members, instead of voting for Feodor, elected Prince Sigismond, a son of John, King of Sweden. This election greatly alarmed Russia, as it allied Poland and Sweden by the most intimate ties, and might eventually place the crown of both of those powerful kingdoms upon the same brow. These apprehensions were increased by the fact that the Crimean Tartars soon again began to make hostile demonstrations, and it was feared that they were moving only in accordance with suggestions which had been sent to them from Poland and Sweden, and that thus a triple alliance was about to desolate the empire. The Tartars commenced their march. But Boris met them with such energy that they were driven back in utter discomfiture.

The nothern portion of Asia consisted of a vast, desolate, thinly-peopled country called Siberia. It was bounded by the Caucasian and Altai mountains on the south, the Ural mountains on the west, the Pacific Ocean on the east, and the Frozen Ocean on the north. Most of the region was within the limits of the frozen zone, and the most southern sections were cold and inhospitable, enjoying but a gleam of summer sunshine. This country, embracing over four millions of square miles, being thus larger than the whole of Europe, contained but about two millions of inhabitants. It was watered by some of the most majestic rivers on the globe, the Oby, Enisei and the Lena. The population consisted mostly of wandering Mohammedan Tartars, in a very low state of civilization. At that time there were but two important towns in this region, Tura and Tobolsk. Some of the barbarians of this region descended to the shores of the Volga, in a desolating, predatory excursion. A Russian army drove them back, pursued them to their homes, took both of these towns, erected fortresses, and gradually brought the whole of Siberia under Russian sway. This great conquest was achieved almost without bloodshed.

Boris Gudenow now exercised all the functions of sovereign authority. His energy had enriched Russia with the accession of Siberia. He now resolved to lay aside the feeble prince Feodor, who nominally occupied the throne, and to place the crown upon his own brow. It seemed to him an easy thing to appropriate the emblems of power, since he already enjoyed all the prerogatives of royalty. Under the pretense of rewarding, with important posts of trust, the most efficient of the nobles, he removed all those whose influence he had most to dread, to distant provinces and foreign embassies. He then endeavored, by many favors, to win the affections of the populace of Moscow.

The young prince Dmitri had now attained his ninth year, and was residing, under the care of his tutors, at the city of Uglitz, about two hundred miles from Moscow. Uglitz, with its dependencies, had been assigned to him for his appanage. Gudenow deemed it essential, to his secure occupancy of the throne, that this young prince should be put out of the way. He accordingly employed a Russian officer, by the promise of immense rewards, to assassinate the child And then, the deed having been performed, to prevent the possibility of his agency in it being divulged, he caused another low-born murderer to track the path of the officer and plunge a dagger into his bosom. Both murders were successfully accomplished.

The news of the assassination of the young prince soon reached Moscow, and caused intense excitement. Gudenow was by many suspected, though he endeavored to stifle the report by clamorous expressions of horror and indignation, and by apparently making the most strenuous efforts to discover the murderers. As an expression of his rage, he sent troops to demolish the fortress of Uglitz, and to drive the inhabitants from the city, because they had, as he asserted, harbored the assassins. Soon after this Feodor was suddenly taken ill. He lingered upon his bed for a few days in great pain, and then died. When the king was lying upon this dying bed, Boris Gudenow, who, it will be recollected, was the father of the wife of Feodor, succeeded in obtaining from him a sort of bequest of the throne, and immediately upon the death of the king, he assumed the state of royalty as a duty enjoined upon him by this bequest. The death of Feodor terminated the reign of the house of Ruric, which had now governed Russia for more than seven hundred years.

Not a little artifice was still requisite to quell the indignant passions which were rising in the bosoms of the nobles. But Gudenow was a consummate master of his art, and through the intrigues of years had the programme of operations all arranged. According to custom, six weeks were devoted to mourning for Feodor. Boris then assembled the nobility and principal citizens of Moscow, in the Kremlin, and, to the unutterable surprise of many of them, declared that he could not consent to assume the weighty cares and infinite responsibilities of royalty; that the empire was unfortunately left without a sovereign, and that they must proceed to designate the one to whom the crown should be transferred; that he, worn down with the toils of State, had decided to retire to a monastery, and devote the remainder of his days to poverty, retirement and to God. He immediately took leave of the astonished and perplexed assembly, and withdrew to a convent about three miles from Moscow.

The partisans of Boris were prepared to act their part. They stated that intelligence had arrived that the Tartars, with an immense army, had commenced the invasion of Russia; that Boris alone was familiar with the condition and resources of the empire, and with the details of administration —that he was a veteran soldier, and that his military genius and vigorous arm were requisite to beat back the foe. These considerations were influential, and a deputation was chosen to urge Boris, as he loved his country, to continue in power and accept the scepter, which, as prime minister, he had so long successfully wielded. Boris affected the most extreme reluctance. The populace of Moscow, whose favor he had purchased, surrounded the convent in crowds, and with vehemence, characteristic of their impulsive, childish natures, threw themselves upon the ground, tore their hair, beat their breasts, and declared that they would never return to their homes unless Boris would consent to be their sovereign.

Pretending, at last, to be overcome by these entreaties, Boris consented to raise and lead an army to repel the Tartars, and he promised that should Providence prosper him in this enterprise, he would regard it as an indication that it was the will of Heaven that he should ascend the throne. He immediately called all his tremendous energies into exercise, and in a few months collected an army, of the nobles and of the militia, amounting to five hundred thousand men. With great pomp he rode through the ranks of this mighty host, receiving their enthusiastic applause. In that day, as neither telegraphs, newspapers or stage-coaches existed, intelligence was transmitted with difficulty, and very slowly.

The story of the Tartar invasion proved a sham. Boris had originated it to accomplish his purposes. He amused and conciliated the soldiers with magnificent parades, intimating that the Tartars, alarmed by his vast preparations, had not dared to advance against him. A year's pay was ordered for each one of the soldiers. The nobles received gratuities and were entertained by the tzar in festivals, at which parties of ten thousand, day after day, were feasted, during an interval of six weeks. Boris then returned to Moscow. The people met him several miles from the city, and conducted him in triumph to the Kremlin. He was crowned, with great pomp, Emperor of Russia, on the 1st of September, 1577.

Boris watched, with an eagle eye, all those who could by any possibility disturb his reign or endanger the permanence of the new dynasty which he wished to establish. Some of the princes of the old royal family were forbidden to marry ; others were banished to Siberia. The diadem, thus usurped, proved indeed a crown of thorns. That which is founded in crime, can generally by crime alone be perpetuated. The manners of the usurper were soon entirely altered. He had been affable, easy of access, and very popular. But now he became haughty, reserved and suspicious. Wishing to strengthen his dynasty by royal alliances, he proposed the marriage of his daughter to Gustavus, son of Erie XIV., King of Sweden. He accordingly invited Gustavus to Moscow, making him pompous promises. The young prince was received with magnificent display and loaded with presents. But there was soon a falling out between Boris and his intended son-in-law, and the young prince was dismissed in disgrace. He however succeeded in establishing a treaty of peace with the Poles, which was to continue twenty years He also was successful in contracting an alliance for his daughter Axinia, with Duke John of Denmark. The marriage was celebrated in Moscow in 1602 with great splendor. But even before the marriage festivities were closed, the duke was taken sick and died, to the inexpressible disappointment of Boris.

The Turks from Constantinople sent an embassy to Moscow with rich presents, proposing a treaty of friendship and alliance. But Boris declined the presents and dismissed the embassadors, saying that he could never be friendly to the Turks, as they were the enemies of Christianity. Like many other men, he could trample upon the precepts of the gospel, and yet be zealous of Christianity as a doctrinal code or an institution.

A report was now circulated that the young Dmitri was still alive, that his mother, conscious of the danger of his assassination, had placed the prince in a position of safety, and that another child had been assassinated in his stead. This rumor overwhelmed the guilty soul of Boris with melancholy. His fears were so strongly excited, that several nobles, who were supposed to be in the interests of the young prince, were put to the rack to extort a confession. But no positive information respecting Dmitri could be gained. The mother of Dmitri was banished to an obscure fortress six hundred miles from Moscow.

The emissaries of Boris were everywhere busy to detect, if possible, the hiding place of Dmitri. Intelligence was at length brought to the Kremlin that two monks had escaped from a convent and had fled to Poland, and that it was apprehended that one of them was the young prince in disguise; it was also said that Weisnowiski, prince of Kief, was protector of Dmitri, and, in concert with others, was preparing a movement to place him upon the throne of his ancestors. Boris was thrown into paroxysms of terror. Not knowing what else to do, he franticly sent a party of Cossacks to murder Weisnowiski; but the prince was on his guard, and the enterprise failed.

The question, "Have we a Bourbon among us?" has agitated the whole of the United States. The question, "Have we a Dmitri among us?" then agitated Russia far more intensely. It was a question of the utmost practical importance, involving civil war and the removal of the new dynasty for the restoration of the old. Whether the person said to be Dmitri were really such, is a question which can now never be settled. The monk Griska Utropeja, who declared himself to be the young prince, sustained his claim with such an array of evidence as to secure the support of a large portion of the Russians, and also the coöperation of the court of Poland. The claims of Griska were brought up before the Polish diet and carefully examined. He was then acknowledged by them as the legitimate heir to the crown of Russia. An army was raised to restore him to his ancestral throne. Sigismond, the King of Poland, with ardor espoused his cause.

Boris immediately dispatched an embassy to Warsaw to remind Sigismond of the treaty of alliance into which he had entered, and to insist upon his delivering up the pretended Dmitri, dead or alive. A threat was added to the entreaty: "If you countenance this impostor," said Boris, "you will draw down upon you a war which you may have cause to repent."

Sigismond replied, that though he had no doubt that Griska was truly the Prince Dmitri, and, as such, entitled to the throne of Russia, still he had no disposition personally to embark in the advocacy of his rights; but, that if any of his nobles felt disposed to espouse his claims with arms or money, he certainly should do nothing to thwart them. The Polish nobles, thus encouraged, raised an army of forty thousand men, which they surrendered to Griska. He, assuming the name of Dmitri, placed himself at their head, and boldly commenced a march upon Moscow. As soon as he entered the Russian territories many nobles hastened to his banners, and several important cities declared for him.

Boris was excessively alarmed. With characteristic energy he speedily raised an army of two hundred thousand men, and then was in the utmost terror lest this very army should pass over to the ranks of his foes. He applied to Sweden and to Denmark to help him, but both kingdoms refused. Dmitri advanced triumphantly, and laid siege to Novgorod on the 21st of December, 1605. For five months the war continued with varying success. Boris made every attempt to secure the assassination of Griska, but the wary chieftain was on his guard, and all such endeavors were frustrated. Griska at length decided to resort to the same weapons. An officer was sent to the Kremlin with a feigned account of a victory obtained over the troops of Dmitri. This officer succeeded in mingling poison with the food of Boris. The drug was so deadly that the usurper dropped and expired almost without a struggle and without a groan.

As soon as Boris was dead, his widow, a woman of great ambition and energy, lost not an hour in proclaiming the succession of her son, Feodor. The officers of the army were promptly summoned to take the oath of allegiance to the new sovereign. Feodor was but fifteen years of age, a thoroughly spoilt boy, proud, domineering, selfish and cruel. There was now a revolt in the army of the late tzar. Several of the officers embraced the cause of Griska, declaring their full conviction that he was the Prince Dmitri, and they carried over to his ranks a large body of the soldiers.

The defection of the army caused great consternation at court. The courtiers, eager to secure the favor of the prince whose star was so evidently in the ascendant, at once abandoned the hapless Feodor and his enraged mother; and the halls of the Kremlin and the streets of Moscow were soon resounding with the name of Dmitri. A proclamation was published declaring general amnesty, and rich rewards to all who should recognize and support the rights of their legitimate prince, but that his opponents must expect no mercy. The populace immediately rose in revolt against Feodor.

They assailed the Kremlin. In a resistless inundation they forced its gates, seized the young tzar, with his mother, sister and other relatives, and hurried them all to prison.

Dmitri was at Thula when he received intelligence of this revolution. He immediately sent an officer, Basilius Galitzan, to Moscow to receive the oath of fidelity of the city, and, at the same time, he diabolically sent an assassin, one Ivan Bogdanoff, with orders to strangle Feodor and his mother in the prison, but with directions not to hurt his sister. Bogdanoff reluctantly executed his mission. On the 15th of July, 1605, Dmitri made his triumphal entry into Moscow. He was received with all the noisy demonstrations of public rejoicing, and, on the 29th of July, was crowned, with extraordinary grandeur, Emperor of all the Russias.

The ceremonies of the triumphal entrance are perhaps worthy of record. A detachment of Polish horse in brilliant uniform led the procession, headed by a numerous band of trumpeters. Then came the gorgeous coach of Dmitri, empty, drawn by six horses, richly caparisoned, and preceded, followed and flanked by dense columns of musqueteers. Next came a procession of the clergy in their ecclesiastical robes, and with the banners of the church. This procession was led by the bishops, who bore effigies of the Virgin Mary and of St. Nicholas, the patron saint of Russia. Following the clergy appeared Dmitri, mounted on a white charger, and surrounded by a splendid retinue. He proceeded first to the church of Notre Dame, where a Te Deum was chanted, and where the new monarch received the sacrament. He then visited the tomb of Ivan IV., and kneeling upon it, as the tomb of his father, implored God's blessing. Perceiving that the body of Boris Gudenow had received interment in the royal cemetery, he ordered his remains, with those of his wife and son, all three of whom Dmitri had caused to be assassinated, to be removed to a common churchyard without the city.

Either to silence those who might doubt his legitimacy

or being truly the son of Ivan IV., he sent two of the nobles, with a brilliant retinue, to the convent, more than six hundred miles from Moscow, to which Boris had banished the widow of Ivan. They were to conduct the queen dowager to the capital. As she approached the city, Dmitri went out to receive her, accompanied by a great number of his nobles. As soon as he perceived her coach, he alighted, went on foot to meet his alleged mother, and threw himself into her arms with every demonstration of joy and affection, which embraces she returned with equal tenderness. Then, with his head uncovered, and walking by the side of her carriage, he conducted her to the city and to the Kremlin. He ever after treated her with the deference due to a mother, and received from her corresponding proofs of confidence and affection.

But Dmitri was thoroughly a bad man, and every day became more unpopular. He debauched the young sister of Feodor, and then shut her up in a convent. He banished seventy noble families who were accused of being the friends of Boris, and gave their estates and dignities to his Polish partisans. A party was soon organized against him, who busily circulated reports that he was an impostor, and a conspiracy was formed to take his life. Perplexities and perils now gathered rapidly around his throne. He surrounded himself with Polish guards, and thus increased the exasperation of his subjects.

To add to his perplexities, another claimant of the crown appeared, who declared himself to be the son of the late tzar, Feodor, son of Ivan IV. This young man, named Peter, was seventeen years of age. He had raised his standard on the other side of the Volga, and had rallied four thousand partisans around him. In the meantime, Dmitri had made arrangements for his marriage with Mariana Meneiski, a Polish princess, of the Roman church. This princess was married to the tzar by proxy, in Cracow, and in January, 1606, with a numerous retinue set out on her journey to Moscow. She did not reach the capital of Moscow until the 1st of May. Her father's whole family, and several thousand armed Polanders, by way of guard, accompanied her. Many of the Polish nobles also took this opportunity of visiting Russia, and a multitude of merchants put themselves in her train for purposes of traffic.

The tzarina was met, at some distance from Moscow, by the royal guard, and escorted to the city, where she was received with ringing of bells, shoutings, discharge of cannons and all the ordinary and extraordinary demonstrations of popular joy. On the 8th of May, the ceremony of blessing the marriage was performed by the patriarch, and immediately after she was crowned tzarina with greater pomp than Russia had ever witnessed before. But the appearance of this immense train of armed Poles incensed the Russians; and the clergy, who were jealous of the encroachments of the church of Rome, were alarmed in behalf of their religion. An intrepid noble, Zuski, now resolved, by the energies of a popular insurrection, to rid the throne of Dmitri. With great sagacity and energy the conspiracy was formed. The tzarina was to give a grand entertainment on the evening of the 17th of May, and the conspirators fixed upon that occasion for the consummation of their plan. Twenty thousand troops were under the orders of Zuski, and he had led them all into the city, under the pretense of having them assist in the festival.

At six o'clock in the morning of the appointed day these troops, accompanied by some thousands of the populace, surrounded the palace and seized its gates. A division was then sent in, who commenced the indiscriminate massacre of all who were, or who looked like Polanders. It was taken for granted that all in the palace were either Poles or their partisans. The alarm bells were now rung, and Zuski traversed the streets with a drawn saber in one hand and a cross in the other, rousing the ignorant populace by the cry that the Poles had taken up arms to murder the Russians. Dmitri, in his chamber, hearing the cries of the dying and the shrieks of those who fled before the assassins, leaped from his window into the court yard, and, by his fall, dislocated his thigh. He was immediately seized, conveyed into the grand hall of audience, and a strong guard was set over him.

The murderers ransacked the palace, penetrating every room, killing every Polish man and treating the Polish ladies with the utmost brutality. They inquired eagerly for the tzarina, but she was nowhere to be found. She had concealed herself beneath the hoop of an elderly lady whose gray hairs and withered cheek had preserved her from violence. Zuski now went to the dowager tzarina, the widow of Ivan IV., and demanded that she should take her oath upon the Gospels whether Dmitri were her son. He reported that, thus pressed, she confessed that he was an impostor, and that her true son had perished many years before. The conspirators now fell upon Dmitri and his body was pierced with a thousand dagger thrusts. His mangled remains were then dragged through the streets and burned. Mariana was soon after arrested and sent to prison. It is said that nearly two thousand Poles perished in this massacre.

Even to the present day opinion is divided in Russia in regard to Dmitri, whether he was an impostor or the son of Ivan IV. Respecting his character there is no dispute. All that can be said in his favor is that he would not commit an atrocious crime unless impelled to it by very strong temptation. There was now no one who seemed to have any legitimate title to the throne of Russia.

The nobles and the senators who were at Moscow then met to proceed to the election of a new sovereign. It was an event almost without a parallel in Russian history. The lords, though very friendly in their deliberations, found it difficult to decide into whose hands to intrust the scepter. It was at last unanimously concluded to make an appeal to the people. Their voice was for Zuski. He was accordingly declared tzar and was soon after crowned with a degree of unanimity which, though well authenticated, seems inexplicable.

The Poles were exasperated beyond measure at the massacre of so many of their nobles and at the insult offered to Mariana, the tzarina. But Poland was at that time distracted by civil strife, and the king found it expedient to postpone the hour of vengeance. Zuski commenced his reign by adopting measures which gave him great popularity with the adjoining kingdoms, while they did not diminish the favorable regards of the people. But suddenly affairs assumed a new aspect, so strange that a writer of fiction would hardly have ventured to imagine it. An artful man, a schoolmaster in Poland, who could speak the Russian language, declared that he was Dmitri; that he had escaped from the massacre in his palace, and that it was another man, mistaken for him, whom the assassins had killed. Poland, inspired by revenge, eagerly embraced this man's cause. Mariana, who had been liberated from prison, was let into the secret, and willing to ascend again to the grandeur from which she had fallen, entered with cordial coöperation into this new intrigue. The widowed tzarina and the Polish adventurer contrived their first meeting in the presence of a large concourse of nobles and citizens. They rushed together in a warm embrace, while tears of affected transport bedewed their cheeks. The farce was so admirably performed that many were deceived, and this new Dmitri and the tzarina occupied for several days the same tent in the Polish encampment, apparently as husband and wife.

CHAPTER XVII.

A CHANGE OF DYNASTY.

FROM 1608 TO 1680.

CONQUESTS BY POLAND.—SWEDEN IN ALLIANCE WITH RUSSIA.—GRANDEUR OF POLAND.—LADISLAUS ELECTED KING OF RUSSIA.—COMMOTIONS AND INSURRECTIONS.—REJECTION OF LADISLAUS AND ELECTION OF MICHAEL FEODOR ROMANOW.—SORROW OF HIS MOTHER.—PACIFIC CHARACTER OF ROMANOW.—CHOICE OF A BRIDE.—EUDOCHIA STRESCHNEW.—THE ARCHBISHOP FEODOR.—DEATH OF MICHAEL AND ACCESSION OF ALEXIS.—LOVE IN THE PALACE.—SUCCESSFUL INTRIGUE.—MOBS IN MOSCOW.—CHANGE IN THE CHARACTER OF THE TZAR.—TURKISH INVASIONS.—ALLIANCE BETWEEN RUSSIA AND POLAND.

THIS public testimonial of conjugal love led men, who had before doubted the pretender, to repose confidence in his claims. The King of Poland took advantage of the confusion now reigning in Russia to extend his dominions by wresting still more border territory from his great rival. In this exigence, Zuski purchased the loan of an army of five thousand men from Sweden by surrendering Livonia to the Swedes. With these succors united to his own troops, he marched to meet the pretended Dmitri. There was now universal confusion in Russia. The two hostile armies, avoiding a decisive engagement, were maneuvering and engaging in incessant petty skirmishes, which resulted only in bloodshed and misery. Thus five years of national woe lingered away. The people became weary of both the claimants for the crown, and the nobles boldly met, regardless of the rival combatants, and resolved to choose a new sovereign.

Poland had then attained the summit of its greatness. As an energetic military power, it was superior to Russia. To conciliate Poland, whose aggressions were greatly feared, the Russian nobles chose, for their sovereign, Ladislaus, son of Sigismond, the King of Poland. They hoped thus to withdraw the Polish armies from the banners of the pretended Dmitri, and also to secure peace for their war-blasted kingdom.

Ladislaus accepted the crown. Zuski was seized, deposed, shaved, dressed in a friar's robe and shut up in a convent to count his beads. He soon died of that malignant poison, grief. Dmitri made a show of opposition, but he was soon assassinated by his own men, who were convinced of the hopelessness of his cause. His party, however, lasted for many years, bringing forward a young man who was called his son. At one time there was quite an enthusiasm in his favor, crowds flocked to his camp, and he even sent embassadors to Gustavus IX., King of Sweden, proposing an alliance. At last he was betrayed by some of his own party, and was sent to Moscow, where he was hanged.

Sigismond was much perplexed in deciding whether to consent to his son's accepting the crown of Russia. That kingdom was now in such a state of confusion and weakness that he was quite sanguine that he would be able to conquer it by force of arms and bring the whole empire under the dominion of his own scepter. His armies were already besieging Smolensk, and the city was hourly expected to fall into their hands. This would open to them almost an unobstructed march to Moscow. The Poles, generally warlike and ambitious of conquest, represented to Sigismond that it would be far more glorious for him to be the conqueror of Russia than to be merely the father of its tzar.

Sigismond, with trivial excuses, detained his son in Poland, while, under various pretexts, he continued to pour his troops into Russia. Ten thousand armed Poles were sent to Moscow to be in readiness to receive the newly-elected monarch upon his arrival. Their general, Stanislaus, artfully contrived even to place a thousand of these Polish troops in garrison in the citadel of Moscow. These foreign soldiers at last became so insolent that there was a general rising of the populace, and they were threatened with utter extermination. The storm of passion thus raised, no earthly power could quell. The awful slaughter was commenced, and the Poles, conscious of their danger, resorted to the horrible but only measure which could save them from destruction. They immediately set fire to the city in many different places. The city then consisted of one hundred and eighty thousand houses, most of them being of wood. As the flames rose, sweeping from house to house and from street to street, the inhabitants, distracted by the endeavor to save their wives, their children and their property, threw down their arms and dispersed. When thus helpless, the Poles fell upon them, and one of the most awful massacres ensued of which history gives any record. A hundred thousand of the wretched people of Moscow perished beneath the Polish cimeters. For fifteen days the depopulated and smouldering capital was surrendered to pillage. The royal treasury, the churches, the convents were all plundered. The Poles, then, laden with booty, but leaving a garrison in the citadel, evacuated the ruined city and commenced their march to Poland.

These horrors roused the Russians. An army under a heroic general, Zachary Lippenow, besieged the Polish garrison, starved them into a surrender, and put them all to death. The nobles then met, declared the election of Ladislaus void, on account of his not coming to Moscow to accept it, and again proceeded to the choice of a sovereign. After long deliberation, one man ventured to propose a candidate very different from any who had before been thought of. It was Michael Feodor Romanow. He was a studious, philosophic young man, seventeen years of age. His father was archbishop of Rostow, a man of exalted reputation, both for genius and piety. Michael, with his mother, was in a convent at Castroma. It was modestly urged that in this young man there were centered all the qualifications essential for the promotion of the tranquillity of the State. There were but three males of his family living, and thus the State would avoid the evil of having numerous relatives of the prince to be cared for. He was entirely free from embroilments in the late troubles. As his father was a clergyman of known piety and virtue, he would counsel his son to peace, and would conscientiously seek the best good of the empire.

The proposition, sustained by such views, was accepted with general acclaim. There were several nobles from Castroma who testified that though they were not personally acquainted with young Romanow, they believed him to be a youth of unusual intelligence, discretion and moral worth. As the nobles were anxious not to act hastily in a matter of such great importance, they dispatched two of their number to Castroma with a letter to the mother of Michael, urging her to repair immediately with her son to Moscow.

The affectionate, judicious mother, upon the reception of this letter, burst into tears of anguish, lamenting the calamity which was impending.

"My son," she said, "my only son is to be taken from me to be placed upon the throne, only to be miserably slaughtered like so many of the tzars who have preceded him."

She wrote to the electors entreating them that her son might be excused, saying that he was altogether too young to reign, that his father was a prisoner in Poland, and that her son had no relations capable of assisting him with their advice. This letter, on the whole, did but confirm the assembly of nobles in their conviction that they could not make a better choice than that of the young Romanow. They accordingly, with great unanimity, elected Michael Feodor Romanow, sovereign of all the Russias; then, repairing in a body to the cathedral, they proclaimed him to the people as their sovereign. The announcement was received with rapturous applause. It was thus that the house of Romanow was placed upon the throne of Russia. It retains the throne to the present day.

Michael, incited by singular sagacity and by true Christian philanthropy, commenced his reign by the most efficient measures to secure the peace of the empire. As soon as he had notified his election to the King of Poland, his father, archbishop of Rostow, was set at liberty and sent home. He was immediately created by his son patriarch of all Russia, an office in the Greek church almost equivalent to that of the pope in the Romish hierarchy. While these scenes were transpiring, Charles IX. died, and Gustavus Adolphus succeeded to the throne of Sweden. Gustavus and Michael both desired peace, the preliminaries were soon settled, and peace was established upon a basis far more advantageous to the Swedes than to the Russians. By this treaty, Russia ceded to Sweden territory, which deprived Russia of all access to the Baltic Sea. Thus the only point now upon which Russia touched the ocean, was on the North Sea. No enemies remained to Russia but the Poles. Here there was trouble enough. Ladislaus still demanded the throne, and invaded the empire with an immense army. He advanced, ravaging the country, even to the gates of Moscow. But, finding that he had no partisans in the kingdom, and that powerful armies were combining against him, he consented to a truce for fourteen years.

Russia was now at peace with all the world. The young tzar, aided by the counsels of his excellent father, devoted himself with untiring energy to the promotion of the prosperity of his subjects. It was deemed a matter of much political importance that the tzar should be immediately married. According to the custom of the empire, all the most beautiful girls were collected for the monarch to make his choice. They were received in the palace, and were lodged separately though they all dined together. The tzar saw them, either incognito or without disguise, as suited his pleasure. The day for the nuptials was appointed, and the bridal robes prepared when no one knew upon whom the monarch's choice had been fixed. On the morning of the nuptial day the robes were presented to the empress elect, who then, for the first time, learned that she had proved the successful candidate. The rejected maidens were returned to their homes laden with rich presents.

The young lady selected, was Eudocia Streschnew, who chanced to be the daughter of a very worthy gentleman, in quite straitened circumstances, residing nearly two hundred miles from Moscow. The messenger who was sent to inform him that his daughter was Empress of Russia, found him in the field at work with his domestics. The good old man was conducted to Moscow; but he soon grew weary of the splendors of the court, and entreated permission to return again to his humble rural home. Eudocia, reared in virtuous retirement, proved as lovely in character as she was beautiful in person, and she soon won the love of the nation. The first year of her marriage, she gave birth to a daughter. The three next children proved also daughters, to the great disappointment of their parents. But in the year 1630, a son was born, and not only the court, but all Russia, was filled with rejoicing. In the year 1634, the tzar met with one of the greatest of afflictions in the loss of his father by death. His reverence for the venerable patriarch Feodor, had been such that he was ever his principal counselor, and all his public acts were proclaimed in the name of the tzar and his majesty's father, the most holy patriarch.

"As he had joined," writes an ancient historian, "the miter to the sword, having been a general in the army before he was an ecclesiastic, the affable and modest behaviour, so becoming the ministers of the altar, had tempered and corrected the fire of the warrior, and rendered his manners amiable to all that came near him."

The reign of Michael proved almost a constant success.

His wisdom and probity caused him to be respected by the neighboring States, while the empire, in the enjoyment of peace, was rapidly developing all its resources, and increasing in wealth, population and power. His court was constantly filled with embassadors from all the monarchies of Europe and even of Asia. The tzar, rightly considering peace as almost the choicest of all earthly blessings, resisted all temptations to draw the sword. There were a few trivial interruptions of peace during his reign; but the dark clouds of war, by his energies, were soon dispelled. This pacific prince, one of the most worthy who ever sat upon any throne, died revered by his subjects on the 12th of July, 1645, in the forty-ninth year of his age and the thirty-third of his reign. He left but two children—a son, Alexis, who succeeded him, and a daughter, Irene, who a few years after died unmarried.

Alexis was but sixteen years of age when he succeeded to the throne. To prevent the possibility of any cabals being formed, in consequence of his youth, he was crowned the day after his father's death. In one week from that time Eudocia also died, her death being hastened by grief for the loss of her husband. An ambitious noble, Morośon, supremely selfish, but cool, calculating and persevering, attained the post of prime minister or counselor of the young tzar. The great object of his aim was to make himself the first subject in the empire. In the accomplishment of this object there were two leading measures to which he resorted. The first was to keep the young tzar as much as possible from taking any part in the transactions of state, by involving him in an incessant round of pleasures. The next step was to secure for the tzar a wife who would be under his own influence. The love of pleasure incident to youth rendered the first measure not difficult of accomplishment. Peculiar circumstances seemed remarkably to favor the second measure. There was a nobleman of high rank but of small fortune, strongly attached to Moroson, who had two daughters of marvelous beauty.

Moroson doubted not that he could lead his ardent young monarch to marry one of these lovely sisters, and he resolved himself to marry the other. He would thus become the brother-in-law of the emperor. Through his wife he would be able to influence her sister, the empress. The family would also all feel that they were indebted to him for their elevation. The plan was triumphantly successful.

The two young ladies were invited to court, and were decorated to make the most impressive display of their loveliness. With the young tzar, a boy of sixteen, it was love at first sight, and that very day he told Moroson that he wished to marry Maria, the eldest of the beauties. Rich presents were immediately lavished upon the whole family, so that they could make their appearance at court with suitable splendor. The tzar and Maria were immediately betrothed, and in just eight days the ardent lover led his bride from the altar. At the end of another week Moroson married the other sister. Moroson and Miloslouski, the father of the two brides, now ruled Russia, while the tzar surrendered himself to amusements.

The people soon became exasperated by the haughtiness and insolence of the duumvirate, and murmurs growing deeper and louder, ere long led to an insurrection. On the 6th of July, 1648, the tzar, engaged in some civic celebration, was escorted in a procession to one of the monasteries of Moscow. The populace assembled in immense numbers to see him pass. On his return the crowd broke through the attendant guards, seized the bridle of his horse, and entreated him to listen to their complaints concerning the outrages perpetrated by his ministers. The tzar, much alarmed by their violence, listened impatiently to their complaints and promised to render them satisfaction. The people were appeased, and were quietly retiring when the partisans of the ministers rode among them, assailing them with abusive language, crowding them with their horses, and even striking at them with their whips.

The populace, incensed, began to pelt them with stones, and though the guard of the tzar came to their rescue, they escaped with difficulty to the palace. The mob was now thoroughly aroused. They rushed to the palace of Moroson, burst down the doors, and sacked every apartment. They even tore from the person of his wife her jewels, throwing them into the street, but in other respects treating her with civility. They then passed to the palace of Miloslauski, treating it in the same manner. The mob had now possession of Moscow. Palace after palace of the partisans of the ministers was sacked, and several of the most distinguished members of the court were massacred.

The tzar, entirely deficient in energy, remained trembling in the Kremlin during the whole of the night of the 6th of July, only entreating his friends to strengthen the guards and to secure the palace from the outrages of the populace. Afraid to trust the Russian troops, who might be found in sympathy with the people, Alexis sent for a regiment of German troops who were in his employ, and stationed them around the palace. He then sent out an officer to disperse the crowd, assuring them that the disorders of which they complained should be redressed. They demanded that the offending ministers should be delivered to them, to be punished for the injuries they had inflicted upon the empire. Alexis assured them, through his messenger, upon his oath, that Moroson and Miloslauski had escaped, but promised that the third minister whom they demanded, a noble by the name of Plesseon, who was judge of the supreme court of judicature of Moscow, should be brought out directly, and that those who had escaped should be delivered up as soon as they could be arrested. The guilty, wretched man, thus doomed to be the victim to appease the rage of the mob, in a quarter of an hour was led out bareheaded by the servants of the tzar to the market-place. The mob fell upon him with clubs, beat him to the earth, dragged him over the pavements, and finally cut off his head. Thus satiated, about eleven o'clock in the morning they dispersed and returned to their homes.

In the afternoon, however, the reign of violence was resumed. The city was set on fire in several places, and the mob collected for plunder, making no effort to extinguish the flames. The fire spread with such alarming rapidity that the whole city was endangered. At length, however, after terrible destruction of property and the loss of many lives, the fury of the conflagration was arrested. The affrighted tzar now filled the important posts of the ministry with men who had a reputation for justice, and the clergy immediately espousing the cause of order, exhorted the populace to that respect and obedience to the higher powers which their religion enjoined. Alexis personally appeared before the people and addressed them in a speech, in which he made no apology for the outrages which had been committed by the government, but, assuming that the people were right in their demands, promised to repeal the onerous duties, to abolish the obnoxious monopolies, and even to increase the privileges which they had formerly enjoyed. The people received this announcement with great applause. The tzar, taking advantage of this return to friendliness, remarked,

"I have promised to deliver up to you Moroson and his confederates in the government. Their acts I admit to have been very unjust, but their personal relations to me renders it peculiarly trying for me to condemn them. I hope the people will not deny the first request I have ever made to them, which is, that these men, whom I have displaced, may be pardoned. I will answer for them for the future, and assure you that their conduct shall be such as to give you cause to rejoice at your lenity."

The people were so moved by this address, which the tzar pronounced with tears, that, as with one accord, they shouted, "God grant his majesty a long and happy life. The will of God and of the tzar be done." Peace was thus restored between the government and the people, and great good accrued to Russia from this successful insurrection.

During the early reign of Alexis, there were no foreign wars of any note. The Poles were all the time busy in endeavors to beat back the Turks, who, in wave after wave of invasion, were crossing the Danube. Upon the death of Ladislaus, King of Poland, Alexis, who had then a fine army at his command, offered to march to repel the Turks, if the Poles would choose him King of Poland. But at the same time France made a still more alluring offer, in case they would choose John Casimir, a prince in the interests of France, as their sovereign. The choice fell upon John Casimir. The provinces of Smolensk, Kiof and Tchernigov were then in possession of tho Poles, having been, in former wars, wrested from Russia. The Poles had conquered them by taking advantage of internal troubles in Russia, which enabled them with success to invade the empire.

Alexis now thought it right, in his turn, to take advantage of the weakness of Poland, harassed by the Turks, to recover these lost provinces. He accordingly marched to the city of Smŏlensk, and encamped before it with an army of three hundred thousand men. Smolensk was one of the strongest places which military art had then been able to rear. The Poles had received sufficient warning of the attack to enable them to garrison the fortifications to their utmost capacity and to supply the town abundantly with all the materials of war. The siege was continued for a full year, with all the usual accompaniments of carnage and misery which attend a beleaguered fortress. At last the city, battered into ruins, surrendered, and the victorious Russians immediately swept over Lithuanian Poland, meeting no force to obstruct its march. Another army, equally resistless, swept the banks of the Dnieper, and recovered Tchernigov and Kiof.

Misfortunes seemed now to be falling like an avalanche upon Poland. While the Turks were assailing them on the south, and the Russians were wresting from them opulent and populous provinces on the north, Charles Gustavus of Sweden, was crossing her eastern frontiers with invading hosts. The impetuous Swedish king, in three months, overran nearly the whole of Poland, threatening the utter extinction of the kingdom. This alarmed the surrounding kingdoms, lest Sweden should become too powerful for their safety. Alexis immediately entered into a truce with Poland, which guaranteed to him the peaceable possession of the provinces he had regained, and then united his armies with those of his humiliated rival, to arrest the strides of the Swedish conqueror.

Sieges, cannonades and battles innumerable ensued, over hundreds of leagues of territory, bordering the shores of the Baltic. For several years the maddened strife continued, producing its usual fruits of gory fields, smouldering cities, desolated homes, with orphanage, widowhood, starvation, pestilence, and every conceivable form of human misery. At length, all parties being exhausted, peace was concluded on the 2d of June, 1661.

The great insurrection in Moscow had taught the tzar Alexis a good lesson, and he profited by it wisely. He was led to devote himself earnestly to the welfare of his people. His recovery of the lost provinces of Russia was considered just, and added immeasurably to his renown. Conscious of the imperfection of his education, he engaged earnestly in study, causing many important scientific treatises to be translated into the Russian language, and perusing them with diligence and delight. He had the laws of the several provinces collected and published together. Many new manufactures were introduced, particularly those of silk and linen. Though rigidly economical in his expenses, he maintained a magnificent court and a numerous army. He took great interest in the promotion of agriculture, bringing many desert wastes into cultivation, and peopling them with the prisoners taken in the Polish and Swedish wars. It was the custom in those barbaric times to drive, as captives of war, the men, women and children of whole provinces, to be slaves in the territory of the conqueror. Often they occupied the position of a vassal peasantry, tilling the soil for the benefit of their lords. With singular foresight, Alexis planned for the construction of a fleet both on the Caspian and the Black Sea. With this object in view, he sent for ship carpenters from Holland and other places.

All Europe was now trembling in view of the encroachments of the Turks. Several very angry messages had passed between the sultan and the tzar, and the Turks had proved themselves ever eager to combine with the Tartars in bloody raids into the southern regions of the empire. Alexis resolved to combine Christian Europe, if possible, in a war of extermination against the Turks. To this end he sent embassadors to every court in Christendom. As his embassador was presented to Pope Clement X., the pope extended his foot for the customary kiss. The proud Russian drew back, exclaiming,

"So ignoble an act of homage is beneath the dignity of the prince whom I have the honor to serve."

He then informed the pope that the Emperor of Russia had resolved to make war against the Turks, that he wished to see all Christian princes unite against those enemies of humanity and religion, that for that purpose he had sent embassadors to all the potentates of Europe, and that he exhorted his holiness to place himself at the head of a league so powerful, so necessary for the protection of the church, and from which every Christian State might derive the greatest advantages. Foolish punctilios of etiquette interfered with any efficient arrangements with the court of Rome, and though the embassadors of other powers were received with the most marked respect, these powers were all too much engrossed with their own internal affairs to enlist in this enterprise for the public good. The Turks were, however, alarmed by these formidable movements, and, fearing such an alliance, were somewhat checked in their career of conquest.

On the 10th of November, 1674, the King of Poland died, and again there was an attempt on the part of Russia to unite Poland and the empire under the same crown. All the monarchies in Europe were involved in intrigues for the Polish crown. The electors, however, chose John Sobieski, a renowned Polish general, for their sovereign. The tzar was very apprehensive that the Poles would make peace with the Turks, and thus leave the sultan at liberty to concentrate all his tremendous resources upon Russia. Alexis raised three large armies, amounting in all to one hundred and fifty thousand men, which he sent into the Ukraine, as the frontier country, watered by the lower Dnieper, was then called.

The Turkish army, which was spread over the country between the Danube and the Dniester, now crossed this latter stream, and, in solid battalions, four hundred thousand strong, penetrated the Ukraine. They immediately commenced the fiend-like work of reducing the whole province to a desert. The process of destruction is swift. Flames, in a few hours, will consume a city which centuries alone have reared. A squadron of cavalry will, in a few moments, trample fields of grain which have been slowly growing and ripening for months. In less than a fortnight nearly the whole of the Ukraine was a depopulated waste, the troops of the tzar being shut up in narrow fortresses. The King of Poland, apprehensive that this vast Turkish army would soon turn with all their energies of destruction upon his own territories, resolved to march, with all the forces of his kingdom, to the aid of the Russians. One hundred thousand Polish troops immediately besieged the great city of Humau, which the Turks had taken, midway between the Dnieper and the Dniester.

John Sobieski, the newly-elected King of Poland, was a veteran soldier of great military renown. He placed himself at the head of other divisions of the army, and endeavored to distract the enemy and to divide their forces. At the same time, Alexis himself hastened to the theater of war that he might animate his troops by his presence. The Turks, finding themselves unable to advance any further, sullenly returned to their own country by the way of the Danube. Upon the retirement of the Turks, the Russians and the Poles began to quarrel respecting the possession of the Ukraine. Affairs were in this condition when the tzar Alexis, in all the vigor of manhood, was taken sick and died. He was then in the forty-sixth year of his age. His first wife, Maria Miloslouski, had died several years before him, leaving two sons and four daughters. His second wife, Natalia Nariskin, to whom he was married in the year 1671, still lived with her two children, a son, Peter, who was subsequently entitled the Great, as being the most illustrious monarch Russia has known, and a daughter Natalia.

Alexis, notwithstanding the unpropitious promise of his youth, proved one of the wisest and best princes Russia had known for years. He was a lover of peace, and yet prosecuted war with energy when it was forced upon him. His oldest surviving son, Feodor, who was but eighteen years of age at the time of his father's death, succeeded to the crown. Feodor, following the counsel which his father gave him on his dying bed, soon took military possession of nearly all of the Ukraine. The Turks entered the country again, but were repulsed with severe loss. Apprehensive that they would speedily return, the tzar made great efforts to secure a friendly alliance with Poland, in which he succeeded by paying a large sum of money in requital for the provinces of Smolensk and Kiof which his arms had recovered.

In the spring of 1678, the Turks again entered the Ukraine with a still more formidable army than the year before. The campaign was opened by laying siege to the city Czeherin, which was encompassed by nearly four hundred thousand men, and, after a destructive cannonade, was carried by storm.

The garrison, consisting of thirty thousand men, were put to the sword. The Russian troops were so panic-stricken by this defeat, that they speedily retreated. The Turks pursued them a long distance, constantly harassing their rear. But the Turks, in their turn, were compelled to retire, being driven back by famine, a foe against whom their weapons could make no impression.

The Ottoman Porte soon found that little was gained by waging war with an empire so vast and sparsely settled as Russia, and that their conquest of the desolated and depopulated lands of the Ukraine, was by no means worth the expenses of the war. The Porte was therefore inclined to make peace with Russia, that the Turkish armies might fall upon Poland again, which presented a much more inviting field of conquest. The Poles were informed of this through their embassador at Constantinople, and earnestly appealed to the tzar of Russia, and to all the princes in Christendom to come to their aid. The selfishness which every court manifested is humiliating to human nature. Each court seemed only to think of its own aggrandizement. Feodor consented to aid them only on condition that the Poles should renounce all pretension to any places then in possession of Russia. To this the Polish king assented, and the armies of Russia and Poland were again combined to repel the Turks.

CHAPTER XVIII.

THE REGENCY OF SOPHIA.

FROM 1680 TO 1697.

ADMINISTRATION OF FEODOR.—DEATH OF FEODOR.—INCAPACITY OF IVAN.—SUCCESSION OF PETER.—USURPATION OF SOPHIA.—INSURRECTION OF THE STRELITZES.—MASSACRE IN MOSCOW.—SUCCESS OF THE INSURRECTION.—IVAN AND PETER DECLARED SOVEREIGNS UNDER THE REGENCY OF SOPHIA.—GENERAL DISCONTENT.—CONSPIRACY AGAINST SOPHIA.—HER FLIGHT TO THE CONVENT.—THE CONSPIRACY QUELLED.—NEW CONSPIRACY.—ENERGY OF PETER.—HE ASSUMES THE CROWN.—SOPHIA BANISHED TO A CONVENT.—COMMENCEMENT OF THE REIGN OF PETER.

FEODOR, influenced by the wise counsels of his father, devoted much attention to the beautifying of his capital, and to developing the internal resources of the empire. He paved the streets of Moscow, erected several large buildings of stone in place of the old wooden structures. Commerce and arts were patronized, he even loaning, from the public treasury, sums of money to enterprising men to encourage them in their industrial enterprises. Foreigners of distinction, both scholars and artisans, were invited to take up their residence in the empire. The tzar was particularly fond of fine horses, and was very successful in improving, by importations, the breed in Russia.

Feodor had always been of an exceedingly frail constitution, and it was evident that he could not anticipate long life. In the year 1681 he married a daughter of one of the nobles. His bride, Opimia Routoski, was also frail in health, though very beautiful. Six months had hardly passed away ere the youthful empress exchanged her bridal robes and couch for the shroud and the tomb. The emperor himself, grief-stricken, was rapidly sinking in a decline. His ministers almost forced him to another immediate marriage, hoping that, by the birth of a son, the succession of his half brother Peter might be prevented. The dying emperor received into his emaciate, feeble arms the new bride who had been selected for him, Marva Matweowna, and after a few weeks of languor and depression died. He was deeply lamented by his subjects, for during his short reign of less than three years he had developed a noble character, and had accomplished more for the real prosperity of Russia than many a monarch in the longest occupation of the throne.

Feodor left two brothers—Ivan, a brother by the same mother, Eudocia, and Peter, the son of the second wife of Alexis. Ivan was very feeble in body and in mind, with dim vision, and subject to epileptic fits. Feodor consequently declared his younger brother Peter, who was but ten years of age, his successor. The custom of the empire allowed him to do this, and rendered this appointment valid. It was generally the doom of the daughters of the Russian emperors, who could seldom find a match equal to their rank, to pass their lives immured in a convent.

Feodor had a sister, Sophia, a very spirited, energetic woman, ambitious and resolute, whose whole soul revolted against such a moping existence. Seeing that Feodor had but a short time to live, she left her convent and returned to the Kremlin, persisting in her resolve to perform all sisterly duties for her dying brother. Ivan, her own brother, was incapable of reigning, from his infirmities. Peter, her half-brother, was but a child. Sophia, with wonderful energy, while tending at the couch of Feodor, made herself familiar with the details of the administration, and, acting on behalf of the dying sovereign, gathered the reins of power into her own hands.

As soon as Feodor expired, and it was announced that Peter was appointed successor to the throne, to the exclusion of his elder brother Ivan, Sophia, through her emissaries, excited the militia of the capital to one of the most bloody revolts Moscow had ever witnessed. It was her intention to gain the throne for the imbecile Ivan, as she doubted not that she could, in that event, govern the empire at her pleasure. Peter, child as he was, had already developed a character of self-reliance which taught Sophia that he would speedily wrest the scepter from her hands.

The second day after the burial of Feodor, the militia, or *strelitzes* as they were called, a body of citizen soldiers in Moscow, corresponding very much with the national guard of Paris, surrounded the Kremlin, in a great tumult, and commenced complaining of nine of their colonels, who owed them some arrears of pay. They demanded that these officers should be surrendered to them, and their demand was so threatening that the court, intimidated, was compelled to yield. The wretched officers were seized by the mob, tied to the ground naked, upon their faces, and whipped with most terrible severity. The soldiers thus overawed opposition, and became a power which no one dared resist. Sophia was their inspiring genius, inciting and directing them through her emissaries. Though some have denied her complicity in these deeds of violence, still the prevailing voice of history is altogether against her.

Sophia, having the terrors of the mob to wield, as her executive power, convened an assembly of the princes of the blood, the generals, the lords, the patriarch and the bishops of the church, and even of the principal merchants. She urged upon them that Ivan, by right of birth, was entitled to the empire. The mother of Peter, Natalia Nariskin, now empress dowager, was still young and beautiful. She had two brothers occupying posts of influence at court. The family of the Nariskins had consequently much authority in the empire. Sophia dreaded the power of her mother-in-law, and her first efforts of intrigue were directed against the Nariskins. Her agents were everywhere busy, in the court and in the army, whispering insinuations against them. It was even intimated that they had caused the death of Feodor, by bribing his physician to poison him, and that they had attempted the life of Ivan. At length Sophia gave to her agents a list of forty lords whom they were to denounce to the insurgent soldiery as enemies to them and to the State.

This was the signal for their massacre. Two were first seized in the palace of the Kremlin, and thrown out of the window. The soldiers received them upon their pikes, and dragged their mutilated corpses through the streets to the great square of the city. They then rushed back to the palace, where they found Athanasius Nariskin, one of the brothers of the queen dowager. He was immediately murdered. They soon after found three of the proscribed in a church, to which they had fled as a sanctuary. Notwithstanding the sacredness of the church, the unhappy lords were instantly hewn to pieces by the swords of the assassins. Thus frenzied with blood, they met a young lord whom they mistook for Ivan Nariskin, the remaining brother of the mother of Peter. He was instantly slain, and then the assassins discovered their error. With some slight sense of justice, perhaps of humanity, they carried the bleeding corpse of the young nobleman to his father. The panic-stricken, heart-broken parent dared not rebuke them for the murder, but thanked them for bringing to him the corpse of his child. The mother, more impulsive and less cautious, broke out into bitter and almost delirious reproaches. The father, to appease her, said to her, in an under tone, "Let us wait till the hour shall come when we shall be able to take revenge."

Some one overheard the imprudent words, and reported them to the mob. They immediately returned, dragged the old man down the stairs of his palace by the hair, and cut his throat upon his own door sill. They were now searching the city, in all directions, for Von Gaden the German physician of the late tzar, who was accused of administering to him poison. They met in the streets, the son of the physician, and demanded of him where his father was. The trembling lad replied that he did not know. They cut him down. Soon they met another German physician.

"You are a doctor," they said. "If you have not poisoned our sovereign you have poisoned others, and deserve death."

He was immediately murdered. At length they discovered Von Gaden. He had attempted to disguise himself in a beggar's garb. The worthy old man, who, like most eminent physicians, was as distinguished for humanity as for eminent medical skill, was dragged to the Kremlin. The princesses themselves came out and mingled with the crowd, begging for the life of the good man, assuring them that he had been a faithful physician and that he had served their sovereign with zeal. The soldiers declared that he deserved to die, as they had positive proof that he was a sorcerer, for, in searching his apartments, they had found the skin of a snake and several reptiles preserved in bottles. Against such proof no earthly testimony could avail.

They also demanded that Ivan Nariskin, whom they had been seeking for two days, should be delivered up to them. They were sure that he was concealed somewhere in the Kremlin, and they threatened to set fire to the palace and burn it to the ground unless he were immediately delivered to them. It was evident that these threats would be promptly put into execution. Firing the palace would certainly insure his death. There was the bare possibility of escape by surrendering him to the mob. The empress herself went to her brother in his concealment and informed him of the direful choice before him. The young prince sent for the patriarch, confessed his sins, partook of the Lord's Supper, received the sacrament of extreme unction in preparation for death, and was then led out, by the patriarch himself, dressed in his pontifical robes and bearing an image of the Virgin Mary, and was delivered by him to the soldiers. The queen and the princesses accompanied the victim, surrounding him, and, falling upon their knees before the soldiers, they united with the patriarch in pleading for his life. But the mob, intoxicated and maddened, dragged the young prince and the physician before a tribunal which they had constituted on the spot, and condemned them to what was expressively called the punishment of "ten thousand slices." Their bodies were speedily cut into the smallest fragments, while their heads were stuck upon the iron spikes of the balustrade.

These outrages were terminated by a proclamation from the soldiery that Ivan and Peter should be joint sovereigns under the regency of Sophia. The regent rewarded her partisans liberally for their efficient and successful measures. Upon the leaders she conferred the confiscated estates of the proscribed. A monument of shame was reared, upon which the names of the assassinated were engraved as traitors to their country. The soldiers were rewarded with double pay.

Sophia unscrupulously usurped all the prerogatives and honors of royalty. All dispatches were sealed with her hand. Her effigy was stamped upon the current coin. She took her seat as presiding officer at the council. To confer a little more dignity upon the character of her imbecile brother, Ivan, she selected for him a wife, a young lady of extraordinary beauty whose father had command of a fortress in Siberia. It was on the 25th of June, 1682, that Sophia assumed the regency. In 1684 Ivan was married. The scenes of violence which had occurred agitated the whole political atmosphere throughout the empire. There was intense exasperation, and many conspiracies were formed for the overthrow of the government. The most formidable of these conspiracies was organized by Couvanski, commander-in-chief of the strelitzes. He was dissatisfied with the rewards he had received, and, conscious that he had placed Sophia upon the throne through the energies of the soldiers he commanded, he believed that he might just as easily have placed himself there. Having become accustomed to blood, the slaughter of a few more persons, that he might place the crown upon his own brow, appeared to him a matter of but little moment. He accordingly planned to murder the two tzars, the regent Sophia and all the remaining princes of the royal family. Then, by lavishing abundant rewards upon the soldiers, he doubted not that he could secure their efficient coöperation in maintaining him on the throne.

The conspiracy was discovered upon the eve of its accomplishment. Sophia immediately fled with the two tzars and the princes, to the monastery of the Trinity. This was a palace, a convent and a fortress. The vast pile, reared of stone, was situated thirty-six miles from Moscow, and was encompassed with deep ditches, and massive ramparts bristling with cannon. The monks were in possession of the whole country for a space of twelve miles around this almost impregnable citadel. From this safe retreat Sophia opened communications with the rebel chief. She succeeded in alluring him to come half way to meet her in conference. A powerful band of soldiers, placed in ambush, seized him. He was immediately beheaded, with one of his sons, and thirty-seven strelitzes who had accompanied him.

As soon as the strelitzes in Moscow, numbering many thousands, heard of the assassination of their general and of their comrades, they flew to arms, and in solid battalions, with infantry, artillery and cavalry, marched to the assault of the convent. The regent rallied her supporters, consisting of the lords who were her partisans, and their vassals, and prepared for a vigorous defense. Russia seemed now upon the eve of a bloody civil war. The nobles generally espoused the cause of the tzars under the regency of Sophia. Their claims seemed those of legitimacy, while the success of the insurrectionary soldiers promised only anarchy. The rise of the people in defense of the government was so sudden and simultaneous, that the strelitzes were panic-stricken, and soon, in the most abject submission, implored pardon, which was wisely granted them. Sophia, with the tzars, surrounded by an army, returned in triumph to Moscow. Tranquillity was thus restored.

Sophia still held the reins of power with a firm grasp. The imbecility of Ivan and the youth of Peter rendered this usurpation easy. Very adroitly she sent the most mutinous regiments of the strelitzes on apparently honorable missions to the distant provinces of the Ukraine, Kesan, and Siberia. Poland, menaced by the Turks, made peace with Russia, and purchased her alliance by the surrender of the vast province of Smolensk and all the conquered territory in the Ukraine. In the year 1687, Sophia sent the first Russian embassy to France, which was then in the meridian of her splendor, under the reign of Louis XIV. Voltaire states that France, at that time, was so unacquainted with Russia, that the Academy of Inscriptions celebrated this embassy by a medal, as if it had come from India.* The Crimean Tartars, in confederacy with the Turks, kept Russia, Poland, Hungary, Transylvania, and the various provinces of the German empire in perpetual alarm. Poland and Russia were so humiliated, that for several years they had purchased exemption from these barbaric forays by paying the Tartars an annual tribute amounting to fifty thousand dollars each. Sophia, anxious to wipe out this disgrace, renewed the effort, which had so often failed, to unite all Europe against the Turks. Immense armies were raised by Russia and Poland and sent to the Tauride. For two years a bloody war raged with about equal slaughter upon both sides, while neither party gained any marked advantage.

Peter had now attained his eighteenth year, and began to manifest pretty decisively a will of his own. He fell in love

* "La France n'avait eu encore aucune correspondance avec la Russie; on ne le connaissait pas; et l'Académie des Inscriptions célébra par une médaille cette ambassade, comme si elle fut venue des Indes."—*Histoire de l'Empire de Russie, sous Pierre le Grand*, page 93.

with a beautiful maiden, Ottokesa Lapuchin, daughter of one of his nobles, and, notwithstanding all the intriguing opposi tion of Sophia, persisted in marrying her. This marriage increased greatly the popularity of the young prince, and it was very manifest that he would soon thrust Sophia aside, and with his own vigorous arm, wield the scepter alone.

The regent, whose hands were already stained with the blood of assassination, now resolved to remove Peter out of the way. The young prince, with his bride, was residing at his country seat, a few miles out from Moscow. Sophia, in that corrupt, barbaric age, found no difficulty in obtaining, with bribes, as many accomplices as she wanted. Two distinguished generals led a party of six hundred strelitzes out of the city, to surround the palace of Peter and to secure his death. The soldiers had already commenced their march, when Peter was informed of his danger. The tzar leaped upon a horse, and spurring him to his utmost speed, accompanied by a few attendants, escaped to the convent of the Trinity, to which we have before alluded as one of the strongest fortresses of Russia. The mother, wife and sister of the tzar, immediately joined him there.

The soldiers were not aware of the mission which their leaders were intending to accomplish. When they arrived at the palace, and it was found that the tzar had fled, and it was whispered about that he had fled to save his life, the soldiers, by nature more strongly attached to a chivalrous young man than to an intriguing, ambitious woman, whose character was of very doubtful reputation, broke out into open revolt, and, abandoning their officers, marched directly to the monastery and offered their services to Peter. The patriarch, whose religious character gave him almost unbounded influence with the people, also found that he was included as one of the victims of the conspiracy; that he was to have been assassinated, and his place conferred upon one of the partisans of Sophia. He also fled to the convent of the Trinity.

Sophia now found herself deserted by the soldiery and the nation. She accordingly, with the most solemn protestations, declared that she had been accused falsely, and after sending messenger after messenger to plead her cause with her brother, resolved to go herself. She had not advanced more than half way, ere she was met by a detachment of Peter's friends who informed her, from him, that she must go directly back to Moscow, as she could not be received into the convent. The next day Peter assembled a council, and it was resolved to bring the traitors to justice. A colonel, with three hundred men, was sent to the Kremlin to arrest the officers implicated in the conspiracy. They were loaded with chains, conducted to the Trinity, and in accordance with the barbaric custom of the times were put to the torture. In agony too dreadful to be borne, they of course made any confession which was demanded.

Peter was reluctant to make a public example of his sister. There ensued a series of punishments of the conspirators too revolting to be narrated. The mildest of these punishments was exile to Siberia, there, in the extremest penury, to linger through scenes of woe so long as God should prolong their lives. The executions being terminated and the exiles out of sight, Sophia was ordered to leave the Kremlin, and retire to the cloisters of Denitz, which she was never again to leave. Peter then made a triumphal entry into Moscow. He was accompanied by a guard of eighteen thousand troops. His feeble brother Ivan received him at the outer gate of the Kremlin. They embraced each other with much affection, and then retired to their respective apartments. The wife and mother of Peter accompanied him on his return to Moscow.

Thus terminated the regency of Sophia. From this time Peter was the real sovereign of Russia. His brother Ivan took no other share in the government than that of lending his name to the public acts. He lived for a few years in great seclusion, almost forgotten, and died in 1696. Peter was physically, as well as intellectually, a remarkable man. He was tall and finely formed, with noble features lighted up with an extremely brilliant eye. His constitution was robust, enabling him to undergo great hardship, and he was, by nature, a man of great activity and energy. His education, however, was exceedingly defective. The regent Sophia had not only exerted all her influence to keep him in ignorance, but also to allure him into the wildest excesses of youthful indulgence. Even his recent marriage had not interfered with the publicity of his amours, and all distinguished foreigners in Moscow were welcomed by him to scenes of feasting and carousing.

Notwithstanding these deplorable defects of character, for which much allowance is to be made from the neglect of his education and his peculiar temptations, still it was manifest to close observers even then, that the seeds of true greatness were implanted in his nature. When five years of age, he was riding with his mother in a coach, and was asleep in her arms. As they were passing over a bridge where there was a heavy fall of water from spring rains, the roar of the cataract awoke him. The noise, with the sudden aspect of the rushing torrent, created such terror that he was thrown into a fever, and, for years, he could not see any standing water, much less a running stream, without being thrown almost into convulsions. To overcome this weakness, he resolutely persisted in plunging into the waves until his aversion was changed into a great fondness for that element.

Ashamed of his ignorance, he vigorously commenced studying German, and, notwithstanding all the seductions of the court, succeeded in acquiring such a mastery of the language as to be able both to speak and write it correctly. Peter's father, Alexis, had been anxious to open the fields of commerce to his subjects. He had, at great expense, engaged the services of ship builders and navigators from Holland. A frigate and a yacht had been constructed, with which the

Volga had been navigated to its mouth at Astrachan. It was his intention to open a trade with Persia through the Caspian Sea. But, in a revolt at Astrachan, the vessels were seized and destroyed, and the captain killed. Thus terminated this enterprise. The master builder, however, remained in Russia, where he lived a long time in obscurity.

One day, Peter, at one of his summer palaces of Ismaelhof, saw upon the shore of the lake the remains of a pleasure boat of peculiar construction. He had never before seen any boat but such as was propelled by oars. The peculiarity of the structure of this arrested his attention, and being informed that it was constructed for sails as well as oars, he ordered it to be repaired, that he might make trial of it. It so chanced that the shipwright, Brandt, from Holland, who had built the boat, was found, and the tzar, to his great delight, enjoyed, for the first time in his life, the pleasures of a sail. He immediately gave directions for the boat to be transported to the great lake near the convent of the Trinity, and here he ordered two frigates and three yachts to be built. For months he amused himself piloting his little fleet over the waves of the lake. Like many a plebeian boy, the tzar had now acquired a passion for the sea, and he longed to get a sight of the ocean.

With this object in view, in 1694 he set out on a journey of nearly a thousand miles to Archangel, on the shores of the White Sea. Taking his shipwrights with him, he had a small vessel constructed, in which he embarked for the exploration of the Frozen Ocean, a body of water which no sovereign had seen before him. A Dutch man-of-war, which chanced to be in the harbor at Archangel, and all the merchant fleet there accompanied the tzar on this expedition. The sovereign himself had already acquired much of the art of working a ship, and on this trip devoted all his energies to improvement in the science and practical skill of navigation.

While the tzar was thus turning his attention to the subject of a navy, he at the same time was adopting measures of extraordinary vigor for the reorganization of the army. Hitherto the army had been composed of bands of vassals, poorly armed and without discipline, led by their lords, who were often entirely without experience in the arts of war. Peter commenced, at his country residence, with a company of fifty picked men, who were put through the most thorough drill by General Gordon, a Scotchman of much military ability, who had secured the confidence of the tzar. Some of the sons of the lords were chosen as their officers, but these young nobles were all trained by the same military discipline, Peter setting them the example by passing through all the degrees of the service from the very lowest rank. He shouldered his musket, and commencing at the humblest post, served as sentinel, sergeant and lieutenant. No one ventured to refuse to follow in the footsteps of his sovereign. This company, thus formed and disciplined, was rapidly increased until it became the royal guard, most terrible on the field of battle. When this regiment numbered five thousand men, another regiment upon the same principle was organized, which contained twelve thousand. It is a remarkable fact stated by Voltaire, that one third of these troops were French refugees, driven from France by the revocation of the Edict of Nantes.

One of the first efforts of the far-sighted monarch was to consolidate the army and to bring it under the energy of one mind, by breaking down the independence of the nobles, who had heretofore acted as petty sovereigns, leading their contingents of vassals. Peter was thus preparing to make the influence of Russia felt among the armies of Europe as it had never been felt before.

The Russian empire, sweeping across Siberian Asia, reached down indefinitely to about the latitude of fifty-two degrees, where it was met by the Chinese claims. Very naturally, a dispute arose respecting the boundaries, and with a degree of good sense which seems almost incredible in view of the developments of history, the two half-civilized nations decided to settle the question by conference rather than by war. A place of meeting, for the embassadors, was appointed on the frontiers of Siberia, about nine hundred miles from the great Chinese wall. Fortunately for both parties, there were some Christian missionaries who accompanied the Chinese as interpreters. Probably through the influence of these men of peace a treaty was soon formed. Both parties pledged themselves to the observance of the treaty in the following words, which were doubtless written by the missionaries:

"If any of us entertain the least thought of renewing the flames of war, we beseech the supreme Lord of all things, who knows the heart of man, to punish the traitor with sudden death."

Two large pillars were erected upon the spot to mark the boundaries between the two empires, and the treaty was engraved upon each of them. Soon after, a treaty of commerce was formed, which commerce, with brief interruptions, has continued to flourish until the present day. Peter now prepared, with his small but highly disciplined army, to make vigorous warfare upon the Turks, and to obtain, if possible, the control of the Black Sea. Early in the summer of 1695 the Russian army commenced its march. Striking the head waters of the Don, they descended the valley of that river to attack the city of Azov, an important port of the Turks, situated on an island at the mouth of the Don.

The tzar accompanied his troops, not as commander-in-chief, but a volunteer soldier. Generals Gordon and Le Fort, veteran officers, had the command of the expedition. Azov was a very strong fortress and was defended by a numerous garrison. It was found necessary to invest the place and commence a regular siege. A foreign officer from Dantzic, by the name of Jacob, had the direction of the battering train. For some violation of military etiquette, he had been condemned to ignominious punishment. The Russians were accustomed to such treatment, but Jacob, burning with revenge, spiked his guns, deserted, joined the enemy, adopted the Mussulman faith, and with great vigor conducted the defense.

Jacob was a man of much military science, and he succeeded in thwarting all the efforts of the besiegers. In the attempt to storm the town the Russians were repulsed with great loss, and at length were compelled to raise the siege and to retire. But Peter was not a man to yield to difficulties. The next summer he was found before Azov, with a still more formidable force. In this attempt the tzar was successful, and on the 28th of July the garrison surrendered without obtaining any of the honors of war. Elated with success Peter increased the fortifications, dug a harbor capable of holding large ships, and prepared to fit out a strong fleet against the Turks; which fleet was to consist of nine sixty gun ships, and forty-one of from thirty to fifty guns. While the fleet was being built he returned to Moscow, and to impress his subjects with a sense of the great victory obtained, he marched the army into Moscow beneath triumphal arches, while the whole city was surrendered to all the demonstrations of joy. Characteristically Peter refused to take any of the credit of the victory which had been gained by the skill and valor of his generals. These officers consequently took the precedency of their sovereign in the triumphal procession, Peter declaring that merit was the only road to military preferment, and that, as yet, he had attained no rank in the army. In imitation of the ancient Romans, the captives taken in the war were led in the train of the victors. The unfortunate Jacob was carried in a cart, with a rope about his neck, and after being broken upon the wheel was ignominiously hung.

CHAPTER XIX.

PETER THE GREAT.

FROM 1697 TO 1702.

YOUNG RUSSIANS SENT TO FOREIGN COUNTRIES.—THE TZAR DECIDES UPON A TOUR OF OBSERVATION.—HIS PLAN OF TRAVEL.—ANECDOTE.—PETER'S MODE OF LIFE IN HOLLAND.—CHARACTERISTIC ANECDOTES.—THE PRESENTATION OF THE EMBASSADOR.—THE TZAR VISITS ENGLAND.—LIFE AT DEPTFORD.—ILLUSTRIOUS FOREIGNERS ENGAGED IN HIS SERVICE.—PETER VISITS VIENNA.—THE GAME OF LANDLORD.—INSURRECTION IN MOSCOW.—RETURN OF THE TZAR, AND MEASURES OF SEVERITY.—WAR WITH SWEDEN.—DISASTROUS DEFEAT OF NARVA.—EFFORTS TO SECURE THE SHORES OF THE BALTIC.—DESIGNS UPON THE BLACK SEA.

IT was a source of mortification to the tzar that he was dependent upon foreigners for the construction of his ships. He accordingly sent sixty young Russians to the sea-ports of Venice and Leghorn, in Italy, to acquire the art of ship-building, and to learn scientific and practical navigation. Soon after this he sent forty more to Holland for the same purpose. He sent also a large number of young men to Germany, to learn the military discipline of that warlike people.

He now adopted the extraordinary resolve of traveling himself, *incognito*, through most of the countries of Europe, that he might see how they were governed, and might become acquainted with the progress they had made in the arts and sciences. In this European tour he decided to omit Spain, because the arts there were but little cultivated, and France, because he disliked the pompous ceremonials of the court of Louis XIV. His plan of travel was as ingenuous as it was odd. An extraordinary embassage was sent by him, as Emperor of Russia, to all the leading courts of Europe. These embassadors received minute instructions, and were fitted out for their expedition with splendor which should add to the renown of the Russian monarchy. Peter followed in the retinue of this embassage as a private gentleman of wealth, with the servants suitable for his station.

Three nobles of the highest dignity were selected as embassadors. Their retinue consisted of four secretaries, twelve gentlemen, two pages for each embassador, and a company of fifty of the royal guard. The whole embassage embraced two hundred persons. The tzar was lost to view in this crowd. He reserved for himself one valet de chambre, one servant in livery, and a dwarf. "It was," says Voltaire, "a thing unparalleled in history, either ancient or modern, for a sovereign, of five and twenty years of age, to withdraw from his kingdoms, only to learn the art of government." The regency, during his absence, was entrusted to two of the lords in whom he reposed confidence, who were to consult, in cases of importance, with the rest of the nobility. General Gordon, the Scotch officer, was placed in command of four thousand of the royal troops, to secure the peace of the capital.

The embassadors commenced their journey in April, 1697. Passing directly west from Moscow to Novgorod, they thence traversed the province of Livonia until they reached Riga, at the mouth of the Dwina. Peter was anxious to examine the important fortifications of this place, but the governor peremptorily forbade it, Riga then belonging to Sweden. Peter did not forget the affront. Continuing their journey, they arrived at Konigsburg, the capital of the feeble electorate of Brandenburg, which has since grown into the kingdom of Prussia. The elector, an ambitious man, who subsequently took the title of king, received them with an extravagant display of splendor. At one of the bacchanalian feasts, given on the occasion, the bad and good qualities of Peter were very conspicuously displayed. Heated with wine, and provoked by a remark made by La Fort, who was one of his embassadors, he drew his sword and called upon La Fort to defend himself. The embassador humbly bowed, folded his hands upon his breast, and said,

"Far be it from me. Rather let me perish by the hand of my master." The tzar, enraged and intoxicated, raised his arm to strike, when one of the retinue seized the uplifted hand and averted the blow. Peter immediately recovered his self-possession, and sheathing his sword said to his embassador,

"I ask your pardon. It is my great desire to reform my subjects, and yet I am ashamed to confess that I am unable to reform myself."

From Konigsburg they continued their route to Berlin, and thence to Hamburg, near the mouth of the Elbe, which was, even then, an important maritime town. They then turned their steps towards Amsterdam. As soon as they reached Emmeric, on the Rhine, the tzar, impatient of the slow progress of the embassage, forsook his companions, and hiring a small boat, sailed down the Rhine and proceeded to Amsterdam, reaching that city fifteen days before the embassy. "He flew through the city," says one of the annalists of those days, "like lightning," and proceeded to a small but active sea-port town on the coast, Zaandam. The first person they saw here was a man fishing from a small skiff, at a short distance from the shore. The tzar, who was dressed like a common Dutch skipper, in a red jacket and white linen trowsers, hailed the man, and engaged lodgings of him, consisting of two small rooms with a loft over them, and an adjoining shed. Strangely enough, this man, whose name was Kist, had been in Russia working as a smith, and he knew the tzar. He was strictly enjoined on no account to let it be known who his lodger was.

A group soon gathered around the strangers, with many questions. Peter told them that they were carpenters and laborers from a foreign country in search of work. But no one believed this, for the attendants of the tzar still wore the rich robes which constituted the costume of Russia. With sympathy as beautiful as it is rare, Peter called upon several families of ship carpenters who had worked for him and with him at Archangel, and to some of these families he gave valuable presents, which he said that the tzar of Russia had sent to them. He clothed himself, and ordered his companions to clothe themselves, in the ordinary dress of the dockyard, and purchasing carpenters' tools they all went vigorously to work.

The next day was the Sabbath. The arrival of these strangers, so peculiar in aspect and conduct, was noised abroad, and when Peter awoke in the morning he was greatly annoyed by finding a large crowd assembled before his door. Indeed the rumor of the Russian embassage, and that the tzar himself was to accompany it, had already reached Amsterdam, and it was shrewdly suspected that these strangers were in some way connected with the expected arrival of the embassadors. One of the barbers in Amsterdam had received from a ship carpenter in Archangel a portrait of the tzar, which had been for some time hanging in his shop. He was with the crowd around the door. The moment his eye rested upon Peter, he exclaimed, with astonishment, "*that is the tzar!*" His form, features and character were all so marked that he could not easily be mistaken.

No further efforts were made at concealment, though Peter was often very much annoyed by the crowds who followed his footsteps and watched all his actions. He was persuaded to change his lodgings to more suitable apartments, though he still wore his workman's dress and toiled in the ship-yard with energy, and also with skill which no one could surpass. The extraordinary rapidity of his motions astonished and amused the Dutch. "Such running, jumping and clambering over the shipping," they said, "we never witnessed before." To the patriarch in Moscow he wrote,

"I am living in obedience to the commands of God, which were spoken to father Adam: '*In the sweat of thy brow shalt thou eat thy bread.*'"

Very many anecdotes are related of Peter during this portion of his life, which, though they may be apochryphal, are very characteristic of his eccentric nature. At one time he visited a celebrated iron manufactory, and forged himself several bars of iron, directing his companions to assist him in the capacity of journeymen blacksmiths. Upon the bars he forged, he put his own mark, and then he demanded of Muller, the proprietor, payment for his work, at the same rate he paid other workmen. Having received eighteen *altins*, he said, looking at the patched shoes on his feet,

"This will serve me to buy a pair of shoes, of which I stand in great need. I have earned them well, by the sweat of my brow, with hammer and anvil."

When the embassadors entered Amsterdam, Peter thought it proper to take a part in the procession, which was arranged in the highest style of magnificence. The three embassadors rode first, followed by a long train of carriages, with servants in rich livery on foot. The tzar, dressed as a private gentleman, was in one of the last carriages in the train of his embassadors. The eyes of the populace searched for him in vain. From this fête he returned eagerly to his work, with saw, hammer and adz, at Zaandam. He persisted in living like the rest of the workmen, rising early, building his own fire, and often cooking his own meals. One of the inhabitants of Zaandam thus describes his appearance at that time:

"The tzar is very tall and robust, quick and nimble of foot, dexterous and rapid in all his actions. His face is plump and round; fierce in his look, with brown eyebrows, and short, curly hair of a brownish color. He is quick in his gait, swinging his arms, and holding in one of them a cane."

The Dutch were so much interested in him, that a regular diary was kept in Zaandam of all he said and did. Those who were in daily intercourse with him preserved a memorandum of all that occurred. He was generally called by the name of Master Peter. While hard at work in the ship-yard, he received intelligence of troubles in Poland. The renowned king, John Sobieski, died in 1696. The electors were divided in the choice of a successor. Augustus II., Elector of Saxony, by means of bribes and his army, obtained the vote. But there was great dissatisfaction, and a large party of the nation rallied around the prince of Conti, the rival candidate. Peter, learning these facts, immediately sent word, from his carpenter's shop, to Augustus, offering to send an army of thirty thousand men to his assistance. He frequently went from Zaandam to Amsterdam, to attend the anatomical lectures of the celebrated Ruisch. His thirst for knowledge appeared to be universal and insatiable. He even performed, himself, several surgical operations. He also studied natural philosophy under Witsen. Most minds would have been bewildered by such a multiplicity of employments, but his mental organization was of that peculiar class which grasps and retains all within its reach. He worked at the forge, in the rope-walks, at the sawing mills, and in the manufactures for wire drawing, making paper and extracting oil.

While at Zaandam, Peter finished a sixty gun ship, upon which he had worked diligently from the laying of the keel. As the Russians then had no harbor in the Baltic, this ship was sent to Archangel, on the shores of the White Sea. Peter also engaged a large number of French refugees, and Swiss and German artists, to enter his service and sent them to Moscow. Whenever he found a mechanic whose work testified to superior skill, he would secure him at almost any price and send him to Moscow. To geography he devoted great attention, and even then devised the plan of uniting the Caspian and the Black Sea by a ship canal.

Early in January, 1698, Peter, having passed nine months at Zaandam, left for the Hague. King William III. sent his yacht to the Hague, to convey the tzar to England, with a convoy of two ships of war. Peter left the Hague on the 18th of January, and arrived in London on the 21st. Though he attempted here no secrecy as to his rank, he requested to be treated only as a private gentleman. A large mansion was engaged for him, near the royal navy yard at Deptford, a small town upon the Thames, about four miles from London. The London Postman, one of the leading metropolitan journals of that day, thus announces this extraordinary visit:

"The tzar of Muscovy, desiring to raise the glory of his nation, and avenge the Christians of all the injuries they have received from the Turks, has abrogated the wild manners of his predecessors, and having concluded, from the behavior of his engineers and officers, who were sent him by the Elector of Brandenburg, that the western nations of Europe understood the art of war better than others, he resolved to take a journey thither, and not wholly to rely upon the relations which his embassadors might give him; and, at the same time, to send a great number of his nobility into those parts through which he did not intend to travel, that he might have a complete idea of the affairs of Europe, and enrich his subjects with the arts of all other Christian nations; and as navigation is the most useful invention that ever was yet found out, he seems to have chosen it as his own part in the general inquiry he is about. His design is certainly very noble, and discovers the greatness of his genius. But the model he has proposed himself to imitate is a convincing proof of his extraordinary judgment; for what other prince, in the world, was a fitter pattern for the great Emperor of Muscovy, than William the Third, King of Great Britain?"*

In London and Deptford Peter followed essentially the same mode of life which he had adopted in Amsterdam. There was not a single article belonging to a ship, from the casting of a cannon to the making of cables, to which he did not devote special attention. He also devoted some time to watch making. A number of English artificers, and also several literary and scientific gentlemen from England, were taken into

* Postman, No. 417.

his service. He made arrangements with a distinguished Scotch geometrician and two mathematicians from Christ Church hospital, to remove to Moscow, who laid the foundation in Russia of the Marine Academy. To astronomy, the calculation of eclipses, and the laws of gravitation he devoted much thought, guided by the most scientific men England could then produce. Perry, an English engineer, was sent to Russia to survey a route for a ship canal from the ocean to the Caspian and from the Caspian to the Black Sea. A company of merchants paid the tzar seventy-five thousand dollars for permission to import tobacco into Russia. The sale of this narcotic had heretofore been discouraged in Russia, by the church, as demoralizing in its tendency and inducing untidy habits. Peter was occasionally induced to attend the theater, but he had no relish for that amusement. He visited the various churches and observed the mode of conducting religious worship by the several sects.

Before leaving England the tzar was entertained by King William with the spectacle of a sham sea fight. In this scene Peter was in his element, and in the excess of his delight he declared that an English admiral must be a happier man than even the tzar of Russia. His Britannic majesty made his guest also a present of a beautiful yacht, called the Royal Transport. In this vessel Peter returned to Holland, in May, 1698, having passed four months in England. He took with him quite a colony of emigrants, consisting of three captains of men of war, twenty-five captains of merchant ships, forty lieutenants, thirty pilots, thirty surgeons, two hundred and fifty gunners, and three hundred artificers. These men from Holland sailed in the Royal Transport to Archangel, from whence they were sent to different places where their services were needed. The officers whom the tzar sent to Italy, also led back to Russia many artists from that country.

From Holland the Emperor of Russia, with his suite, repaired to Vienna to observe the military discipline of the Germans, who had then the reputation of being the best soldiers in Europe. He also wished to enter into a closer alliance with the Austrian court as his natural ally against the Turks. Peter, however, insisted upon laying aside all the ceremonials of royalty, and, as a private person, held an interview with the Emperor Leopold.

Nothing of especial interest occurred during the brief residence of Peter in Vienna. The Emperor of Germany paid the tzar every possible attention which could be conferred upon one who had the strongest reluctance to be gazed upon, or to take part in any parade. For the amusement of the tzar the emperor revived the ancient game of landlord. The royal game is as follows. The emperor is landlord, the empress landlady, the heir apparent to the throne, the archdukes and archduchesses are generally their assistants. They entertain people of all nations, dressed after the most ancient fashion of their respective countries. The invited guests draw lots for tickets, on each of which is written the name or the nation of the character they are to represent. One is a Chinese mandarin, another a Persian mirza, another a Roman senator. A queen perhaps represents a dairy maid or a nursery girl. A king or prince represents a miller, a peasant or a soldier. Characteristic amusements are introduced. The landlord and landlady, with their family, wait upon the table.

On this occasion the emperor's eldest son, Joseph, who was the heir apparent, represented, with the Countess of Traun, the ancient Egyptians. His brother, the Archduke Charles, and the Countess of Walstein appeared as Flemings in the reign of Charles V. His sister Mary and Count Fraun were Tartars. Josephine, another daughter of Leopold, with the Count of Workla, represented Persians. Marianne, a third daughter, and Prince Maximilian of Hanover were North Holland peasants. Peter presented himself as a Friesland boor, a character, we regret to say, which the tzar could personify without making the slightest change in his usual habits, for Peter was quite a stranger to the graces of the polished gentleman.

This game seems to have been quite a favorite in the Austrian court. Maria Antoinette introduced it to Versailles. The tourist is still shown the dairy where that unhappy queen made butter and cheese, the mill where Louis XVI. ground his grist, and the mimic village tavern where the King and Queen of France, as landlord and landlady, received their guests.

Peter was just leaving Vienna to go to Venice when he received intelligence that a rebellion had broken out in Moscow. His ambitious sister Sophia, who had been placed with a shaven head in the cloisters of a monastery, took advantage of the tzar's absence to make another attempt to regain the crown. She represented that the nation was in danger of being overrun with foreigners, that their ancient customs would all be abolished, and that their religion would be subverted. She involved several of the clergy in her plans, and a band of eight thousand insurgents were assembled, who commenced their march towards Moscow, hoping to rouse the metropolis to unite with them. General Gordon, whom Peter had left in command of the royal guard, met them, and a battle ensued in which a large number of the insurgents were slain, and the rest were taken prisoners and conducted to the capital. Hearing these tidings Peter abandoned all plans for visiting Italy, and set out impetuously for Moscow, and arrived at the Kremlin before it was known that he had left Germany.

Peter was a rough, stern man, and he determined to punish the abettors of this rebellion with severity, which should appall all the discontented. General Gordon, in the battle, had slain three thousand of the insurgents and had taken five thousand captive. These prisoners he had punished, decimating them by lot and hanging every tenth man. Peter rewarded magnificently the royal guard, and then commenced the terrible chastisement of all who were judged guilty of sympathizing in the conspiracy. Some were broken on the wheel and then beheaded. Others were hung in chains, on gibbets near the gates of the city, and left, frozen as solid as marble, to swing in the wind through the long months of winter. Stone monuments were erected, on which were engraved the names, the crimes and the punishment of the rebels. A large number were banished to Siberia, to Astrachan, and to the shores of the Sea of Azof. The entire corps of the *strelitzes* was abolished, and their place supplied by the new guard, marshaled and disciplined on the model of the German troops. The long and cumbersome robes which had been in fashion were exchanged for a uniform better adapted for rapid motion. The sons of the nobles were compelled to serve in the ranks as common soldiers before they could be promoted to be officers. Many of the young nobles were sent to the tzar's fleet in the Sea of Azof to serve their apprenticeship for the navy. The revenue of the empire had thus far been raised by the payment of a stipulated sum from each noble according to his amount of land. The noble collected this sum from his vassals or bondmen; but they often failed of paying in the amount demanded. Peter took now the collection of the revenue into his own hands, appointing officers for that purpose.

Reforms in the church he also undertook. The patriarch, Adrian, who was the pope of the Greek church, dying about this time, Peter declared that he should have no successor. Virtually assuming the authority of the head of the church, he gathered the immense revenues of the patriarchal see into the royal treasury. Though professedly intrusting the government of the church to the bishops, he controlled them with despotism which could brook no opposition. Anxious to promote the population of his vast empire, so sparsely inhabited, he caused a decree to be issued, that all the clergy, of every grade, should be married; and that whenever one of the clergy lost a wife his clerical functions should cease until he obtained another. Regarding the monastic vow, which consigned young men and young women to a life of indolence in the cloister, as alike injurious to morality and to the interests of the State, he forbade any one from taking that vow until after the age of fifty had been passed. This salutary regulation has since his time been repealed.

The year, in Russia, had for ages commenced with the 1st of September. Peter ordered that, in conformity with the custom in the rest of Europe, the year should commence with the 1st of January. This alteration took place in the year 1700, and was celebrated with the most imposing solemnities. The national dress of the Russians was a long flowing robe, which required no skill in cutting or making. Razors were also scarce, and every man wore his beard. The tzar ordered long robes and beards to be laid aside. No man was admitted to the palace without a neatly shaven face. Throughout the empire a penalty was imposed upon any one who persisted in wearing his beard. A smooth face thus became in Russia, and has continued, to the present day, the badge of culture and refinement. Peter also introduced social parties, to which ladies with their daughters were invited, dressed in the fashions of southern Europe.

Heretofore, whenever a Russian addressed the tzar, he always said, " Your *slave* begs," etc. Peter abolished this word, and ordered *subject* to be used instead. Public inns were established on the highways, and relays of horses for the convenience of travelers. Conscious of the power of splendor to awe the public mind, he added very considerably to the magnificence of his court, and instituted an order of knighthood. In all these measures Peter wielded the energies of an unrelenting despotism, and yet of a despotism which was constantly devoted, not to his own personal aggrandizement, but to the welfare of his country.

The tzar established his great ship-yard at Voronise, on the Don, from which place he could float his ships down to the Sea of Azof, hoping to establish there a fleet which would soon give him the command of the Black Sea. In March, 1699, he had thirty-six ships launched and rigged, carrying each from thirty to sixty guns; and there were then twenty more ships on the stocks. There were, also, either finished or in process of construction, eighteen large galleys, one hundred smaller brigantines, seven bomb ships and four fire ships. At the same time Peter was directing his attention to the Volga and the Caspian, and still more vigorously to the Baltic, upon whose shores he had succeeded in obtaining a foothold.

And now the kingdom of Sweden came, with a rush, into the political arena. Poland had ceded to Sweden nearly the whole of Livonia. The Livonians were very much dissatisfied with the administration of the government under Charles XI., and sent a deputation to Stockholm to present respectful remonstrances. The indignant king consigned all of the deputation, consisting of eight gentlemen, to prison, and condemned the leader, John Patgul, to an ignominious death. Patgul escaped from prison, and hastening to Poland, urged the new sovereign, Augustus, to reconquer the province of Livonia, which Poland had lost, assuring him the Livonians would aid with all their energies to throw off the Swedish yoke. Patgul hastened from Poland to Moscow, and urged Peter to unite with Augustus, in a war against Sweden, assuring him that thus he could easily regain the provinces of Ingria and Carelia, which Sweden had wrested from his ancestors. Denmark also, under its new sovereign, Frederic IV., was induced to enter into the alliance with Russia and Poland against Sweden. Just at that time, Charles XI. died, and his son, Charles XII., a young man of eighteen, ascended the throne. The youth and inexperience of the new monarch encouraged the allies in the hope that they might make an easy conquest.

Charles XII., a man of indomitable, of maniacal energy, and who speedily infused into his soldiers his own spirit, came down upon Denmark like northern wolves into southern flocks and herds. In less than six weeks the war was terminated and the Danes thoroughly humbled. Then with his fleet of thirty sail of the line and a vast number of transports, he crossed the Baltic, entered the Gulf of Finland, and marching over ice and snow encountered the Russians at Narva, a small town about eighty miles south-west of the present site of the city of St. Petersburg. The Russians were drawn up eighty thousand strong, behind intrenchments lined with one hundred and forty-five pieces of artillery; Charles XII. had but nine thousand men. Taking advantage of one of the fiercest of wintry storms, which blew directly into the faces of the Russians, smothering them with snow and sleet mingled with smoke, and which concealed both the numbers and the movements of the Swedes, Charles XII. hurled his battalions with such impetuosity upon the foe, that in less than an hour the camp was taken by storm. One of the most awful routs known in the annals of war ensued. The Swedes toiled to utter exhaustion in cutting down the flying fugitives. Thirty thousand Russians perished on that bloody field. Nearly all of the remainder were taken captive, with all their artillery. Disarmed and with uncovered heads, thirty thousand of these prisoners defiled before the victorious king.*

Peter, the day before this disastrous battle, had left the intrenchments at Narva to go to Novgorod, ostensibly to hasten forward the march of some reinforcements. When Peter was informed of the annihilation of his army he replied, with characteristic coolness,

"I know very well that the Swedes will have the advantage of us for a considerable time; but they will teach us, at length, to beat them."

He immediately collected the fragments of his army at Novgorod, and repairing to Moscow issued orders for a cer-

* These are the numbers as accurately as they can now be ascertained by the most careful sifting of the contradictory accounts. The forces of the Russians have been variously estimated at from forty thousand to one hundred thousand. That the Swedes had but nine thousand is admitted on all hands.

tain proportion of the bells of the churches and convents throughout the empire to be cast into cannon and mortars. In a few months one hundred pieces of cannon for sieges, and forty-two field pieces, with twelve mortars and thirteen howitzers, were sent to the army, which was rapidly being rendezvoused at Novgorod.

Charles XII., having struck this terrific blow, left the tzar to recover as best he could, and turned his attention to Poland, resolved to hurl Augustus from the throne. Peter himself hurried to Poland to encourage Augustus to the most vigorous prosecution of the war, promising to send him speedily twenty thousand troops. In the midst of these disasters and turmoil, the tzar continued to prosecute his plans for the internal improvement of his empire, and commenced the vast enterprise of digging a canal which should unite the waters of the Baltic with the Caspian, first, by connecting the Don with the Volga, and then by connecting the Don with the Dwina, which empties into the Baltic near Riga.

War continued to rage very fiercely for many months between the Swedes on one side, and Russia and Poland on the other, Charles XII. gaining almost constant victories. The Swedes so signally proved their superiority in these conflicts, that when, on one occasion, eight thousand Russians repulsed four thousand Swedes, the tzar said,

"Well, we have at last beaten the Swedes, when we were two to one against them. We shall by and by be able to face them man to man."

In these conflicts, it was the constant aim of Peter to get a foothold upon the shores of the Baltic, that he might open to his empire the advantages of commerce. He launched a large fleet upon Lake Ladoga, a large inland sea, which, by the river Neva, connects with the Gulf of Finland. The fleets of Sweden penetrated these remote waters, and for months their solitudes resounded with the roar of naval conflicts. We can not refrain from recording the heroic conduct of Colonel Schlippenbuch, the Swedish commander of the town of Notteburg, on this lake. The town was invested by a large Russian army. For a month the Russians battered the town night and day, until it presented the aspect of a pile of ruins, and the garrison was reduced to one hundred men. Yet, so indomitable was this little band, that, standing in the breaches, they extorted honorable terms of capitulation from their conqueror. They would not surrender but on condition of being allowed to send for two Swedish officers, who should examine their remaining means of defense, and inform their master, Charles XII., that it was impossible for them any longer to preserve the town.

Peter was a man of too strong sense to be elated and vainglorious in view of such success. He knew full well that Charles XII., since the battle of Narva, looked with utter contempt upon the Russian soldiers, and he was himself fully conscious of the vast superiority of the Swedish troops. But while Charles XII., with a monarch's energies, was battering down the fortresses and cutting to pieces the armies of Poland, Peter had gained several victories over small detachments of Swedish troops left in Russia. To inspire his soldiers with more confidence, he ordered a very magnificent celebration of these victories in Moscow. It was one of the most gorgeous fête days the metropolis had ever witnessed. The Swedish banners, taken in several conflicts on sea and land, were borne in front of the procession, while all the prisoners, taken in the campaign, were marched in humiliation in the train of the victors.

While thus employed, the stern, indefatigable tzar was pressing forward the building of his fleet on the Don for the conquest of the Black Sea, and was unwearied in his endeavors to promote the elevation of his still semi-barbaric realms, by the introduction of the sciences, the arts, the manufactures and the social refinements of southern Europe.

CHAPTER XX.

CONQUESTS AND ACHIEVEMENTS OF PETER THE GREAT.

FROM 1702 TO 1718.

PETER TAKES LAKE LADOGA AND THE NEVA.—FOUNDATION OF ST. PETERSBURG.—CONQUEST OF LIVONIA.—MARIENBURG TAKEN BY STORM.—THE EMPRESS CATHARINE.—EXTRAORDINARY EFFORTS IN BUILDING ST. PETERSBURG.—THREAT OF CHARLES XII.—DEPOSITION OF AUGUSTUS.—ENTHRONEMENT OF STANISLAUS.—BATTLE OF PULTOWA.—FLIGHT OF CHARLES XII TO TURKEY.—INCREASED RENOWN OF RUSSIA.—DISASTROUS CONFLICT WITH THE TURKS.—MARRIAGE OF ALEXIS.—HIS CHARACTER.—DEATH OF HIS WIFE.—THE EMPRESS ACKNOWLEDGED.—CONQUEST OF FINLAND.—TOUR OF THE TZAR TO SOUTHERN EUROPE.

CHARLES XII., despising the Russians, devoted all his energies to the humiliation of Augustus of Poland, resolving to pursue him until he had driven him for ever from his throne. Peter was thus enabled to get the command of the lake of Ladoga, and of the river Neva, which connects that lake with the Baltic. He immediately laid the foundations of a city, St. Petersburg, to be his great commercial emporium, at the mouth of the Neva, near the head of the Gulf of Finland. The land was low and marshy, but in other respects the location was admirable. Its approaches could easily be defended against any naval attack, and water communications were opened with the interior through the Neva and lake Ladoga.

Livonia was a large province, about the size of the State of Maine, nearly encircled by the Gulf of Riga, the Baltic, the Gulf of Finland and Lake Tchude. The possession of this province, which contained some five hundred thousand inhabitants, was essential to Peter in the prosecution of his commercial enterprises. During the prosecution of this war the small town of Marienburg, on the confines of Livonia, situated on the shores of a lake, was taken by storm. The town was utterly destroyed and nearly all the inhabitants slain, a few only being taken prisoners. The Russian commanding officer saw among these captives a young girl of extraordinary beauty, who was weeping bitterly. Attracted by such rare loveliness and uncontrollable grief he called her to him, and learned from her that she was born in a village in the vicinity on the borders of the lake; that she had never known her father, and that her mother died when she was but three years of age. The protestant minister of Marienburg, Dr. Gluck, chancing to see her one day, and ascertaining that she was left an orphan and friendless, received her into his own house, and cherished her with true parental tenderness.

The very evening before the town of Marienburg was assaulted and taken by storm, she was married to a young Livonian sergeant, a very excellent young man, of reputable family and possessing a little property. In the horrors of the tempest of war which immediately succeeded the nuptial ceremonies, her husband was slain, and as his body could never be found, it probably was consumed in the flames, which laid the town in ashes. General Boyer, moved with compassion, took her under his protection. He ascertained that her character had always been irreproachable, and he ever maintained that she continued to be a pattern of virtue. She was but seventeen years of age when Peter saw her. Her beauty immediately vanquished him. His wife he had repudiated after a long disagreement, and she had retired to a convent. Peter took the lovely child, still a child in years, under his own care, and soon privately married her, with how much sacredness of nuptial rites is not now known. Such was the early history of Catharine, who subsequently became the recognized and renowned Empress of Russia.

"That a poor stranger," says Voltaire, "who had been discovered amid the ruins of a plundered town, should become the absolute sovereign of that very empire into which she was led captive, is an incident which fortune and merit have never before produced in the annals of the world."

The city of Petersburg was founded on the 22d of May, 1703, on a desert and marshy spot of ground, in the sixtieth degree of latitude. The first building was a fort which now stands in the center of the city. Though Peter was involved in all the hurry and confusion of war, he devoted himself with marvelous energy to the work of rearing an imperial city upon the bogs and the swamps of the Neva. It required the merciless vigor of despotism to accomplish such an enterprise. Workmen were marched by thousands from Kesan, from Astrachan, from the Ukraine, to assist in building the city. No difficulties, no obstacles were allowed to impede the work. The tzar had a low hut, built of plank, just sufficient to shelter him from the weather, where he superintended the operations. This hut is still preserved as one of the curiosities of St. Petersburg. In less than a year thirty thousand houses were reared, and these were all crowded by the many thousands Peter had ordered to the rising city, from all parts of the empire. Death made terrible ravages among them ; but the remote provinces furnished an abundant supply to fill the places of the dead. Exposure, toil, and the insalubrity of the marshy ground, consigned one hundred thousand to the grave during this first year.

The morass had to be drained, and the ground raised by bringing earth from a distance. Wheelbarrows were not in use there, and the laborers conveyed the earth in baskets, bags and even in the skirts of their clothes, scooping it up with their hands and with wooden paddles. The tzar always manifested great respect for the outward observances of religion, and was constant in his attendance upon divine service. As we have mentioned, the first building the tzar erected was a fort, the second was a church, the third a hotel. In the meantime private individuals were busily employed, by thousands, in putting up shops and houses. The city of Amsterdam was essentially the model upon which St. Petersburg was built. The wharves, the canals, the bridges and the rectangular streets lined with trees were arranged by architects brought from the Dutch metropolis. When Charles XII. was informed of the rapid progress the tzar was making in building a city on the banks of the Neva, he said,

"Let him amuse himself as he thinks fit in building his city. I shall soon find time to take it from him and to put his wooden houses in a blaze."

Five months had not passed away, from the commencement of operations upon these vast morasses at the mouth of the Neva, ere, one day, it was reported to the tzar that a large ship under Dutch colors was in full sail entering the harbor. Peter was overjoyed at this realization of the dearest wish of his heart. With ardor he set off to meet the welcome stranger. He found that the ship had been sent by one of his old friends at Zaandam. The cargo consisted of salt, wine and provisions generally. The cargo was landed free from all duties and was speedily sold to the great profit of the owners. To protect his capital, Peter immediately commenced his defenses at Cronstadt, about thirty miles down the bay. From that hour until this, Russia has been at work upon those fortifications, and they can now probably bid defiance to all the navies of the world.

Charles XII., sweeping Poland with fire and the sword, drove Augustus out of the kingdom to his hereditary electorate of Saxony, and then, convening the Polish nobles, caused Stanislaus Leczinsky, one of his own followers, to be elected sovereign, and sustained him on the throne by all the power of the Swedish armies.* The Swedish warrior now fitted out a fleet for the destruction of Cronstadt and Petersburg. The defense of the province was intrusted to Menzikoff. This man subsequently passed through a career so full of vicissitudes

* See Empire of Austria, page 382.

that a sketch of his variêd life thus far seems important. He was the son of one of the humblest of the peasants living in the vicinity of Moscow. When but thirteen years of age he was taken into the service of a pastry cook to sell pies and cakes about the streets, and he was accustomed to attract customers by singing jocular songs. The tzar chanced to hear him one day, and, diverted by his song and struck by his bright, intelligent appearance, called for the boy, and offered to purchase his whole stock, both cakes and basket.

The boy replied,

"It is my business to sell the cakes, and I have no right to sell the basket without my master's permission. Yet, as every thing belongs to our prince, your majesty has only to give the command, and it is my duty to obey."

This adroit, apt answer so pleased the tzar that he took the lad into his service, giving him at first some humble employment. But being daily more pleased with his wit and shrewdness, he raised him, step by step, to the highest preferment. Under the tuition of General Le Fort, he attained great skill in military affairs, and became one of the bravest and most successful of the Russian generals.

Early in the spring of 1705 the Swedish fleet, consisting of twenty-two ships of war, each carrying about sixty guns, besides six frigates, two bomb ketches and two fire ships, approached Cronstadt. At the same time a large number of transports landed a strong body of troops to assail the forts in the rear. This was the most formidable attack Charles XII. had yet attempted in his wars. Though the Swedes almost invariably conquered the Russians in the open field, Menzikoff, from behind his well-constructed redoubts, beat back his assailants, and St. Petersburg was saved. The summer passed away with many but undecisive battles, until the storms of the long northern winter separated the combatants. The state of exasperation was now such that the most revolting cruelties were perpetrated on both sides.

The campaign of 1706 opened most disastrously to Russia. In four successive pitched battles the forces of the tzar had been defeated. Augustus was humbled to the dust, and was compelled to write a letter to Stanislaus congratulating him upon his accession to the throne. He also ignominiously consented to deliver up the unfortunate Livonian noble, Patgul, whose only crime was his love for the rights and privileges of his country. Charles XII. caused this unhappy noble to be broken upon the wheel, thus inflicting a stain upon his own character which can never be effaced. The haughty Swedish monarch seemed now to be sovereign over all of northern Europe excepting Russia. Augustus, driven from the throne of Poland, was permitted to hold the electorate of Saxony only in consequence of his abject submission to Charles XII. Stanislaus, the new Polish sovereign, was merely a vassal of Sweden. And even the Emperor Joseph of Germany paid implicit obedience to the will of a monarch who had such terrible armies at his command.

Under these circumstances some of the powers endeavored to secure peace between Sweden and Russia. The French envoy at the court of Sweden introduced the subject. Charles XII. proudly replied, "I shall treat with the tzar in the city of Moscow."

Peter, being informed of this boast and threat, remarked, "My brother Charles wants to act the part of Alexander, but he shall not find in me a Darius."

Charles XII., from his triumphant invasion of Saxony, marched with an army of forty-five thousand men through Poland, which was utterly desolated by war, and crossing the frontiers of Russia, directed his march to Moscow. Driving all opposition before him, he arrived upon the banks of the Dnieper, and without much difficulty effected the passage of the stream. Peter himself, with Menzikoff, now hastened to the theater of conflict, and summoned his mightiest energies to repel the foe. Battle after battle ensued with varying results. But the situation of the Swedish conqueror was fast growing desperate. He was far from home. His regiments were daily diminishing beneath the terrible storms of war, while recruits were pouring in, from all directions, to swell the ranks of the tzar. It was the month of December. The villages had been all burned and the country turned into a desert. The cold was so intense that on one particular march two thousand men dropped down dead in their ranks. The wintry storms soon became so severe that both parties were compelled to remain for some time in inaction. Every poor peasant, within fifty miles, was robbed by detachments of starving soldiers.

The moment the weather permitted, both armies were again in action. Charles XII. had taken a circuitous route towards Moscow, through the Ukraine, hoping to rouse the people of this region to join his standards. This plan, however, proved an utter failure. About the middle of June the two armies, led by their respective sovereigns, met at Pultowa, upon the Worskla, near its point of junction with the Dnieper, about four hundred miles south of Moscow. Several days were passed in maneuvering and skirmishing in preparation for a decisive struggle. It was evident to all Europe that the great battle to ensue would decide the fate of Russia, Poland and Sweden. Thirty thousand war-worn veterans were marshaled under the banners of Charles XII. The tzar led sixty thousand troops into the conflict. Fully aware of the superiority of the Swedish troops, he awaited the attack of his formidable foe behind his redoubts. In one of the skirmishes, two days before the great battle, a bullet struck Charles XII., shattering the bone of his heel. It was an exceedingly painful wound, which was followed by an equally painful operation. Though the indomitable warrior was suffering severely, he caused himself to be borne in a litter to the head of his troops, and led the charge. The attack upon the intrenchments was made with all the characteristic impetuosity of these demoniac fighters. Notwithstanding the storm of grape shot which was hurled into their faces, covering the ground with the mangled and the dead, two of the redoubts were taken, and shouts of victory ran along the lines of the Swedes.

The action continued with fiend-like ferocity for two hours. Charles XII., with a pistol in his hand, was borne on his litter from rank to rank, animating his troops, until a cannon ball, striking down one of his bearers, also shattered the litter into fragments, and dashed the bandaged monarch to the ground. With as much calmness as though this were an ordinary, every-day occurrence, Charles ordered his guards immediately to make another litter with their pikes. He was placed upon it, and continued to direct the battle, paying no more attention to bullets, balls and bombshells, than if they had been snow flakes.

Peter was equally prodigal of danger. Death in that hour was more desirable to him than defeat, for Charles XII., victorious, would march direct to Moscow, and Russia would share the fate of Poland. The tzar was conspicuous at every point where the battle raged most fiercely. Several bullets pierced his clothes; one passing through his hat just grazed the crown of his head. At length, the Swedes, overpowered by numbers, gave way, and fled in great confusion. Charles, though agonized by his wound, was compelled to mount on horseback as the only means of escape from capture. The black hour of woe came, which sooner or later meets almost every warrior, however successful for a time his career may be. The blow was fatal to Charles XII. More than nine thousand of the Swedes were left dead upon the field of battle. Eighteen thousand were taken prisoners. The Swedish king, with a few hundred troops in his retinue, cut off from his retreat towards Sweden, crossed the Dnieper and fled to Turkey. Peter did not pursue him, but being informed of his desperate resolve to seek refuge in the territory of the Turks, he magnanimously wrote a letter to him, urging him not to take so perilous a step, assuring him, upon his honor, that he would not detain him as a prisoner, but that all their difficulties should be settled by a reasonable peace. A special courier was dispatched with this letter, but he could not overtake the fugitives. When the courier arrived at the river Boy, which separates the deserts of Ukraine from the territories of the Grand Seignor, the Swedes had already crossed the river. In the character of Peter there was a singular compound of magnanimity and of the most brutal insensibility and mercilessness. He ordered all the Swedish generals, who were his captives, to be introduced to him, returned to them their swords and invited them to dine. With a gracefulness of courtesy rarely surpassed, he offered as a toast the sentiment, "To the health of my masters in the art of war." And yet, soon after, he consigned nearly all these captives to the horrors of Siberian exile.

This utter defeat of Charles XII. produced a sudden revolution in Poland, Sweden and Saxony. Peter immediately dispatched a large body of cavalry, under Menzikoff, to Poland, to assist Augustus in regaining his crown. Soon after, he followed himself, at the head of an army, and entering Warsaw in triumph, on the 7th of October, 1709, replaced Augustus upon the throne from which Charles XII. had ejected him. The whole kingdom acknowledged Peter for their protector. Peter then marched to the electorate of Brandenburg, which had recently been elevated into the kingdom of Prussia, and performing the functions of his own embassador, entered into a treaty with Frederic I., grandfather of Frederic the Great. He then returned with all eagerness to St. Petersburg, and pressed forward the erection of new buildings and the enlargement of the fleet.

A magnificent festival was here arranged in commemoration of the great victory of Pultowa. Nine arches were reared, beneath which the procession marched, in the most gorgeous array of civic and military pageantry. The artillery of the vanquished, their standards, the shattered litter of the king, and the vast array of captives, soldiers and officers, all on foot, followed in the train of the triumphal procession, while the ringing of bells, the explosion of an hundred pieces of artillery, and the shouts of an innumerable multitude, added to the enthusiasm which the scene inspired.

The battle of Pultowa gave Peter great renown throughout Europe, and added immeasurably to the reputation of Russia. An occurrence had taken place in London which had deeply offended the tzar, who, wielding himself the energies of despotism, could form no idea of that government of law which was irrespective of the will of the sovereign. The Russian embassador at the court of Queen Anne had been arrested at the suit of a tradesman in London, and had been obliged to give bail to save himself from the debtor's prison. Peter, regarding this as a personal insult, demanded of Queen Anne satisfaction. She expressed her regret for the occurrence, but stated, that according to the laws of England, a creditor had a right to sue for his just demands, and that there was no statute exempting foreign embassadors from being arrested for debt. Peter, who had no respect for constitutional liberty, was not at all satisfied with this declaration, but postponed further action until his conflict with Sweden should be terminated.

Now, in the hour of victory, he turned again to Queen Anne and demanded reparation for what he deemed the insult offered to his government. He threatened, in retaliation, to take vengeance upon all the merchants and British subjects within his dominions. This was an appalling menace. Queen Anne accordingly sent Lord Whitworth on a formal embassy to the tzar, with a diplomatic lie in his mouth. Addressing Peter in the flattering words of "most high and mighty emperor," he assured him, that the offending tradesman had been punished with imprisonment and rendered infamous, and that an act of Parliament should be passed, rendering it no longer lawful to arrest a foreign embassador. The offender had not been punished, but the act was subsequently passed.

The acknowledgment, accompanied by such flattering testimonials of respect, was deemed satisfactory. The tzar had demanded the death of the offender. Every Englishman must read with pride the declaration of Queen Anne in reference to this demand.

"There are," said she, "insuperable difficulties with respect to the ancient and fundamental laws of the government of our people, which we fear do not *permit* so severe and rigorous a sentence to be given, as your imperial majesty first seemed to expect in this case. And we persuade ourselves that your imperial majesty, who are a prince famous for clemency and exact justice, will not require us, who are the *guardian and protector of the laws*, to inflict a punishment on our subjects which the law does not empower us to do."

The whole of Livonia speedily fell into the hands of the tzar and was reannexed to Russia. Pestilence, which usually follows in the train of war, now rose from the putridity of battle fields, and sweeping, like the angel of death, over the war-scathed and starving inhabitants of Livonia, penetrated Sweden. Whole provinces were depopulated, and in Stockholm alone thirty thousand perished. The war of the Spanish Succession was now raging, and every nation in Europe was engaged in the work of destruction and butchery. Spain, Portugal, Italy, France, the German empire, England, Holland, Denmark, Sweden, Poland, were all in arms, and hundreds of millions of men were directly or indirectly employed in the work of mutual destruction. The fugitive king, Charles XII., was endeavoring to enlist the energies of the Ottoman Porte in his behalf, and the Grand Seignor had promised to throw his armies also, two hundred thousand strong, into the arena of flame and blood, and to march for the conquest of Russia.

Peter, conscious of the danger of an attack from Turkey,

raised an army of one hundred and twenty-five thousand men, when he was informed that the Turks, with a combined army of two hundred and ten thousand troops, were ravaging the province of Azof. Urging his troops impetuously onward, he crossed the Pruth and entered Jassi, the capital of Moldavia. The grand vizier, with an army three times more numerous, crossed the Danube and advanced to meet him. For three days the contending hosts poured their shot into each other's bosoms. The tzar, outnumbered and surrounded, though enabled to hold his position behind his intrenchments, saw clearly that famine would soon compel him to surrender. His position was desperate.

Catharine had accompanied her husband on this expedition, and, at her earnest solicitation, the tzar sent proposals of peace to the grand vizier, accompanied with a valuable present of money and jewels. The Turk, dreading the energies which despair might develop in so powerful a foe, was willing to come into an accommodation, and entered into a treaty, which, though greatly to the advantage of the Ottoman Porte, rescued the tzar from the greatest peril in which he had ever been placed. The grand vizier good-naturedly sent several wagons of provisions to the camp of his humbled foes, and the Russians returned to their homes, having lost twenty thousand men.

Alexis, the oldest son of Peter, had ever been a bad boy, and he had now grown up into an exceedingly dissolute and vicious young man. Indolent, licentious, bacchanalian in his habits, and overbearing, his father had often threatened to deprive him of his right of succession, and to shave his crown and consign him to a convent. Hoping to improve his character, he urged his marriage, and selected for him a beautiful princess of Wolfenbuttle, as the possessions of the dukes of Brunswick were then called. The old ducal castle still stands on the banks of the Oka about forty miles south-east of Hanover. The princess of Wolfenbuttle, who was but eighteen years of age, was sister to the Empress of Germany, consort of Charles VI. The young Russian prince was dragged very reluctantly to this marriage, for he wished to be shackled by no such ties. He was the son of Peter's first wife, not of the Empress Catharine, whom the tzar had now acknowledged. Peter and Catharine attended these untoward nuptials, which were celebrated in the palace of the Queen of Poland, in which a princess as lovely in character as in person was sacrificed to one who made the few remaining months of her life a continued martyrdom. But little more than a year nad passed after their marriage ere she was brought to bed of a son. Her heart was already broken, and she was quite unprepared for the anguish of such an hour. Though the sweetness of her disposition and the gentleness of her manners had endeared her to all her household, her husband treated her with the most brutal neglect and cruelty. Unblushingly he introduced into the palace his mistresses, and the saloons ever resounded with the uproar of his drunken companions. The woe-stricken princess, then but twenty years of age, covered her face with the bed clothes, and, weeping bitterly, refused to take any nourishment, and begged the physicians to permit her to die in peace. Intelligence was immediately sent to the tzar of the confinement of his daughter in-law, and of her dangerous situation. He hastened to her chamber. The interview was short, but so affecting that the tzar, losing all self-control, burst into an agony of grief and wept like a child. The dying princess commended to his care her babe and her servants, and, as the clock struck the hour of midnight, her spirit departed, we trust to that world "where the wicked cease from troubling and the weary are at rest." The orphan babe was baptized as Peter Alexis, and subsequently, on the death of the Empress Catharine, became Emperor of Russia.

On the 20th of February, 1712, Peter, who had previously acknowledged his private marriage with Catharine, had the marriage publicly solemnized at St. Petersburg with the utmost pomp. Soon after this, to the inexpressible joy of both parents, Catharine gave birth to a son. The war with Sweden still continued, notwithstanding Charles XII. was a fugitive in Turkey unable to return to his own country. Finland, a vast realm containing one hundred and thirty-five thousand square miles and almost embraced by the Gulfs of Bothnia and of Finland, then belonged to Sweden. Peter fitted out an expedition from St. Petersburg for the conquest of that country. With three hundred ships, conveying thirteen thousand men, he effected a landing in the vicinity of Abo notwithstanding the opposition of the Swedish force there, and, establishing his troops in redoubts with ample supplies, he returned to St. Petersburg for reinforcements. He soon returned, and, with an army augmented to twenty thousand foot and four thousand horse, with a powerful train of artillery, commenced a career of conquest. The city of Abo, on the coast, the capital of Finland, fell unresistingly into his hands with a large quantity of provisions. There was a flourishing university here containing a valuable library. Peter sent the books to St. Petersburg, and they became the foundation of the present royal library in that place.

The tzar, leaving the prosecution of the war to his generals, returned to St. Petersburg. Many and bloody battles were fought in those northern wilds during the summer, in most of which the Russians had the advantage, gaining citadel after citadel until winter drove the combatants from the field.

With indefatigable zeal Peter pressed forward in his plan to give splendor and power to his new city of Petersburg. One thousand families were moved there from Moscow. Very flattering offers were made to induce foreigners to settle there, and a decree was issued declaring Petersburg to be the only port of entry in the empire. He ordered that no more wooden houses should be built, and that all should be covered with tile; and to secure the best architects from Europe, he offered them houses rent free, and entire exemption from taxes for fourteen years. The campaign of another summer, that of 1714, rendered the tzar the master of the whole province of Finland.

In the autumn of this year, Charles XII., escaped from Turkey, where he had performed pranks outrivaling Don Quixote, and had finally been held a prisoner. He traversed Hungary and Germany in disguise, and traveling day and night, in such haste that but one of his attendants could keep up with him, arrived, exhausted and haggard, in Sweden. He was received with the liveliest demonstrations of joy, and immediately placed himself again at the head of the Swedish armies.

The tzar, however, conscious that he now had not much to fear from Sweden, left the conduct of the desultory war with his generals, and set out on another tour of observation to southern Europe. The lovely Catharine, who, with the fairy form and sylph-like grace of a girl of seventeen, had won the love of Peter, was now a staid and worthy matron of middle life. She had, however, secured the abiding affection of the tzar, and he loved to take her with him on all his journeys. Catharine, though on the eve of again becoming a mother, accompanied her husband as far as Holland. Through Stralsund, Mecklenburg and Hamburg, they proceeded to Rostock, where a fleet of forty-five galleys awaited him. The emperor took the command, and hoisting his flag, sailed to Copenhagen. Here he was entertained for two months with profuse hospitality by the King of Denmark, during which time he studied, with sleepless vigilance, the institutions and the artistic attainments of the country.

About the middle of December he arrived at Amsterdam. The city gave him a splendid reception, and he was welcomed by the Earl of Albemarle in a very complimentary speech, pompous and flowery. The uncourteous tzar bluntly replied,

"I thank you heartily, though I do n't understand much of what you say. I learned my Dutch among ship-builders, but the sort of language you have spoken I am sure I never learned."

Some of his old companions, who were ship-builders, and had acquired wealth, invited him to dine. They addressed him as "your majesty." Peter cut them short, saying,

"Come, brothers, let us converse like plain and honest ship-carpenters."

A servant brought him some wine. "Give me the jug," said he laughing, "and then I can drink as much as I please, and no one can tell how much I have taken."

He hastened to Zaandam, where he was received with the utmost joy by his old friends from whom he had parted nineteen years before. An old woman pressed forward to greet him.

"My good woman," said the tzar, "how do you know who I am?"

"I am the widow," she said, "of Baas Pool, at whose table your majesty so often sat nineteen years ago."

The emperor kissed her upon the forehead and invited her to dine with him that very day. One of his first visits was to the little cottage, or rather hut, which he had occupied while residing there. The cottage is still carefully preserved, having been purchased in 1823 by the sister of the Emperor Alexander, and enclosed in another building with large arched windows. The room was even then regarded as sacred. In the center stood the oaken table and the three wooden chairs which constituted the furniture when Peter occupied it. The loft was ascended by a ladder which still remains.

With all the roughness of Peter's exterior, he had always been a man of deep religious feelings, and through all his life was in habits of daily prayer. This loft had been his place of private devotion to which he daily ascended. Upon entering the cottage and finding every thing just as he had left it, the tzar was for a moment much affected. He ascended the ladder to his closet of prayer in the loft, and there remained alone with his God for a full half hour. Eventful indeed and varied had his life been since there, a young man of twenty-five, he had daily sought divine guidance.

CHAPTER XXI.

THE TRIAL AND CONDEMNATION OF ALEXIS AND DEATH OF THE TZAR.

FROM 1718 TO 1725.

THE TZAR'S SECOND VISIT TO HOLLAND.—RECEPTION IN FRANCE.—DESCRIPTION OF CATHARINE.—DOMESTIC GRIEF.—CONDUCT OF ALEXIS.—LETTERS FROM HIS FATHER. —FLIGHT TO GERMANY.—THENCE TO NAPLES.—ENVOYS SENT TO BRING HIM BACK. ALEXIS EXCLUDED FROM THE SUCCESSION.—HIS TRIAL FOR TREASON.—CONDEMNATION AND UNEXPECTED DEATH.—NEW EFFORTS OF THE TZAR FOR THE WELFARE OF RUSSIA.—SICKNESS OF PETER.—HIS DEATH.—SUCCESSION OF THE EMPRESS CATHARINE.—EPITAPH TO THE EMPEROR.

FROM Holland the tzar went to Paris. Great preparations were made there for his reception, and apartments in the Louvre were gorgeously fitted up for the accommodation of him and his suite. But Peter, annoyed by parade, declined the sumptuous palace, and, the very evening of his arrival, took lodgings at the Hotel de Lesdiguieres. To those who urged his acceptance of the saloons of the Louvre he replied,

"I am a soldier. A little bread and beer satisfy me. I prefer small apartments to large ones. I have no desire to be attended with pomp and ceremony, nor to give trouble to so many people."

Every hour of his stay in Paris was employed in studying the institutions of the realm, and the progress made in the arts and sciences. Standing by the tomb of Richelieu, which is one of the finest pieces of sculpture in Europe, he exclaimed,

"Thou great man! I would have given thee one half of my dominions to learn of thee how to govern the other half."

All the trades and manufactures of the capital he examined with the greatest care, and took back with him to St. Petersburg a large number of the most skillful artists and mechanics. Leaving France he returned to Amsterdam, where he rejoined Catharine, and proceeded with her to Berlin. A haughty German lady, piqued, perhaps, that a woman not of noble birth should be an empress, thus describes the appearance of Catharine at that time:

"The tzarina is short and lusty, remarkably coarse, without grace and animation. One need only see her to be satisfied of her low birth. At the first blush one would take her for a German actress. Her clothes looked as if bought at a doll shop; every thing was so old fashioned and so bedecked with silver and tinsel. She was decorated with a dozen orders, portraits of saints, and relics, which occasioned such a clatter that when she walked one would suppose that an ass with bells was approaching. The tzar, on the contrary, was tall and well made. His countenance is handsome, but there is something in it so rude that it inspires one with dread. He was dressed like a seaman, in a frock, without lace or ornament."*

On Peter's return to Russia, he was compelled to meet and grasp a trouble which for fifteen years had embittered his life. His son, Alexis, had ever been a thorn in his father's side. He was not only indolent and dissipated, but he was utterly opposed to all his father's measures for reform, and was continually engaged in underhand measures to head a party against him. Upon the death of the unhappy princess of Wolfenbuttle, wife of this worthless prince, the grieved and indignant father wrote to him as follows:

"I shall wait a little while longer to see if there be any hopes of your reform. If not, I shall cut you off from the succession as one lops off a dead branch. Do not think that I wish to intimidate you; and do not place too much reliance upon the fact that you are my only son.† If I am willing to

* Memoires de la Margrave de Bareith.

† The empress gave birth to a son shortly after this letter was written.

lay down my own life for Russia, do you think that I shall be willing to sacrifice my country for you? I would rather transmit the crown to an entire stranger worthy of the trust, than to my own child unworthy of it."

This letter produced no effect upon the shameless debauchee. He continued unchecked in his career of infamy. In acknowledging the receipt of his father's letter, he contemptuously replied that he had no wish for the crown, and that he was ready at any time to take an oath that he would renounce it for ever. Matters were in this position when the tzar left for Denmark. He had hardly arrived in Copenhagen when he received dispatches informing him that his son was gathering around him all the disaffected, and was seriously endangering the tranquillity of the State. Once more the anxious father wrote to him in these words:

"I observe in your letter that you say not a word of the affliction your conduct has caused me for so many years. A father's admonitions seem to produce no impression upon you. I have prevailed on myself to write you once more, and for the last time. Those *bushy beards* bind you to their purposes. They are the persons whom you trust, who place their hopes in you; and you have no gratitude to him who gave you life. Since you were of age have you ever aided your father in his toils? Have you not opposed every thing I have done for the good of my people? Have I not reason to believe that should you survive me you will destroy all that I have accomplished? Amend your life. Render yourself worthy of the succession, or turn monk. Reply to this either in person or in writing. If you do not I shall treat you as a criminal."

The reply of Alexis was laconic indeed. It consisted of just four lines, and was as follows:

"Your letter of the 19th I received yesterday. My illness prevents me from writing at length. I intend to embrace the monastic life, and I request your gracious consent to that effect."

Seven months passed away, during which the tzar heard nothing directly from his son, though the father kept himself informed of his conduct. As Peter was returning from France he wrote to his son reproaching him for his long silence, and requesting him, if he wished to amend his ways and secure his father's favor, to meet him at Copenhagen; but that if, on the contrary, he preferred to enter a convent, which was the only alternative, he should inform him by the return courier, that measures might be adopted to carry the plan immediately into effect.

This brought matters to a crisis. The last thing the bloated debauchee wished was to enter a convent. He was equally averse to a sober life, and dared not meet his father lest he should be placed under arrest. He consequently made no reply, but pretending that he was to set out immediately for Copenhagen, he secured all the treasure he could lay his hands upon and fled to Germany, to the court of the Emperor Charles VI., who, it will be remembered, was his brother-in-law, having married a sister of his deceased wife. Here he told a deplorable story of the cruelty of his father, of the persecutions to which he was exposed, and that to save his life he had been compelled to flee from Russia.

The emperor, knowing full well that the young man was an infamous profligate, was not at all disposed to incur the displeasure of Peter by apparently espousing the cause of the son against the father. He consequently gave the miscreant such a cold reception that he found the imperial palace any thing but a pleasant place of residence, and again he set out on his vagabond travels. The next tidings his father heard of him were that he was in Naples, spending, as ever, his substance in riotous living. A father's heart still yearned over the miserable young man, and compassion was blended with disappointment and indignation. He immediately dispatched two members of his court, M. Romanzoff, captain of the royal guards, and M. Toltoi, a privy counselor, to Naples, to make a last effort to reclaim his misguided son. They found the young man in the chateau of Saint Elme, and presented to him a letter from his father. It was dated Spa, July 1, 1717, and contained the following words:

"I write to you for the last time. Toltoi and Romanzoff will make known to you my will. If you obey me, I assure you, and I promise before God, that I will not punish you, but if you will return to me I will love you better than ever. But if you will not return to me, I pronounce upon you, as your father, in virtue of the power I have received from God, my eternal malediction; and, as your sovereign, I assure you that I shall find means to punish you, in which I trust God will assist me."

It required the most earnest persuasion, and even the intervention of the viceroy of Naples, to induce Alexis to return to Russia. The miserable man had a harem of abandoned women with him, with whom he set out on his return. They arrived in Moscow the 13th of February, 1718, and on that very day Peter had an interview with his son. No one knows what passed in that interview. The rumor of the arrival of Alexis spread rapidly through the city, and it was supposed that a reconciliation had taken place. But the next morning, at the earliest dawn, the great bell of Moscow rang an alarm, the royal guards were marshaled and the privy counselors of the emperor were summoned to the Kremlin.

Alexis was led, without his sword and as a prisoner, into the presence of his father. At the same time, all the high ecclesiastics of the church were assembled, in solemn conclave, in the cathedral church. Alexis fell upon his knees before his father, confessed his faults, renounced all claim to the succession and entreated only that his life might be spared. The tzar led his son into an adjoining room, where they for some time remained alone. He then returned to his privy council and read a long statement, very carefully drawn up, minutely recapitulating the conduct of Alexis, his indolence, his shameless libertinism, his low companionship, his treasonable designs, and exhibiting his utter unfitness, in all respects, to be entrusted with the government of an empire. This remarkable document was concluded with the following words:

"Now although our son, by such criminal conduct, merits the punishment of death, yet our paternal affection induces us to pardon his crimes and to exempt him from the penalty which is his due. But considering his unworthiness, as developed in the conduct we have described, we can not, in conscience, bequeath to him the throne of Russia, foreseeing that, by his vicious courses, he would degrade the glory of our nation, endanger its safety and speedily lose those provinces which we have recovered from our foes with so much toil and at so vast an expense of blood and treasure. To inflict upon our faithful subjects the rule of such a sovereign, would be to expose them to a condition worse than Russia has ever yet experienced. We do therefore, by our paternal authority, in virtue of which, by the laws of our empire, any of our subjects may disinherit a son and give his succession to such other of his sons as he pleases, and, in quality of sovereign prince, in consideration of the safety of our dominions, we do deprive our son, Alexis, for his crimes and unworthiness, of the succession after us to our throne of Russia, and we do constitute and declare successor to the said throne after us our second son, Peter.

"We lay upon our said son, Alexis, our paternal curse if ever, at any time, he pretends to, or reclaims said succession, and we desire our faithful subjects, whether ecclesiastics or seculars, of all ranks and conditions, and the whole Russian nation, in conformity to this, our will, to acknowledge our son Peter as lawful successor, and to confirm the whole by oath before the holy altar upon the holy gospel, kissing the cross. And all those who shall ever oppose this, our will, and shall dare to consider our son, Alexis, as successor, we declare traitors to us and to their country. We have ordered these presents to be everywhere promulgated, that no person may pretend ignorance. Given at Moscow, February 3d, 1718."

This document was then taken to the cathedral, where all the higher ecclesiastics had been assembled, and was read to them. Nothing was omitted which could invest the act with solemnity. There is every evidence that the heart of the father was rent with acutest anguish in all these proceedings. Nothing could have been more desirable to him than to transmit the empire his energies had rendered so illustrious, to his own son to carry on the enterprises his-father had commenced. But to place eighteen millions of people in the hands of one who had proved himself so totally unworthy, would have been the greatest cruelty. The exclusion of Alexis from the succession was the noblest act of Peter's life.

But new facts were soon developed which rendered it impossible for the unhappy father to stop even here. Evidence came to light that Alexis had been plotting a conspiracy for the dethronement of his father, and for the seizure of the crown by violence. His mother, whom the tzar had repudiated, and his energetic aunt, Mary, both of whom were in a convent, were involved in the plot. He had applied to his brother-in-law, the Emperor of Germany, for foreign troops to aid him. There were many restless spirits in the empire, turbulent and depraved, the boon companions of Alexis, who were ready for any deeds of desperation which might place Alexis on the throne. The second son of the emperor, the child of Catharine, was an infant of but a few months old. The health of Peter was infirm and his life doubtful. It was manifest that immediately upon the death of the tzar, Alexis would rally his accomplices around him, raise the banner of revolt against the infant king, and that thus the empire would be plunged into all the horrors of a long and bloody civil war.

Peter having commenced the work of self-sacrifice for the salvation of Russia, was not disposed to leave that work half accomplished. All knew that the infamous Alexis would shrink from no crime, and there was ample evidence of his treasonable plots. The father now deliberately resolved to arraign his son for high treason, a crime which doomed him to death. Aware of the awful solemnity of such a moment, and of the severity with which his measures and his motives would be sifted by posterity, he proceeded with the greatest circumspection. A high court of justice was organized for the trial, consisting of two chambers, the one ecclesiastical, the other secular. On the 13th of June, 1718, the court was assembled, and the tzar presented to them the documentary evidence, which had been carefully obtained, of his son's treasonable designs, and thus addressed them:

"Though the flight of Alexis, the son of the tzar, and a part of his crimes be already known, yet there are now discovered such unexpected and surprising attempts, as plainly show with what baseness and villainy he endeavored to impose on us, his sovereign and father, and what perjuries he hath committed against Almighty God, all which shall now be laid before you. Though, according to all laws, civil and divine, and especially those of this empire, which grant fathers absolute jurisdiction over their children, we have full power to judge our son according to our pleasure, yet, as men are liable to prejudice in their own affairs, and as the most eminent physicians rely not on their own judgment concerning themselves, but call in the advice of others, so we, under the awful fear of displeasing God, make known our disease, and apply to you for a cure. As I have promised pardon to my son in case he should declare to me the truth, and though he has forfeited this promise by concealing his rebellious designs, yet, that we may not swerve from our obligation, we pray you to consider this affair with seriousness, and report what punishment he deserves without favor or partiality either to him or me. Let not the reflection that you are passing sentence on the son of your prince have any influence on you, but administer justice without respect of persons. Destroy not your own souls and mine, by doing any thing which may injure our country or upbraid our consciences in the great and terrible day of judgment."

The evidence adduced against the young prince, from his own confession, and the depositions which had been taken, were very carefully considered, nearly a month being occupied in the solemnities of deliberation. A verdict was finally rendered in the form of a report to the emperor. It was a long, carefully-worded document, containing a statement of the facts which the evidence substantiated against the culprit. The conclusion was as follows:

"It is evident, from the whole conduct of the son of the tzar, that he intended to take the crown from the head of his father and place it upon his own, not only by a civil insurrection, but by the assistance of a foreign army which he had actually requested. He has therefore rendered himself unworthy of the clemency promised by the emperor; and, since all laws, divine, ecclesiastical, civil and military, condemn to death, without mercy, not only those who attempt rebellion against their sovereign, but those who are plotting such attempts, what shall be our judgment of one who has conspired for the commission of a crime almost unparalleled in history—the assassination of his sovereign, who was his own father, a father of great indulgence, who reared his son from the cradle with more than paternal tenderness, who, with incredible pains, strove to educate him for government, and to qualify him for the succession to so great an empire? How much more imperatively does such a crime merit death.

"It is therefore with hearts full of affliction, and eyes streaming with tears, that we, as subjects and servants, pronounce this sentence against the son of our most precious sovereign lord, the tzar. Nevertheless, it being his pleasure that we should act in this capacity, we, by these presents, declare our real opinion, and pronounce this sentence of condemnation with a pure conscience as we hope to answer at the tribunal of Almighty God. We submit, however, this sentence to the sovereign will and revisal of his imperial majesty, our most merciful sovereign."

This sentence was signed by all the members of the court, one hundred and eighty in number; and on the 6th of July it was read to the guilty prince in the castle where he was kept confined. The miserable young man, enfeebled in body and mind by debaucheries, was so overwhelmed with terror, as his death warrant was read, that he was thrown into convulsions. All the night long fit succeeded fit, as, delirious with woe, he moaned upon his bed. In the morning a messenger was dispatched to the tzar to inform him that his son was seriously sick; in an hour another messenger was sent stating that he was very dangerously sick; and soon a third messenger was dispatched with the intelligence that Alexis could not survive the day, and was very anxious to see his father. Peter, scarce less wretched than his miserable son, hastened to his room. The dying young man, at the sight of his father, burst into tears, confessed all his crimes, and begged his father's blessing in this hour of death. Tears coursed down the cheeks of the stern emperor, and he addressed his dying child in terms so pathetic, and so fervently implored God's pardon for him, that the stoutest hearts were moved and loud sobbings filled the room.

It was midday of the 7th of July, 1718. The prince was confined in a large chamber of a stone castle, which was at the same time a palace and a fortress. There lay upon the couch the dying Alexis, bloated by the excesses of a life of utter pollution, yet pale and haggard with terror and woe. The iron-hearted father, whose soul this sublime tragedy had melted, sat at his side weeping like a child. The guards who stood at the door, the nobles and ecclesiastics who had accompanied the emperor, were all unmanned, many sobbing aloud, overwhelmed by emotions utterly uncontrollable. This scene stamps the impress of almost celestial greatness upon the soul of the tzar. He knew his son's weakness, incompetency and utter depravity, and even in that hour of agony his spirit did not bend, and he would not sacrifice the happiness of eighteen millions of people through parental tenderness for his debauched and ruined child.

About six o'clock in the evening the wretched Alexis breathed his last, and passed from the tribunals of earth to the judgment-seat of God. The emperor immediately seemed to banish from his mind every remembrance of his crimes, and his funeral was attended with all the customary demonstrations of affection and respect. Peter, fully aware that this most momentous event of his life would be severely criticised throughout the world, sent a statement of the facts to all the courts of Europe. In his letter, which accompanied these statements, he says:

"While we were debating in our mind between the natural emotions of paternal clemency on one side, and the regard we ought to pay to the preservation and the future security of our kingdom on the other, and pondering what resolution to take in an affair of so great difficuly and importance, it pleased the Almighty God, by his especial will and his just judgment, and by his mercy to deliver us out of that embarrassment, and to save our family and kingdom from the shame and the dangers by abridging the life of our said son Alexis, after an illness with which he was seized as soon as he had heard the sentence of death pronounced against him.

"That illness appeared at first like an apoplexy; but he afterwards recovered his senses and received the holy sacraments; and having desired to see us, we went to him immediately, with all our counselors and senators; and then he acknowledged and sincerely confessed all his said faults and crimes, committed against us, with tears and all the marks of a true penitent, and begged our pardon, which, according to Christian and paternal duty, we granted him; after which on the 7th of July, at six in the evening, he surrendered his soul to God."

The tzar endeavored to efface from his memory these tragic scenes by consecrating himself, with new energy, to the promotion of the interests of Russia. Utterly despising all luxurious indulgence, he lived upon coarse fare, occupied plainly-furnished rooms, dressed in the extreme of simplicity and devoted himself to daily toil with diligence, which no mechanic or peasant in the realm could surpass. The war still continued with Sweden. On the night of the 29th of November, of this year, 1718, the madman Charles XII. was instantly killed by a cannon ball which carried away his head as he was leaning upon a parapet, in the siege of Fredericshall in Norway. The death of this indomitable warrior quite changed the aspect of European affairs. New combinations of armies arose and new labyrinths of intrigue were woven, and for several years wars, with their usual successes and disasters, continued to impoverish and depopulate the nations of Europe. At length the tzar effected a peace with Sweden, that kingdom surrendering to him the large and important provinces of Livonia, Esthonia, Ingria and Carelia. This was an immense acquisition for Russia.

With the utmost vigilance the tzar watched the administration of all the internal affairs of his empire, punishing fraud, wherever found, with unrelenting severity. The enterprise which now, above all others, engaged his attention, was to open direct communication, by means of canals, between St. Petersburg and the Caspian Sea. The most skillful European engineers were employed upon this vast undertaking, by which the waters of Lake Ladoga were to flow into the Volga, so that the shores of the Baltic and distant Persia might be united in maritime commerce. The sacred Scriptures were also, by command of the emperor, translated into the Russian language and widely disseminated throughout the empire. The Russian merchants were continually receiving insults, being plundered and often massacred by the barbaric tribes on the shores of the Caspian. Peter fitted out a grand expedition from Astrachan for their chastisement, and went himself to that distant city to superintend the important operations. A war of twelve months brought those tribes into subjection, and extended the Russian dominion over vast and indefinite regions there.

Catharine, whom he seemed to love with all the fervor of youth, accompanied him on this expedition. Returning to St. Petersburg in 1724, Peter resolved to accomplish a design which he for some time had meditated, of placing the imperial crown upon the brow of his beloved wife. Their infant son had died. Their grandson, Peter, the son of Alexis, was still but a child, and the failing health of the tzar admonished him that he had not many years to live. Reposing great confidence in the goodness of Catharine and in the wisdom of those counselors whom, with his advice, she would select, he resolved to transmit the scepter, at his death, to her. In preparation for this event, Catharine was crowned Empress on the 18th of May, 1724, with all possible pomp.

The city of Petersburg had now become one of the most important capitals of Europe. Peter was not only the founder of this city, but, in a great measure, the architect. An observatory for astronomical purposes was reared, on the model of that in Paris. A valuable library was in the rapid progress of collection, and there were several cabinets formed, filled with the choicest treasures of nature and art. There were now in Russia a sufficient number of men of genius and of high literary and scientific attainment to form an academy of the arts and sciences, the rules and institutes of which the emperor drew up with his own hand.

While incessantly engaged in these arduous operations, the emperor was seized with a painful and dangerous sickness —a strangury—which confined him to his room for four months. Feeling a little better one day, he ordered his yacht to be brought up to the Neva, opposite his palace, and embarked to visit some of his works on Lake Ladoga. His physicians, vainly remonstrating against it, accompanied him. It was the middle of October. The weather continuing fine, the emperor remained upon the water, visiting his works upon the shore of the lake and of the Gulf of Finland, until the 5th of November. The exposures of the voyage proved too much for him, and he returned to Petersburg in a state of debility and pain which excited the greatest apprehensions.

The disease made rapid progress. The mind of the emperor, as he approached the dying hour, was clouded, and, with the inarticulate mutterings of delirium, he turned to and fro, restless, upon his bed. His devoted wife, for three days and three nights, did not leave his side, and, on the 28th of January, 1725, at four o'clock in the afternoon, he breathed his last, in her arms.

Before the dethronement of his reason, the tzar had assembled around his bed the chief dignitaries of the empire, and had requested them, as soon as he should be dead, to acknowledge the Empress Catharine as their sovereign. He even took the precaution to exact from them an oath that they would do this. Peter died in the fifty-third year of his age. None of the children whom he had by his first wife survived him. Both of the sons whom he had by the Empress Catharine were also dead. Two daughters still lived. After the Empress Catharine, the next heir to the throne was his grandson, Peter, the orphan child of the guilty Alexis.

Immediately upon the death of the emperor, the senate assembled and unanimously declared Catharine Empress of Russia. In a body, they waited upon Catharine with this announcement, and were presented to her by Prince Menzikoff. The mourning for the tzar was universal and heartfelt. The remains were conveyed to the tomb with all the solemnities becoming the burial of one of the greatest monarchs earth has ever known. Over his remains the empress erected a monument sculptured by the most accomplished artists of Italy, containing the following inscription:

HERE LIETH
ALL THAT COULD DIE OF A MAN IMMORTAL,
PETER ALEXOUITZ;
IT IS ALMOST SUPERFLUOUS TO ADD
GREAT EMPEROR OF RUSSIA;
A TITLE
WHICH, INSTEAD OF ADDING TO HIS GLORY,
BECAME GLORIOUS BY HIS WEARING IT.
LET ANTIQUITY BE DUMB,
NOR BOAST HER ALEXANDER OR HER CÆSAR.
HOW EASY WAS VICTORY
TO LEADERS WHO WERE FOLLOWED BY HEROES,
AND WHOSE SOLDIERS FELT A NOBLE DISDAIN
AT BEING THOUGHT LESS VIGILANT THAN THEIR GENERALS!
BUT HE,
WHO IN THIS PLACE FIRST KNEW REST,
FOUND SUBJECTS BASE AND INACTIVE,
UNWARLIKE, UNLEARNED, UNTRACTABLE,
NEITHER COVETOUS OF FAME NOR FEARLESS OF DANGER—
CREATURES WITH THE NAMES OF MEN,
BUT WITH QUALITIES RATHER BRUTAL THAN RATIONAL
YET EVEN THESE
HE POLISHED FROM THEIR NATIVE RUGGEDNESS,
AND, BREAKING OUT LIKE A NEW SUN
TO ILLUMINE THE MINDS OF A PEOPLE,
DISPELLED THEIR NIGHT OF HEREDITARY DARKNESS,
AND, BY FORCE OF HIS INVINCIBLE INFLUENCE,
TAUGHT THEM TO CONQUER
EVEN THE CONQUERORS OF GERMANY.
OTHER PRINCES HAVE COMMANDED VICTORIOUS ARMIES;
THIS COMMANDER CREATED THEM.
EXULT, O NATURE! FOR THINE WAS THIS PRODIGY.
BLUSH, O ART! AT A HERO WHO OWED THEE NOTHING;

CHAPTER XXII.

THE REIGNS OF CATHARINE I., ANNE, THE INFANT IVAN AND ELIZABETH.

FROM 1725 TO 1762.

ENERGETIC REIGN OF CATHARINE.—HER SUDDEN DEATH.—BRIEF REIGN OF PETER II.—DIFFICULTIES OF HEREDITARY SUCCESSION.—A REPUBLIC CONTEMPLATED.—ANNE, DAUGHTER OF IVAN.—THE INFANT IVAN PROCLAIMED KING.—HIS TERRIBLE DOOM.—ELIZABETH, DAUGHTER OF PETER THE GREAT ENTHRONED.—CHARACTER OF ELIZABETH.—ALLIANCE WITH MARIA THERESA.—WARS WITH PRUSSIA.—GREAT REVERSES OF FREDERIC OF PRUSSIA.—DESPERATE CONDITION OF FREDERIC.—DEATH OF ELIZABETH.—SUCCESSION OF PETER III.

THE new empress, Catharine I., was already exceedingly popular, and she rose rapidly in public esteem by the wisdom and vigor of her administration. Early in June her eldest daughter, Anne, was married with much pomp to the Duke of Holstein. It was a great novelty to the Russians to see a woman upon the throne; and the neighboring States seemed inspired with courage to commence encroachments, thinking that they had but little to apprehend from the feeble arm of a queen. Poland, Sweden and Denmark were all animated with the hope that the time had now come in which they could recover those portions of territory which, during past wars, had been wrested from them by Russia.

Catharine was fully aware of the dangers thus impending, and adopted such vigorous measures for augmenting the army and the fleet as speedily to dispel the illusion. Catharine vigorously prosecuted the measures her husband had introduced for the promotion of the civilization and enlightenment of her subjects. She took great care of the young prince Peter, son of the deceased Alexis, and endeavored in all ways to educate him so that he might be worthy to succeed her upon the throne. This young man, the grandson of Peter the Great, was the only prince in whose veins flowed the blood of the tzars.

The academy of sciences at St. Petersburg, which Peter had founded, was sedulously fostered by Catharine. The health of the empress was feeble when she ascended the throne, and it rapidly declined. She, however, continued to apply herself with great assiduity to public affairs until the middle of April, when she was obliged to take her bed. There is no "royal road" to death. After four weeks of suffering and all the humbling concomitants of disease and approaching dissolution, the empress breathed her last at nine o'clock in the evening of the 16th of May, 1727, after a reign of but little more than two years, and in the forty-second year of her age.

Upon her death-bed Catharine declared Peter II., the son of Alexis, her successor; and as he was but twelve years of age, a regency was established during his minority. Menzikoff, however, the illustrious favorite of Peter the Great, who had been appointed by Catharine generalissimo of all the armies both by land and sea, attained such supremacy that he was in reality sovereign of the empire. During the reign of Catharine Russia presented the extraordinary spectacle of one of the most powerful and aristocratic kingdoms on the globe governed by an empress whose origin was that of a nameless girl found weeping in the streets of a sacked town—while there rode, at the head of the armies of the empire, towering above grand dukes and princes of the blood, the son of a peasant, who had passed his childhood the apprentice of a pastry cook, selling cakes in the streets of Moscow. Such changes would have been extraordinary at any period of time and in any quarter of the world; but that they should have occurred in Russia, where for ages so haughty an aristocracy had dominated, seems almost miraculous. Menzikoff, elated by the power which the minority of the king gave him, assumed such airs as to excite the most bitter spirit of hostility among the nobles. They succeeded in working his ruin; and the boy emperor banished him to Siberia and confiscated his immense estates. The blow was fatal. Sinking into the most profound melancholy, Menzikoff lingered for a few months in the dreary region of his exile, and died in 1729. Peter the Second did not long survive him. But little more than two years elapsed after the death of Catharine, when he, being then a lad of but fourteen years of age, was seized with the small-pox and died the 19th of January, 1730. One daughter of Peter the Great and of Catharine still survived.

Some of the principal of the nobility, seeing how many difficulties attended hereditary succession, which at one time placed the crown upon the brow of a babe in the cradle, again upon a semi-idiot, and again upon a bloated and infamous debauchee, conferred upon the subject of changing the government into a republic. But Russia was not prepared for a reform so sudden and so vast. After much debate it was decided to offer the crown to Anne, Duchess of Courland, who was second daughter of the imbecile Ivan, who, for a short time, had nominally occupied the throne, associated with his brother Peter the Great. She had an elder sister, Catharine, who was married to the Duke of Mecklenburg. So far as the right of birth was concerned, Catharine was first entitled to the succession. But as the Duke of Mecklenburg, whose grand duchy bordered upon the Baltic, and which was equal to about one half the State of Massachusetts, was engaged in a kind of civil war with his nobles, it was therefore thought best to pass her by, lest the empire should become involved in the strife in which her husband was engaged. As Ivan was the elder brother, it was thought that his daughters should have the precedence over those of Peter.

Another consideration also influenced the nobles who took the lead in selecting Anne. They thought that she was a woman whom they could more easily control than Catharine. These nobles accordingly framed a new constitution for the empire, limiting the authority of the queen to suit their purposes. But Anne was no sooner seated upon the throne, than she grasped the scepter with vigor which astounded all. She banished the nobles who had interfered with the royal prerogatives, and canceled all the limitations they had made. She selected a very able ministry, and gave the command of her armies to the most experienced generals. While sagacity and efficiency marked her short administration, and Russia continued to expand and prosper, no events of special importance occurred. She united her armies with those of the Emperor of Germany in resisting the encroachments of France. She waged successful war against the Turks, who had attempted to recover Azof. In this war, the Crimean Tartars were crushed, and Russian influence crowded its way into the immense Crimean peninsula. The energies of Anne caused Russia to be respected throughout Europe.

As the empress had no children, she sent for her niece and namesake, Anne, daughter of her elder sister, Catharine, Duchess of Mecklenburg, and married her to one of the most distinguished nobles of her court, resolved to call the issue of this marriage to the succession. On the 12th of August, 1740, this princess was delivered of a son, who was named Ivan. The empress immediately pronounced him her successor, placing him under the guardianship of his parents. The health of the empress was at this time rapidly failing, and it was evident to all that her death was not far distant. In anticipation of death, she appointed one of her favorites, John Ernestus Biron, regent, during the minority of the prince. Baron Osterman, high chancellor of Russia, had the rank of prime minister, and Count Munich, a soldier of distinguished reputation, was placed in the command of the armies, with the title of field marshal. These were the last administrative acts of Anne. The king of terrors came with his inevitable summons. After a few weeks of languor and suffering, the queen expired in October, 1740.

A babe, two months old, was now Emperor of Russia. The senate immediately met and acknowledged the legitimacy of his claims. The foreign embassadors presented to him their credentials, and the Marquis of Chetardie, the French minister, reverentially approaching the cradle, made the imperially majestic baby a congratulatory speech, addressing him as Ivan V., Emperor of all the Russias, and assuring him of the friendship of Louis XV., sovereign of France.

The regent, as was usually the case, arrogating authority and splendor, soon became excessively unpopular, and a conspiracy of the nobles was formed for his overthrow. On the night of the 17th of November the conspirators met in the palace of the grand duchess, Anne, mother of the infant emperor, unanimously named her regent of the empire, arrested Biron, and condemned him to death, which sentence was subsequently commuted to Siberian exile.

Elizabeth, the daughter of Peter, was now thirty-eight years of age. Though very beautiful, she was unmarried, and resided in the palace in a state of splendid captivity. A party now arose who secretly conspired to overthrow the regency of Anne, and to depose the infant Ivan and place Elizabeth upon the throne. The plot being fully matured, on the night of the 5th of December a body of armed men repaired to the palace, where they met Elizabeth, who was ready to receive them, and marched, with her at their head, to the barracks, where she was enthusiastically received by the soldiers. The spirit of her father seemed at once to inspire her soul. With a voice of authority, as if born to command, she ordered the regiments to march to different quarters of the city and to seize all the prominent officers of the government. Then leading, herself, a regiment to the palace, she took possession of the infant emperor and of his mother, the regent. They were held in captivity, though, at first, treated with all the consideration which became their birth.

This revolution was accepted by the people with the loudest demonstrations of joy. The memory of Peter the Great was enshrined in every heart, and all exulted in placing the crown upon his daughter's brow. The next morning, at the head of the royal guards and all the other troops of the metropolis, Elizabeth was proclaimed Empress of Russia. In one week from this time, the deposed infant emperor, Ivan, who was then thirteen months old, was sent, with his parents, from Petersburg to Riga, where they were for a long time detained in a castle as prisoners. Two efforts which they made for escape were frustrated.

This conspiracy, which was carried to so successful a result, was mainly founded in the hostility with which the Russians regarded the foreigners who had been so freely introduced to the empire by Peter the Great, and who occupied so many of the most important posts in the State. Thus the succession of Elizabeth was, in fact, a counter revolution, arresting the progress of reform and moving Russia back again toward the ancient barbarism. But Elizabeth soon expended her paroxysm of energy, and surrendered herself to luxury and to sensual indulgence unsurpassed by any debauchee who ever occupied a throne. Jealous of sharing her power, she refused to take a husband, though many guilty favorites were received to her utmost intimacy.

The doom of the deposed Ivan and his parents was sad, indeed. They were removed for safe keeping to an island in the White Sea, fifty miles beyond Archangel, a region as desolate as the imagination can well conceive. Here, after a year of captivity, the infant Ivan was torn from his mother and removed to the monastery of Oranienburg, where he was brought up in the utmost seclusion, not being allowed to learn either to read or write. The bereaved mother, Anne, lingered a couple of years until she wept away her life, and found the repose of the grave in 1746. Her husband survived thirty years longer, and died in prison in 1775. It was an awful doom for one who had committed no crime. The whole course of history proves that in this life we see but the commencement of a divine government, and that "after death cometh the judgment."

A humane monk, taking pity upon the unfortunate little Ivan, attempted to escape with him. He had reached Smolensk, when he was arrested. The unhappy prince was then conveyed to the castle of Schlusselburg, where he was immersed in a dungeon which no ray of the sun could ever penetrate. A single lamp burning in his cell only revealed its horrors. The prince could not distinguish day from night, and had no means of computing the passage of the hours. Food was left in his cell, and the attendants, who occasionally entered, were prohibited from holding any conversation with the child. This treatment, absolutely infernal, soon reduced the innocent prince to a state almost of idiocy.

Twice Elizabeth ordered him to be brought to Petersburg, where she conversed with him without letting him know who she was; but she did nothing to alleviate his horrible doom. After the death of Elizabeth, her successor, Peter III., made Ivan a visit, without making himself known. Touched with such an aspect of misery, he ordered an apartment to be built in an angle of the fortress, for Ivan, who had now attained the age of manhood, where he could enjoy air and light. The sudden death of Peter defeated this purpose, and Ivan was left in his misery. Still weary years passed away while the prince, dead to himself as well as to the world, remained breathing in his tomb. Catharine II., after her accession to the throne, called to see Ivan. She thus describes her visit:

"After we had ascended the throne, and offered up to Heaven our just thanksgivings, the first object that employed our thoughts, in consequence of that humanity which is natural to us, was the unhappy situation of that prince, who was dethroned by divine Providence, and had been unfortunate ever since his birth; and we formed the resolution of alleviating his misfortunes as far as possible.

"We immediately made a visit to him in order to judge of his understanding and talents, and to procure him a situation suitable to his character and education. But how great was our surprise to find, that in addition to a defect in his utterance, which rendered it difficult for him to speak, and still more difficult to be understood, we observed an almost total deprivation of sense and reason. Those who accompanied us, during this interview, saw how much our heart suffered at the contemplation of an object so fitted to excite compassion; they were also convinced that the only measure we could take to succor the unfortunate prince was to leave him where we found him, and to procure him all the comforts and conveniences his situation would admit of. We accordingly gave our orders for this purpose, though the state he was in prevented his perceiving the marks of our humanity or being sensible of our attention and care; for he knew nobody, could not distinguish between good and evil, nor did he know the use that might be made of reading, to pass the time with less weariness and disgust. On the contrary, he sought pleasure in objects that discovered with sufficient evidence the disorder of his imagination."

Soon after this poor Ivan was cruelly assassinated. An officer in the Russian army, named Mirovitch, conceived an absurd plan of liberating Ivan from his captivity, restoring him to the throne, and consigning Catharine II. to the dungeon the prince had so long inhabited. Mirovitch had command of the garrison at Schlusselburg, where Ivan was imprisoned. Taking advantage of the absence of the empress, on a journey to Livonia, he proceeded to the castle, with a few soldiers whose coöperation he had secured through the influence of brandy and promises, knocked down the commandant of the fortress with the butt end of a musket, and ordered the officers who had command of the prisoner to bring him to them. These officers had received the secret injunction that should the rescue of the prince ever be attempted, they were to put him to death rather than permit him to be carried off. They accordingly entered his cell, and though the helpless captive made the most desperate resistance, they speedily cut him down with their swords.

History has few narratives so extraordinary as the fate of Ivan. A forced marriage was arranged that a child might be generated to inherit the Russian throne. When this child was but a few days old he was declared emperor of all the Russias, and received the congratulations of the foreign embassadors. When thirteen months of age he was deposed, and for the crime of being a king, was thrown into captivity. To prevent others from using him as the instrument of their purposes, he was thrown into a dungeon, and excluded from all human intercourse, so that like a deaf child he could not even acquire the power of speech. For him there was neither clouds nor sunshine, day nor night, summer nor winter. He had no employment, no amusement, no food for thought, absolutely nothing to mark the passage of the weary hours. The mind became paralyzed and almost idiotic by such enormous woe. Such was his doom for twenty-four years. He was born in 1740, and assassinated under the reign of Catharine II., in 1764. The father of Ivan remained in prison eleven years longer until he died.

From this tragedy let us turn back to the reign of Elizabeth. It was the great object of this princess to undo all that her illustrious father had done, to roll back all the reforms he had commenced, and to restore to the empire its ancient usages and prejudices. The hostility to foreigners became so bitter, that the queen's guard formed a conspiracy for a general massacre, which should sweep them all from the empire. Elizabeth, conscious of the horror such an act would inspire throughout Europe, was greatly alarmed, and was compelled to issue a proclamation in defense of their lives.

"The empress," she said in this proclamation, "can never forget how much foreigners have contributed to the prosperity of Russia. And though her subjects will at all times enjoy her favors in preference to foreigners, yet the foreigners in her service are as dear to her as her own subjects, and may rely on her protection."

In the mean time, Elizabeth was prosecuting with great vigor the hereditary war with Sweden. Russia was constantly gaining in this conflict, and at length the Swedes purchased peace by surrendering to the Russians extensive territories in Finland. The favor of Russia was still more effectually purchased by the Swedes choosing for their king, Adolpus Frederic, Duke of the Russian province of Holstein, and kinsman of Elizabeth. The boundaries of Russia were thus enlarged, and Sweden became almost a tributary province of the gigantic empire.

Maria Theresa was now Empress of Austria, and she succeeded in enlisting the coöperation of Elizabeth in her unrelenting warfare with Frederic of Prussia. Personal hostility also exasperated Elizabeth against the Prussian monarch, for in some of his writings he had spoken disparagingly of the humble birth of Elizabeth's mother, Catharine, the wife of Peter the First; and a still more unpardonable offense he had committed, when, flushed with wine, at a table where the Russian embassador was present, he had indulged in witticisms in reference to the notorious gallantries of the empress. A woman who could plunge into the wildest excesses of licentiousness, still had sensibility enough to resent the taunts of the royal philosopher. In 1753, Elizabeth and Maria Theresa entered into an agreement to resist *all further augmentation* of the Prussian power. In the bloody Seven Years' War between Frederic and Maria Theresa, the heart of Elizabeth was always with the Austrian queen, and for five of those years their armies fought side by side. In the year 1759, Elizabeth sent an army of one hundred thousand men into Prussia. They committed every outrage which fiends could perpetrate; and though victorious over the armies of Frederic, they rendered the country so utterly desolate, that through famine they were compelled to retreat. Burning villages and mangled corpses marked their path.

The next year, 1758, another Russian army invaded Prussia, overran nearly the whole kingdom, and captured Konigsburg. The victorious Russians thinking that all of Prussia was to be annexed to their dominions, began to treat the Prussians tenderly and as countrymen. An order was read from the churches, that if any Prussian had cause of complaint against any Russian, he should present it at the military chancery at Konigsburg, where he would infallibly have redress. The inhabitants of the conquered realm were all obliged to swear fealty to the Empress of Russia. The Prussian army was at this time in Silesia, struggling against the troops of Maria Theresa. The warlike Frederic soon returned at the head of his indomitable hosts, and attacking the Russians about six miles from Kustrin, defeated them in one of the most bloody battles on record, and drove the shattered battalions, humiliated and bleeding, out of the territory.

The summer of 1759 again found the Russian troops spread over the Prussian territory. In great force the two hostile armies soon met on the banks of the Oder. The Russians, posted upon a line of commanding heights, numbered seventy thousand. Frederic fiercely assailed them through the most formidable disadvantages, with but thirty thousand men. The slaughter of the Prussians was fearful, and Frederic, after losing nearly eight thousand of his best troops in killed and wounded and prisoners, sullenly retired. The Russian troops were now strengthened by a reinforcement of twelve thousand of the choicest of the Austrian cavalry, and still presenting, notwithstanding their losses, a solid front of ninety thousand men. Frederic, bringing every nerve into action, succeeded in collecting and bringing again into the field fifty thousand troops.* Notwithstanding the disparity in numbers, it seemed absolutely necessary that the King of Prussia should fight, for the richest part of his dominions was in the hands of the allied Prussians and Austrians, and Berlin was menaced. The field of battle was on the banks of the Oder, near Frankfort.

On the 12th of June, 1759, at two o'clock in the morning, the King of Prussia formed his troops in battle array, behind a forest which concealed his movements from the enemy. The battle was commenced with a fierce cannonade; and in the midst of the thunderings and carnage of this tempest of war, solid columns emerged from the ranks of the Prussians and pierced the Russian lines. The attack was too impetuous to be resisted. From post to post the Prussians advanced, driving the foe before them, and covering the ground with the slain. For six hours of almost unparalleled slaughter the victory was with the Prussians. Seventy-two pieces of cannon fell into the hands of the victors, and at every point the Russians were retreating. Frederic, in his exultation, scribbled a note to the empress, upon the field of battle, with the pommel of his saddle for a tablet, and dispatched it to her by a courier. It was as follows:

"Madam: we have beat the Russians from their entrenchments. In two hours expect to hear of a glorious victory."

But in less than two hours the tide of victory turned. The day was one of excessive heat. An unclouded sun poured its burning rays upon the field, and at midday the troops and the horses, having been engaged for six hours in one of the severest actions which was ever known, were utterly beat out and fainting with exhaustion. Just then the whole body of the Russian and Austrian cavalry, some fourteen thousand

* Some authorities give the Russians eighty thousand and the Prussians forty thousand.

strong, which thus far had remained inactive, came rushing upon the plain as with the roar and the sweep of the whirlwind. The foe fell before them as the withered grass before the prairie fire. Frederic was astounded by this sudden reverse, and in the anguish of his spirit plunged into the thickest of the conflict. Two horses were shot beneath him. His clothes were riddled with balls. Another courier was dispatched to the empress from the sanguinary field, in the hottest speed. The note he bore was as follows:

"Remove from Berlin with the royal family. Let the archives be carried to Potsdam, and the capital make conditions with the enemy."

As night approached, Frederic assembled the fragments of his army, exhausted and bleeding, upon some heights, and threw up redoubts for their protection. Twenty thousand of his troops were left upon the field or in the hands of the enemy. Every cannon he had was taken. Scarcely a general or an inferior officer escaped unwounded, and a large number of his most valuable officers were slain. It was an awful defeat and an awful slaughter.

Fortunately for Frederic the losses of the Russians had also been so terrible that they did not venture to pursue the foe. Early the next morning the Prussian king crossed the Oder; and the Russians, encumbered with the thousands of their own mutilated and dying troops, thought it not prudent to march upon Berlin. The war still raged furiously, the allies being inspirited by hope and Frederic by despair. At length the affairs of Prussia became quite hopeless, and the Prussian monarch was in a position from which no earthly energy or sagacity could extricate him. The Russians and Austrians, in resistless numbers, were spread over all his provinces excepting Saxony, where the great Frederic was entirely hemmed up.

The Prussian king was fully conscious of the desperation of his affairs, and, though one of the most stoical and stern of men, he experienced the acutest anguish. For hours he paced the floor of his tent, absorbed in thought, seldom exchanging a word with his generals, who stood silently by, having no word to utter of counsel or encouragement. Just then God mysteriously interposed and saved Prussia from dismemberment, and the name of her monarch from ignominy. The Empress of Russia had been for some time in failing health, and the year 1762 had but just dawned, when the enrapturing tidings were conveyed to the camp of the despairing Prussians that Elizabeth was dead. This event dispelled midnight gloom and caused the sun to shine brightly upon the Prussian fortunes.

The nephew of the empress, Peter III., who succeeded her on her throne, had long expressed his warm admiration of Frederic of Prussia, had visited his court at Berlin, where he was received with the most flattering attentions, and had enthroned the warlike Frederic in his heart as the model of a hero. He had even, during the war, secretly written letters to Frederic expressive of his admiration, and had communicated to him secrets of the Russian cabinet and their plans of operation. The elevation of Peter III. to the throne was the signal, not only for the withdrawal of the Russian troops from the Austrian alliance, but for the direct marching of those troops as allies into the camp of the Prussians. Thus sudden are the mutations of war; thus inexplicable are the combinations of destiny.

Elizabeth died in the fifty-second year of her age, after a reign of twenty years. She was during her whole reign mainly devoted to sensual pleasure, drinking intoxicating liquors immoderately, and surrendering herself to the most extraordinary licentiousness. Though ever refusing to recognize the claims of marriage, she was the mother of several children, and her favorites can not easily be enumerated. Her ministers managed the affairs of State for her, in obedience to her caprices. She seemed to have some chronic disease of the humane feelings which induced her to declare that not one of her subjects should during her reign be doomed to death, while at the same time, with the most gentle self complacency, she could order the tongues of thousands to be torn out by the roots, could cut off the nostrils with red hot pincers, could lop off ears, lips and noses, and could twist the arms of her victims behind them, by dislocating them at the shoulders. There were tens of thousands of prisoners thus horridly mutilated.

The empress was fond of music, and introduced to Russia the opera and the theater. She was as intolerent to the Jews as her father had been, banishing them all from the country. She lived in constant fear of conspiracies and revolutions, and, as a desperate safeguard, established a secret inquisitorial court to punish all who should express any displeasure with the measures of government. Spies and informers of the most worthless character filled the land, and multitudes of the most virtuous inhabitants of the empire, falsely accused, or denounced for a look, a shrug, or a harmless word, were consigned to mutilation more dreadful and to exile more gloomy than the grave.

CHAPTER XXIII.

PETER III. AND HIS BRIDE.

FROM 1728 TO 1762.

LINEAGE OF PETER III.—CHOSEN BY ELIZABETH AS HER SUCCESSOR.—THE BRIDE CHOSEN FOR PETER.—HER LINEAGE.—THE COURTSHIP.—THE MARRIAGE.—AUTOBIOGRAPHY OF CATHARINE.—ANECDOTES OF PETER.—HIS NEGLECT OF CATHARINE AND HIS DEBAUCHERIES.—AMUSEMENTS OF THE RUSSIAN COURT.—MILITARY EXECUTION OF A RAT.—ACCESSION OF PETER III. TO THE THRONE.—SUPREMACY OF CATHARINE.—HER REPUDIATION THREATENED.—THE CONSPIRACY.—ITS SUCCESSFUL ACCOMPLISHMENT.

PETER the Third was grandson of Peter the Great. His mother, Anne, the eldest daughter of Peter and Catharine, married the Duke of Holstein, who inherited a duchy on the eastern shores of the Baltic containing some four thousand square miles of territory and about three hundred thousand inhabitants. Their son and only child, Peter, was born in the ducal castle at Kiel, the capital of the duchy, in the year 1728. The blood of Peter the Great of Russia, and of Charles the Twelfth of Sweden mingled in the veins of the young duke, of which fact he was exceedingly proud. Soon after the birth of Peter, his mother, Anne, died. The father of Peter was son of the eldest sister of Charles XII., and, as such, being the nearest heir, would probably have succeeded to the throne of Sweden had not the king's sudden death, by a cannon ball, prevented him from designating his successor. The widowed father of Peter, thus disappointed in his hopes of obtaining the crown of Sweden, which his aunt Ulrica, his mother's sister, successfully grasped, lived in great retirement. The idea had not occurred to him that the crown of imperial Russia could, by any chance, descend to his son, and the education of Peter was conducted to qualify him to preside over his little patrimonial duchy.

When young Peter was fourteen years of age, the Empress Elizabeth, his maternal aunt, to the surprise and delight of the family, summoned the young prince to St. Petersburg, intimating her intention to transmit to him her crown. But Peter was a thoroughly worthless boy. All ignoble qualities seemed to be combined in his nature without any redeeming virtues. Elizabeth having thus provided twenty millions of people with a sovereign, looked about to find for that sovereign a suitable wife. Upon the banks of the Oder there was a small *principality*, as it was called, containing some thirteen hundred square miles, about the size of the State of Rhode Island. Christian Augustus, the prince of this little domain, had a daughter, Sophia, a child rather remarkable both for beauty and vivacity. She was one year younger than Peter, and Elizabeth fixed her choice upon Sophia as the future spouse of her nephew. Peter was, at this time, with the empress in Moscow, and Sophia was sent for to spend some time in the Russian capital before the marriage, that she might become acquainted with the Russian language and customs.

Both of these children had been educated Protestants, but they were required to renounce the Lutheran faith and accept that of the Greek church. Children as they were, they did this, of course, as readily as they would have changed their dresses. With this change of religion Sophia received a new name, that of Catharine, and by this name she was ever afterward called. When these children, to whom the government of the Russian empire was to be intrusted, first met, Peter was fifteen years of age and Catharine fourteen. Catharine subsequently commenced a minute journal, an autobiography of these her youthful days, which opens vividly to our view the corruptions of the Russian court. Nothing can be more wearisome than the life there developed. No thought whatever seemed to be directed by the court to the interests of the Russian people. They were no more thought of than the jaded horses who dragged the chariots of the nobles. It is amazing that the indignation of the millions can have slumbered so long.

Catharine, in her memoirs, naively describes young Peter, when she first saw him, as "weak, ugly, little and sickly." From the age of ten he had been addicted to intoxicating drinks. It was the 9th of February, 1744, when Catharine was taken to Moscow. Peter, or, as he was then called, the grand duke, was quite delighted to see the pretty girl who was his destined wife, and began immediately to entertain Catharine, as she says, "by informing me that he was in love with one of the maids of honor to the empress, and that he would have been very glad to have married her, but that he was resigned to marry me instead, as his aunt wished it."

The grand duke had the faculty of making himself excessively disagreeable to every one around him, and the affianced *haters* were in a constant quarrel. Peter could develop nothing but stupid malignity. Catharine could wield the weapons of keen and cutting sarcasm, which Peter felt as the mule feels the lash. Catharine's mother had accompanied her to Moscow, but the bridal wardrobe, for a princess, was extremely limited.

"I had arrived," she writes, "in Russia very badly provided for. If I had three or four dresses in the world, it was the very outside, and this at a court where people changed their dress three times a day. A dozen chemises constituted the whole of my linen, and I had to use my mother's sheets."

Soon after Catharine's arrival, the grand duke was taken with the small-pox, and his natural ugliness was rendered still more revolting by the disfigurement it caused. On the 10th of February, 1745, when Catharine had been one year at Moscow, the grand duke celebrated his seventeenth birthday. In her journal Catharine writes that Peter seldom saw her, and was always glad of any excuse by which he could avoid paying her any attention. Though Catharine cared as little for him, still, with girlish ambition, she was eager to marry him, as she very frankly records, in consideration of the crown which he would place upon her brow, and her womanly nature was stung by his neglect.

"I fully perceived," she writes, "his want of interest, and how little I was cared for. My self-esteem and vanity grieved in silence; but I was too proud to complain. I should have thought myself degraded had any one shown me a friendship which I could have taken for pity. Nevertheless I shed tears when alone, then quietly dried them up, and went to romp with my maids.

"I labored, however," writes Catharine, "to gain the affection of every one. Great or small I neglected no one, but laid it down to myself as a rule to believe that I stood in need of every one, and so to act, in consequence, as to obtain the good will of all, and I succeeded in doing so."

The 21st of August of this year was fixed for the nuptial day. Catharine looked forward to it with extreme repugnance. Peter was revolting in his aspect, disgusting in manners, a drunkard, and licentious to such a degree that he took no pains to conceal his amours. But the crown of Russia was in the eyes of Catharine so glittering a prize, though then she had not entered her sixteenth year, that she was willing to purchase it even at the price of marrying Peter, the only price at which it could be obtained. She was fully persuaded that Peter, with a feeble constitution and wallowing in debauchery, could not live long, and that, at his death, she would be undisputed empress.

"As the day of our nuptials approached," she writes, "I became more and more melancholy. My heart predicted but little happiness; ambition alone sustained me. In my inmost soul there was something which led me never to doubt, for a single moment, that sooner or later I should become sovereign empress of Russia in my own right."

The marriage was celebrated with much pomp; but a more cold and heartless union was perhaps never solemnized. Catharine very distinctly intimates that her husband, who was as low in his tastes and companionship as he was degraded in his vices, left her at the altar, to return to his more congenial harem.

"My beloved spouse," she writes, "did not trouble himself in the slightest degree about me; but was constantly with his valets, playing at soldiers, exercising them in his room, or changing his uniform twenty times a day. I yawned and grew weary, having no one to speak to."

Again she writes, "A fortnight after our marriage he confessed to me that he was in love with Mademoiselle Carr, maid of honor to her imperial majesty. He said that there was no comparison between that lady and me. Surely, said I to myself, it would be impossible for me not to be wretched with such a man as this were I to give way to sentiments of tenderness thus requited. I might die of jealousy without benefit to any one. I endeavored to master my feelings so as not to be jealous of the man who did not love me. I was naturally well-disposed, but I should have required a husband who had common sense, which this one had not."

For amusement, the grand duke played cruelly with dogs in his room, pretending to train them, whipping them from corner to corner. When tired of this he would scrape execrably on a violin. He had many little puppet soldiers, whom, hour after hour, he would marshal on the floor in mimic war. He would dress his own servants and the maids of Catharine in masks, and set them dancing, while he would dance with them, playing at the same time on the fiddle.

"With rare perseverance," writes Catharine, "the grand duke trained a pack of dogs, and with heavy blows of his whip, and cries like those of the huntsmen, made them fly from one end to the other of his two rooms, which were all he had. Such of the dogs as became tired, or got out of rank, were severely punished, which made them howl still more. On one occasion, hearing one of these animals howl piteously and for a long time, I opened the door of my bed-room, where I was seated, and which adjoined the apartment in which this scene was enacted, and saw him holding this dog by the collar, suspended in the air, while a boy, who was in his service, a Kalmuck by birth, held the animal by the tail. It was a poor little King Charles spaniel, and the duke was beating him with all his might with the heavy handle of a whip. I interceded for the poor beast; but this only made him redouble his blows. Unable to bear so cruel a scene, I returned to my room with tears in my eyes. In general, tears and cries, instead of moving the duke to pity, put him in a passion. Pity was a feeling that was painful and even insupportable in his mind."

At one time there was a little hunchback girl in the court, upon whom the duke fixed his vagrant desires, and she became his unconcealed favorite. The duke was ever in the habit of talking freely with Catharine about his paramours and praising their excellent qualities.

"Madame Vladisma said to me," writes Catharine, "that every one was disgusted to see this little hunchback preferred to me. 'It can not be helped,' I said, as the tears started to my eyes. I went to bed; scarcely was I asleep, when the grand duke also came to bed. As he was tipsy and knew not what he was doing, he spoke to me for the purpose of expatiating on the eminent qualities of his favorite. To check his garrulity I pretended to be fast asleep. He spoke still louder in order to wake me; but finding that I slept, he gave me two or three rather hard blows in the side with his fist, and dropped asleep himself. I wept long and bitterly that night, as well on account of the matter itself and the blows he had given me, as on that of my general situation, which was, in all respects, as disagreeable as it was wearisome."

One of the ridiculous and disgraceful amusements of the vulgar men and women collected in the court of Elizabeth, was what was called masquerade balls, in which all the men were required to dress as women, and all the women as men, and yet no masks were worn.

"The men," Catharine writes, "wore large whaleboned petticoats, with women's gowns, and the head-dresses worn on court days, while the women appeared in the court costume of men. The men did not like these reversals of their sex, and the greater part of them were in the worst possible humor on these occasions, because they felt themselves to be hideous in such disguises. The women looked like scrubby little boys, while the more aged among them had thick short legs which were any thing but ornamental. The only woman who looked really well, and completely a man, was the empress herself. As she was very tall and somewhat powerful, male attire suited her wonderfully well. She had the handsomest leg I have ever seen with any man, and her foot was admirably proportioned. She danced to perfection, and every thing she did had a special grace, equally so whether she dressed as a man or a woman."

Enervating and degrading pleasure and ambitious or revengeful wars, engrossed the whole attention of the Russian court during the reign of Elizabeth. The welfare of the people was not even thought of. The following anecdote, illustrative of the character of Peter III., is worthy of record in the words of Catharine:

"One day, when I went into the apartments of his imperial highness, I beheld a great rat which he had hung, with all the paraphernalia of an execution. I asked what all this meant. He told me that this rat had committed a great crime, which, according to the laws of war, deserved capital punishment. It had climbed the ramparts of a fortress of card-board, which he had on a table in his cabinet, and had eaten two sentinels, made of pith, who were on duty in the bastions. His setter had caught the criminal, he had been tried by martial law and immediately hung; and, as I saw, was to remain three days exposed as a public example. In justification of the rat," continues Catharine, "it may at least be said, that he was hung without having been questioned or heard in his own defense."

It is not surprising that a woman, young, beautiful and vivacious, living in a court where corruption was all around her, where an unmarried empress was rendering herself notorious by her gallantries, stung to the quick by the utter neglect of her husband, insulted by the presence of his mistresses, and disgusted by his unmitigated boobyism, should have sought solace in the friendship of others. And it is not strange that such friendships should have ripened into love, and that one thus tempted should have fallen. Catharine in her memoirs does not deny her fall, though she can not refrain from allowing an occasional word to drop from her pen, evidently intended in extenuation. Much which is called virtue consists in the absence of temptation.

Catharine's first son, Paul, was born on the 20th of September, 1753. He was unquestionably the son of Count Sottikoff, a nobleman alike distinguished for the graces of his person and of his mind. Through a thousand perils and cunning intrigues, Catharine and the count prosecuted their amour. Woe was, as usual, to both of them the result. The empress gives a very touching account of her sufferings, in both body and mind, on the occasion of the birth of her child.

"As for me," she writes, "I did nothing but weep and moan in my bed. I neither could or would see anybody, I felt so miserable. I buried myself in my bed, where I did nothing but grieve. When the forty days of my confinement were over, the empress came a second time into my chamber. My child was brought into my room; it was the first time I had seen him since his birth."

One day Peter brought into his wife's room, for her amusement, a letter which he had just received from one of his mistresses, Madame Teploff. Showing the letter to Catharine, he said,

"Only think! she writes me a letter of four whole pages, and expects that I should read it, and, what is more, answer it also; I, who have to go to parade, then dine, then attend the rehearsal of an opera, and the ballet which the cadets will dance at. I will tell her plainly that I have not time, and, if she is vexed, I will quarrel with her till next winter."

"That will certainly be the shortest way," Catharine coolly replied. "These traits," she very truly adds in her narrative, "are characteristic, and they will not therefore be out of place."

Such was the man and such the woman wno succeeded to the throne of Russia upon the death of the Empress Elizabeth. She had hardly emitted her last breath, ere the courtiers, impatiently awaiting the event, rushed to the apartments of the grand duke to congratulate him upon his accession to the crown. He immediately mounted on horseback and traversed the streets of St. Petersburg, scattering money among the crowd. The soldiers gathered around him exclaiming, "Take care of us and we will take care of you." Though the grand duke had been very unpopular there was no outburst of opposition. The only claim Peter III. had to the confidence of the nation was the fact that he was grandson of Peter the Great. Conspiracies were, however, immediately set on foot to eject him from the throne and give Catharine his seat. Catharine had a high reputation for talent, and being very affectionate in her disposition and cordial in her manners, had troops of friends. Indeed, it is not strange that public sentiment should not only have extenuated her faults, but should almost have applauded them. Forgetting the commandments of God, and only remembering that her brutal husband richly merited retaliation, the public almost applauded the spirit with which she conducted her intrigues. The same sentiment pervaded England when the miserable

George IV. goaded his wife to frenzy, and led her, in uncontrollable exasperation, to pay him back in his own coin.

Fortunately for the imbecile Peter, he had enough sense to appreciate the abilities of Catharine; and a sort of maudlin idea of justice, if it were not, perhaps, utter stupidity, dissuaded him from resenting her freedom in the choice of favorites. Upon commencing his reign, he yielded himself to the guidance of her imperial mind, hoping to obtain some dignity by the renown which her measures might reflect upon him. Catharine advised him very wisely. She caused seventeen thousand exiles to be recalled from Siberia, and abolished the odious secret court of chancery—that court of political inquisition which, for years, had kept all Russia trembling.

For a time, Russia resounded with the praises of the new sovereign, and when Peter III. entered the senate and read an act permitting the nobility to bear arms, or not, at their own discretion, and to visit foreign countries whenever they pleased, a privilege which they had not enjoyed before, the gratitude of the nobles was unbounded. It should, however, be recorded that this edict proved to be but a dead letter. It was expected that the nobles, as a matter of courtesy, should always ask permission to leave, and this request was frequently not granted. The secret tribunal, to which we have referred, exposed persons of all ranks and both sexes to be arrested upon the slightest suspicion. The accused was exposed to the most horrible tortures to compel a confession. When every bone was broken and every joint dislocated, and his body was mangled by the crushing wheel, if he still had endurance to persist in his denial, the accuser was, in his turn, placed upon the wheel, and every nerve of agony was tortured to force a recantation of the charge.

Though Peter III. promulgated the wise edicts which were placed in his hands, he had become so thoroughly imbruted by his dissolute life that he made no attempt to tear himself away from his mistresses and his drunken orgies.

Peter III. was quite infatuated in his admiration of Frederic of Prussia. One of his first acts upon attaining the reins of government was to dispatch an order forbidding the Russian armies any longer to coöperate with Austria against Prussia. This command was speedily followed by another, directing the Russian generals to hold themselves and their troops obedient to the instructions of Frederic, and to coöperate in every way with him to repel their former allies, the Austrians. It was the caprice of a drunken semi-idiot which thus rescued Frederic the Great from disgrace and utter ruin. The Emperor of Prussia had sufficient sagacity to foresee that Peter III. would not long maintain his seat upon the throne. He accordingly directed his minister at St. Petersburg, while continuing to live in great intimacy with the tzar, to pay the most deferential attention to the empress.

There was no end to the caprices of Peter the drunkard. At one time he would leave the whole administration of affairs in the hands of Catharine, and again he would treat her in the most contemptuous and insulting manner. In one of the pompous ceremonials of the court, when the empress, adorned with all the marks of imperial dignity, shared the throne with Peter, the tzar called one of his mistresses to the conspicuous seat he occupied with the empress, and made her sit down by his side. Catharine immediately rose and retired. At a public festival that same evening, Peter, half drunk, publicly and loudly launched at her an epithet the grossest which could be addressed to a woman. Catharine was so shocked that she burst into tears. The sympathy of the spectators was deeply excited in her behalf, and their indignation roused against the tzar.

While Peter III. was developing his true character of brute and buffoon, gathering around him the lowest profligates, and reveling in the most debasing and vulgar vices, Catharine, though guilty and unhappy, was holding her court with dignity and affability, which charmed all who approached her. She paid profound respect to the external observances of religion, daily performing her devotions in the churches, accosting the poor with benignity, treating the clergy with marked respect, and winning all hearts by her kindness and sympathy.

One of the mistresses of Peter III., the Countess Vorontzof, had gained such a boundless influence over her paramour, that she had extorted from him the promise that he would repudiate Catharine, marry her, and crown her as empress. Elated by this promise, she had the imprudence to boast of it. Her father and several of the courtiers whose fortunes her favor would secure, were busy in paving her way to the throne. The numerous friends of Catharine were excited, and were equally active in thwarting the plans of the tzar. Peter took no pains to conceal his intentions, and gloried in proclaiming the illegitimacy of Paul, the son of the empress. Loathsome as his own life was, he seemed to think that his denunciations of Catharine, whose purity he had insulted and whose heart he had crushed, would secure for him the moral support of his subjects and of Europe. But he was mistaken. The sinning Catharine was an angel of purity compared with the beastly Peter.

It was necessary for Peter to move with caution, for Catharine had ability, energy, innumerable friends, and was one of the last women in the world quietly to submit to be plunged into a dungeon, and then to be led to the scaffold, and by such a man as her despicable spouse. Peter III. was by no means a match for Catharine. About twelve miles from St. Petersburg, on the southern shore of the Bay of Cronstadt, and nearly opposite the renowned fortresses of Cronstadt which command the approaches to St. Petersburg, was the imperial summer palace of Peterhof, which for some time had been the favorite residence of Catharine. A few miles further down the bay, which runs east and west, was the palace of Oranienbaum, in the decoration of which many succeeding monarchs had lavished large sums. This was Peter's favorite resort, and its halls ever echoed with the carousings of the prince and his boon companions. Every year, on the 8th of July, there is a grand festival at Peterhof in honor of Peter and Paul, the patron saints of the imperial house. This was the time fixed upon by Catharine and her friends for the accomplishment of their plans. The tzar, on the evening of the 8th of July, was at Oranienbaum, surrounded by a bevy of the most beautiful females of his court. Catharine was at Peterhof. It was a warm summer's night, and the queen lodged in a small *cottage orné* called Montplaisir, which was situated in the garden. They had not intended to carry their plot into execution that night, but an alarm precipitated their action. At two o'clock in the morning Catharine was awoke from a sound sleep, by some one of her friends entering her room, exclaiming,

"Your majesty has not a moment to lose. Rise and follow me!"

Catharine, alarmed, called her confidential attendant, dressed hurriedly in disguise, and entered a carriage which was waiting for her at the garden gate. The horses were goaded to their utmost speed on the road to St. Petersburg, and so inconsiderately that soon one of them fell in utter exhaustion. They were still at some distance from the city, and the energetic empress alighted and pressed forward on foot. Soon they chanced to meet a peasant, driving a light cart. Count Orloff, who was a reputed lover of Catharine, and was guiding in this movement, seized the horse, placed the empress in the cart, and drove on. These delays had occupied so much time that it was seven o'clock in the morning before they reached St. Petersburg. The empress, with her companions, immediately proceeded to the barracks, where most of the soldiers were quartered, and whose officers had been gained over, and threw herself upon their protection.

"Danger," she said to the soldiers, "has compelled me to

fly to you for help. The tzar had intended to put me to death, together with my son. I had no other means of escaping death than by flight. I throw myself into your arms!"

Such an appeal from a woman, beautiful, beloved and imploring protection from the murderous hands of one who was hated and despised, inspired every bosom with indignation and with enthusiasm in her behalf. With one impulse they took an oath to die, if necessary, in her defense; and cries of "Long live the empress" filled the air. In two hours Catharine found herself at the head of several thousand veteran soldiers. She was also in possession of the arsenals; and the great mass of the population of St. Petersburg were clamorously advocating her cause.

Accompanied by a numerous and brilliant suite, the empress then repaired to the metropolitan church, where the archbishop and a great number of ecclesiastics, whose cooperation had been secured, received her, and the venerable archbishop, a man of imposing character and appearance, dressed in his sacerdotal robes, led her to the altar, and placing the imperial crown upon her head, proclaimed her sovereign of all the Russias, with the title of Catharine the Second. A *Te Deum* was then chanted, and the shouts of the multitude proclaimed the cordiality with which the populace accepted the revolution. The empress then repaired to the imperial palace, which was thrown open to all the people, and which, for hours, was thronged with the masses, who fell upon their knees before her, taking their oath of allegiance.

The friends of Catharine were, in the meantime, everywhere busy in putting the city in a state of defense, and in posting cannon to sweep the streets should Peter attempt resistance. The tzar seemed to be left without a friend. No one even took the trouble to inform him of what was transpiring. Troops in the vicinity were marched into the city, and before the end of the day, Catharine found herself at the head of fifteen thousand men; the most formidable defenses were arranged, strict order prevailed, and not a drop of blood had been shed. The manifesto of the empress, which had been secretly printed, was distributed throughout the city, and a day appointed when the foreign embassadors would be received by Catharine. The revolution seemed already accomplished without a struggle and almost without an effort.

CHAPTER XXIV.

THE CONSPIRACY; AND ACCESSION OF CATHARINE II.

FROM 1762 TO 1765.

PETER III. AT ORANIENBAUM.—CATHARINE AT PETERHOF.—THE SUCCESSFUL ACCOMPLISHMENT OF THE CONSPIRACY.—TERROR OF PETER.—HIS VACILLATING AND FEEBLE CHARACTER.—FLIGHT TO CRONSTADT.—REPULSE.—HEROIC COUNSEL OF MUNICH.—PETER'S RETURN TO ORANIENBAUM.—HIS SUPPLIANT LETTERS TO CATHARINE.—HIS ARREST.—IMPRISONMENT.—ASSASSINATION.—PROCLAMATION OF THE EMPRESS. HER COMPLICITY IN THE CRIME.—ENERGY OF CATHARINE'S ADMINISTRATION.—HER EXPANSIVE VIEWS AND SAGACIOUS POLICY.—CONTEMPLATED MARRIAGE WITH COUNT ORLOF.

IT was the morning of the 19th of July, 1762. Peter, at Oranienbaum, had passed most of the night, with his boon companions and his concubines, in intemperate carousings. He awoke at a late hour in the morning, and after breakfast set out in a carriage, with several of his women, accompanied by a troop of courtiers in other carriages, for Peterhof. The gay party were riding at a rapid rate over the beautiful shore road, looking out upon the Bay of Cronstadt, when they were met by a messenger from Peterhof, sent to inform them that the empress had suddenly disappeared during the night. Peter, upon receiving this surprising intelligence, turned pale as ashes, and alighting, conversed for some time anxiously with the messenger. Entering his carriage again, he drove with the utmost speed to Peterhof, and with characteristic silliness began to search the cupboards, closets, and under the bed for the empress. Those of greater penetration foresaw what had happened, but were silent, that they might not add to his alarm.

In the meantime some peasants, who had come from St.

Petersburg, related to a group of servants rumors they had heard of the insurrection in that city. A fearful gloom oppressed all, and Peter was in such a state of terror that he feared to ask any questions. As they were standing thus mute with confusion and dismay, a countryman rode up, and making a profound bow to the tzar, presented him with a note. Peter ran his eyes hastily over it, and then read it aloud. It communicated the appalling intelligence which we have just recorded.

The consternation into which the whole imperial party was thrown no language can describe. The women were in tears. The courtiers could offer not a word of encouragement or counsel. One, the king's chancellor, with the tzar's consent, set off for St. Petersburg to attempt to rouse the partisans of the tzar; but he could find none there. The wretched Peter was now continually receiving corroborative intelligence of the insurrection, and he strode up and down the walks of the garden, forming innumerable plans and adhering to none.

The tzar had a guard of three thousand troops at his palace of Oranienbaum. At noon these approached Peterhof led by their veteran commander, Munich. This energetic officer urged an immediate march upon St. Petersburg.

"Believe me," said Munich, "you have many friends in the city. The royal guard will rally around your standard when they see it approaching; and if we are forced to fight, the rebels will make but a short resistance."

While he was urging this energetic measure, and the women and the courtiers were trying to dissuade him from the step, and were entreating him to go back to Oranienbaum, news arrived that the troops of the empress, twenty thousand in number, were on the march to arrest him.

"Well," said Munich to the tzar, "if you wish to decline a battle, it is not wise at any rate to remain here, where you have no means of defense. Neither Oranienbaum nor Peterhof can withstand a siege. But Cronstadt offers you a safe retreat. Cronstadt is still under your command. You have there a formidable fleet and a numerous garrison. From Cronstadt you will find it easy to bring Petersburg back to duty."

The fortresses of Cronstadt are situated on an island of the same name, at the mouth of a bay which presents the only approach to St. Petersburg. This fortress, distant about thirty miles west of St. Petersburg, may be said to be impregnable. In the late war with Russia it bade defiance to the combined fleets of France and England. As we have before mentioned, Peterhof and Oranienbaum were pleasure-palaces, situated on the eastern shore of the Bay of Cronstadt, but a few miles from the fortress and but a few miles from each other. The gardens of these palaces extend to the waters of the bay, where there are ever riding at anchor a fleet of pleasure-boats and royal yachts.

The advice of Munich was instantly adopted. A boat was sent off conveying an officer to take command of the fortress, while, in the meantime, two yachts were got ready for the departure of the tzar and his party. Peter and his affrighted court hastened on board, continually looking over their shoulders fearing to catch a sight of the troops of the queen, whose appearance they every moment apprehended. But the energetic Catharine had anticipated this movement, and her emissaries had already gained the soldiers of the garrison, and were in possession of Cronstadt.

As the two yachts, which conveyed Peter and his party, entered the harbor, they found the garrison, under arms, lining the coast. The cannons were leveled, the matches lighted, and the moment the foremost yacht, which contained the emperor, cast anchor, a sentinel cried out,

"Who comes there?"

"The emperor," was the answer from the yacht.

"There is no emperor," the sentinel replied.

Peter III. started forward upon the deck, and, throwing back his cloak, exhibited the badges of his order, exclaiming,

"What! do you not know me?"

"No!" cried a thousand voices; "we know of no emperor. Long live the Empress Catharine II."

They then threatened immediately to sink the yacht unless the tzar retired.

The heroic Munich urged the tzar to an act of courage of which he was totally incapable.

"Let us leap on shore," said he; "none will dare to fire on you, and Cronstadt will still be your majesty's."

But Peter, in dismay, fled into the cabin, hid himself among his women, and ordered the cable instantly to be cut, and the yacht to be pulled out to sea by the oars. They were soon beyond the reach of the guns. It was now night, serene and beautiful; the sea was smooth as glass, and the stars shone with unusual splendor in the clear sky. The poltroon monarch of all the Russias had not yet ventured upon deck, but was trembling in his cabin, surrounded by his dismayed mistresses, when the helmsman entered the cabin and said to the tzar,

"Sire, to what port is it your majesty's pleasure that I should take the vessel?"

Peter gazed, for a moment, in consternation and bewilderment, and then sent for Munich.

"Field marshal," said he, "I perceive that I was too late in following your advice. You see to what extremities I am reduced. Tell me, I beseech you, what I ought to do."

About two hundred miles from where they were, directly down the Gulf of Finland, was the city of Revel, one of the naval depots of Russia. A large squadron of ships of war was riding at anchor there. Munich, as prompt in council as he was energetic in action, replied,

"Proceed immediately to join the squadron at Revel.

There take a ship, and go on to Pomerania.* Put yourself at the head of your army, return to Russia, and I promise you that in six weeks Petersburg and all the rest of the empire will be in subjection to you."

The women and the courtiers, with characteristic timidity, remonstrated against a measure so decisive, and, believing that the empress would not be very implacable, entreated the tzar to negotiate rather than fight. Peter yielded to their senseless solicitations, and ordered them to make immediately for Oranienbaum. They reached the dock at four o'clock in the morning. Peter hastened to his apartment, and wrote a letter to the empress, which he dispatched by a courier. In this letter he made a humble confession of his faults, and promised to share the sovereign authority with Catharine if she would consent to reconciliation. The empress was, at this time, at the head of her army within about twenty miles of Oranienbaum. During the night, she had slept for a few hours upon some cloaks which the officers of her suite had spread for her bed. Catharine, knowing well that perjury was one of the most trivial of the faults of the tzar, made no reply, but pressed forward with her troops.

Peter, soon receiving information of the advance of the army, ordered one of his fleetest horses to be saddled, and dressed himself in disguise, intending thus to effect his escape to the frontiers of Poland. But, with his constitutional irresolution, he soon abandoned this plan, and, ordering the fortress of Oranienbaum to be dismantled, to convince Catharine that he intended to make no resistance, he wrote to the empress another letter still more humble and sycophantic than the first. He implored her forgiveness in terms of the most abject humiliation. He assured her that he was ready to resign to her unconditionally the crown of Russia, and that

* Pomerania was one of the duchies of Prussia, where the Russian army, in coöperation with the King of Prussia, was assembled. Frederic might, perhaps, have sent his troops to aid Peter in the recovery of his crown.

he only asked permission to retire to his native duchy of Holstein, and that the empress would graciously grant him a pension for his support.

Catharine read the letter, but deigning no reply, sent back the chamberlain who brought it, with a verbal message to her husband that she could enter into no negotiations with him, and could only accept his unconditional submission. The chamberlain, Ismailof, returned to Oranienbaum. The tzar had with him there only his Holstein guard consisting of six hundred men. Ismailof urged the tzar, as the only measure of safety which now remained, to abandon his troops, who could render him no defense, and repair to the empress, throwing himself upon her mercy. For a short time the impotent mind of the degraded prince was in great turmoil. But as was to be expected, he surrendered himself to the humiliation. Entering his carriage, he rode towards Peterhof to meet the empress. Soon he encountered the battalions on the march for his capture. Silently they opened their ranks and allowed him to enter, and then, closing around him, they stunned him with shouts of, "Long live Catharine."

The miserable man had the effrontery to take with him, in his carriage, one of his mistresses. As she alighted at the palace of Peterhof, some of the soldiers tore the ribbons from her dress. The tzar was led up the grand stair-case, stripped of the insignia of imperial power, and was shut up, and carefully guarded in one of the chambers of the palace. Count Panin then visited him, by order of the empress, and demanded of him the abdication of the crown, informing him that having thus abdicated, he would be sent back to his native duchy and would enjoy the dignity of Duke of Holstein for the remainder of his days. Peter was now as pliant as wax. Aided by the count, he wrote and signed the following declaration:

"During the short space of my absolute reign over the

empire of Russia, I became sensible that I was not able to support so great a burden, and that my abilities were not equal to the task of governing so great an empire, either as a sovereign or in any other capacity whatever. I also foresaw the great troubles which must thence have arisen, and have been followed with the total ruin of the empire, and my own eternal disgrace. After having therefore seriously reflected thereon, I declare, without constraint, and in the most solemn manner, to the Russian empire and to the whole universe, that I for ever renounce the government of the said empire, never desiring hereafter to reign therein, either as an absolute sovereign, or under any other form of government; never wishing to aspire thereto, or to use any means, of any sort, for that purpose. As a pledge of which I swear sincerely before God and all the world to this present renunciation, written and signed this 29th day of June, O. S. 1762."*

Peter III., having placed this abdication in the hands of Count Panin, seemed quite serene, fancying himself safe, at least from bodily harm. In the evening, however, an officer, with a strong escort, came and conveyed him a prisoner to Ropscha, a small imperial palace about fifteen miles from Peterhof. Peter, after his disgraceful reign of six months, was now imprisoned in a palace; and his wife, whom he had intended to repudiate and probably to behead, was now sovereign Empress of Russia. In the evening, the thunderings of the cannon upon the ramparts of St. Petersburg announced the victory of Catharine. She however slept that night at Peterhof, and in the morning received the homage of the nobility, who from all quarters flocked around her to give in their adhesion to her reign.

Field Marshal Munich, who with true fealty had stood by

* By the Gregorian Calendar or New Style, adopted by Pope Gregory XIII. in 1582, ten days were dropped after the 4th of October, and the 5th was reckoned as the 15th. Thus the 29th of June, O. S. would be July 8, N. S.

Peter III. to the last, urging him to unfurl the banner of the tzar and fight heroically for his crown, appeared with the rest. The noble old man with an unblushing brow entered the presence of Catharine. As soon as she perceived him she called aloud,

"Field marshal, it was you, then, who wanted to fight me?"

"Yes, madam," Munich answered, in a manly tone; "could I do less for the prince who delivered me from captivity? But it is henceforth my duty to fight for you, and you will find in me a fidelity equal to that with which I had devoted my services to him."*

In the afternoon, the empress returned to St. Petersburg. She entered the city on horseback, accompanied by a brilliant retinue of nobles, and followed by her large army of fifteen thousand troops. All the soldiers wore garlands of oak leaves. The immense crowds in the city formed lines for the passage of the empress, scattered flowers in her path, and greeted her with constant bursts of acclaim. All the streets through which she passed were garlanded and spanned with triumphal arches, the bells rang their merriest peals, and military salutes bellowed from all the ramparts. As the high ecclesiastics crowded to meet her, they kissed her hand, while she, in accordance with Russian courtesy, kissed their cheeks.

* Marshal Munich was eighty-two years of age. Elizabeth had sent him to Siberian exile. Peter liberated him. Upon his return to Moscow, after twenty years of exile, he found one son living, and twenty-two grandchildren and great grandchildren whom he had never seen. When the heroic old man presented himself before the tzar dressed in the sheep-skin coat he had worn in Siberia, Peter said,

"I hope, notwithstanding your age, you may still serve me."

Munich replied,

"Since your majesty has brought me from darkness to light, and called me from the depths of a cavern, to admit me to the foot of the throne, you will find me ever ready to expose my life in your service. Neither a tedious exile nor the severity of a Siberian climate have been able to extinguish, or even to damp, the ardor I have formerly shown for the interests of Russia and the glory of its monarch."

Catharine summoned the senate, and presided over its deliberations with wonderful dignity and grace. The foreign ministers, confident in the stability of her reign, hastened to present their congratulations. Peter found even a few hours in the solitude of the palace of Ropscha exceedingly oppressive; he accordingly sent to the empress, soliciting the presence of a negro servant to whom he was much attached, and asking also for his dog, his violin, a Bible and a few novels.

"I am disgusted," he wrote, "with the wickedness of mankind, and am resolved henceforth to devote myself to a philosophical life."

After Peter had been six days at Ropscha, one morning two nobles, who had been most active in the revolution which had dethroned the tzar, entered his apartment, and, after conversing for a time, brandy was brought in. The cup of which the tzar drank was poisoned! He was soon seized with violent colic pains. The assassins then threw him upon the floor, tied a napkin around his neck, and strangled him. Count Orlof, the most intimate friend of the empress, and who was reputed to be her paramour, was one of these murderers. He immediately mounted his horse, and rode to St. Petersburg to inform the empress that Peter was dead. Whether Catharine was a party to this assassination, or whether it was perpetrated entirely without her knowledge, is a question which now can probably never be decided. It is very certain that the grief she manifested was all feigned, and that the assassins were rewarded for their devotion to her interests. She shut herself up for a few days, assuming the aspect of a mourner, and issued to her subjects a declaration announcing the death of the late tzar. When one enters upon the declivity of crime, the descent is ever rapid. The innocent girl, who, but a few years before, had entered the Russian court from her secluded ancestral castle a spotless child of fifteen, was now most deeply involved in intrigues and sins. It is probable, indeed, that she had not intended the death of her husband, but had designed sending him to Holstein and providing for him abundantly, for the rest of his days, with dogs and wine, and leaving him to his own indulgences. It is certain, however, that the empress did not punish, or even dismiss from her favor, the murderers of Peter. She announced to the nation his death in the following terms:

"*By the Grace of God, Catharine II., Empress of all the Russias, to our loving Subjects, Greeting:*

"The seventh day after our accession to the throne of all the Russias, we received information that the late emperor, Peter III., was attacked with a most violent colic. That we might not be wanting in Christian duty, or disobedient to the divine command by which we are enjoined to preserve the life of our neighbor, we immediately ordered that the said Peter should be furnished with every thing that might be judged necessary to restore his health by the aids of medicine. But, to our great regret and affliction, we were yesterday evening apprised that, by the permission of the Almighty, the late emperor departed this life. We have therefore ordered his body to be conveyed to the monastery of Nefsky, in order to its interment in that place. At the same time, with our imperial and maternal voice, we exhort our faithful subjects to forgive and forget what is past, to pay the last duties to his body, and to pray to God sincerely for the repose of his soul, wishing them, however, to consider this unexpected and sudden death as an especial effect of the providence of God, whose impenetrable decrees are working for us, for our throne, and for our country things known only to his holy will.

"Done at St. Petersburg, July 7th (N. S., July 18th), 1762."

The news of the revolution soon spread throughout Russia, and the nobles generally acquiesced in it without a murmur. The masses of the people no more thought of expressing or having an opinion than did the sheep. One of the first acts of the empress was to send an embassy to Frederic of Prussia, announcing,

"That she was resolved to observe inviolably the peace recently concluded with Prussia; but that nevertheless she had decided to bring back to Russia all her troops in Silesia, Prussia and Pomerania."

All the sovereigns of Europe acknowledged the title of Catharine II., and some sent especial congratulations on her accession to the throne. Maria Theresa, of Austria, was at first quite delighted, hoping that Catharine would again unite the Russian troops with hers in hostility to her great rival, Frederic. But in this expectation she was doomed to bitter disappointment. The King of Prussia, in a confidential note to Count Finkenstein, wrote of Catharine and the new reign as follows:

"The Emperor of Russia has been dethroned by his consort. It was to be expected. That princess has much good sense, and the same friendly relations towards us as the deceased. She has no religion, but acts the devotee. The chancellor Bestuchef is her greatest favorite, and, as he has a strong propensity to *guinées*, I flatter myself that I shall be able to retain the friendship of the court. The poor emperor wanted to imitate Peter I., but he had not the capacity for it."

The empress, taking with her her son Paul, and a very brilliant and numerous suite of nobles, repaired to Moscow, where she was crowned with unusual splendor. By marked attention to the soldiers, providing most liberally for their comfort, she soon secured the enthusiastic attachment of the army. By the most scrupulous observance of all the external rites of religion, she won the confidence of the clergy. In every movement Catharine exhibited wonderful sagacity and energy. It was not to be supposed that the partisans of Peter III. would be ejected from their places to give room for others, without making desperate efforts to regain what they had lost.

A very formidable conspiracy was soon organized, and the friends of Catharine were thrown into the greatest state of alarm. But her courage did not, for one moment, forsake her.

"Why are you alarmed?" said she. "Think you that I fear to face this danger; or rather do you apprehend that I know not how to overcome it? Recollect that you have seen me, in moments far more terrible than these, in full possession of all the vigor of my mind; and that I can support the most cruel reverses of fortune with as much serenity as I have supported her favors. Think you that a few mutinous soldiers are to deprive me of a crown that I accepted with reluctance, and only as the means of delivering the Russian nation from their miseries? They cause me no alarm. That Providence which has called me to reign, will preserve me for the glory and the happiness of the empire. That almighty arm which has hitherto been my defense will now confound my foes!"

The revolt was speedily quelled. The celebrity of her administration soon resounded from one end of Europe to the other. She presided over the senate; assisted at all the deliberations of the council; read the dispatches of the embassadors; wrote, with her own hand, or dictated the answers, and watched carefully to see that all her orders were faithfully executed. She studied the lives of the most distinguished men, and was emulous of the renown of those who had been friends and benefactors of the human race. There has seldom been a sovereign on any throne more assiduously devoted to the cares of empire than was Catharine II. In one of her first manifestoes, issued the 10th of August of this year, she uttered the words, which her conduct proved to be essentially true,

"Not only all that we have or may have, but also our life itself, we have devoted to our dear country. We value nothing on our own account. We serve not ourself. But we labor with all pains, with all diligence and care for the glory and happiness of our people."

Catharine found corruption and bribery everywhere, and

she engaged in the work of reform with the energies of Hercules in cleansing the Augean stables. She abolished, indignantly the custom, which had existed for ages, of attempting to extort confession of crime by torture. It is one of the marvels of human depravity that intelligent minds could have been so imbruted as to tolerate, for a day, so fiend-like a wrong. The whole system of inquisitorial investigations, in both Church and State, was utterly abrogated. Foreigners were invited to settle in the empire. The lands were carefully explored, that the best districts might be pointed out for tillage, for forest and for pasture. The following proclamation, inviting foreigners to settle in Russia, shows the liberality and the comprehensive views which animated the empress:

"Any one who is destitute shall receive money for the expenses of his journey, and shall be forwarded to these free lands at the expense of the crown. On his arrival he shall receive a competent assistance, and even an advance of capital, free of interest, for ten years. The stranger is exempted from all service, either military or civil, and from all taxes for a certain time. In these new tracts of land the colonists may live according to their own good-will, under their own jurisdiction for thirty years. All religions are tolerated."

Thus encouraged, thousands flocked from Germany to the fresh and fertile acres on the banks of the Volga and the Samara. The emigration became so great that several of the petty German princes issued prohibitions. In the rush of adventurers, of the indolent, the improvident and the vicious, great suffering ensued. Desert wilds were, however, peopled, and the children of the emigrants succeeded to homes of comparative comfort. Settlers crowded to these lands even from France, Poland and Sweden. Ten thousand families emigrated to the district of Saratof alone.

"The world," said Catharine one day to the French minister, "will not be able properly to judge of my administration till after five years. It will require at least so much time to reduce the empire to order. In the mean time I shall behave, with all the princes of Europe, like a finished coquette. I have the finest army in the world. I have a greater taste for war than for peace; but, I am restrained from war by humanity, justice and reason. I shall not allow myself, like Elizabeth, to be pressed into a war. I shall enter upon it when it will prove advantageous to me, but never from complaisance to others."

A large number of the nobles, led by the chancellor of the empire, now presented a petition to Catharine, urging her again to marry. After a glowing eulogium on all the empress had done for the renown and prosperity of Russia, they reminded her of the feeble constitution of her son Paul, of the terrible calamity a disputed succession might impose upon Russia, and entreated her to give an additional proof of her devotion to the good of her subjects, by sacrificing her own liberty to their welfare, in taking a spouse. This advice was quite in harmony with the inclinations of the empress. Count Orlof, one of the most conspicuous nobles of the court, and the prime actor in the conspiracy which had overthrown and assassinated Peter III., was the recognized favorite of Catharine. But Count Orlof had assumed such haughty airs, regarding Catharine as indebted to him for her crown, that he had rendered himself extremely unpopular; and so much discontent was manifested in view of his elevation to the throne, that Catharine did not dare to proceed with the measure. It is generally supposed, however, that there was a sort of private marriage instituted, of no real validity, between Catharine and Orlof, by which the count became virtually the husband of the empress.

Catharine was now firmly established on the throne. The beneficial effects of her administration were daily becoming more apparent in all parts of Russia. Nothing which could be promotive of the prosperity of the empire escaped her observation. With questions of commerce, finance and politics she seemed equally familiar. On the 11th of August, 1673, she issued an imperial edict written by her own hand, in which it is said,

"On the whole surface of the earth there is no country better adapted for commerce than our empire. Russia has spacious harbors in Europe, and, overland, the way is open through Poland to every region. Siberia extends, on one side, over all Asia, and India is not very remote from Orenburg. On the other side, Russia seems to touch on America. Across the Euxine is a passage, though as yet unexplored, to Egypt and Africa, and bountiful Providence has blessed the extensive provinces of our empire with such gifts of nature as can rarely be found in all the four quarters of the world."

CHAPTER XXV.

REIGN OF CATHARINE II.

FROM 1765 TO 1774.

ENERGY OF CATHARINE'S ADMINISTRATION.—TITLES OF HONOR DECREED TO HER.—CODE OF LAWS INSTITUTED.—THE ASSASSINATION OF THE EMPRESS ATTEMPTED.—ENCOURAGEMENT OF LEARNED MEN.—CATHARINE INOCULATED FOR THE SMALL-POX.—NEW WAR WITH TURKEY.—CAPTURE OF THE CRIMEA.—SAILING OF THE RUSSIAN FLEET.—GREAT NAVAL VICTORY.—VISIT OF THE PRUSSIAN PRINCE HENRY.—THE SLEIGH RIDE.—PLANS FOR THE PARTITION OF POLAND.—THE HERMITAGE.—MARRIAGE OF THE GRAND DUKE PAUL.—CORRESPONDENCE WITH VOLTAIRE AND DIDEROT.

THE friends and the foes of Catharine are alike lavish in their encomiums upon her attempts to elevate Russia in prosperity and in national greatness. Under her guidance an assembly was convened to frame a code of laws, based on justice, and which should be supreme throughout all Russia. The assembly prosecuted its work with great energy, and, ere its dissolution, passed a resolution decreeing to the empress the titles of "Great, Wise, Prudent, and Mother of the Country."

To this decree Catharine modestly replied, "If I have rendered myself worthy of the first title, it belongs to posterity to confer it upon me. Wisdom and prudence are the gifts of Heaven, for which I daily give thanks, without presuming to derive any merit from them myself. The title of *Mother of the Country* is, in my eyes, the most dear of all, —the only one I can accept, and which I regard as the most benign and glorious recompense for my labors and solicitudes in behalf of a people whom I love."

The code of laws thus framed is a noble monument to the genius and humanity of Catharine II. The principles of enlightened philanthropy pervades the code, which recognizes the immutable principles of right, and which seems designed to undermine the very foundations of despotism. In the instructions which Catharine drew up for the guidance of the assembly, she wrote,

"Laws should be framed with the sole object of conducting mankind to the greatest happiness. It is our duty to mitigate the lot of those who live in a state of dependence. The liberty and security of the citizens ought to be the grand and precious object of all laws; they should all tend to render life, honor and property as stable and secure as the constitution of the government itself. It is incomparably better to prevent crimes than to punish them. The use of torture is contrary to sound reason. Humanity cries out against this practice, and insists on its being abolished."

The condition of the peasantry, heavily taxed by the nobles, excited her deepest commiseration. She wished their entire enfranchisement, but was fully conscious that she was not strong enough to undertake so sweeping a measure of reform. She insisted, however, "that laws should be prescribed to the nobility, obliging them to act more circumspectly in the manner of levying their dues, and to protect the peasant, so that his condition might be improved and that he might be enabled to acquire property."

A ruffian attempted to assassinate Catharine. He was arrested in the palace, with a long dagger concealed in his dress, and without hesitation confessed his design. Catharine had the assassin brought into her presence, conversed mildly with him, and seeing that there was no hope of disarming his fanaticism, banished him to Siberia. But the innocent daughter of the guilty man she took under her protection, and subsequently appointed her one of her maids of honor. In the year 1767, she sent a delegation of scientific men on a geological survey into the interior of the empire, with directions to determine the geographical position of the principal places, to mark their temperature, their productions, their wealth, and the manners and characters of the several people by whom they were inhabited. Russia was then, as now, a world by itself, peopled by innumerable tribes or nations, with a great diversity of climates, and with an infinite variety of manners and customs. A large portion of the country was immersed in the profoundest barbarism, almost inaccessible to the traveler. In other portions vagrant hordes wandered without any fixed habitations. Here was seen the castle of the noble with all its imposing architecture, and its enginery of offense and defense. The mud hovels of the peasants were clustered around the massive pile; and they passed their lives in the most degrading bondage.

From all parts of Europe the most learned men were invited to the court of Catharine. The renowned mathematician, Euler, was lured from Berlin to St. Petersburg. The empress settled upon him a large annual stipend, and made him a present of a house. Catharine was fully conscious that the glory of a country consists, not in its military achievements, but in advancement in science and in the useful and elegant arts. The annual sum of five thousand dollars was assigned to encourage the translation of foreign literary works into the Russian language. The small-pox was making fearful ravages in Russia. The empress had heard of inoculation. She sent to England for a physician, Dr. Thomas Dimsdale, who had practiced inoculation for the small-pox with great success in London. Immediately upon his arrival the empress sent for him, and with skill which astonished the physician, questioned him respecting his mode of practice. He was invited to dine with the empress; and the doctor thus describes the dinner party:

"The empress sat singly at the upper end of a long table, at which about twelve of the nobility were guests. The entertainment consisted of a variety of excellent dishes, served up after the French manner, and was concluded by a dessert of the finest fruits and sweetmeats, such as I little expected to find in that northern climate. Most of these luxuries were, however, the produce of the empress's own dominions. Pine-apples, indeed, are chiefly imported from England, though those of the growth of Russia, of which we had one that day, are of good flavor but generally small. Water-melons and grapes are brought from Astrachan; great plenty of melons from Moscow; and apples and pears from the Ukraine.

"But what most enlivened the whole entertainment, was the unaffected ease and affability of the empress herself. Each of her guests had a share of her attention and politeness. The conversation was kept up with freedom and cheerfulness to be expected rather from persons of the same rank, than from subjects admitted to the honor of their sovereign's company."

The empress after conversing with Dr. Dimsdale, decided to introduce the practice of small-pox inoculation* into Russia, and heroically resolved that the experiment should first be tried upon herself. Dr. Dimsdale, oppressed by the immense responsibility thus thrown upon him, for though the disease, thus introduced, was generally mild, in not a few cases it proved fatal, requested the assistance of the court physicians.

"It is not necessary," the empress replied; "you come well recommended. The conversation I have had increases my confidence in you. It is impossible that my physicians should have much skill in this operation. My life is my own, and with the utmost cheerfulness I entrust myself to your care. I wish to be inoculated as soon as you judge it convenient, and desire to have it kept a secret."

The anxious physician begged that the experiment might

* Vaccination, or inoculation with the cow-pox, was not introduced to Europe until many years after this. The celebrated treatise of Jenner, entitled *An inquiry into the causes and effects of Variolæ Vaccinæ*, was published in 1798.

first be tried by inoculating some of her own sex and age, and, as near as possible, of her own constitutional habits. The empress replied,

"The practice is not novel, and no doubt remains of its general success. It is, therefore, not necessary that there should be any delay on that account."

Catharine was inoculated on the 12th of October, 1768, and went immediately to a secluded private palace at some distance from the city, under the pretense that she wished to superintend some repairs. She took with her only the necessary attendants. Soon, however, several of the nobility, some of whom she suspected had not had the small-pox, followed. As a week was to elapse after the operation before the disease would begin to manifest itself, the empress said to Dr. Dimsdale,

"I must rely on you to give me notice when it is possible for me to communicate the disease. Though I could wish to keep my inoculation a secret, yet far be it from me to conceal it a moment when it may become hazardous to others."

In the mean time she took part in every amusement with her wonted affability and without the slightest indication of alarm. She dined with the rest of the company, and enlivened the whole court with those conversational charms for which she was distinguished. The disease proved light, and she was carried through it very successfully. Soon after, she wrote to Voltaire,

"I have not kept my bed a single instant, and I have received company every day. I am about to have my only son inoculated. Count Orlof, that hero who resembles the ancient Romans in the best times of the republic, both in courage and generosity, doubting whether he had ever had the small-pox, has put himself under the hands of our Englishman, and, the next day after the operation, went to the hunt in a very deep fall of snow. A great number of courtiers have followed his example, and many others are preparing to do so. Besides this, inoculation is now carried on at Petersburg in three seminaries of education, and in an hospital established under the protection of Dr. Dimsdale."

The empress testified her gratitude for the benefits Dr. Dimsdale had conferred upon Russia by making him a present of fifty thousand dollars, and settling upon him a pension of one thousand dollars a year. On the 3d of December, 1768, a thanksgiving service was performed in the chapel of the palace, in gratitude for the recovery of her majesty and her son Paul from the small-pox.

The Turks began now to manifest great apprehensions in view of the rapid growth of the Russian empire. Poland was so entirely overshadowed that its monarchs were elected and its government administered under the influence of a Russian army. In truth, Poland had become but little more than one of the provinces of Catharine's empire. The Grand Seignior formed an alliance with the disaffected Poles, arrested the Russian embassador at Constantinople, and mustered his hosts for war. Catharine II. was prepared for the emergency. Early in 1769 the Russian army commenced its march towards the banks of the Cuban, in the wilds of Circassia. The Tartars of the Crimea were the first foes whom the armies of Catharine encountered. The Sea of Azof, with its surrounding shores, soon fell into the possession of Russia. One of the generals of Catharine, General Drevitch, a man whose name deserves to be held up to eternal infamy, took nine Polish gentlemen as captives, and, cutting off their hands at the wrist, sent them home, thus mutilated, to strike terror into the Poles. Already Frederic of Prussia and Catharine were secretly conferring upon a united attack upon Poland and the division of the territory between them.

Frederic sent his brother Henry to St. Petersburg to confer with Catharine upon this contemplated robbery, sufficiently gigantic in character to be worthy of the energies of the royal bandits. Catharine received Henry with splendor which the world has seldom seen equaled. One of the entertainments with which she honored him was a moonlight sleigh ride arranged upon a scale of imperial grandeur. The sleigh which conveyed Catharine and the Prussian prince was an immense parlor drawn by sixteen horses, covered and inclosed by double glasses, which, with numberless mirrors, reflected all objects within and without. This sledge was followed by a retinue of two thousand others. Every person, in all the sledges, was dressed in fancy costume, and masked. When two miles from the city, the train passed beneath a triumphal arch illuminated with all conceivable splendor. At the distance of every mile, some grand structure appeared in a blaze of light, a pyramid, or a temple, or colonnades, or the most brilliant displays of fireworks. Opposite each of these structures ball rooms had been reared, which were crowded with the rustic peasantry, amusing themselves with music, dancing and all the games of the country. Each of the spacious houses of entertainment personated some particular Russian nation, where the dress, music and amusements of that nation were represented. All sorts of gymnastic feats were also exhibited, such as vaulting, tumbling and feats upon the slack and tight rope.

Through such scenes the imperial pleasure party rode, until a high mountain appeared through an avenue cut in the forest, representing Mount Vesuvius during an eruption. Vast billows of flame were rolling to the skies, and the whole region was illumined with a blaze of light. The spectators had hardly recovered from the astonishment which this display caused, when the train suddenly entered a Chinese village, which proved to be but the portal to the imperial palace of Tzarkoselo. The palace was lighted with an infinite number of wax candles. For two hours the guests amused themselves with dancing. Suddenly there was a grand discharge of cannon. The candles were immediately extinguished, and a magnificent display of fireworks, extending along the whole breadth of the palace, converted night into day. Again there was a thundering discharge of artillery, when, as by enchantment, the candles blazed anew, and a sumptuous supper was served up. After the entertainment, dancing was renewed, and was continued until morning.

The empress had a private palace at St. Petersburg which she called her Hermitage, where she received none but her choicest friends. This sumptuous edifice merits some minuteness of description. It consisted of a suite of apartments containing every thing which the most voluptuous and exquisite taste could combine. The spacious building was connected with the imperial palace by a covered arch. It would require a volume to describe the treasures of art and industry with which it abounded. Here the empress had her private library and her private picture gallery. Raphael's celebrated gallery in the Vatican at Rome was exactly repeated here with the most accurate copies of all the paintings, corner pieces and other ornaments of the same size and in the same situations. Medals, engravings, curious pieces of art, models of mechanical inventions and collections of specimens of minerals and of objects of natural history crowded the cabinets. Chambers were arranged for all species of amusements. A pleasure garden was constructed upon arches, with furnaces beneath them in winter, that the plants might ever enjoy genial heat. This garden was covered with fine brass wire, that the birds from all countries, singing among the trees and shrubs, or hopping along the grass plots and gravel walks, and which the empress was accustomed to feed with her own hand, might not escape. While the storms of a Russian winter were howling without, the empress here could tread upon verdant lawns and gravel walks beneath luxuriant vegetation, listening to bird songs and partaking of fruits and flowers of every kind.

In this artificial Eden the empress often received Henry, the Prussian prince, and matured her plan for the partition of

Poland. The festivities which dazzled the eyes of the frivolous courtiers were hardly thought of by Catharine and Henry. Mr. Richardson, an English gentleman who was in the family of Lord Cathcart, then the British embassador at the Russian court, had sufficient sagacity to detect that, beneath this display of amusements, political intrigues of great moment were being woven. He wrote from St. Petersburg, on the 1st of January, 1771, as follows:

"This city, since the beginning of winter, has exhibited a continued scene of festivities; feasts, balls, concerts, plays, and masquerades in continued succession; and all in honor of, and to divert his royal highness, Prince Henry of Prussia, the famous brother of the present king. Yet his royal highness does not seem to be much diverted. He looks at them as an old cat looks at the gambols of a young kitten; or as one who has higher sport going on in his mind than the pastime of fiddling and dancing. He came here on pretense of a friendly visit to the empress; to have the happiness of waiting on so magnanimous a princess, and to see, with his own eyes, the progress of those immense improvements, so highly celebrated by Voltaire and those French writers who receive gifts from her majesty.

"But do you seriously imagine that this creature of skin and bone should travel through Sweden, Finland and Poland, all for the pleasure of seeing the metropolis and the empress of Russia? Other princes may pursue such pastime; but the princes of the house of Brandenburg fly at a nobler quarry. Or is the King of Prussia, as a tame spectator, to reap no advantage from the troubles in Poland and the Turkish war? What is the meaning of his late conferences with the Emperor of Germany? Depend upon it these planetary conjunctions are the forerunners of great events. A few months may unfold the secret. You will recollect the signs when, after this, you shall hear of changes, usurpations and revolutions."

In one of these interviews, in which the dismemberment of Poland was resolved on, Catharine said,

"I will frighten Turkey and flatter England. Do you take it upon yourself to buy over Austria, and amuse France."

Though the arrangements for the partition were at this time all made, the portion which was to be assigned to Austria agreed upon, and the extent of territory which each was to appropriate to itself settled, the formal treaty was not signed till two years afterwards.

The war still continued to rage on the frontiers of Turkey. After ten months of almost incessant slaughter, the Turkish army was nearly destroyed. The empress collected two squadrons of Russian men-of-war at Archangel on the White Sea, and at Revel on the Baltic, and sent them through the straits of Gibraltar into the Mediterranean. All Europe was astonished at this wonderful apparition suddenly presenting itself amidst the islands of the Archipelago. The inhabitants of the Greek islands were encouraged to rise, and they drove out their Mussulman oppressors with great slaughter. Catharine was alike victorious on the land and on the sea; and she began very seriously to contemplate driving the Turks out of Europe and taking possession of Constantinople. Her land troops speedily overran the immense provinces of Bessarabia, Moldavia and Wallachia, and annexed them to the Russian empire.

The Turkish fleet encountered the Russians in the narrow channel which separates the island of Scio from Natolia. In one of the fiercest naval battles on record, and which raged for five hours, the Turkish fleet was entirely destroyed. A courier was instantly dispatched to St. Petersburg with the exultant tidings. The rejoicings in St. Petersburg, over this naval victory, were unbounded. The empress was so elated that she resolved to liberate both Greece and Egypt from the sway of the Turks. The Turks were in a terrible panic, and resorted to the most desperate measures to defend the Dardanelles, that the Russian fleet might not ascend to Constantinople. At the same time the plague broke out in Constantinople with horrible violence, a thousand dying daily, for several weeks.

The immense Crimean peninsula contains fifteen thousand square miles, being twice as large as the State of Massachusetts. The isthmus of Perikop, which connects it with the mainland, is but five miles in width. The Turks had fortified this passage by a ditch seventy-two feet wide, and forty-two feet deep, and had stationed along this line an army of fifty thousand Tartars. But the Russians forced the barrier, and the Crimea became a Russian province. The victorious army, however, soon encountered a foe whom no courage could vanquish. The plague broke out in their camp, and spread through all Russia, with desolation which seems incredible, although well authenticated. In Moscow, not more than one fourth of the inhabitants were left alive. More than sixty thousand died in that city in less than a year. For days the dead lay in the streets where they had fallen, there not being carts or people enough to carry them away. The pestilence gradually subsided before the intensity of wintry frosts.

The devastations of war and of the plague rendered both the Russians and Turks desirous of peace. On the 2d of August, 1772, the Russian and Turkish plenipotentiaries met under tents, on a plain about nineteen miles north of Bucharest, the capital of Wallachia. The Russian ministers approached in four grand coaches, preceded by hussars, and attended by one hundred and sixty servants in livery. The Turkish ministers came on horseback, with about sixty servants, all dressed in great simplicity. The two parties, however, could not agree, and the conference was broken up. The negotiations were soon resumed at Bucharest, but this attempt was also equally unsuccessful with the first.

The plot for the partition of Poland was now ripe. Rus

sia, Prussia and Austria had agreed to march their armies into the kingdom and divide a very large portion of the territory between them. It was as high-handed a robbery as the world ever witnessed. There is some consolation, however, in the reflection, that the masses of the people in Poland were quite unaffected by the change. They were no more oppressed by their new despots than they had been for ages by their old ones. By this act, Russia annexed to her territory the enormous addition of three thousand four hundred and forty square leagues, sparsely inhabited, indeed, yet containing a population of one million five hundred thousand. Austria obtained less territory, but nearly twice as many inhabitants. Prussia obtained the contiguous provinces she coveted, with about nine hundred thousand inhabitants. They still left to the King of Poland, in this first partition, a small fragment of his kingdom. The King of Prussia removed from his portion the first year twelve thousand families, who were sent to populate the uninhabited wilds of his hereditary dominions. All the young men were seized and sent to the Prussian army. The same general course was pursued by Russia. That the Polish population might be incorporated with that of Russia, and all national individuality lost, the Poles were removed into ancient Russia, while whole provinces of Russians were sent to populate Poland.

The vast wealth which at this time the Russian court was able to extort from labor, may be inferred from the fact, that while the empress was carrying on the most expensive wars, her disbursements to favorites, generals and literary men—in encouraging the arts, purchasing libraries, pictures, statues, antiques and jewels, vastly exceeded that of any European prince excepting Louis XIV. A diamond of very large size and purity, weighing seven hundred and seventy-nine carats, was brought from Ispahan by a Greek. Catharine purchased it for five hundred thousand dollars, settling at the same time a pension of five thousand dollars for life, upon the fortunate Greek of whom she bought it.

The war still raged fiercely in Turkey with the usual vicissitudes of battles. The Danube at length became the boundary between the hostile armies, its wide expanse of water, its islands and its wooded shores affording endless opportunity for surprises, ambuscades, flight and pursuit. Under these circumstances war was prosecuted with an enormous loss of life; but as the wasting armies were continually being replenished, it seemed as though there could be no end to the strife.

Catharine had for some time been meditating a marriage for her son, the Grand Duke Paul. There was a grand duchy in Germany, on the Rhine, almost equally divided by that stream, called Darmstadt. It contained three thousand nine hundred square miles, being about half the size of the State of Massachusetts, and embraced a population of nearly a million. The Duke of Darmstadt had three very attractive daughters, either one of whom, Catharine thought, would make a very suitable match for her son. She accordingly invited the three young ladies, with their mother, to visit her court, that her son might, after a careful scrutiny, take his pick. The brilliance of the prospective match with the tzar of all the Russias outweighed every scruple, and the invitation was eagerly acceptd. Paul was cold as an iceberg, stubborn as a mule and crack-brained, but he could place on the brow of his spouse the crown of an empress. Catharine received her guests with the greatest magnificence, loaded them with presents, and finally chose one of them, Wilhelmina, for the bride of Paul. The marriage was solemnized on the 10th of November, 1773, with all the splendor with which the Russian court could invest the occasion, the festivities being continued from the 10th to the 21st of the month.

Catharine, with her own hand, kept up a regular correspondence with many literary and scientific men in other parts of Europe, particularly with Voltaire and Diderot, the illustrious philosophers of France. Several times she sent them earnest invitations to visit her court. Diderot accepted her invitation, and was received with confiding and friendly attentions which no merely crowned head could have secured. Diderot sat at the table of the empress, and daily held long social interviews with her, conversing upon politics, philosophy, legislation, freedom of conscience and the rights of nations. Catharine was charmed with the enthusiasm and eloquence of her guest, but she perfectly appreciated the genius and the puerility combined in his character.

"Diderot," said she, "is a hundred years old in many respects, but in others he is no more than ten."

The following letter from Catharine to Diderot, written with all the freedom of the most confidential correspondence, gives a clearer view of the character of Catharine's mind, ana of her energy, than any description could give.

"Now we are speaking of haughtiness, I have a mind to make a general confession to you on that head. I have had great successes during this war; that I am glad of it, you will very naturally conclude. I find that Russia will be well known by this war. It will be seen how indefatigable a nation it is; that she possesses men of eminent merit, and who have all the qualities which go to the forming of heroes. It will be seen that she is deficient in no resources, but that she can defend herself and prosecute a war with vigor whenever she is unjustly attacked.

"Brimful of these ideas, I have never once thought of Catharine, who, at the age of forty-two, can increase neither in body nor in mind, but, in the natural order of things, ought to remain, and will remain, as she is. Do her affairs go on well? she says, so much the better. If they prosper less, she would employ all her faculties to put them in a better train.

"This is my ambition, and I have none other. What I

tell you, is the truth. I will go further, and say that, for the sparing of human blood, I sincerely wish for peace. But this peace is still a long way off, though the Turks, from different motives, are ardently desirous of it. Those people know not how to go about it.

"I wish as much for the pacification of the unreasonable contentions of Poland. I have to do there with brainless heads, each of which, instead of contributing to the common peace, on the contrary, throws impediments in the way of it by caprice and levity. My embassador has published a declaration adapted to open their eyes. But it is to be presumed that they will rather expose themselves to the last extremity than adopt, without delay, a wise and consistent rule of conduct. The vortices of Descartes never existed anywhere but in Poland. There every head is a vortex turning continually around itself. It is stopped by chance alone, and never by reason or judgment.

"I have not yet received your *Questions*,* or your watches from Ferney. I have no doubt that the work of your artificers is perfect, since they work under your eyes. Do not scold your rustics for having sent me a surplus of watches. The expense of them will not ruin me. It would be very unfortunate for me if I were so far reduced as not to have, for sudden emergencies, such small sums whenever I want them. Judge not, I beseech you, of our finances by those of the other ruined potentates of Europe. Though we have been engaged in war for three years, we proceed in our buildings, and every thing else goes on as in a time of profound peace. It is two years since any new impost was levied. The war, at present, has its fixed establishment; that once regulated, it never disturbs the course of other affairs. If we capture another Kesa or two, the war is paid for.

"I shall be satisfied with myself whenever I meet with your approbation, monsieur. I likewise, a few weeks ago,

* Questions sur l'Encyclopedie.

read over again my instructions for the code, because I then thought peace to be nearer at hand than it is, and I found that I was right in composing them. I confess that this code will give me a considerable deal of trouble before it is brought to that degree of perfection at which I wish to see it. But no matter, it must be completed.

"Perhaps, in a little time, the khan of the Crimea will be brought to me in person. I learn, this moment, that he did not cross the sea with the Turks, but that he remained in the mountains with a very small number of followers, nearly as was the case with the Pretender, in Scotland, after the defeat at Culloden. If he comes to me, we will try to polish him this winter, and, to take my revenge of him, I will make him dance, and he shall go to the French comedy.

"Just as I was about to fold up this letter, I received yours of the 10th of July, in which you inform me of the adventure that happened to my 'Instruction'* in France. I knew that anecdote, and even the appendix to it, in consequence of the order of the Duke of Choiseul. I own that I laughed on reading it in the newspapers, and I found that I was amply revenged."

* Her majesty's instruction for a code of laws.

CHAPTER XXVI.

REIGN OF CATHARINE II.

FROM 1774 TO 1781.

PEACE WITH TURKEY.—COURT OF CATHARINE II.—HER PERSONAL APPEARANCE AND HABITS.—CONSPIRACY AND REBELLION.—DEFEAT OF THE REBELS.—MAGNANIMITY OF CATHARINE II.—AMBITION OF THE EMPRESS.—COURT FAVORITE.—DIVISION OF RUSSIA INTO PROVINCES.—INTERNAL IMPROVEMENTS.—NEW PARTITION OF POLAND. DEATH OF THE WIFE OF PAUL. SECOND MARRIAGE OF THE GRAND DUKE.—SPLENDOR OF THE RUSSIAN COURT. RUSSIA AND AUSTRIA SECRETLY COMBINE TO DRIVE THE TURKS OUT OF EUROPE. THE EMPEROR JOSEPH II.

IN 1774 peace was concluded with Turkey, on terms which added greatly to the renown and grandeur of Russia. By this treaty the Crimea was severed from the Ottoman Porte, and declared to be independent. Russia obtained the free navigation of the Black Sea, the Bosporus and the Dardanelles. Immense tracts of land, lying on the Euxine, were ceded to Russia, and the Grand Seignior also paid Catharine a large sum of money to defray the expenses of the war. No language can describe the exultation which this treaty created in St. Petersburg. Eight days were devoted, by order of the empress, to feasts and rejoicings. The doors of the prisons were thrown open, and even the Siberian exiles were permitted to return.

The court of Catharine II. at this period was the most brilliant in Europe. In no other court was more attention paid to the most polished and agreeable manners. The expenditure on her court establishment amounted to nearly four millions of dollars a year. In personal appearance the empress was endowed with the attractions both of beauty and of queenly dignity. A cotemporary writer thus describes her:

"She is of that stature which is necessarily requisite to perfect elegance of form in a lady. She has fine large blue eyes, with eyebrows and hair of a brownish color. Her mouth is well-proportioned, chin round, with a forehead regular and open. Her hands and arms are round and white, and her figure plump. Her bosom is full, her neck high, and she carries her head with peculiar grace.

"The empress never wears rich clothes except on solemn festivals, when her head and corset are entirely set with brilliants, and she wears a crown of diamonds and precious stones. Her gait is majestic; and, in the whole of her form and manner there is something so dignified and noble, that if she were to be seen without ornament or any outward marks of distinction, among a great number of ladies of rank, she would be immediately esteemed the chief. She seems born to command, though in her character there is more of liveliness than of gravity. She is courteous, gentle, benevolent and outwardly devout."

Like almost every one who has attained distinction, Catharine was very systematic in the employment of her time. She usually rose at about five o'clock both in summer and winter; and what seems most remarkable, prepared her own simple breakfast, as she was not fond of being waited upon. But a short time was devoted to her toilet. From eight to eleven in the forenoon she was busy in her cabinet, signing commissions and issuing orders of various purport. The hour, from eleven to twelve, was daily devoted to divine worship in her chapel. Then, until one o'clock, she gave audience to the ministers of the various departments. From half past one till two she dined. She then returned to her cabinet, where she was busily employed in cares of state until four o'clock, when she took an airing in a coach or sledge. At six she usually exhibited herself for a short time to her subjects at the theater, and at ten o'clock she retired. Court balls were not unfrequently given, but the empress never condescended to dance, though occasionally she would make one at a game of cards. She, however, took but little interest in the game, being much more fond of talking with the ladies, generals and ministers who surrounded her. Even from these court balls the very sensible empress usually retired, by a slide door, at ten o'clock.

The empress informed herself minutely of every thing which concerned the administration of government. Her ministers were merely instruments in her hands executing her imperial will. All matters relating to the army, the navy, the finances, the punishment of crime and to foreign affairs, were reported to her by her ministers, and were guided by her decisions.

There must always be, in every government, an opposition party—that is, a party who wish to eject from office those in power, that they themselves may enjoy the loaves and fishes of governmental favor. This is peculiarly the case in an empire where a large class of haughty nobles are struggling for the preëminence. Many of the bigoted clergy were exasperated by the toleration which the empress enjoined, and they united with the disaffected lords in a conspiracy for a revolution. The clergy in the provinces had great influence over the unlettered boors, and the conspiracy soon assumed a very threatening aspect. The first rising of rebellion was by the wild population scattered along the banks of the Don. The rebellion was headed by an impostor, who declared that he was Peter III., and that, having escaped from those who had attempted his assassination, he had concealed himself for a long time, waiting for vengeance. This barbaric chieftain, who was called Pugatshef, very soon found himself at the head of fourteen thousand fierce warriors, and commenced ravaging oriental Russia. For a season his march was a constant victory. Many thousand Siberian exiles escaped from their gloomy realms and joined his standards. So astonishing was his success, that even Catharine trembled.

Pugatshef waged a war of extermination against the nobles who were the supporters of Catharine, in cold blood beheading their wives and children, and conferring their titles and estates upon his followers. The empress found it necessary to rouse all her energies to meet this peril. She issued a manifesto, which was circulated through all the towns of the empire, and raised a large army, which was dispatched to crush the rebellion. Battle after battle ensued, until, at last, in a decisive conflict, the hosts of Pugatshef were utterly cut up.

Still, this indefatigable warrior soon raised another army from the untamed barbarians of the Don, and, rapidly descending the Volga, attacked, by surprise, some Russian regiments encamped upon its banks, and routed them with fearful slaughter. The astronomer, Lovitch, a member of the imperial academy of sciences at St. Petersburg, was, at that time, under the protection of these regiments, surveying the route for a canal between the Don and the Volga. Pugatshef ordered his dragoons to thrust their pikes into the unfortunate man, and raise him upon them into the air, "in order," said he, "that he may be nearer the stars." They did this, and then cut him to pieces with their sabers.

The troops of Catharine pursued the rebels, encountered them in some intricate passes of the mountains, whence escape was impossible, and overwhelmed them with destruction. Their vigorous leader, leaping from crag to crag, escaped, swam the Volga, crossed, in solitude, vast deserts, and made new attempts to rally partisans around him. But his last hour was sounded. Deserted by all, he was wandering from place to place, pursued like a wild beast, when some of his own confederates, basely betraying him, seized him, after a violent struggle, put him in irons, and delivered him to one of the officers of the Russian army. The wretched man, preserving impenetrable silence, was conveyed to Moscow in an iron cage. Refusing to eat, food was forced down his stomach.

The empress immediately appointed a commission for the trial of the rebel. She instructed the court to be satisfied with whatever voluntary confession of his crime he might make, forbidding them to apply the torture, or to require him to name his accomplices. The culprit was sentenced to have his hands and feet cut off, and then to be quartered. By order of the empress, however, he was first beheaded. Eight of his accomplices were also executed, eighteen underwent the knout, and were then exiled to Siberia. Thus terminated a rebellion which cost the lives of more than a hundred thousand men.

Over those wide regions, whose exact boundaries are even now scarcely known, numerous nations are scattered, quite distinct in language, religion and customs, and so separated by almost impassable deserts, that they know but little of each other. These wilds, peopled by war-loving races, afford the most attractive field for military adventures. The energy and sagacity with which Catharine crushed this formidable rebellion added greatly to her renown. Tranquillity being restored, the empress, in order to crown a general pardon, forbade any further allusion whatever to be made to the rebellion, consigning all its painful events to utter oblivion. She even forbade the publication of the details of the trial, saying,

"I shall keep the depositions of Pugatshef secret, that they may not aggravate the disgrace of those who spurred him on."

The empress was ambitious to make her influence felt in every European movement, and she was conscious that, in order to command the respect of other courts, she must ever have a formidable army at her disposal. In all the great movements of kings and courts this wonderful woman performed her part with dignity which no monarch, male or female, has ever surpassed. It is strange that it has taken so many centuries for the nations to learn that peace, not war, enriches realms. Had Russia abstained from those wars in which she has unnecessarily engaged, she might now have been the most wealthy and powerful nation on the globe. Admitting that there have been many wars which, involving her national existence, she could not have avoided, still she has squandered countless millions of money and of lives in battles which were quite unnecessary. Russia, like the United States, is safe from all attacks from without. Had Russia employed the yearly earnings of the empire in cultivating the fields, rearing towns, and in extending the arts of industry and refinement, infinitely more would have been accomplished for her happiness and renown than by the most brilliant conquests. But Catharine, in her high ambition, seemed to be afraid that Europe might forget her, and she was eager to have her voice heard in the deliberations of every cabinet, and to have her banners unfurled in the march of every army.

There was an office, in the court of the empress, sanctioned by time in Russia, which has not existed in any other court in Europe. It perhaps originated from the fact that for about three fourths of a century Russia was almost exclusively governed by women. The court favorite was not merely the prime minister, but the confidential friend and companion of the empress. On the day of his installation he received a purse containing one hundred thousand dollars, and a salary of twelve thousand dollars a month. A marshal was also commissioned to provide him a table of twenty-four covers, and to defray all the expenses of his household. The twelve thousand dollars a month were for what the ladies call *pin money*. The favorite occupied in the palace an apartment beneath that of the empress, to which it communicated by a private staircase. He attended the empress on all parties of amusement, at the opera, the theater, balls, promenades and excursions of pleasure, and he was not allowed to leave the palace without express permission. It was also understood that he should pay no attention to any lady but the empress.

The year 1775 dawned upon Russia with peace at home and abroad. Catharine devoted herself anew to the improvement of her subjects in education and all physical comforts. Prince Gregory Orlof had been for many years the favorite of the empress, but he was now laid aside, and Count Potemkin took his place.

Catharine now divided her extensive realms into forty-three great provinces, over each of which a governor was appointed. These provinces embraced from six to eight hundred thousand inhabitants. There was then a subdivision into districts or circles, as they were called. There were some ten of these districts in each province, and they contained from forty to sixty thousand inhabitants. An entire system of government was established for each province, with its laws and tribunals, that provision might be made for every thing essential to the improvement and embellishment of the country. The governors of these provinces were invested with great dignity and splendor. The gubernatorial courts, if they may so be called, established centers of elegance and refinement, which it was hoped would exert a powerful influence in polishing a people exceedingly rude and uncultivated. There were also immense advantages derived from the uniform administration of justice thus established. This new division of the empire was the most comprehensive reform Russia had yet experienced. Thus the most extensive empire on the globe, with its geographical divisions so vast and dissimilar, was cemented into one homogeneous body politic.

Until this great reform the inhabitants of the most distant provinces had been compelled to travel to Petersburg and Moscow in their appeals to the tribunals of justice. Now there were superior courts in all the provinces, and inferior courts in all the districts. In all important cases there was an appeal to the council of the empress. Russian ships, laden with the luxuries of the Mediterranean, passed through the Dardanelles and the Bosporus, and landed their precious freights upon the shores of Azof, from whence they were transported into the heart of Russia, thus opening a very lucrative commerce.

The Polish nobles, a very turbulent and intractable race of men, were overawed by the power of Catharine, and the masses of the Polish people were doubtless benefited by their transference to new masters. Russia was far more benignant in its treatment of the conquered provinces, than were her banditti accomplices, Prussia and Austria.

The road to China, traversed by caravans, was long and perilous, through pathless and inhospitable wilds, where, for leagues, no inhabitant could be seen, and yet where a fertile soil and a genial clime promised, to the hand of industry, all the comforts and luxuries of life. All along this road she planted villages, and, by the most alluring offers, induced settlers to establish themselves on all portions of the route. Large sums of money were expended in rendering the rivers navigable.

In the year 1776, the grand duchess, consort of Paul, who was heir to the throne, died in childbirth, and was buried in the same grave with her babe. About the same time Prince Henry of Prussia visited the Russian court to confer with Catharine upon some difficulties which had arisen in the demarcations of Poland. It will be remembered that in the division which had now taken place, the whole kingdom had not been seized, but a remnant had been left as the humble patrimony of Poniatowski, the king. In this interview with the empress, Prince Henry said,

"Madam, I see one sure method of obviating all difficulty. It may perhaps be displeasing to you on account of Poniatowski.* But you will nevertheless do well to give it your approbation, since compensations may be offered to that monarch of greater value to him than the throne which is continually

* Poniatowski had been formerly a favorite of the empress.

tottering under him. The remainder of Poland must be partitioned."

The empress cordially embraced the plan, and the annihilation of Poland was decreed. It was necessary to move slowly and with caution in the execution of the plan. In the meantime, as the grand duchess had died, leaving no heir to the empire, the empress deemed it a matter of the utmost moment to secure another wife for the Grand Duke Paul, lest Russia should be exposed to the perils of a disputed succession. Natalia was hardly cold in her grave ere the empress proposed to Prince Henry, that his niece, the princess of Wirtemberg, should become the spouse of the grand duke. The princess was already betrothed to the hereditary prince of Hesse Darmstadt, but both Henry and his imperial brother, Frederic of Prussia, deemed the marriage of their niece with the prospective Emperor of Russia a match far too brilliant to be thwarted by so slight an obstacle. Frederic himself informed the prince of the exalted offer which had been made to his betrothed, and without much difficulty secured his relinquishment of his contemplated bride. Frederic deemed it a matter of infinite moment that the ties subsisting between Russia and Prussia should be more closely drawn. He wrote to his brother Henry of his success, and by the same courier invited the Grand Duke Paul to visit Berlin that he might see the new spouse designed for him. He also expressed his own ardent desire to become acquainted with the grand duke.

Catharine, highly gratified with this success, placed a purse of fifty thousand dollars in the hands of her son to defray the expenses of his journey. It was at the close of the summer of 1776 when the grand duke left the palaces of St. Petersburg to visit those of Berlin. His mother, who made all the arrangements, dispatched her son on this visit in a style of regal splendor. When the party reached Riga, a courier overtook them with the following characteristic letter, written by the empress's own hand to Prince Henry:

"JUNE 11, 1776.

"I take the liberty of transmitting to your royal highness the four letters of which I spoke to you, and which you promised to take care of. The first is for the king, your brother, and the others for the prince and princesses of Wirtemberg. I venture to pray you, that if my son should bestow his heart on the Princess Sophia, as I have no doubt but what he will, to deliver the three letters according to their directions, and to support the contents of them with that persuasive eloquence with which God has endowed you.

"The convincing and reiterated proofs which you have given me of your friendship, the high esteem which I have conceived for your virtues, and the extent of the confidence which you have taught me to repose in you, leave me no doubt on the success of a business which I have so much at heart. Was it possible for me to place it in better hands?

"Your royal highness is surely an unique in the art of negotiation. Pardon me that expression of my friendship. But I think that there has never been an affair of this nature transacted as this is; which is the production of the most intimate friendship and confidence.

"That princess will be the pledge of it. I shall not be able to see her without recollecting in what manner this business was begun, continued and terminated, between the royal house of Prussia and that of Russia. May it perpetuate the connections which unite us!

"I conclude by very tenderly thanking your royal highness for all the cares and all the troubles you have given yourself; and I beseech you to be assured that my gratitude, my friendship, my esteem, and the high consideration which I have for you, will terminate only with my life.

"CATHARINE."

The Grand Duke Paul was received in Berlin with all the honors due his rank as heir to the imperial throne of Russia. The great Frederic even came to the door of his apartment to greet his guest. The grand duke was escorted into the city with much pomp. Thirty-four trumpeters, winding their bugles, preceded him, all in rich uniform. Then came a strong array of soldiers. These were followed by a civic procession, in brilliant decorations. Three superb state coaches, containing the dignitaries of Berlin, came next in the train, followed by a detachment of the life-guards, who preceded the magnificent chariot of the duke, which chariot was regarded as the most superb which had then ever been seen, and which was drawn by eight of the finest horses Prussia could produce. This carriage conveyed Paul and Prince Henry. A hundred dragoons, as a guard of honor, closed the procession. At the gates of the city the magistracy received Paul beneath a triumphal arch, where seventy beautiful girls, dressed like nymphs and shepherdesses, presented the grand duke with complimentary verses, and crowned him with a garland of flowers. The ringing of bells, the pealing of cannon, strains of martial music, and the acclamations of the multitude, greeted Paul from the time he entered the gates until he reached the royal palace.

"Sire," exclaimed Paul, as he took the hand of the King of Prussia, "the motives which bring me from the extremities of the North to these happy dominions, are the desire of assuring your majesty of the friendship and alliance to subsist henceforth and for ever between Russia and Prussia, and the eagerness to see a princess destined to ascend the throne of the Russian empire. By my receiving her at your hands, I assure you that she will be more dear to myself and to the nation over which she is to reign. It has also been one of the most ardent aspirations of my soul to contemplate the greatest of heroes, the admiration of our age and the astonishment of posterity."

Here the king interrupted him, replying,

"Instead of which, you behold a hoary-headed valitudinarian, who could never have wished for a superior happiness than that of welcoming within these walls the hopeful heir of a mighty empire, the only son of my best friend, Catharine."

After half an hour's conversation, the grand duke was led into the apartment of the queen, where the court was assembled. Here he was introduced to his contemplated bride, Sophia, Princess of Wirtemberg, and immediately, in the name of the Empress of Russia, demanded her in marriage of the grand duke. The marriage contract was signed the same day. The whole company then supped with the queen in great magnificence. Feasts and entertainments succeeded for many days without interruption.

On the 3d of August, Paul returned to St. Petersburg, where his affianced bride soon joined him. As he took leave, the King of Prussia presented him with dessert service and a coffee service, with ten porcelain vases of Berlin manufacture, a ring, containing the king's portrait, surmounted with a diamond valued at thirty thousand crowns, and also a stud of Prussian horses and four pieces of rich tapestry. Upon the arrival of the princess, she was received into the Greek church, assuming the name of Maria, by which she was ever after called. The marriage soon took place, and from this marriage arose the two distinguished emperors, Alexander and Nicholas.

The empress was exceedingly gratified by the successful accomplishment of this plan. With energy which seemed never to tire, she urged forward her plans for national improvements, establishing schools all over the empire, which were munificently supported at the imperial expense. The splendor of the Russian court, during the reign of Catharine, surpassed all ordinary powers of description. Almost boundless wealth was lavished upon gorgeous dresses—lords and ladies glittering alike in most costly jewelry. Many cour tiers appeared almost literally covered with diamonds. They sparkled, in most lavish profusion, upon their buttons, their buckles, the scabbards of their swords, their epaulets, and many even wore a triple row as a band around the hat. Frequently eight thousand tickets were given out for a ball at the palace, and yet there was no crowd, for twenty saloons, of magnificent dimensions, brilliantly lighted, afforded room for all. Her majesty usually entered the saloons about seven o'clock, and retired about ten.

The empress never ceased to look with a wistful eye upon the regions which the Turks had wrested from the Christians. The commercial greatness of Russia, in her view, imperiously required that Constantinople and its adjacent shores should be in her possession. In May, 1780, Catharine had an interview with Joseph II., Emperor of Germany, at Mohilef. Both sovereigns traveled with great pomp to meet at this place. After several confidential interviews, they agreed to unite their forces to drive the Turks out of Europe, and to share the spoil between them. It was also agreed to reëstablish the ancient republics of Greece. The emperor, Joseph II., received an earnest invitation to visit Moscow, which he accepted, but, with characteristic eccentricity, refused to travel with the queen, as he was excessively annoyed by the trammels of etiquette and ceremonial pomp. The empress, consequently, returned to St. Petersburg, and Joseph II. set out for Moscow in the following fashion:

Leaving his carriages with his suite to follow, he proceeded alone, *incognito*, on horse-back, as the *avant courier*. At each station he would announce that his master the emperor, with the imperial carriages, was coming on, and that dinner, supper or lodgings must be provided for so many persons. Calling for a slice of ham and a cup of beer, he would throw himself upon a bench for a few hours' repose, constantly refusing to take a bed, as the expedition he must make would not allow this indulgence.

At Mohilef, the empress had provided magnificent apartments, in the palace, for the emperor; but he insisted upon taking lodgings at an ordinary inn. At St. Petersburg, notwithstanding the emperor's repugnance to pomp, Catharine received him with entertainments of the greatest magnificence. Joseph, however, took but little interest in such displays, devoting his attention almost exclusively to useful establishments and monuments of art. He was surprised to find at Tula, manufactories of hardware unsurpassed by those of Sheffield and Birmingham. He expressed his surprise, on his return home, at the mixture of refinement and barbarism Russia had presented to his view.

The empress, seeing that so many princes visited foreign countries, decided to send her son Paul, with Maria, to make the tour of Europe. Obedient to the maternal commands, they commenced their travels through Poland and Austria to Italy, and returned to St. Petersburg, through France and Holland, after an absence of fourteen months. The empress had a confidential agent in their company, who kept her informed, minutely, of every event which transpired. A courier was dispatched every day to inform her where they were and how they were employed.

The relations between Turkey and Russia were continually growing more threatening. Turkey had been compelled to yield the Crimea, and also to surrender the navigation of the Euxine, with the Bosporus and the Dardanelles, to her powerful rival. Galled by these concessions, which had been forced upon her by bullet and bayonet, the Ottoman Porte was ever watching to regain her lost power. Russia, instead of being satisfied with her acquisitions, was eagerly grasping at more. The Greek Christians also, throughout the Turkish empire, hating their Mussulman oppressors, were ever watching for opportunities when they could shake off the burden and the insult of slavery. Thus peace between Russia and Turkey was never more than an armistice. The two powers constantly faced each other in a hostile attitude, ever ready to appeal to arms.

CHAPTER XXVII.

TERMINATION OF THE REIGN OF CATHARINE II.

From 1781 to 1786.

Statue of Peter the Great.—Alliance between Austria and Russia.—Independence of the Crimea.—The Khan of the Crimea.—Vast Preparations for War.—National Jealousies.—Tolerant Spirit of Catharine.—Magnificent Excursion to the Crimea.—Commencement of Hostilities.—Anecdote of Paul.—Peace.—New Partition of Poland.—Treaty with Austria and France.—Hostility to Liberty in France.—Death of Catharine.—Her Character.

CATHARINE found time, amidst all the cares of empire, to devote special attention to the education of her grandchildren Alexander and Constantine, who had been born during the five years which had now elapsed since the marriage of Paul and Maria. For their instruction as they advanced in years, she wrote several historical and moral essays of no small merit. The "Tales of Chlor, Son of the Tzar," and "The Little Samoyede," are beautiful compositions from her pen, alike attractive to the mature and the youthful mind. The histories and essays she wrote for these children have since been collected and printed in French, under the title of "Bibliotheque des grands-ducs Alexandre et Constantin."

The empress, about this time, resolved to erect, in St. Petersburg, a statue of Peter the Great, which should be worthy of his renown. A French artist, M. Falconet, was engaged to execute this important work. He conceived the design of having, for a pedestal, a rugged rock, to indicate the rude and unpolished character of the people to whom the emperor had introduced so many of the arts of civilization. Immediate search was made to find a suitable rock.

About eight miles from the city a huge boulder was discovered, forty-two feet long, thirty-four feet broad, and twenty-one feet high. It was found, by geometric calculation, that this enormous mass weighed three millions two hundred thousand pounds. It was necessary to transport it over heights and across morasses to the Neva, and there to float it down to the place of its destination. The boulder lay imbedded a few feet in the ground, absolutely detached from all other rock, and with no similar substance anywhere in the vicinity.

It would seem impossible that a mass so stupendous could be moved. But difficulties only roused the energies of Catharine. In the first place, a solid road was made for its passage. After four months' labor, with very ingenious machinery, the rock was so far raised as to enable them to slip under it heavy plates of brass, which rested upon cannon balls five inches in diameter, and which balls ran in grooves of solid metal. Then, by windlasses, worked by four hundred men, it was slowly forced along its way. Having arrived at the Neva, is was floated down the river by what are called camels, that is immense floating fabrics constructed with air chambers so as to render them very buoyant.

This statue as completed is regarded as one of the grandest ever executed. The tzar is represented as on horseback, ascending a steep rock, the summit of which he is resolved to attain. In an Asiatic dress and crowned with laurel, he is pointing forward with his right hand, while with his left he holds the bridle of the magnificent charger on which he is mounted. The horse stands on his hind feet bounding forward, trampling beneath a brazen serpent, emblematic of the opposition the monarch encountered and overcame. It bears the simple inscription, "To Peter the First, by Catharine the Second, 1782." The whole expense of the statue amounted to over four hundred thousand dollars, an immense sum for that day, when a dollar was worth more than many dollars now.

At the close of the year 1782, the Emperor of Germany and Catharine II. entered into an alliance for the more energetic prosecution of the war against the Turks. They issued very spirited proclamations enumerating their grievances, and immediately appeared on the Turkish frontiers with vast armies. The attention of Catharine was constantly directed towards Constantinople, the acquisition of which city, with the Bosporus and the Dardanelles, was the object which, of all others, was the nearest to her heart. On the banks of the Dnieper, eighteen hundred miles from St. Petersburg, she laid the foundations of Kherson as a maritime port, and in an almost incredibly short time a city rose there containing forty thousand inhabitants. From its ship-yards vessels of war were launched which struck terror into the Ottoman empire.

By previous wars, it will be remembered, the Crimea had been wrested from the Turks and declared to be independent, remaining nominally in the hands of the Tartars. Catharine II. immediately took the Tartar khan of the Crimea under her special protection, loaded him with favors, and thus assumed the guidance of his movements. He became enervated by luxury, learned to despise the rude manners of his countrymen, engaged a Russian cook, and was served from silver plate. Instead of riding on horseback he traveled in a splendid chariot, and even solicited a commission in the Russian army. Catharine contrived to foment a revolt against her protegé the khan, and then, very kindly, marched an army into the Crimea for his relief. She then, without any apology, took possession of the whole of the Crimea, and received the oath of allegiance from all the officers of the government. Indeed, there appears to have been no opposition to this measure. The Tartar khan yielded with so much docility that he soon issued a manifesto in which he abdicated his throne, and transferred the whole dominion of his country to Catharine. Turkey, exasperated, prepared herself furiously for war. Russia formed an alliance with the Emperor of Germany, and armies were soon in movement upon a scale such as even those war-scathed regions had never witnessed before. The Danube, throughout its whole course, was burdened with the barges of the Emperor of Germany, heavily laden with artillery, military stores and troops. More than a hundred thousand men were marched down to the theater of conflict from Hungary. Fifteen hundred pieces of artillery were in the train of these vast armies of the German emperor. The Russian force was equally efficient, as it directed its march through the plains of Poland, and floated down upon the waters of the Don and the Dnieper. The Turkish sultan was not wanting in energy. From all his wide-spread domains in Europe and Asia, he marshaled his hosts, and engaged from other nations of Europe, and particularly from France, the most skillful officers and engineers, to introduce into his armies European discipline and improvements in weapons of war.

The Ottoman Porte issued a manifesto, which was a very remarkable document both in vigor of style and nobility of sentiment. After severely denouncing the enormous encroachments of Russia, extending her dominions unscrupulously in every direction, the sultan asked indignantly,

"What right can Russia have to territories annexed for ages to the dominions of the Porte? Should the Porte make such claims on any portion of the Russian dominions, would they not be repulsed? And can it be presumed that the Sublime Porte, however desirous of peace, will acquiesce in wrong which, however it may be disguised, reason and equity must deem absolute usurpation? What northern power has the Porte offended? Whose territories have the Ottoman troops invaded? In the country of what prince is the Turkish standard displayed? Content with the boundaries of empire assigned by God and the Prophet, the wishes of the Porte are for peace; but if the court of Russia be determined in her claim, and will not recede without the acquisition of territories which do not belong to her, the Sublime Porte, appealing to the world for the justice of its proceedings, must prepare for war, relying on the decrees of Heaven, and confident in the interposition of the Prophet of prophets, that he will protect his faithful followers in the hour of every difficulty."

No Mohammedan pen could have produced so vigorous a document. It was written by the English minister at Constantinople, Sir Robert Ainslie. Catharine II., apprehensive that, while all her armies were engaged on the banks of the Euxine, Sweden might attack her on the shores of the Baltic, decided to form a new treaty of peace with Gustavus III. An interview was arranged to take place at Frederiksham, a small but strongly fortified town upon the Gulf of Finland, the last town occupied by the Russians towards the frontiers of Sweden. The empress repaired thither in a yacht the 29th of June, 1783. Gustavus III., with his suite, met her at the appointed hour. Two contiguous houses were prepared, furnished with the utmost splendor, and connected by a gallery, so that, during the four days these sovereigns remained at Frederiksham, they could meet and converse at any time. There is still a picture existing, painted by order of Catharine, representing the empress and the Swedish monarch in one of their most confidential interviews. Catharine II. promised Gustavus that if he would faithfully remain neutral during her war with Turkey she would, at its close, aid Sweden in gaining possession of Norway. The two sovereigns, having exchanged rich presents, separated, mutually delighted with each other.

The empress had now seventy thousand men on the frontiers of the Crimea, and a reserve of forty thousand on the march to strengthen them. A third army of great power was rendezvoused at Kief. A large squadron of ships of war was ready for battle in the Sea of Azof, and another squadron was prepared to sail from the Baltic for the Mediterranean. England, alarmed by the growth of Russia, did every thing in her power to stimulate the Turks to action. But the Porte, overawed by the force brought against her, notwithstanding the brave manifesto it had been induced to issue, sued for peace. Yielding to all the demands of Russia a treaty was soon signed. Catharine gained undisputed possession of the Crimea, large portions of Circassia, the whole of the Black Sea, and also the free passage of the Dardanelles. Thus, without firing a gun, Russia gained several thousand square miles of territory, and an addition of more than a million and a half of inhabitants, with commercial privileges which added greatly to the wealth of the empire.

Catharine's fleet now rode triumphantly upon the Caspian, and she resolved to extend her dominions along the western shores of that inland sea. These vast regions were peopled by warlike tribes, ever engaged in hostilities against each other. Slowly but surely she advanced her conquests and reared her fortresses through those barbaric wilds. At the same time she was pushing her acquisitions with equal sagacity and success along the shores of Kamtschatka. With great vigor she encouraged her commercial caravans to penetrate China, and even opened relations with Japan, obtaining from that jealous people permission to send a trading ship to their coast every year.

No persons are so jealous of the encroachments of others as those who are least scrupulous in regard to the encroachments which they themselves make. The English government, whose boast it is that the sun, in its circuit of the globe, never ceases to shine on their domains, watches with an eagle eye lest any other government on the globe should venture upon the most humble act of annexation. So it was with Catharine. Though adding to her vast dominions in every quarter; though appropriating, alike in peace and in war, all the territory she could lay her hands upon, she could inveigh against the inordinate ambition of other nations with the most surprising volubility.

The increasing fame and power of Frederic II. had for some time disturbed her equanimity, and she manifested great anxiety lest he should be guilty of the impropriety of annexing some petty duchy to his domains. Since he had united with Catharine and Austria in the banditti partition of Poland, he had continually been making all the encroachments in his power; adding acres to his domains as Catharine added square leagues to hers. In precisely the same spirit, England, who was grasping at all the world, protested, with the most edifying devotion to the claims of justice and humanity, against the ambitious spirit of Russia. The "beam" did not exclude the vision of the "mote." Cathraine, offended by the opposition of England, retaliated by entering into a treaty of commerce with France, which deprived England of an important part of the Russian trade.

The spirit of toleration manifested by Catharine is worthy of all praise. During the whole of her reign she would not allow any one to be persecuted, in the slightest degree, on account of religious opinions. All the conquered provinces were protected in the free exercise of their religion. Lutherans, Calvinists, Moravians, Papists, Mohammedans, and Pagans of all kinds, not only enjoyed freedom of opinion and of worship, but could alike aspire to any post, civil or military, of which they could prove themselves worthy. At one time, when urged by the hateful spirit of religious bigotry to frown upon some heresy, she replied smiling,

"Poor wretches! since we know that they are to suffer so much and so long in the world to come, it is but reasonable that we should endeavor, by all means, to make their situation here as comfortable as we can."

Though Catharine II. had many great defects of character, she had many virtues which those who have denounced her most severely might do well to imitate. Her crowning vice, and the one which, notwithstanding her virtues, has consigned her name to shame, was that she had a constant succession of lovers who by secret and very informal nuptial rites were bound to her for a season, each one of whom was exchanged for another as caprice incited. The spirit of national aggrandizement which influenced Catharine, was a spirit possessed, to an equal extent, at that time, by every cabinet in Christendom. It was the great motive power of the age. Dismembered Poland excites our sympathy; but Poland was as eager to share in the partition of other States as she was reluctant to submit to that operation herself. In personal character Catharine was humane, tolerant, self-denying, and earnestly devoted to the welfare of her empire. Religious teachers, of all denominations, freely met at her table. This Christian liberality, thus encouraged in the palace, spread through the realm, producing the most beneficial results. On the occasion of a celebrated festival, Catharine gave a grand dinner party to ecclesiastics of all communions at the palace. This entertainment she called the "Dinner of Toleration." The representatives of eight different forms of worship met around this hospitable board.

The instruction of the masses of the people occupied much of the attention of this extraordinary woman. She commenced with founding schools in the large towns; and then proceeded to the establishment of them in various parts of the country. Many normal schools were established for the education of teachers. The empress herself attended the examinations and questioned the scholars. On one of these occasions, when a learned German professor of history was giving a lecture to some pupils, gathered from the tribes of Siberia, the empress proposed an objection to some views he advanced. The courtiers were shocked at the learned man's presumption in replying to the objection in the most conclusive manner. The empress, ever eager in the acquisition of knowledge, admitted her mistake, and thanked the professor for having rectified it with so much ability.

She purchased, at a high price, the libraries of D'Alembert, and of Voltaire, immediately after the death of those illustrious men. She also purchased the valuable cabinet of natural curiosities collected by Professor Pallas. The most accomplished engineers she could obtain were sent to explore the mountains of Caucasus, and even to the frontiers of China. When we consider the trackless deserts to be explored, the inhospitable climes and barbarous nations to be encountered, these were enterprises far more perilous than the circumnavigation of the globe. The scientific expedition to China was escorted by a corps of eight hundred and ten chosen men, led by one hundred and seven distinguished officers. The *savans* were provided with every thing which could be thought of to promote their comfort and to aid them in their explorations, and three years were alloted as the probable term of service required by the mission. At the same time a naval expedition was fitted out to explore the northern seas, and ascertain the limits of the Russian empire. But the greatest work of Catharine's reign was the completion of the canal which united the waters of the Volga and the Neva, and thus established an inland navigation through all the countries which lie between the Caspian Sea and the Baltic.

In the year 1786 the empress announced her intention of making a magnificent journey to the Crimea, in order to be crowned sovereign of her new conquests. This design was to be executed in the highest style of oriental pomp, as the empress was resolved to extend her sway over all the nations of the Tartars. But the Tartars of those unmeasured realms, informed of the contemplated movement, were alarmed, and immediately combined their energies for a determined resistance. The Grand Seignior was also goaded to the most desperate exertions, for the empress had formed the design, and the report was universally promulgated, of placing her second grandchild, Constantine, on the throne of Constantinople.

The empress set out on her triumphal journey to the Crimea, on the 18th of January, 1787, accompanied by a magnificent suite. The sledges, large, commodious and so lined with furs as to furnish luxurious couches for repose, traveled night and day. Relays of horses were collected at all the stations and immense bonfires blazed at night all along the road. Twenty-one days were occupied in the journey to Kief, where the empress was met by all the nobles of that portion of the empire. Here fifty magnificent galleys, upon the ice of the Dnieper, awaited the arrival of the empress and the opening of the river. On the 6th of May the ice was gone, the barges were afloat, and the empress with her suite embarked. The King of Poland, who had now assumed his old name of Count Poniatowski, here met, in the barge of the empress, his rival, Stanislaus Augustus.

The passage down the river, in this lovely month of spring, was like a fairy scene. The banks of the Dnieper were lined with villages constructed for the occasion. Peasants, in the most picturesque costumes, tended their flocks, or attended to various industrial arts as the flotilla drifted by. The Emperor of Germany, Joseph II., met the empress at Kaidak, from whence they proceeded together, by land, to Kherson. Here Catharine lodged in a palace where a throne had been erected for the occasion which cost fourteen thousand dollars. The whole expense of this one journey exceeded seven millions of dollars. From Kherson the empress proceeded to the inland part of the Crimean peninsula. Her body guard consisted of an army of one hundred and fifty thousand men, stationed at but a short distance from her. The entertainments in the Crimea were of the most gorgeous character, and were arranged without any regard to expense. On the return of the empress she reached St. Petersburg the end of July, having been absent six months and four days. All Europe was surprised at the supineness which the sultan had manifested in allowing Catharine to prosecute her journey unobstructed; but Turkey was not then prepared for the commencement of hostilities.

A squadron of thirty ships of war soon sailed from Constantinople and entered the Euxine. The Turks were apprehensive that the Greeks might rise and disarmed them all before commencing the campaign. The empress had equipped, at Azof and Kherson, eight ships of the line, twelve frigates, and two hundred gun-boats. She had, in addition, a large squadron at Cronstadt, ready to sail for the Mediterranean. Eighty thousand soldiers were also on the march from Germany to Moldavia. Every thing indicated that the entire overthrow of the Ottoman empire was at hand.

The thunders of battle soon commenced on the sea and on the land. Both parties fought with desperation. Russia and Austria endeavored to unite France with them, in the attempt to dismember the Turkish empire as Poland had been partitioned, but France now stood in dread of the gigantic growth both of Russia and of Austria, and was by no means disposed to strengthen those powers. England was also secretly aiding the Turks and sending them supplies. Influenced by the same jealousy against Russia, Sweden ventured to enter into an alliance with the Turks, while Prussia, from the same motive, secretly lent Gustavus III. money, and England sent him a fleet. Thus, all of a sudden, new and appalling dangers blazed upon Russia. So many troops had been sent to the Crimea that Catharine was quite unprepared for an attack from the Swedish frontier.

The Grand Duke Paul begged permission of his mother that he might join the army against the Turks. The empress refused her consent.

"My intention," wrote again the grand duke, "of going to fight against the Ottomans is publicly known. What will Europe say, in seeing that I do not carry it into effect?"

"Europe will say," Catharine replied, "that the grand duke of Russia is a dutiful son."

The appearance of the powerful Swedish fleet in the Baltic rendered it necessary for Catharine to recall the order for the squadron at Cronstadt to sail for the Mediterranean. The roar of artillery now reverberated alike along the shores of the Baltic and over the waves of the Euxine. Denmark and Norway were brought into the conflict, and all Europe was again the theater of intrigues and battles. It would be a weary story to relate the numerous conflicts, defeats and victories which ensued. Famine and pestilence desolated the regions where the Turkish and Russian armies were struggling. Army after army was destroyed until men began to grow scarce in the Russian empire. Even the wilds of Siberia were ransacked for exiles, and many of them were brought back to replenish the armies of the empress. At length, after a warfare of two years, with about equal success on both sides, Catharine and Gustavus came to terms, both equally glad to escape the blows which each gave the other. This peace enabled Russia to concentrate her energies upon Turkey.

The Turks now fell like grass before the scythe. But the Russian generals and soldiers were often as brutal as demons. Nominal Christianity was no more merciful than was paganism. Count Potemkin, the leader of the Russian army, was one of the worst specimens of the old aristocracy, which now, in many parts of Europe, have gone down into a grave whence, it is to be hoped, there can be no resurrection. The Turkish town of Ismael was taken in September, 1790, after enormous slaughter. The French Revolution was at this time in rapid progress, and several Frenchmen were in the Russian army. To one of these, Colonel Langeron, Potemkin said,

"Colonel, your countrymen are a pack of madmen. I would require only my grooms to stand by me, and we should soon bring them to their senses."

Langeron replied, "Prince, I do not think you would be able to do it with all your army!"

These words so exasperated the Russian general that he rose in a rage, and threatened to send Langeron to Siberia. Conscious of his peril the French colonel fled, and entered into the service of the Austrians.

Emissaries of Catharine were sent through all the Greek

isles, to urge the Greeks to rise against the enemies of the cross and restore their country to independence. Many of the Greeks rose, and Constantinople was in consternation. A Grecian embassage waited upon Catharine, imploring her aid for the enfranchisement of their country, and that she would give them her grandson Constantine for a sovereign. On the 20th of February, 1790, Joseph II., Emperor of Austria, died, and was succeeded by Leopold II., who, yielding to the influence of Prussia, concluded a separate peace with the Porte, and left Catharine to contend alone with the Ottomans. The empress now saw that, notwithstanding her victories, Russia was exhausted, and that she could not hope for the immediate accomplishment of her ambitious projects, and she became desirous of peace. Through the mediation of England terms of peace were proposed, and acceded to in January, 1792. In this war it is estimated that Russia lost two hundred thousand men, Austria one hundred and thirty thousand, and Turkey three hundred and thirty thousand. Russia expended in this war, beneficial to none and ruinous alike to all, two hundred millions of dollars.

The empress, thwarted in her designs upon Turkey, now turned to Poland. War was soon declared, and her armies were soon sweeping over that ill-fated territory. Kosciusko fought like a hero for his country, but his troops were mercilessly butchered by Russian and Prussian armies. In triumph the allies entered the gory streets of Warsaw, sent the king, Stanislaus Augustus, to exile on a small pension, and divided the remainder of Poland between them. Catharine now entered into the coalition of the European powers against republican France. She consented to a treaty with England and Austria, by which she engaged to furnish an army of eighty thousand men to crush the spirit of French liberty, on condition that those two powers should consent to her driving the Turks out of Europe. Catharine was highly elated with this treaty. It was drawn up and was to be signed on the 6th of November, 1796.

On the morning of that day the empress, in her usual health and spirits, rose from the breakfast table, and retired to her closet. Not returning as soon as usual, some of her attendants entered and found her on the floor senseless. She had fallen in a fit of apoplexy, and died at ten o'clock in the evening of the next day without regaining consciousness or uttering a word, in the sixty-seventh year of her age, and after a reign of thirty-five years.

Paul, who was at his country palace, being informed of his mother's death, and of his accession to the throne, hastened to St. Petersburg. He ordered the tomb of Peter III. to be opened and placed the coffin by the side of that of the empress, with a true love knot reaching from one to the other, containing the inscription, under the circumstances supremely ridiculous, "divided in life—united in death." They were both buried together with the most sumptuous funeral honors.

The character of Catharine II. is sufficiently portrayed in her marvelous history. The annals of past ages may be searched in vain for her parallel. Two passions were ever predominant with her, love and ambition. Her mind seemed incapable of exhaustion, and notwithstanding the number of her successive favorites, with whom she entered into the most guilty connections, no monarch ever reigned with more dignity or with a more undisputed sway. Under her reign, notwithstanding the desolating wars, Russia made rapid advances in power and civilization. She protected commerce, excited industry, cultivated the arts, encouraged learning, promoted manufactures, founded cities, dug canals, and developed in a thousand ways the wealth and resources of the country. She had so many vices that some have consigned her name to infamy, and so many virtues, that others have advocated her canonization.

By the most careful calculation it is estimated that during the thirty-five years of the reign of Catharine, she added over four hundred thousand square miles to the territory of Russia, and six millions of inhabitants. It would be difficult to estimate the multitude of lives and the amount of treasure expended in her ambitious wars. We know of no more affecting comment to be made upon the history of our world, than that it presents such a bloody tragedy, that even the career of Catharine does not stand out in any peculiar prominence of atrocity. God made man but little lower than the angels. He is indeed fallen.

CHAPTER XXVIII.

THE REIGN OF PAUL I.

FROM 1796 TO 1801.

ACCESSION OF PAUL I. TO THE THRONE.—INFLUENCE OF THE HEREDITARY TRANSMISSION OF POWER.—EXTRAVAGANCE OF PAUL.—HIS DESPOTISM.—THE HORSE COURT MARTIALED.—PROGRESS OF THE FRENCH REVOLUTION.—FEARS AND VIOLENCE OF PAUL—HOSTILITY TO FOREIGNERS.—RUSSIA JOINS THE COALITION AGAINST FRANCE.—MARCH OF SUWARROW.—CHARACTER OF SUWARROW.—BATTLE ON THE ADDA.—BATTLE OF NOVI.—SUWARROW MARCHES TO THE RHINE.—HIS DEFEAT AND DEATH.—PAUL ABANDONS THE COALITION AND JOINS FRANCE.—CONSPIRACIES AT ST. PETERSBURG.

FEW sovereigns have ever ascended the throne more ignorant of affairs of state than was Paul I. Catharine had endeavored to protract his childhood, entrusting him with no responsibilities, and regulating herself minutely all his domestic and private concerns. He was carefully excluded from any participation in national affairs and was not permitted to superintend even his own household. Catharine took his children under her own protection as soon as they were born, and the parents were seldom allowed to see them. Paul I. had experienced, in his own person, all the burden of despotism ere he ascended Russia's despotic throne. Naturally desirous to secure popularity, he commenced his reign with acts which were much applauded. He introduced economy into the expenditures of the court, forbade the depreciation of the currency and the further issue of paper money, and withdrew the army which Catharine had sent to Persia on a career of conquest.

Paul I. did not love his mother. He did not believe that he was her legitimate child. Still, as his only title to the throne was founded on his being the reputed child of Peter III., he did what he could to rescue the memory of that prince from the infamy to which it had been very properly consigned. He had felt so humiliated by the domineering spirit of Catharine, that he resolved that Russia should not again fall under the reign of a woman, and issued a decree that henceforth the crown should descend in the male line only, and from father to son. The new emperor manifested his hostility to his mother, by endeavoring in various ways to undo what she had done.

The history of Europe is but a continued comment upon the folly of the law of the hereditary descent of power, a law which is more likely to place the crown upon the brow of a knave, a fool or a madman, than upon that of one qualified to govern. Russia soon awoke to the consciousness that the destinies of thirty millions of people were in the hands of a maniac, whose conduct seemed to prove that his only proper place was in one of the wards of Bedlam. The grossest contradictions followed each other in constant succession. To-day he would caress his wife, to-morrow place her under military arrest. At one hour he would load his children with favors, and the next endeavor to expose them publicly to shame.

Though Paul severely blamed his mother for the vast sums she lavished upon her court, these complaints did not prevent him from surpassing her in extravagance. The innumerable palaces she had reared and embellished with more than oriental splendor, were not sufficient for him. Neither the Winter palace, nor the Summer palace, nor the palace of Anitschkoff, nor the Marble palace, nor the Hermitage, whose fairy-like gorgeousness amazed all beholders, nor a crowd of other royal residences, too numerous to mention, and nearly all world-renowned, were deemed worthy of the residence of the new monarch. Pretending that he had received a celestial injunction to construct a new palace, he built, reckless of expense, the chateau of St. Michael.

The crown of Catharine was the wonder of Europe, but it was not rich enough for the brow of Paul. A new one was constructed, and his coronation at Moscow was attended with freaks of expenditure which impoverished provinces. Boundless gifts were lavished upon his favorites. But that he might enrich a single noble, ten thousand peasants were robbed. The crown peasants were vassals, enjoying very considerable freedom and many privileges. The peasantry of the nobles were slaves, nearly as much so as those on a Cuban plantation, with the single exception that custom prevented their being sold except with the land. Like the buildings, the oaks and the elms, they were inseparably attached to the soil. The emperor, at his coronation, gave away eighty thousand families to his favorites. Their labor henceforth, for life, was all to go to enrich their masters. These courtiers, reveling in boundless luxury, surrendered their slaves to overseers, whose reputation depended upon extorting as much as possible from the miserable boors.

The extravagance of Catharine II. had rendered it necessary for her to triple the capitation, or, as we should call it, the poll-tax, imposed upon the peasants. Paul now doubled this tax, which his mother had already tripled. The King of Prussia had issued a decree that no subject should fall upon his knees before him, but that every man should maintain in his presence and in that of the law the dignity of humanity. Paul, on the contrary, reëstablished, in all its rigor, the oriental etiquette, which Peter I. and Catharine had allowed to pass into disuse, which required every individual, whether a citizen or a stranger, to fall instantly upon his knees whenever the tzar made his appearance. Thus, when Paul passed along the streets on horseback or in his carriage, every man, woman and child, within sight of the royal cortege, was compelled to kneel, whether in mud or snow, until the cortege had passed. No one was exempted from the rule. Strangers and citizens, nobles and peasants, were compelled to the degrading homage.

Those on horseback or in carriages were required instantly to dismount and prostrate themselves before the despot.

A noble lady who came to St. Petersburg in her carriage, in great haste, to seek medical aid for her husband, who had been suddenly taken sick, in her trouble not having recognized the imperial livery, was dragged from her carriage and thrust into prison. Her four servants, who accompanied her, were seized and sent to the army, although they plead earnestly that, coming from a distance, they were ignorant of the law, the infraction of which was attributed to them as a crime. The unhappy lady, thus separated from her sick husband, and plunged into a dungeon, was so overwhelmed with anguish that she was thrown into a fever. Reason was dethroned, and she became a hopeless maniac. The husband died, being deprived of the succor his wife had attempted to obtain.

The son of a rich merchant, passing rapidly in his sleigh, muffled in furs, did not perceive the carriage of the emperor which he met, until it had passed. The police seized him; his sleigh and horses were confiscated. He was placed in close confinement for a month, and then, after receiving fifty blows from the terrible knout, was delivered to his friends a mangled form, barely alive.

A young lady, by some accident, had not thrown herself upon her knees quick enough at the appearance of the imperial carriage in the streets of Moscow. She was an orphan and resided with an aunt. They were both imprisoned for a month and fed upon bread and water; the young lady for failing in respect to the emperor, and the aunt for not having better instructed her niece. How strange is this power of despotism, by which one madman compels forty millions of people to tremble before him!

One of the freaks of this crazy prince was to court-martial his horse. The noble steed had tripped beneath his rider. A council was convened, composed of the equerries of the palace. The horse was proved guilty of failing in respect to his majesty, and was condemned to receive fifty blows from a heavy whip. Paul stood by, as the sentence was executed, counting off the blows.*

Twelve Polish gentlemen were condemned, for being "wanting in respect to his majesty," to have their noses and ears cut off, and were then sent to perpetual Siberian exile. When any one was admitted to an audience with the tzar, it was necessary for him to fall upon his knees so suddenly and heavily that his bones would ring upon the floor like the butt of a musket. No gentle genuflexion satisfied the tzar. A prince Gallatin was imprisoned for "kneeling and kissing the emperor's hand too negligently." This contempt for humanity soon rendered Paul very unpopular. He well knew that his legitimacy was doubted, and that if an illegitimate child he had no right whatever to the throne. He seemed to wish to prove that he was the son of Peter III. by imitating all the silly and cruel caprices of that most contemptible prince.

The French Revolution was now in progress, the crushed people of that kingdom endeavoring to throw off the yoke of intolerable oppression. All the despots in Europe were alarmed lest popular liberty in France should undermine their thrones. None were more alarmed than Paul. He was so fearful that democratic ideas might enter his kingdom that he forbade the introduction into his realms of any French journal or pamphlet. All Frenchmen in his kingdom were also ordered immediately to depart. All ships arriving were searched and if any French subjects were on board, men or women, they were not permitted to land, but were immediately sent out of the kingdom. Merchants, who had left their families and their business for a temporary absence, were not permitted again to set foot in the kingdom. The suffering which this cruel edict occasioned was very great.

Day after day new decrees were issued, of ever increasing violence. The tzar became suspicious of all strangers of what-

* Memoires Secret, tome i., page 334.

ever nation, and endeavored to rear a wall of separation around his whole kingdom which should exclude it from all intercourse with other parts of Europe. The German universities were all declared to be tainted with superstition, and all Russians were prohibited, under penalty of the confiscation of their estates, from sending their sons to those institutions. No foreigner, of whatever nation, was allowed to take part in any civil or ecclesiastical service. The young Russians who were already in the German universities, were commanded immediately to return to their homes.

Apprehensive that knowledge itself, by whomsoever communicated, might make the people restless under their enormous wrongs, Paul suppressed nearly all the schools which had been founded by Catharine II., reserving only a few to communicate instruction in the military art. All books, but those issued under the surveillance of the government, were interdicted. The greatest efforts were made to draw a broad line of distinction between the people and the nobles, and to place a barrier there which no plebeian could pass. Some one informed Paul that in France the revolutionists wore the chapeau, or three-cornered hat, with one of the corners in front. The tzar immediately issued a decree that in Russia the hat should be worn with the corner behind.

We have said that Paul was bitterly hostile to all foreigners. The emigrants, however, who fled from France, with arms in their hands, imploring the courts of Europe to crush republican liberty in France, he welcomed with the greatest cordiality and loaded with favors. The princes and nobles of the French court received from Paul large pensions, while, at the same time, he ignobly made them feel that he was their master and they were his slaves. His dread of French liberty was so great, that with all his soul he entered into the widespread European coalition which the genius of Pitt had organized against France, and which embraced even Turkey. And now for the first time the spectacle was seen of the Russian and Turkish squadrons combining against a common foe Paul sent an army of one hundred thousand men to coöperate with the allies. Republican France gathered up her energies to resist Europe in arms. The young Napoleon, heading a heroic band of half-famished soldiers, turned the Alps and fell like a thunderbolt into the Austrian camp upon the plains of Italy. In a series of victories which astounded the world he swept the foe before him, and compelled the Austrians to sue for peace. The embassadors of France and Germany met at Rastadt, in congress, and after spending many months in negotiations, the congress was dissolved by the Emperor of Germany, in April, 1799. The French embassadors set out to return, and were less than a quarter of a mile from the city, when a troop of Austrian hussars fell upon them, and two of their number, Roberjeot and Bonnier, were treacherously assassinated. The third, Delry, though left for dead, revived so far as to be able, covered with wounds and blood, to crawl back to Rastadt.*

Napoleon was at this time in Egypt, endeavoring to assail England, the most formidable foe of France, in India, the only vulnerable point which could be reached. Fifty thousand Russians, in a single band, were marching through Germany to coöperate with the Austrians on the French frontiers. The more polished Germans were astonished at the barbaric character of their allies. A Russian officer, in a freak of passion,

* "Our plenipotentiaries were massacred at Rastadt, and notwithstanding the indignation expressed by all France at that atrocity, vengeance was still very tardy in overtaking the assassins. The two Councils were the first to render a melancholy tribute of honor to the victims. Who that saw that ceremony ever forgot its solemnity ? Who can recollect without emotion the religious silence which reigned throughout the hall and galleries when the vote was put? The president then turned towards the curule chairs of the victims, on which lay the official costume of the assassinated representatives, covered with black crape, bent over them, pronounced the names of Roberjeot and Bonnier, and added, in a voice, the tone of which was always thrilling, *Assassinated at the Congress of Rastadt.* Immediately all the representatives responded, *May their blood be upon the heads of their murderers.*' —*Duchess of Abrantes*, p. 206.

shot an Austrian postilion, and then took out his purse and enquired of the employer of the postilion what damage was to be paid, as coolly as if he had merely killed a horse or a cow. Even German law was compelled to wink at such outrages, for an ally so essential as Russia it was needful to conciliate at all hazards. Paul deemed himself the most illustrious monarch of Europe, and resolved that none but a Russian general should lead the allied armies. The Germans, on the contrary, regarded the Russians as barbarians of wolfish courage and gigantic strength, but far too ignorant of military science to be entrusted with the plan of a campaign. After much contention the Emperor of Austria was compelled to yield, and an old Russian general, Suwarrow, was placed in command of the armies of the two most powerful empires then on the globe.

And who was Suwarrow? Behold his portrait. Born in a village of the Ukraine, the boy was sent by his father, an army officer, to the military academy at St. Petersburg, whence he entered the army as a common soldier, and ever after, for more than sixty years, he lived in incessant battles in Sweden, Turkey, Poland. In the storm of Ismael, forty thousand men, women and children fell in indiscriminate massacre at his command. In the campaign which resulted in the partition of Poland, twenty thousand Poles were cut down by his dragoons. A stranger to fear, grossly illiterate, and with no human sympathies, he appears on the arena but as a thunderbolt of war. Next to the emperor Paul, he was perhaps the most fantastic man on the continent. In a war with the Turks he killed a large number with his own hands, and brought, on his shoulders, a sackful of heads, which he rolled out at the feet of his general. This was the commencement of his reputation.* His whole military career was in accordance with this act. He had but one passion, love of war. He would often, even in mid-winter, have one or two pailsful of

* Histoire Philosophique et Politique de Russie. Tome cinquième, p. 233.

cold water poured upon him, as he rose from his bed, and then, in his shirt, leap upon an unsaddled horse and scour the camp with the speed of the wind. Sometimes he would appear, in the early morning, at the door of his tent, stark naked, and crow like a cock. This was a signal for the tented host to spring to arms. Occasionally he would visit the hospital, pretending that he was a physician, and would prescribe medicine for those whom he thought sick, and scourgings for those whom he imagined to be feigning sickness. Sometimes he would turn all the patients out of the doors, sick and well, saying that it was not permitted for the soldiers of Suwarrow to be sick. He was as merciless to himself as he was to his soldiers. Hunger, cold, fatigue, seemed to him to be pleasures. Hardships which to many would render life a scene of insupportable torture, were to him joys. He usually traveled in a coarse cart, which he made his home, sleeping in it at night, with but the slightest protection from the weather. Whenever he lodged in a house, his *aides* took the precaution to remove the windows from his room, as he would otherwise inevitably smash every glass.

Notwithstanding this ostentatious display of his hatred of all luxury, he was excessively fond of diamonds and other precious stones. He was also exceedingly superstitious, ever falling upon his knees before whatever priest he might meet, and imploring his benediction. Such men generally feel that the observance of ceremonial rites absolves them from the guilt of social crimes. With these democratic manners Suwarrow utterly detested liberty. The French, as the most liberty-loving people of Europe, he abhorred above all others. He foamed with rage when he spoke of them. In the sham fights with which he frequently exercised the army, when he gave the order to "*charge the miserable French*," every soldier was to make two thrusts of the bayonet in advance, as if twice to pierce the heart of the foe, and a third thrust into the ground, that the man, twice bayoneted, might be pinned in death to the earth. Such was the general whom Paul sent "to destroy the impious government," as he expressed it, "which dominated over France."

With blind confidence Suwarrow marched down upon the plains of Lombardy, dreaming that in those fertile realms nothing awaited him but an easy triumph over those who had been guilty of the crime of abolishing despotism. The French had heard appalling rumors of the prowess and ferocity of these warriors of the North, and awaited the shock with no little solicitude.* The two armies met on the banks of the Adda, which flows into the northern part of the Lake of Como. Suwarrow led sixty thousand Russians and Austrians. The French general, Moreau, to oppose them, had the wreck of an army, consisting of twenty-five thousand men, disheartened by defeat. On the 17th of April, 1799, the first Russian regiment appeared in sight of the bridge of Lecco. The French, indignant at the interference of the Russians in a quarrel with which they had no concern, dashed upon them with their bayonets, and repulsed them with great carnage. But the hosts of Russia and Austria came pouring on in such overwhelming numbers, that Moreau, with his forces reduced to twenty thousand men, was compelled to retreat before an army which could concentrate ninety thousand troops in line of battle. Pressed by the enemy, he retreated through Milan to Turin. Suwarrow tarried in Milan to enjoy a triumph accorded to him by the priests and the nobles, the creatures of Austria.

Moreau entrenched himself at Alexandria, awaiting the arrival of General Macdonald with reinforcements. Suwarrow

* "Suwarrow was a genuine barbarian, fortunately incapable of calculating the employment of his forces, otherwise the republic might perhaps have succumbed. His army was like himself. It had a bravery that was extraordinary and bordered on fanaticism, but no instruction. It was expert only at the use of the bayonet. Suwarrow, extremely insolent to the allies, gave Russian officers to the Austrians to teach them the use of the bayonet. Fortunately his brutal energy, after doing a great deal of mischief, had to encounter the energy of skill and calculation, and was foiled by the latter."—*Thiers' History French Revolution*, vol. iv., p. 346.

approached with an army now exceeding one hundred thousand men. Again Moreau was compelled to retreat, pursued by Suwarrow, and took refuge on the crest of the Apennines, in the vicinity of Genoa. By immense exertions he had assembled forty thousand men. Suwarrow came thundering upon him with sixty thousand. The French army was formed in a semicircle on the slopes of the Monte Rotundo, about twenty miles north of Genoa. The Austro-Russian army spread over the whole plain below. At five o'clock in the morning of the 15th of August, 1799, the fierce battle of Novi commenced. Suwarrow, a fierce fighter, but totally unacquainted with the science of strategy, in characteristic words gave the order of battle. "Kray," said he, "will attack the left—the Russians the center—Melas the right." To the soldiers he said, "God wills, the emperor orders, Suwarrow commands, that to-morrow the enemy be conquered." Dressed in his usual costume, in his shirt down to the waist, he led his troops into battle. Enormous slaughter ensued; numbers prevailing against science, and the French, driven out of Italy, took refuge along the ridges of the Apennines.

Suwarrow, satisfied with his dearly-bought victory, for he had lost ten thousand men in the conflict, did not venture to pursue the retiring foe, but with his bleeding and exhausted army fell back to Coni; and thence established garrisons throughout Piedmont and Lombardy. Paul was almost delirious with joy at this great victory. He issued a decree declaring Suwarrow to be the greatest general "of all times, of all peoples and of all quarters of the globe." In his pride he declared that republican France, for the crime of rebelling against legitimate authority, should receive punishment which should warn all nations against following her example. The Russian squadron combined with that of the Turks, formed a junction with the victorious fleet of Nelson, and sailing from the bay of Aboukir, swept the French fleet from the Mediterranean.

The Austrians and Russians, thus victorious, now marched to assail Massena at Zurich on the Rhine, intending there to cross the stream and invade France. For a month, in September and October, 1799, there was a series of incessant battles. But the republican armies were triumphant. The banners of France struggled proudly through many scenes of blood and woe, and the shores of Lake Zurich and the fastnesses of the Alps, were strewed with the dead bodies of the Russians. In fourteen days twenty thousand Russians and six thousand Austrians were slain. Suwarrow, the intrepid barbarian, with but ten thousand men saved from his proud army, retreated overwhelmed with confusion and rage. Republican France was saved. The rage which Suwarrow displayed is represented as truly maniacal. He foamed at the mouth and roared like a bull. As a wounded lion turns upon his pursuers, from time to time he stopped in his retreat, and rushed back upon the foe. He was crushed in body and mind by this defeat. Having wearied himself in denouncing, in unmeasured terms, all his generals and soldiers, he became taciturn and moody. Secluding himself from his fellow-men he courted solitude, and surrendered himself to a fantastic and superstitious devotion. Enveloped in a cloak, and with his eyes fixed upon the ground, he would occasionally pass through the camp, condescending to notice no one.

Paul had also sent an army into Holland, against France, which had been utterly repulsed by General Brune, with the loss of many slain and taken prisoners. The tidings of these disasters roused, in the bosom of Paul, fury equal to that which Suwarrow had displayed. He bitterly cursed his allies, England and Austria, declaring that they, in the pursuit of their own selfish interests, had abandoned his armies to destruction. Suwarrow, deprived of further command, and overwhelmed with disgrace, retired to one of his rural retreats where he soon died of chagrin.

The Austrian and English embassadors at the court of St.

Petersburg, Paul loaded with reproaches and even with insults. His conduct became so whimsical as to lead many to suppose that he was actually insane. He had long hated the French republicans, but now, with a new and a fresher fury, he hated the allies. The wrecks of his armies were ordered to return to Russia, and he ceased to take an active part in the prosecution of the war, without however professing, in any way, to withdraw from the coalition. Neither the Austrian nor the English embassador could obtain an audience with the emperor. He treated them with utter neglect, and, the court following the example of the sovereign, these embassadors were left in perfect solitude. They could not even secure an audience with any of the ministry.

Paul had been very justly called the Don Quixote of the coalition, and the other powers were now not a little apprehensive of the course he might adopt, for madman as he was, he was the powerful monarch of some forty millions of people. Soon he ordered the Russian fleet, which in coöperation with the squadrons of the allies was blockading Malta, to withdraw from the conflict. Then he recalled his ministers from London and Vienna, declaring that neither England nor Austria was contending for any principle, but that they were fighting merely for their own selfish interests. England had already openly declared her intention of appropriating Malta to herself.

Napoleon had now returned from Egypt and had been invested with the supreme power in France as First Consul. There were many French prisoners in the hands of the allies. France had also ten thousand Russian prisoners. Napoleon proposed an exchange. Both England and Austria refused to exchange French prisoners for Russians.

"What," exclaimed Napoleon, "do you refuse to liberate the Russians, who were your allies, who were fighting in your ranks and under your commanders? Do you refuse to restore to their country those men to whom you are indebted for your victories and conquests in Italy, and who have left in your hands a multitude of French prisoners whom they have taken? Such injustice excites my indignation."

With characteristic magnanimity he added, "I will restore them to the tzar without exchange. He shall see how I esteem brave men."

These Russian prisoners were assembled at Aix la Chapelle. They were all furnished with a complete suit of new clothing, in the uniform of their own regiments, and were thoroughly supplied with weapons of the best French manufacture. And thus they were returned to their homes. Paul was exactly in that mood of mind which best enabled him to appreciate such a deed. He at once abandoned the alliance, and with his own hand wrote to Napoleon as follows:

"Citizen First Consul,—I do not write to you to discuss the rights of men or of citizens. Every country governs itself as it pleases. Whenever I see, at the head of a nation, a man who knows how to rule and how to fight, my heart is attracted towards him. I write to acquaint you with my dissatisfaction with England, who violates every article of the law of nations and has no guide but her egotism and her interest. I wish to unite with you to put an end to the unjust proceedings of that government."

Friendly relations were immediately established between France and Russia, and they exchanged embassadors. Paul had conferred an annual pension of two hundred thousand rubles (about $150,000) upon the Count of Provence, subsequently Louis XVIII., and had given him an asylum at Mittau. He now withdrew that pension and protection. He induced the King of Denmark to forbid the English fleet from passing the Sound, which led into the Baltic Sea, engaging, should the English attempt to force the passage, to send a fleet of twenty-one ships to assist the Danes. The battle of Hohenlinden and the peace of Luneville detached Austria from the coalition, and England was left to struggle alone against the new opinions in France.

The nobles of Russia, harmonizing with the aristocracy of Europe, were quite dissatisfied with this alliance between Russia and France. Though the form of the republic was changed to that of the consulate, they saw that the principles of popular liberty remained unchanged in France. The wife of Paul and her children, victims of the inexplicable caprice of the tzar, lived in constant constraint and fear. The empress had three sons—Alexander, Constantine and Nicholas. The heir apparent, Alexander, was watched with the most rigorous scrutiny, and was exposed to a thousand mortifications. The suspicious father became the jailer of his son, examining all his correspondence, and superintending his mode of life in its minutest details. The most whimsical and annoying orders were issued, which rendered life, in the vicinity of the court, almost a burden. The army officers were forbidden to attend evening parties lest they should be too weary for morning parade. Every one who passed the imperial palace, even in the most inclement weather, was compelled to go with head uncovered. The enforcement of his arbitrary measures rendered the intervention of the troops often necessary. The palace was so fortified and guarded as to resemble a prison. St. Petersburg, filled with the machinery of war, presented the aspect of a city besieged. Every one was exposed to arrest. No one was sure of passing the night in tranquillity, there were so many domiciliary visits; and many persons, silently arrested, disappeared without it ever being known what became of them. Spies moved about everywhere, and their number was infinite. Paul thus enlisted against himself the animosity of all classes of his subjects—his own family, foreigners, the court, the nobles and the bourgeois. Such were the influences which originated the conspiracy which resulted in the assassination of the tzar.

CHAPTER XXIX.

ASSASSINATION OF PAUL AND ACCESSION OF ALEXANDER.

FROM 1801 TO 1807.

ASSASSINATION OF PAUL I.—IMPLICATION OF ALEXANDER IN THE CONSPIRACY.—ANECDOTES.—ACCESSION OF ALEXANDER.—THE FRENCH REVOLUTION.—ALEXANDER JOINS THE ALLIES AGAINST FRANCE.—STATE OF RUSSIA.—USEFUL MEASURES OF ALEXANDER.—PEACE OF AMIENS.—RENEWAL OF HOSTILITIES.—BATTLE OF AUSTERLITZ.—MAGNANIMITY OF NAPOLEON.—NEW COALITION.—AMBITION OF ALEXANDER.—BATTLES OF JENA AND EYLAU.—DEFEAT OF THE RUSSIANS.

WE have before mentioned that Paul I. had three sons—Alexander, Constantine and Nicholas. The eldest of these, Alexander, was a very promising young man, of popular character, twenty-three years of age. His father feared his popularity and treated him with the greatest severity, and was now threatening him and his mother with imprisonment. General Pahlen, governor of St. Petersburg, obtained the confidence of the young prince, and urged upon him, as a necessary measure of self-defense, that he should place himself at the head of a conspiracy for the dethronement of his insane father. The sufferings of the young prince were so severe and his perils so great, and the desire for a change so universal throughout the empire, that it was not found difficult to enlist him in the enterprise. Alexander consented to the dethronement of his father, but with the express condition that his life should be spared. He might perhaps have flattered himself with the belief that this could be done; but the conspirators knew full well that the dagger of the assassin was the only instrument which could remove Paul from the throne. The conspiracy was very extensive, embracing nearly all the functionaries of the government at St. Petersburg, the entire senate, and the diplomatic corps. All the principal officers of the royal guard, with their colonel at their head, were included in the plot. The hour for the execution of the conspiracy was fixed for the night of the 23d of March, 1801.

A regiment devoted to the conspirators was that night on guard at the palace. The confederates who were to execute the plot, composed of the most distinguished men in the court and the army, met at the house of Prince Talitzin ostensibly for a supper. With wine and wassail they nerved themselves for the desperate deed. Just at midnight a select number entered the garden of the palace, by a private gate, and stealing silently along, beneath the trees, approached a portal which was left unbarred and undefended. One of the guardians of the palace led their steps and conducted them to an apartment adjoining that in which the tzar slept. A single hussar guarded the door. He was instantly struck down, and the conspirators in a body rushed into the royal chamber.

Paul sprang from his bed, and seizing his sword, endeavored to escape by another door than that through which the conspirators entered. Foiled in this attempt, in the darkness, for all lights had been extinguished, he hid himself behind a movable screen. He was however soon seized, lights were brought in, and an act of abdication was read to him which he was required to sign. The intrepid tzar sprang at Zoubow, who was reading the act, and cuffed his ears. A struggle immediately ensued, and an officer's sash was passed around the neck of the monarch, and after a desperate resistance he was strangled. The dress of one of the conspirators caused him to be mistaken, by the emperor, for his son Constantine, and the last words which the wretched sovereign uttered were, "And you too, Constantine."

The two grand dukes, Alexander and Constantine, were in the room below, and heard all the noise of the struggle in which their father was assassinated. It was with much difficulty that these young princes were induced to give their consent to the conspiracy, and they yielded only on condition that their father's life should be spared. But self-defense required some vigorous action on their part, for Paul had threatened to send Alexander to Siberia, to immure Constantine in a convent, and the empress mother in a cloister.

The conspirators having accomplished the deed, descended into the apartment, where the grand dukes were awaiting their return. Alexander enquired eagerly if they had saved his father's life. The silence of the conspirators told the melancholy tale. The grief manifested by both Alexander and Constantine was apparently sincere and intense. In passionate exclamations they gave vent to sorrow and remorse. But Pahlen, the governor, who had led the conspiracy, calm and collected, represented that the interests of the empire demanded a change of policy, that the death of Paul was a fatality, and that nothing now remained but for Alexander to assume the reins of government.

"I shall be accused," exclaimed Alexander bitterly, "of being the assassin of my father. You promised me not to attempt his life. I am the most unhappy man in the world."

The dead body of the emperor was placed upon a table, and an English physician, named Wylie, was called in to arrange the features so that it should appear that he had died of apoplexy. The judgment of the world has ever been and probably ever will be divided respecting the nature of Alexander's complicity in this murder. Many suppose that he could not have been ignorant that the death of his father was the inevitable end of the conspiracy, and that he accepted that result as a sad necessity. Certain it is that the conspirators were all rewarded richly, by being entrusted with the chief offices of the state; and the new monarch surrounded his throne with counselors whose hands were imbrued in his father's blood. A lady at St. Petersburg wrote to Fouché on the occasion of some ceremony which soon ensued,

"The young emperor walked preceded by the assassins

of his grandfather, followed by those of his father, and surrounded by his own."

"Behold," said Fouché, "a woman who speaks Tacitus."

At St. Helena, O'Meara enquired of Napoleon if he thought that Paul had been insane. "Latterly," Napoleon replied, "I believe that he was. At first he was strongly prejudiced against the Revolution, and every person concerned in it; but afterwards I had rendered him reasonable, and had changed his opinions altogether. If Paul had lived the English would have lost India before now. An agreement was made between Paul and myself to invade it. I furnished the plan. I was to have sent thirty thousand good troops. He was to send a similar number of the best Russian soldiers, and forty thousand Cossacks. I was to subscribe ten millions for the purchase of camels and other requisites for crossing the desert. The King of Prussia was to have been applied to by both of us to grant a passage for my troops through his dominions, which would have been immediately granted. I had, at the same time, made a demand to the King of Persia for a passage through his country, which would also have been granted, although the negotiations were not entirely concluded, but would have succeeded, as the Persians were desirious of profiting by it themselves."*

On another occasion, speaking upon this same subject, Napoleon said to Las Casas, "Paul had been promised Malta the moment it was taken possession of by the English. Malta reduced, the English ministers denied that they had promised it to him. It is confidently stated that, on the reading ot this shameful falsehood, Paul felt so indignant that, seizing the dispatch in full council, he ran his sword through it, and ordered it to be sent back, in that condition, by way of answer. If this be a folly, it must be allowed that it is the folly of a noble soul. It is the indignation of virtue, which was incapable until then of suspecting such baseness.

* "Napoleon at St. Helena," p. 534.

"At the same time the English ministers, treating with us for the exchange of prisoners, refused to include the Russian prisoners taken in Holland, who were in the actual service and fought for the sole cause of the English. I had hit upon the bent of Paul's character. I seized time by the forelock. I collected these Russians. I clothed them and sent them back without any expense. From that instant that generous heart was altogether devoted to me, and, as I had no interest in opposition to Russia, and should never have spoken or acted but with justice, there is no doubt that I should have been enabled, for the future, to dispose of the cabinet of St. Petersburg. Our enemies were sensible of the danger, and it has been thought that this good-will of Paul proved fatal to him. It might well have been the case, for there are cabinets with whom nothing is sacred."

The death of Paul brought the enemies of France and the friends of England into power at St. Petersburg. The new emperor, the first day after his accession to the throne, issued a proclamation declaring his intention to follow in the footsteps of his grandmother, Catharine. He liberated all the English sailors whom Paul had taken from the ships laid under sequestration. All the decrees against the free importation of English merchandise were abolished; and the young emperor soon wrote, with his own hand, a letter to the King of England, expressing his earnest desire again to establish friendly relations between the courts of Russia and England. This declaration was received in London with shouts of joy.

Alexander was twenty-three years of age when he ascended the throne. A Swiss, by the name of Laharpe, a man of great intelligence and lofty spirit, and a republican in principle, had been for many years the prominent tutor of the young prince, and had obtained a great control over his mind. The instructions of Laharpe, who wished to make a Washington of his pupil, were much counteracted by the despotic lessons he had received from Catharine, and by the luxury, servility and corruption which crowded the Russian court. Naturally amiable, and possessed of by no means a strong character, the young monarch was easily moulded by the influences which surrounded him. He evidently commenced his reign with the best intentions, resolved, in every way, to promote the prosperity of his subjects. It is painful to observe the almost inevitable tendency of power to deprave the soul. History is filled with the records of those sovereigns who have fallen from virtue to vice.

The commencement of the reign of Alexander was hailed with general joy. All his first proclamations breathe the spirit of benevolence, of generosity, of the desire to ameliorate the condition of the oppressed millions. The ridiculous ordinances which Paul had issued were promptly abrogated. By a special edict all Russians were permitted to dress as they pleased, to wear twilled waistcoats and pantaloons, instead of short clothes, if they preferred them. They were permitted to wear round hats, to lead dogs with a leash, and to fasten their shoes with strings instead of buckles. A large number of exiles, whom Paul had sent to Siberia, were recalled, and many of the most burdensome requirements of etiquette, in the court, were annulled.

Though Alexander was an absolute monarch, who could issue any decree, subject to no restraint, he conferred upon the senate the power to revise these decrees, and to suggest any amendment; and he also created a legislature who were permitted to advise respecting any regulations which they might think promotive of the interests of the empire. The will of the emperor was, however, absolute and unchecked. Still the appointment of these deliberative and advising bodies was considered an immense stride towards constitutional freedom. The censorship of the press was greatly mitigated, and foreign books and journals were more freely introduced to the empire.

Two new ministries were established by Alexander, with

extensive responsibilities—the Ministry of the Interior, and that of Public Instruction. All the officers of government were rendered accountable to the senate, and responsible to the sovereign. These elements of accountability and of responsibility had hitherto been almost unknown in Russia. Charitable institutions were established, and schools of different grades, for the instruction of all classes of the people. Ambitious of rendering the Russian court as brilliant in all the appliances of luxury and art as any court in Europe, the emperor was indefatigable in the collection of paintings, statuary, medals and all artistic curiosities. The contrast thus became very marked between the semi-barbarism of the provinces and the enlightenment and voluptuousness of the capital.

It is worthy of remark that when Alexander ascended the throne there did not exist in all Russia, not even in St. Petersburg, a single book-store.* The Russian sovereigns had wished to take from civilization only that which would add to their despotic power. Desiring to perpetuate the monopoly of authority, they sought to retain in their own hands the privileges of instruction. The impulse which Alexander had given to the cause of education spread throughout the empire, and the nobles, in the distant provinces, interested themselves in establishing schools. These schools were, however, very exclusive in their character, admitting none but the children of the nobles. The military schools which Catharine had established, with so much care, Alexander encouraged and supported with the utmost assiduity.

As Catharine II. had endeavored to obliterate every trace of the government of her murdered husband, Peter III., so Alexander strove to efface all vestiges of his assassinated father, Paul. He entered into the closest alliance with England, and manifested much eagerness in his desire to gratify

* *Histoire Philosophique et Politique de Russie, Depuis les Temps les Plus Reculés jusqu'au nos Jours. Par J. Esneaux et Chenechot. Tome cinquième,* p. 293.

all the wishes of the cabinet of St. James. He even went so far as to consent to pay a sum of eight hundred thousand rubles ($600,000), as an indemnity to England for the loss the English merchants had incurred by the embargo placed by Paul upon their ships. Every day the partiality of the young emperor for England became more manifest. In the meantime Napoleon was unwearied in his endeavors to secure the good-will of a monarch whose sword would have so important an influence in settling the quarrel between aristocracy and democracy which then agitated Europe. Napoleon was so far successful that, on the 8th of October, 1801, a treaty of friendly alliance was signed at Paris between France and Russia. The battle of Marengo had compelled Austria to withdraw from the coalition against France; and the peace of Luneville, which Napoleon signed with Austria in February, 1801, followed by peace with Spain and Naples in March, with the pope in July, with Bavaria in August and with Portugal in September, left England to struggle alone against those republican principles which in the eyes of aristocratic Europe seemed equally obnoxious whether moulded under the form of the republic, the consulate or the empire.

The English cabinet, thus left to struggle alone, was compelled, though very reluctantly, by the murmurs of the British people, to consent to peace with France; and the treaty of Amiens, which restored peace to entire Europe, was signed in March, 1802. A few days after this event, peace was signed with Turkey, and thus through the sagacity and energy of Napoleon, every hostile sword was sheathed in Europe and on the confines of Asia. But the treaty of Amiens was a sore humiliation to the cabinet of St. James, and hardly a year had elapsed ere the British government, in May, 1803, again drew the sword, and all Europe was again involved in war. It was a war, said William Pitt truly, "of armed opinions."

The Russian embassador at Paris, M. Marcow, who under

Catharine II. had shown himself bitterly hostile to the French republic, was declared to be guilty of entering into intrigues to assist the English, now making war upon France, and he was ordered immediately to leave the kingdom. Alexander did not resent this act, so obviously proper, but rewarded the dismissed minister with an annual pension of twelve thousand rubles ($9,000).

During this short interval of peace Alexander was raising an army of five hundred thousand men, to extend and consolidate his dominions on the side of Turkey. His frontiers there were dimly defined, and his authority but feebly exerted. He pushed his armies into Georgia and took firm possession of that vast province extending between the Black Sea and the Caspian, and embracing some eighteen thousand square miles. At the same time the blasts of his bugles were heard reverberating through the defiles of the Balkan, and his fortresses were reared and his banners planted there. The monarchs of Russia, for many generations, had fixed a wistful eye upon Constantinople, but no one had coveted the possession of that important city so intensely as now did Alexander. "Constantinople," said he often, "is the key of my house."

The arrest of the Duke d'Enghien, in the territory of the Duke of Baden, and his execution as a traitor for being in arms against his own country, excited the indignation of Alexander. Napoleon, immediately after the arrest, had made an apology to the Duke of Baden for the violation of a neutral territory, and this apology was accepted by the duke as satisfactory. Nevertheless, Alexander through his embassador, sent the following message to the court of the First Consul:

"The Emperor Alexander, as mediator and guarantee of the continental peace, has notified the States of the German empire that he considers the action of the First Consul as endangering their safety and independence, and that he does not doubt that the First Consul will take prompt measures to reassure those governments by giving satisfactory explanations."

Napoleon regarded this interference of Alexander as impertinent, and caused his minister to reply,

"What would Alexander have said if the First Consul had imperiously demanded explanations respecting the murder of Paul I., and had pretended to constitute himself an avenger? How is it, that when the sovereign of the territory, which it is said has been violated, makes no complaint; when all the princes, his neighbors and his allies, are silent—how is it that the Emperor of Russia, least of all interested in the affair, raises his voice alone? Does it not arise from complicity with England, that machinator of conspiracies against the power and the life of the First Consul? Is not Russia engaged in similar conspiracies at Rome, at Dresden and at Paris? If Russia desires war, why does she not frankly say so, instead of endeavoring to secure that end indirectly?"

In May of 1804, Napoleon assumed the imperial title. Alexander, denying the right of the people to elect their own sovereign, refused to recognize the empire. Hence increasing irritation arose. England, trembling in view of the camp at Boulogne, roused all her energies to rally Europe to strike France in the rear. In this effort she was signally successful. Russia, Sweden, Austria, Turkey and Rome, were engaged in vigorous coöperation with England against France. Holland, Switzerland and Bavaria ranged themselves on the side of Napoleon.

On the 8th of September, 1805, the armies of Austria and Russia were on the march for France, and the Austrian troops, in overwhelming numbers, invaded Bavaria. Napoleon was prepared for the blow. The camp at Boulogne was broken up, and his troops were instantly on the march towards the Rhine. In the marvelous campaign of Ulm the Austrian army was crushed, almost annihilated, and the victorious battalions of Napoleon marched resistlessly to Vienna. Alexander, with a vast army, was hurrying forward, by forced marches, to assist his Austrian ally. At Olmutz he met the Emperor of Austria on the retreat with thirty thousand men, the wreck of that magnificent army with which he had commenced his march upon France. Here the two armies formed a junction—seventy thousand Russians receiving into their ranks thirty thousand Austrians. The two emperors, Alexander and Francis, rode at the head of this formidable force.

On the 1st of December, Napoleon, leading an army of seventy thousand men, encountered these, his combined foes, on the plains of Austerlitz. "To-morrow," said he, "before nightfall, that army shall be mine!" A day of carnage, such as war has seldom seen, ensued. From an eminence the Emperors of Russia and Austria witnessed the destruction of their hosts. No language can describe the tumult which pervaded the ranks of the retreating foe. The Russians, wild with dismay, rent the skies with their barbaric shouts, and wreaked their vengeance upon all the helpless villages they encountered in their path.

Francis, the Emperor of Austria, utterly ruined, sought an interview with his conqueror, and implored peace. Napoleon, as ever, was magnanimous, and was eager to sheathe the sword which he had only drawn in self-defense. Francis endeavored to throw the blame of the war upon England.

"The English," said he, "are a nation of merchants. To secure for themselves the commerce of the world they are willing to set the continent in flames!"

The Austrian monarch, having obtained very favorable terms for himself, interceded for Alexander. "The Russian army," Napoleon replied, "is surrounded. Not a man can escape me. If, however, your majesty will promise me that Alexander shall immediately return to Russia, I will stop the advance of my columns."

The pledge was given, and Napoleon then sent General

Savary to the head-quarters of Alexander, to inquire if he would ratify the armistice.

"I am happy to see you," said the emperor to the envoy. "The occasion has been very glorious for your arms. That day will take nothing from the reputation your master has earned in so many battles. It was my first engagement. I confess that the rapidity of his maneuvers gave me no time to succor the menaced points. Everywhere you were at least double the number of our forces."

"Sire," Savary replied, "our force was twenty-five thousand less than yours. And even of that the whole was not very warmly engaged. But we maneuvered much, and the same division combated at several different points. Therein lies the art of war. The emperor, who has seen forty pitched battles, is never wanting in that particular. He is still ready to march against the Archduke Charles, if your majesty does not accept the armistice."

"What guarantee does your master require," continued Alexander, "and what security can I have that your troops will not prosecute their movements against me?"

"He asks only your word of honor," Savary replied. "He has instructed me the moment it is given to suspend the pursuit."

"I give it with pleasure," rejoined the emperor, "and should it ever be your fortune to visit St. Petersburg, I hope that I may be able to render my capital agreeable to you."

Hostilities immediately ceased, and the broken columns of the Russian troops returned to their homes. The Austro-Russian army, in the disastrous day of Austerlitz, lost in killed, wounded and prisoners, over forty thousand men. It is stated that Alexander, when flying from the bloody field with his discomfited troops, his path being strewed with the wounded and the dead, posted placards along the route, with the inscription,

"I commend my unfortunate soldiers to the generosity of the Emperor Napoleon!"

Alexander, young and ambitious, was very much chagrined by this utter discomfiture. Austerlitz was his first battle; and instead of covering him with renown it had overwhelmed him with disgrace. He was anxious for an opportunity to wipe away the stain. A new coalition was soon formed against France, consisting of England, Russia, Prussia and Sweden. Alexander eagerly entered into this coalition, hoping for an opportunity to acquire that military fame which, in this lost world, has been ever deemed so essential to the reputation of a sovereign. The remonstrance of Napoleon, with Russia, was noble and unanswerable.

"Why," said he, "should hostilities arise between France and Russia? Perfectly independent of each other, they are impotent to inflict evil, but all-powerful to communicate benefits. If the Emperor of France exercises a great influence in Italy, the tzar exerts a still greater influence over Turkey and Persia. If the cabinet of Russia pretends to have a right to affix limits to the power of France, without doubt it is equally disposed to allow the Emperor of the French to prescribe the bounds beyond which Russia is not to pass. Russia has partitioned Poland. Can she then complain that France possesses Belgium and the left banks of the Rhine? Russia has seized upon the Crimea, the Caucasus, and the northern provinces of Persia. Can she deny that the right of self-preservation gives France a right to demand an equivalent in Europe? . . . . .

"Let every power begin by restoring the conquests which it has made during the last fifty years. Let them reëstablish Poland, restore Venice to its senate, Trinidad to Spain, Ceylon to Holland, the Crimea to the Porte, the Caucasus and Georgia to Persia, the kingdom of Mysore to the sons of Tippoo Saib, and the Mahratta States to their lawful owners; and then the other powers may have some title to insist that France shall retire within her ancient limits. It is the fashion to speak of the ambition of France. Had she chosen to preserve her conquests, the half of Austria, the Venetian States, the States of Holland and Switzerland and the kingdom of Naples would have been in her possession. The limits of France are, in reality, the Adige and the Rhine. Has it passed either of these limits? Had it fixed on the Solza and the Drave, it would not have exceeded the bounds of its conquests."

In September, 1806, the Prussian army, two hundred thousand strong, commenced their march for the invasion of France. Alexander had also marshaled his barbarian legions and was eagerly following, with two hundred thousand of the most highly disciplined Russian troops in his train. Napoleon contemplated with sorrow the rising of this new storm of war and woe; but with characteristic vigor he prepared to meet it. As he left Paris for the campaign, in a parting message to the senate he said,

"In so just a war, which we have not provoked by any act, by any pretense, the true cause of which it would be impossible to assign, and where we only take arms to defend ourselves, we depend entirely upon the support of the laws, and upon that of the people whom circumstances call upon to give fresh proofs of their devotion and courage."

In the battle of Jena, which took place on the 14th of October, the Prussian army was nearly annihilated, leaving in a few hours more than forty thousand men in killed, wounded and prisoners. In less than a month the conquest of entire Prussia was achieved, and Napoleon was pursuing Frederic William, who, with the wreck of the Prussian army was hastening to take refuge in the bosom of the Russian hosts which were approaching. December had now come with its icy blasts, and Napoleon, leading his victorious troops to the banks of the Vistula, more than a thousand miles from France, established them in winter quarters, waiting until spring for the renewal of the campaign.

Alexander, terrified by the destruction of his Prussian allies, halted his troops upon the other side of the Vistula, and from his vast realms collected recruits. For a few weeks the storms of winter secured a tacit armistice.

In February, 1807, Alexander assumed the offensive and endeavored to surprise Napoleon in his encampment. But Napoleon was on the alert. A series of terrific battles ensued, in which the French were invariably the victors. The retreating Russians, hotly pursued, at last rallied on the field of Eylau. Napoleon had already driven them two hundred and forty miles from his encampment on the Vistula.

"It was the 7th of February, 1807. The night was dark and intensely cold as the Russians, exhausted by the retreat of the day, took their positions for the desperate battle of the morrow. There was a gentle swell of land extending two or three miles, which skirted a vast, bleak, unsheltered plain, over which the wintry gale drifted the snow. Upon this ridge the Russians in double lines formed themselves in battle array. Five hundred pieces of cannon were ranged in battery, to hurl destruction into the bosoms of their foes. They then threw themselves upon the icy ground for their frigid bivouac. A fierce storm had already risen, which spread over the sleeping host its mantle of snow."

Napoleon came also upon the field, in the darkness of the night and of the storm, and placed his army in position for the battle which the dawn would usher in. Two hundred pieces of artillery were planted to reply to the Russian batteries. There were eighty thousand Russians on the ridge, sixty thousand Frenchmen on the plain, and separated by a distance of less than half a cannon shot. The sentinels of either army could almost touch each other with their muskets.

The morning had not yet dawned when the cannonade commenced. The earth shook beneath its roar. A storm of snow at the same time swept over the plain blinding and smothering assailants and assailed. The smoke of the battle blended with the storm had spread over the contending hosts a sulphurous canopy black as midnight. Even the flash of the guns could hardly be discerned through the gloom. All the day long, and until ten o'clock at night, the battle raged with undiminished fury. One half of the Russian army was now destroyed, and the remainder, unable longer to endure the conflict, sullenly retreated. Napoleon remained master of the field, which exhibited such a scene of misery as had never before met even his eye. When congratulated upon his victory by one of his officers he replied sadly,

"To a father who loses his children, victory has no charms. When the heart speaks, glory itself is an illusion."

CHAPTER XXX.

REIGN OF ALEXANDER I.

FROM 1807 TO 1825.

The Field of Eylau.—Letter to the King of Prussia.—Renewal of the War.—Discomfiture of the Allies.—Battle of Friedland.—The Raft at Tilsit.—Intimacy of the Emperors.—Alexander's Designs upon Turkey.—Alliance between France and Russia.—Object of the Continental System.—Perplexities of Alexander.—Driven by the Nobles to War.—Results of the Russian Campaign.—Napoleon Vanquished.—Last Days of Alexander.—His Sickness and Death.

FROM the field of Eylau, the Russians and Prussians retreated to the Niemen. Napoleon remained some days upon the field to nurse the wounded, and, anxious for peace, wrote to the King of Prussia in the following terms:

"I desire to put a period to the misfortunes of your family, and to organize, as speedily as possible, the Prussian monarchy. I desire peace with Russia, and, provided that the cabinet of St. Petersburg has no designs upon the Turkish empire, I see no difficulty in obtaining it. I have no hesitation in sending a minister to Memil to take part in a congress of France, England, Sweden, Russia, Prussia and Turkey. But as such a congress may last many years, which would not suit the present condition of Prussia, your majesty will, I am persuaded, be of the opinion that I have taken the simplest method, and one which is most likely to secure the prosperity of your subjects. At all events I entreat your majesty to believe in my sincere desire to reëstablish amicable relations with so friendly a power as Prussia, and that I wish to do the same with Russia and England."

These advances were haughtily rejected by both Prussia

and Russia; and Napoleon returned to the Vistula to wait until the opening of spring, when the question was again to be referred to the arbitrament of battle. Both parties made vigorous preparations for the strife. Alexander succeeded in gathering around him one hundred and forty thousand soldiers. But Napoleon had assembled one hundred and sixty thousand whom he could rapidly concentrate upon any point between the Vistula and the Niemen.

In June the storm of war commenced with an assault by the allies. Field after field was red with blood as the hosts of France drove their vanquished foes before them. On the 10th of June, Alexander, with Frederic William riding by his side, had concentrated ninety thousand men upon the plains of Friedland, on the banks of the Aller. Here the Russians were compelled to make a final stand and await a decisive conflict. As Napoleon rode upon a height and surveyed his foes, caught in an elbow of the river, he said energetically, "We have not a moment to lose. One does not twice catch an enemy in such a trap." He immediately communicated to his aids his plan of attack. Grasping the arm of Ney, he pointed to the dense masses of the Russians clustered before the town of Friedland, and said,

"Yonder is the goal. March to it without looking about you. Break into that thick mass whatever it costs. Enter Friedland; take the bridges and give yourself no concern about what may happen on your right, your left or your rear. The army and I shall be there to attend to that."

The whole French line now simultaneously advanced. It was one of the most sublime and awful of the spectacles of war. For a few hours there was the gleam and the roar of war's most terrific tempest and the Russian army was destroyed. A frightful spectacle of ruin was exhibited. The shattered bands rushed in dismay into the stream, where thousands were swept away by the current, while a storm of bullets from the French batteries swept the river, and the water ran red with blood. It was in vain for Alexander to make any further assaults. In ten days Napoleon had taken one hundred and twenty pieces of cannon, and had killed, wounded or taken prisoners, sixty thousand Russians.

Alexander now implored peace. It was all that Napoleon desired. The Niemen alone now separated the victorious French and the routed Russians. A raft was moored in the middle of the stream upon which a tent was erected with magnificent decorations, and here the two young emperors met to arrange the terms of peace. Alexander, like Francis of Austria, endeavored to throw the blame of the war upon England. Almost his first words to Napoleon were,

"I hate the English as much as you do. I am ready to second you in all your enterprises against them."

"In that case," Napoleon replied, "every thing will be easily arranged and peace is already made."

The interview lasted two hours, and Alexander was fascinated by the genius of Napoleon. "Never," he afterwards said, "did I love any man as I loved that man." Alexander was then but thirty years of age, and apparently he became inspired with an enthusiastic admiration of Napoleon which had never been surpassed. At the close of the interview, he crossed to the French side of the river, and took up his residence with Napoleon at Tilsit. Every day they rode side by side, dined together, and passed almost every hour in confiding conversation. It was Napoleon's great object to withdraw Alexander from the English alliance. In these long interviews the fate of Turkey was a continual topic of conversation. Alexander was ready to make almost any concession if Napoleon would consent that Russia should take Constantinople. But Napoleon was irreconcilably opposed to this. It was investing Russia with too formidable power. He was willing that the emperor should take the provinces on the Danube, but could not consent that he should pass the Balkan and annex the proud city of Constantine to his realms.

One day when the two emperors were closeted together with the map of Europe spread out before them, Napoleon placed his finger upon Constantinople, and was overheard by Meneval to say, with great earnestness, "Constantinople! never! It is the empire of the world."

"All the Emperor Alexander's thoughts," said Napoleon at St. Helena, "are directed to the conquest of Turkey. We have had many discussions about it. At first I was pleased with his proposals, because I thought it would enlighten the world to drive these brutes out of Egypt. But when I reflected upon its consequences and saw what a tremendous weight of power it would give to Russia, on account of the number of Greeks in the Turkish dominions who would naturally join the Russians, I refused to consent to it, especially as Alexander wanted to get Constantinople, which I would not allow, as it would destroy the equilibrium of power in Europe."

For three weeks the emperors remained together at Tilsit, and then they separated devoted friends. Turkey had for some time been disposed to regard France as its protector against the encroachments of Russia, and was disposed to enter into friendly alliance. By the treaty of Tilsit, Russia consented to make peace with Turkey, and also to exert all her influence to promote peace between France and England. The efforts of Alexander not being successful in this respect, he broke off his connection with Great Britain, and became still more intimately allied with France. The British embassador, Lord Gower, was informed that his presence was no longer desired at St. Petersburg. The second bombardment of Copenhagen, and the seizure of the Danish fleet gave occasion for Alexander to declare war against England. The war, however, which ensued between the two countries, amounted chiefly to a cessation of trade. England, protected by her fleet, was invulnerable; and Napoleon and Alexander both agreed that the only possible way of compelling England to assent to peace, was to shut her out from commerce with the rest of Europe. This was the origin of the famous continental system, by which it was endeavored to force the belligerent islanders to peace by cutting off their trade.

Alexander called upon Sweden to unite in this confederacy against England. The Swedes declined. Alexander overran the whole of Finland with his troops, and in 1809 it was permanently annexed to the Russian empire. Just before this event, in September, 1808, Napoleon and Alexander held another interview at Erfurth. The loss of British commerce was almost as great a calamity to Russia as to England, and the Russian people murmured loudly. England wished to arrest the progress of democratic ideas in France by restoring the rejected Bourbons to the throne. In these views the nobles of Russia sympathized cordially, and they were exasperated that Alexander should allow personal friendship for Napoleon to interfere with the commerce of their country, and with the maintenance of aristocratic privilege in Europe. The Russian nobles had nothing to gain by the establishment of free institutions in France, and the discontent with the measures of Alexander became so general and so loudly expressed that he began to waver.

The only hope of Napoleon was in combining Europe in a league which should starve England into peace. He watched the vacillating spirit of Alexander with alarm, and arranged the interview at Erfurth that he might strengthen him in his friendly purposes. Alexander was by the most solemn pledges bound to be faithful to this alliance. He had attacked Napoleon and had been conquered; and the southern provinces of Russia were at the mercy of the conqueror. Under these circumstances the treaty of Tilsit was made, in which Alexander, in consideration of benefits received, agreed to coöperate with Napoleon in that continental system which seemed vital to the safety of France. Napoleon was well aware of the immense pressure which was brought to bear upon the mind of the Russian tzar to induce him to swerve from his agreement. Hence the conference at Erfurth. During the deliberations at Erfurth it appears that Alexander consented that Napoleon should place the crown of Spain upon the brow of his brother Joseph, in consideration of Napoleon consenting that Russia should take possession of the two Turkish provinces of Moldavia and Wallachia. And again the most strenuous efforts were made by the united emperors to induce inflexible England to sheathe the sword. All the nations on the continent were at peace. England alone was prosecuting the war. But the English aristocracy felt that they could not remain firm in their possessions while principles of democratic freedom were dominant in France. The fundamental principle of the government of the empire was honor to *merit*, not to *birth*. The two emperors wrote as follows to the King of England, imploring peace:

"Sire—The present situation of Europe has brought us together at Erfurth. Our first wish is to fulfill the desire of all nations, and, by a speedy pacification with your majesty to take the most effectual means of relieving the sufferings of Europe. The long and bloody war which has convulsed the continent is at an end, and can not be renewed. Many changes have taken place in Europe; many governments have been destroyed. The cause is to be found in the uneasiness and the sufferings occasioned by the stagnation of maritime commerce. Greater changes still may take place, and all will be unfavorable to the politics of England. Peace, therefore, is at the same time the common cause of the nations of the continent and of Great Britain. We unite in requesting your majesty to lend an ear to the voice of humanity, to suppress that of the passions, to reconcile contending interests, and to secure the welfare of Europe and of the generations over which Providence has placed us."

The only notice taken of this letter was in a communication to the ministers of France and Russia, in which it was stated that the "English ministers could not reply to the two sovereigns, since one of them was not recognized by England." A new coalition was soon formed, and Austria commenced another march upon France, which led to the campaign of Wagram, in which Austria was humbled as never before. Austria was now compelled, in conjunction with France and Russia, and most of the other European powers, to take part in the continental blockade. Alexander, shackled by his nobles, had not been able to render Napoleon the assistance he had promised in this war. Loud murmurs and threats of assassination were rising around him, and instead of rigorously enforcing the exclusion of English goods, he allowed them to be smuggled into the country. This was ruinous to Napoleon's system. Remonstrances and recriminations ensued. At length English goods were freely introduced, provided they entered under American colors. Napoleon, to put a stop to this smuggling, which the local authorities pretended they could not prevent, seized several of the principal ports of northern Germany, and incorporated the possessions of the Duke of Oldenburg, a near relative of Alexander, with France.*

These measures increased the alienation between France

* Colonel Napier, in his "Peninsular War," very justly observes, "The real principle of Napoleon's government, and secret of his popularity, made him the people's monarch, not the sovereign of the aristocracy. Hence Mr. Pitt called him 'the child and the champion of democracy,' a truth as evident as that Mr. Pitt and his successors 'were the children and the champions of aristocracy.' Hence also the *privileged* classes of Europe consistently turned their natural and implacable hatred of the French Revolution to his person; for they saw that in him innovation had found a protector; that he alone, having given preëminence to a system so hateful to them, was really what he called himself, *The State.* The treaty of Tilsit, therefore, although it placed Napoleon in a commanding situation with regard to the potentates of Europe, unmasked the real nature of the war, and brought him and England, the respective champions of Equality and Privilege, into more direct contact. Peace could not be between them while they were both strong, and all that the French emperor had hitherto gained only enabled him to choose his future field of battle."

and Austria. In the mean time Alexander was waging war with Turkey, and was pushing his conquests rapidly on towards the city of Constantine. These encroachments France contemplated with alarm. By the peace of Bucharest, signed May 28th, 1812, the whole of Bessarabia was annexed to Russia, and the limits of the empire were extended from the Dnieper to the Pruth. The Russian nobles were all eager to join the European aristocracy in a war against democratic France, and it was now evident that soon a collision must take place between the cabinet of the Tuileries and that of St. Petersburg. It was almost impossible for Alexander to resist the pressure which urged him to open his ports to the English. The closing of those ports was Napoleon's only hope of compelling England to sheathe the sword. Hence war became a fatality.

Russia, in anticipation of a rupture, began to arm, and ordered a levy of four men out of every hundred. In preparation for war she made peace with Persia and Turkey, and entered into an alliance with Sweden. England was highly gratified by this change, and was soon on most friendly terms with the Russian cabinet. A treaty was speedily formed by England, with both Russia and Sweden, by which these latter powers agreed to open their ports for free commercial relations with England, and they entered into an alliance offensive and defensive with that power. As England was still in arms against France, this was virtually a declaration of war. This violation also of the treaty of Tilsit was the utter ruin of Napoleon's plans. To compel Russia to return to the continental system, Napoleon prepared for that Russian campaign which is one of the most awful tragedies of history. The world is so full of the narratives of that sublime drama, that the story need not be repeated here. It is just to say that Napoleon exhausted all the arts of diplomacy to accomplish his purpose before he put his armies in motion.

The Emperor Alexander followed the French in their retreat from Moscow, and with all the powers of Europe allied, crossed the Rhine, and on the 31st of March, 1814, at the head of an allied army of half a million of men entered Paris a conqueror. His sympathies were warmly enlisted in behalf of his fallen friend Napoleon. In the negotiations which ensued he exerted himself strongly in his favor. It was only by assuming the most energetic attitude against England, Austria and Prussia, that he succeeded in obtaining for Napoleon the sovereignty of Elba. Alexander was very magnanimous, but his voice was lost in the clamor of the sovereigns who surrounded him.

Napoleon retired to Elba. The Bourbons reascended the throne of France. Alexander, with the King of Prussia, visited England, where he was received with great distinction. Returning to Russia he devoted himself to the welfare of his kingdom in the vain attempt to reconcile popular progress with political despotism. Alexander was evidently saddened by the fate of Napoleon, and on his return to St. Petersburg persistently refused to accept the public rejoicings which were proffered him.

Napoleon escaped from Elba, where the influence of Alexander had placed him, and again was on the throne of France. Alexander hesitated whether again to march aginst him. He yielded, however, to the solicitations of his associated sovereigns, and at the head of an army of one hundred and sixty thousand men, was again on the march for Paris. He was apprehensive that the dismemberment of the French empire, which was contemplated, might render Austria and Prussia too powerful for the repose of Europe. Upon the second capitulation of Paris, after the battle of Waterloo, Alexander insisted that France should at least retain the limits she had in 1790. Upon this basis the new treaty was concluded.

It is an interesting fact that the celebrated Juliana, Baroness of Krudoner, was mainly instrumental in the organization of the Holy Alliance, which was at this time formed.

She had wealth, wit and beauty, and had been supremely devoted to pleasure, shining among the most brilliant ornaments of St. Petersburg, Paris and Vienna. Weary of a life of gayety, she seems to have turned to religion and to have become a devout and earnest Christian. Her enthusiasm was roused with the idea of putting a stop to war, and of truly Christianizing Europe. She hastened to Paris, when the allied sovereigns were there, and obtained an interview with the Russian tzar. Alexander was by nature of a devotional turn of mind, and the terrific scenes through which he had passed had given him a meditative and pensive spirit. He listened eagerly to the suggestions of Madame Krudoner, and, aided by her, sketched as follows the plan of the Holy Alliance:

"In the name of the sacred and invisible Trinity, their majesties, the Emperor of Austria, the King of Prussia, and the Emperor of Russia, considering the momentous events which have occured in Europe during the last three years, and especially the blessing which it has pleased Providence to confer on those States which trust in him, and being fully convinced of the necessity of taking, as the rule of life, in all their affairs, the sublime truths which the holy religion of our Saviour teaches us,

"Declare solemnly that the present act has no other object than to proclaim to the whole world their unalterable resolution to take, as their only guide, both in the internal administration of their respective States, and in their political relations with other governments, those principles of justice, Christian charity and peace, which, far from being exclusively applicable to private individuals, should have an immediate influence upon the counsels of princes, and should regulate all their measures, as being the only means of consolidating human institutions and remedying their imperfections. Consequently their majesties have agreed upon the following resolutions:

"Article I. In conformity with the declaration of the

holy Scriptures, which command all men to regard each other as brothers, the three contracting monarchs will remain united to each other by the ties of sincere and indissoluble fraternity Regarding themselves as private individuals, they will render each other, at all times, and in all places, aid and assistance; and considering themselves, in respect to their people and armies, as fathers of families, they will rule in the same spirit of fraternity, that religion, peace and justice may be protected.

"Article II. Also the only obligation of rigor, whether it be between these governments or their subjects, shall consist in rendering each other all sorts of service, and of testifying towards each other that unalterable benevolence and that mutual affection which shall lead them to guard one another as members of one and the same Christian family. The three allied princes, regarding themselves as delegated by Providence to govern three branches of this family, Austria, Prussia and Russia, recognize that the Christian world, of which they and their people compose a part, can have, in reality, no other sovereign than him to whom belongs all power, because in him alone are the treasures of love, of science and of infinite wisdom—that is to say, God, our divine Saviour, the word of the Most High, the word of life. Consequently their majesties recommend to their people, with the greatest solicitude, and as the only means of enjoying that peace which springs from a good conscience, and which alone is durable, to strengthen themselves daily more and more in the exercise of those duties taught to the human family by the divine Saviour.

"Article III. All the powers who believe that they ought solemnly to profess the principles which have dictated this act, and who recognize how important it is for the welfare of nations, too long agitated, that these truths should hereafter exercise over the destinies of the human family that influence which they ought to exert, shall be received, with the same ardor and affection, into this Holy Alliance. Done at Paris, in the year of our Lord, 1814, September 25, and signed, Francis, Frederic William and Alexander."

Such was the bond of the Holy Alliance. It was drawn up in the hand-writing of Alexander. Subsequently it was signed by the Kings of England and France, and by nearly all the sovereigns of Europe. The pope declined signing, as it was not consistent with his dignity to be a member of a confederacy of which he was not the head. These principles, apparently so true and salutary, became vitiated by the underlying of principles which gave them all their force. The alliance became in reality a conspiracy of the crowned heads of Europe against the liberties of their subjects; and thus despotism sat enthroned. The liberal spirit, which was then breaking out all over the continent of Europe, was thus, for a time, effectually crushed. It can hardly be supposed that Alexander intended the Holy Alliance to accomplish the work which it subsequently performed.

Alexander, on his return to Russia, devoted himself energetically to the government of his vast realms, taking long and fatiguing journeys, and manifesting much interest in the elevation of the serfs to freedom. The latter years of Alexander were clouded with sorrow. He was not on good terms with his wife, and the death of all his children rendered his home desolate. His health failed and some deep grief seemed ever to prey upon his spirits. It is supposed that the melancholy fate of Napoleon, dying in a hut at St. Helena, and of whom he had said, "Never did I love a man as I have loved that man!" weighed heavily upon him. He was constantly haunted by fears of a rising of the oppressed people, and to repel that danger was becoming continually more despotic.

In the year 1825, Alexander, sick, anxious and melancholy, took a long journey, with his wife, to Tanganroy, a small town upon the Sea of Azof, fifteen hundred miles from St. Petersburg. He had for some time looked forward with dread to his appearance before the bar of God. A sense of sin oppressed him, and he had long sought relief with prayers and tears. His despondency led him to many forebodings that he should not live to return from this journey.

The morning before he left St. Petersburg, at the early hour of four o'clock, he visited the monastery where the remains of his children were entombed, and at their grave spent some time in prayer. Wrapped in his cloak, in unbroken silence he listened to the "chant for the dead," and then commenced his journey. No peasant whom he met on the way had a heavier heart than throbbed in the bosom of the sovereign. For hours he sat in the carriage with the empress, with whom in grief he had become reconciled, and hardly a word was uttered. At length they arrived upon the shores of Azof. The emperor took a rapid tour through these provinces, visiting among other places Sevastopol, which he had long been fortifying. He was so much struck with the magnificence of this place that he remarked, "Should I ever resign the reins of government, I should wish to retire to this city, that I might here terminate my career!"

Returning to his wife at Tanganroy, he was seized with a fever, probably caused by care and toil. The disease was so rapid in its progress as to lead many to suppose that he was falling a victim to poison. On the approach of death, perceiving that he was dying, he requested that he might be raised upon his pillow, that he might once more behold the light of the sun. He simply remarked, "How beautiful is the day!" and fell back upon his pillow to die. The empress was weeping by his side. He took her hand, pressed it tenderly as if bidding her an eternal adieu, and died. It was the 1st of December, 1825.

The empress Elizabeth in this sad hour forgot all her wrongs; for the emperor had by no means been to her a faithful husband. She wrote to her friends, "Our angel is in heaven; and, as for me, I still linger on earth: but I hope soon to be reunited with him in the skies!"

The cry immediately resounded through Europe that Alexander had fallen by poison. As the emperor had no children living, the crown, by hereditary descent, passed to his next brother, Constantine. Alexander had long been conscious that Constantine did not possess suitable qualifications to govern, and Constantine himself, frivolous and pleasure-loving, was not at all emulous of imperial power. When a mere boy he had been married to a German princess, but fifteen years of age. They endured each other through the angry strifes of four years and then separated. Constantine became enamored of the daughter of a Polish count, and sought a divorce. Alexander consented to this arrangement on condition that Constantine would resign all right to the throne. The terms were gladly accepted, and Constantine signed the following renunciation, which was kept secret until the occasion should arise for it to be promulated.

"Conscious that I do not possess the genius, the talents or the strength necessary to fit me for the dignity of a sovereign, to which my birth would give me a right, I entreat your imperial majesty to transfer that right to him to whom it belongs after me, and thus assure for ever the stability of the empire. As to myself, I shall add, by this renunciation, a new guarantee and a new force to the engagements which I spontaneously and solemnly contracted on the occasion of my divorce from my first wife. All the circumstances in which I find myself strengthen my determination to adhere to this resolution, which will prove to the empire and to the whole world the sincerity of my sentiments."

Another document had also been prepared which declared Alexander's second brother, Nicholas, heir to the empire. Napoleon, at St. Helena, speaking of the King of Prussia and of Alexander, said,

"Frederic William, as a private character, is an honorable,

good and worthy man, but in his political capacity he is naturally disposed to yield to necessity. He is always commanded by whoever has power on his side, and is about to strike.

"As to the Emperor of Russia, he is a man infinitely superior to Frederic William or Francis. He possesses wit, grace, information, and is fascinating, but he is not to be trusted. He is devoid of candor, a true *Greek of the Lower Empire.* At the same time he is not without ideology, real or assumed; after all it may only be a smattering, derived from his education and his preceptor. Would you believe what I had to discuss with him? He maintained that *inheritance* was an abuse in monarchy, and I had to spend more than an hour, and employ all my eloquence and logic in proving to him that this right constituted the peace and happiness of the people. It may be too that he was mystifying, for he is cunning, false, adroit and hypocritical. I repeat it, he is a Greek of the Lower Empire.

"If I die here he will be my real heir in Europe. I alone was able to stop him with his deluge of Tartars. The crisis is great, and will have lasting effects upon the continent of Europe, especially upon Constantinople. He was solicitous with me for the possession of it. I have had much coaxing upon this subject, but I constantly turned a deaf ear to it. The Turkish empire, shattered as it appeared, would constantly have remained a point of separation between us. It was the marsh which prevented my right from being turned.

"As to Greece it is another matter. Greece awaits a liberator. There will be a brilliant crown of glory. He will inscribe his name for ever with those of Homer, Plato and Epaminondas. I perhaps was not far from it. When, during my campaign in Italy, I arrived on the shores of the Adriatic, I wrote to the Directory, that I had before my eyes the kingdom of Alexander. Still later I entered into engagements with Ali Pacha; and when Corfu was taken, they must have found there ammunition, and a complete equipment for an army of forty or fifty thousand men. I had caused maps to be made of Macedonia, Servia, Albania. Greece, the Peloponnesus at least, must be the lot of the European power which shall possess Egypt. It should be ours; and then an independent kingdom in the north, Constantinople, with its provinces, to serve as a barrier to the power of Russia, as they have pretended to do with respect to France, by creating the kingdom of Belgium."

CHAPTER XXXI.

NICHOLAS.

FROM 1825 TO 1855.

ABDICATION OF CONSTANTINE.—ACCESSION OF NICHOLAS.—INSURRECTION QUELLED.—NICHOLAS AND THE CONSPIRATOR.—ANECDOTE.—THE PALACE OF PETERHOFF.—THE WINTER PALACE.—PRESENTATION AT COURT.—MAGNITUDE OF RUSSIA.—DESCRIPTION OF THE HELLESPONT AND THE DARDANELLES.—THE TURKISH INVASION.—AIMS OF RUSSIA.—VIEWS OF ENGLAND AND FRANCE.—WARS OF NICHOLAS.—THE POLISH INSURRECTION.—WAR OF THE CRIMEA.—JEALOUSIES OF THE LEADING NATIONS.—ENCROACHMENTS.—DEATH OF NICHOLAS.—ACCESSION OF ALEXANDER II.

CONSTANTINE was at Warsaw when the news arrived of the death of his brother. The mother of Alexander was still living. Even Nicholas either affected not to know, or did not know, that his wild, eccentric brother Constantine had renounced the throne in his favor, for he immediately, upon the news of the death of Alexander, summoned the imperial guard into the palace chapel, and, with them, took the oath of allegiance to his older brother, the Grand Duke Constantine. On his return, his mother, who is represented as being quite frantic in her inconsolable grief, exclaimed,

"Nicholas, what have you done? Do you not know that there is a document which names you presumptive heir?"

"If there be one," Nicholas replied, "I do not know it, neither does any one else. But this we all know, that our legitimate sovereign, after Alexander, is my brother Constantine. We have therefore done our duty, come what may."

Nicholas was persistent in his resolution not to take the crown until he received from his brother a confirmation of his renunciation of the throne. Three weeks elapsed before this intelligence arrived. It then came full and decisive, and

Nicholas no longer hesitated, though the interval had revealed to him that fearful dangers were impending. He was informed by several of his generals that a wide-spread conspiracy extended throughout the army in favor of a constitutional government. Many of the officers and soldiers, in their wars against Napoleon and in their invasion of France, had become acquainted with those principles of popular liberty which were diffused throughout France, and which it was the object of the allies to crush. Upon their return to Russia, the utter despotism of the tzar seemed more than ever hateful to them. Several conspiracies had been organized for his assassination, and now the plan was formed to assassinate the whole imperial family, and introduce a republic.

Nicholas was seriously alarmed by the danger which threatened, though he was fully conscious that his only safety was to be found in courage and energy. He accordingly made preparation for the administration of the oath of allgiance to the army. "I shall soon," said he, "be an emperor or a corpse." On the morning when the oath was to be administered, and when it was evident that the insurrection would break out, he said, "If I am emperor only for an hour, I will show that I am worthy of it."

The morning of the 25th of December dawned upon St. Petersburg in tumult. Bands of soldiers were parading the streets shouting, "Constantine for ever." The insurrection had assumed the most formidable aspect, for many who were not republicans, were led to believe that Nicholas was attempting to usurp the crown which, of right, belonged to Constantine. Two generals, who had attempted to quell the movement, had already been massacred, and vast mobs, led by the well-armed regiments, were, from all quarters of the city, pressing toward the imperial palace. Nicholas, who was then twenty-nine years of age, met the crisis with the energy of Napoleon. Placing himself at the head of a small body of faithful guards, he rode to encounter his rebellious subjects in the stern strife of war. Instead of meeting a mob of unarmed men, he found marshaled against him the best disciplined troops in his army.

A terrible conflict ensued, in which blood flowed in torrents. The emperor, heading his own troops, exposed himself, equally with them, to all perils. As soon as it was evident that he would be compelled to fire upon his subjects, he sent word to his wife of the cruel necessity. She was in the palace, surrounded by the most distinguished ladies of the court, tremblingly awaiting the issue. When the thunder of the artillery commenced in the streets, she threw herself upon her knees, and, weeping bitterly, continued in prayer until she was informed that the revolt was crushed, and that her husband was safe. The number slain is not known. That it might be concealed, the bodies were immediately thrust through holes cut in the ice of the Neva.

Though the friends of liberty can not but regret that free principles have obtained so slender a foothold in Russia, it is manifest that this attempt could lead only to anarchy. The masses of the nobles were thoroughly corrupt, and the masses of the people ignorant and debased. The Russian word for constitution, *constitutsya*, has a feminine termination. Many of the people, it is reported, who were shouting, "Constantine and the constitution for ever," thought that the constitution was the wife of Constantine. It must be admitted that such ignorance presents but a poor qualification for republican institutions.

At the close of this bloody day, one of the leading conspirators, a general of high position in the army was led a captive into the presence of Nicholas. The heroic republican met, without quailing, the proud eye of his sovereign.

"Your father," said Nicholas sternly, "was a faithful servant, but he has left behind him a degenerate son. For such an enterprise as yours large resources were requisite. On what did you rely?"

"Sire," replied the prisoner, "matters of this kind can not be spoken of before witnesses."

Nicholas led the conspirator into a private apartment, and for a long time conversed with him alone. Here the tzar had opened before him, in the clearest manner, the intolerable burdens of the people, the oppression of the nobles, the impotency of the laws, the venality of the judges, the corruption which pervaded all departments of the government, legislative, executive and judiciary. The noble conspirator, whose mind was illumined with those views of human rights which, from the French Revolution, were radiating throughout Europe, revealed all the corruptions of the State in the earnest and honest language of a man who was making a dying declaration. Nicholas listened to truths such as seldom reach the ears of a monarch; and these truths probably produced a powerful impression upon him in his subsequent career.

Many of the conspirators, in accordance with the barbaric code of Russia, were punished with awful severity. Some were whipped to death. Some were mutilated and exiled to Siberia, and many perished on the scaffold. Fifteen officers of high rank were placed together beneath the gibbet, with ropes around their necks. As the drop fell, the rope of one broke, and he fell to the ground. Bruised and half stunned he rose upon his knees, and looking sadly around exclaimed,

"Truly nothing ever succeeds with me, not even death."

Another rope was procured, and this unhappy man, whose words indicated an entire life of disappointment and woe, was launched into the world of spirits.

We have before spoken of the palace of Peterhoff, a few miles from St. Petersburg, on the southern shores of the bay of Cronstadt. It is now the St. Cloud of Russia, the favorite rural retreat of the Russian tzars. This palace, which has been the slow growth of ages, consists of a pile of buildings of every conceivable order of architecture. It is furnished with all the appliances of luxury which Europe or Asia can produce. The pleasure grounds, in their artistic embellishments, are perhaps unsurpassed by any others in the world. Fountains, groves, lawns, lakes, cascades and statues, bewilder and delight the spectator.

There is an annual fête on this ground in July, which assembles all the élite of Russian society. The spacious gardens are by night illuminated with almost inconceivable splendor. The whole forest blazes with innumerable torches, and every leaf, twig and drop of spray twinkles with colored lights. Here is that famous artificial tree which has so often been described. It is so constructed with root, trunk and branch, leaf and bud as to deceive the most practiced eye. Its shade, with an inviting seat placed beneath it, lures the loiterer, through these Eden groves, to approach and rest. The moment he takes his seat he presses a spring which converts the tree into a shower bath, and from every twig jets of water in a cloud of spray, envelops the astonished stranger.

The Winter Palace at St. Petersburg is also a palace of unsurpassed splendor. More than a thousand persons habitually dwell beneath the imperial roof. No saloons more sumptuous in architecture and adornment are probably to be found in the world; neither are the exactions of court etiquette anywhere more punctiliously observed. In entering this palace a massive gateway ushers one into a hall of magnificent dimensions, so embellished with shrubs and flowers, multiplied by mirrors, that the guest is deceived into the belief that he is sauntering through the walks of a spacious flower garden. A flight of marble stairs conducts to an apartment of princely splendor, called the hall of the Marshals. Passing through this hall, one enters a suite of rooms, apparently interminable, all of extraordinary grandeur and sumptuousness, which are merely antechambers to the grand audience saloon.

In this grand saloon the emperor holds his court. Presentation day exhibits one of the most brilliant spectacles of earthly splendor and luxury. When the hour of presentation arrives some massive folding doors are thrown open, revealing the imperial chapel thronged with those who are to take part in the ceremony. First, there enters from the chapel a crowd of army officers, often a thousand in number, in their most brilliant uniform, the vanguard of the escort of the tzar. They quietly pass through the vast apartment and disappear amidst the recesses of the palace. Still the almost interminable throng, glittering in gala dresses, press on. At length the grand master of ceremonies makes his appearance announcing the approach of the emperor and empress.

The royal pair immediately enter, and bow to the representatives of other courts who may be present, and receive those who are honored with a presentation. No one is permitted to speak to their majesties but in reply to questions which they may ask. The Emperor Nicholas was very stately and reserved in his manners, and said but little. The empress, more affable, would present her ungloved hand to her guest, who would receive it and press it with fervor to his lips.

The Emperor Nicholas, during his reign, was supposed to have some ninety millions of the human family subject to his sway. With a standing army of a million of men, two hundred thousand of whom were cavalry, he possessed power unequaled by that of any other single kingdom on the globe. In the recent struggle at Sevastopol all the energies of England, France and Turkey were expended against Russia alone, and yet it was long doubtful whose banners would be victorious.

It is estimated that the territory of Russia now comprises one seventh of the habitable globe, extending from the Baltic Sea across the whole breadth of Europe and of Asia to Behring's Straits, and from the eternal ices of the north pole, almost down to the sunny shores of the Mediterranean. As the previous narrative has shown, for many ages this gigantic power has been steadily advancing towards Constantinople. The Russian flag now girdles the Euxine Sea, and notwithstanding the recent check at Sevastopol, Russia is pressing on with resistless strides towards the possession of the Hellespont. A brief sketch of the geography of those realms will give one a more vivid idea of the nature of that conflict, which now, under the title of the eastern or Turkish question, engrosses the attention of Europe.

The strait which connects the Mediterranean Sea with the Sea of Marmora was originally called the Hellespont, from the fabulous legend of a young lady, named Helle, falling into it in attempting to escape from a cruel mother-in-law. At the mouth of the Hellespont there are four strong Turkish forts, two on the European and two on the Asiatic side. These forts are called the Dardanelles, and hence, from them, the straits frequently receive the name of the Dardanelles. This strait is thirty-three miles long, occasionally expanding in width to five miles, and again being crowded by the approaching hills into a narrow channel less than half a mile in breadth. Through the serpentine navigation of these straits, with fortresses frowning upon every headland, one ascends to the Sea of Marmora, a vast inland body of water one hundred and eighty miles in length and sixty miles in breadth. Crossing this sea to the northern shore, you enter the beautiful straits of the Bosporus. Just at the point where the Bosporus enters the Sea of Marmora, upon the western shore of the straits, sits enthroned upon the hills, in peerless beauty, the imperial city of Constantine with its majestic domes, arrowy minarets and palaces of snow-white marble glittering like a fairy vision beneath the light of an oriental sun.

The straits of the Bosporus, which connect the Sea of Marmora with the Black Sea, are but fifteen miles long and of an average width of but about one fourth of a mile. In natural scenery and artistic embellishments this is probably the most beautiful reach of water upon the globe. It is the uncontradicted testimony of all tourists that the scenery of the Bosporus, in its highly-cultivated shores, its graceful sweep of hills and mountain ranges, in its gorgeous architecture, its atmospheric brilliance and in its vast accumulations of the costumes and customs of all Europe and Asia, presents a scene which can nowhere else be paralleled.

On the Asiatic shore, opposite Constantinople, lies Scutari, a beautiful city embowered in the foliage of the cyprus. An arm of the strait reaches around the northern portion of Constantinople, and furnishes for the city one of the finest harbors in the world. This bay, deep and broad, is called the Golden Horn. Until within a few years, no embassador of Christian powers was allowed to contaminate the Moslem city by taking up his residence in it. The little suburb of Pera, on the opposite side of the Golden Horn, was assigned to these embassadors, and the Turk, on this account, denominated it *The swine's quarter.*

Passing through the Bosporus fifteen miles, there expands before you the Euxine, or Black Sea. This inland ocean, with but one narrow outlet, receives into its bosom the Danube, the Dniester, the Dnieper, the Don and the Cuban. These streams, rolling through unmeasured leagues of Russian territory, open them to the commerce of the world. This brief sketch reveals the infinite importance of the Dardanelles and the Bosporus to Russia. This great empire, "leaning against the north pole," touches the Baltic Sea only far away amidst the ices of the North. St. Petersburg, during a large portion of the year, is blockaded by ice. Ninety millions of people are thus excluded from all the benefits of foreign commerce for a large portion of the year unless they can open a gateway to distant shores through the Bosporus and the Dardanelles.

America, with thousands of miles of Atlantic coast, manifests the greatest uneasiness in having the island of Cuba in the hands of a foreign power, lest, in case of war, her commerce in the Gulf should be embarrassed. But the Dardanelles are, in reality, the only gateway for the commerce of nearly all Russia. All her great navigable rivers, without exception, flow into the Black Sea, and thence through the Bosporus, the Marmora and the Hellespont, into the Mediterranean. And yet Russia, with her ninety millions of population—three times that of the United States—can not send a boat load of corn into the Mediterranean without bowing her flag to all the Turkish forts which frown along her pathway. And in case of war with Turkey her commerce is entirely cut off. Russia is evidently unembarrassed with any very troublesome scruples of conscience in reference to reclaiming those beautiful realms, once the home of the Christian, which the Turk has so ruthlessly and bloodily invaded. In assailing the Turk, the Russian feels that he is fighting for his religion.

The tzar indignantly inquires, "What title deed can the Turk show to the city of Constantine?" None but the dripping cimeter. The annals of war can tell no sadder tale of woe than the rush of the barbaric Turk into Christian Greece. He came, a merciless robber with gory hands, plundering and burning. Fathers and mothers were butchered. Christian maidens, shrieking with terror, were dragged to the Moslem harems. Christian boys were compelled to adopt the Mohammedan faith, and then, crowded into the army, were compelled to fight the Mohammedan battles. For centuries the Christians, thus trampled beneath the heel of oppression, have suffered every conceivable indignity from their cruel oppressors. Earnestly have they appealed to their Christian brethren of Russia for protection.

It is so essential to the advancing civilization of Russia that she should possess a maritime port which may give her access to commerce, that it is not easy for us to withhold our sympathies from her in her endeavor to open a gateway to and from her vast territories through the Dardanelles. When France, England and Turkey combined to batter down Sevastopol and burn the Russian fleet, that Russia might still be barred up in her northern wilds by Turkish forts, there was an instinct in the American heart which caused the sympathies of this country to flow in favor of Russia, notwithstanding all the eloquent pleadings of the French and English press.

The cabinet of St. James regards these encroachments of Russia with great apprehension. The view England takes of the subject may be seen in the following extracts from the *Quarterly Review:*

"The possession of the Dardanelles would give to Russia the means of creating and organizing an almost unlimited marine. It would enable her to prepare in the Black Sea an armament of any extent, without its being possible for any power in Europe to interrupt her proceedings, or even to watch or discover her designs. Our naval officers, of the highest authority, have declared that an effective blockade of the Dardanelles can not be maintained throughout the year. Even supposing we could maintain permanently in those seas a fleet capable of encountering that of Russia, it is obvious that, in the event of a war, it would be in the power of Russia to throw the whole weight of her disposable forces on any point in the Mediterranean, without any probability of our being able to prevent it, and that the power of thus issuing forth with an overwhelming force, at any moment, would enable her to command the Mediteranean Sea for a limited time whenever it might please her so to do. Her whole southern empire would be defended by a single impregnable fortress. The road to India would then be open to her, with all Asia at her back. The finest materials in the world for an army destined to serve in the East would be at her disposal. Our power to overawe her in Europe would be gone, and by even a demonstration against India she could augment our national expenditure by many millions annually, and render the government of that country difficult beyond all calculation."

Such is the view which England takes of this subject. The

statesmen of England and France contemplate with alarm the rapid growth of Russia, and yet know not how to arrest its progress. They see the Russian tzars, year after year, annexing new nations to their territory, and about all they can do is to remonstrate. All agree that the only effectual measure to check the growth of Russia is to prevent her from taking possession of the Dardanelles. To accomplish this, England and France are endeavoring to bind together the crumbling and discordant elements of Ottoman power, to infuse the vigor of youth into the veins of an old man dying of debauchery and age. But the crescent is inevitably on the wane. The doom of the Moslem is sealed.

There are four great nations now advancing with marvelous strides in the appropriation of this globe to themselves. Russia has already taken possession of one seventh of the world's territory, and she needs now but to annex Turkey in Europe and Turkey in Asia to complete her share. France is spreading her influence throughout southern Europe, and, with a firm grasp, is seizing the provinces of northern Africa. England claims half of the islands of the ocean, boasts that the sun never sets upon her dominions, and *has* professed that the ocean is her private property. Her armies, invincible, sweep the remotest plains of Asia, removing and setting down landmarks at her pleasure. Her advances are so gigantic that the annexation of a few thousand leagues, at any time, hardly attracts attention. America is looking with a wistful eye upon the whole of North and South America, the islands of the Caribbean Sea and the groups of the Pacific.*

* The jealousy of the leading nations in regard to their mutual encroachments is amusingly illustrated in an interview between Senator Douglas and Sir Henry Bulwer in reference to the Clayton-Bulwer treaty. An article was inserted in this treaty by the English government, binding both England and America not to colonize, annex or exercise any dominion over any portion of Central America. Sir Henry argued that the pledge was fair and just since it was reciprocal, England asking no more than she was ready herself to grant.

"To test your principle," said Senator Douglas, "I would propose an

Immediately after the accession of Nicholas to the throne, war broke out with Persia. It was of short duration. The Persian monarch, utterly discomfited, was compelled to cede to Russia large provinces in the Caucasus, and extensive territory on the south-western shore of the Caspian, and to pay all the expenses of the war. Immediately after this, on the 7th of May, 1828, war was declared against Turkey. The Russian army, one hundred and sixty thousand strong, flushed with victory, crossed the Pruth and took possession of the entire left bank of the Danube, for some hundreds of miles from its mouth, with all its fertile fields and populous cities. They then crossed the river, and overran the whole region of Bulgaria. The storms of winter, however, compelled a retreat, which the Russians effected after most terrific conflicts, and, re-crossing the Danube, they established themselves in winter quarters on its left banks, having lost in the campaign one half of their number. The Turks took possession of the right bank, and remained, during the winter, in face of their foes. In the spring of 1829 the Russians, having obtained a reinforcement of seventy thousand men, opened the campaign anew upon the land, while a fleet of forty-two vessels, carrying fifteen hundred guns, coöperated on the Black Sea.

Through fields of blood, where the Turks, with the energies of despair, contested every step, the victorious Russians advanced nearly three hundred miles. They entered the defiles of the Balkan mountains, and forced the passage. Concentrating their strength at the base of the southern

amendment of simply two words. Let the article read, 'Neither England nor the United States will ever colonize any part of Central America *or Asia*.'"

The British minister exclaimed, in surprise, "But you have no colonies in Asia."

"True," replied the United States Senator, "neither have you any colonies in Central America."

"But," rejoined Sir Henry, "you can never establish your government there, in Asia."

"No," Mr. Douglas replied, "neither do we intend that you shall plant your government here, in Central America."

declivities, the path was open before them to Constantinople. Pushing rapidly forward, they entered Adrianople in triumph. They were now within one hundred and fifty miles of Constantinople. The consternation in the Turkish capital was indescribable, and all Europe was looking for the issue with wonder. The advance guard of the Russian army was already within eighty miles of the imperial city when the sultan, Mahmoud IV., implored peace, and assented to the terms his victor extorted.

By this treaty, called the treaty of Adrianople, Turkey paid Russia twenty-nine millions of dollars to defray the expenses of the war, opened the Dardanelles to the free navigation of all Russian merchant ships, and engaged not to maintain any fortified posts on the north of the Danube.

In July, 1830, the Poles rose in a general insurrection, endeavoring to shake off the Russian yoke. With hurricane fury the armies of Nicholas swept the ill-fated territory, and Poland fell to rise no more. The vengeance of the tzar was awful. For some time the roads to Siberia were thronged with noble men driven into exile.

In the year 1833, Constantinople was imperiled by the armies of Mohammed Ali, the energetic pacha of Egypt. The sultan implored aid of Russia. Nicholas sent an army and a fleet, and drove Mohammed Ali back to Egypt. As compensation for this essential aid, the sultan entered into a treaty, by which both powers were bound to afford succor in case either was attacked, and Turkey also agreed to close the Dardanelles against any power with whom Russia might be at war.

The revolution in Paris of 1848, which expelled Louis Philippe from the throne, excited the hopes of the republican party all over Europe. The Hungarians rose, under Kossuth, in the endeavor to shake off the Austrian yoke. Francis Joseph appealed to Russia for aid. Nicholas dispatched two hundred thousand men to crush the Hungarians, and they were crushed. Nicholas asked no remuneration for these services. He felt amply repaid in having arrested the progress of constitutional liberty in Europe.

Various circumstances, each one trivial in itself, conspired to lead Nicholas in 1853 to make a new and menacing demonstration of power in the direction of Constantinople. An army was marshaled on the frontiers, and a large fleet assembled at Odessa and Sevastopol. England and France were alarmed, and a French fleet of observation entered the waters of Greece, while the English fleet at Malta strengthened itself for any emergence. The prominent question professedly at issue between Russia and Turkey was the protection which should be extended to members of the Greek church residing within the Turkish domains. The sultan, strengthened by the secret support of France and England, refused to accede to the terms which Russia demanded, and the armies of Nicholas were put on the march for Constantinople. England and France dispatched their fleets for the protection of Turkey. In the campaign of Sevastopol, with which our readers are all familiar, Russia received a check which will, for a few years, retard her advances.

During the progress of the campaign of Sevastopol, the emperor Nicholas, in February, 1855, was suddenly seized with the influenza. The disease made rapid progress. He could not sleep at night, and an incessant cough racked his frame. On the 22d, notwithstanding the intense severity of the weather, he insisted upon reviewing some troops who were about to set out for the seat of war.

"Sire," said one of his physicians, "there is not a surgeon in the army who would permit a common soldier to leave the hospital in the state in which you are, for he would be sure that his patient would reënter it still worse."

"'Tis well, gentlemen," said the emperor, "you have done your duty, and I shall do mine."

Then wrapping his cloak about him, he entered his

sledge. It was a bleak winter's day. Pale, languid and coughing incessantly, he rode along the lines of his troops. He returned in a profuse perspiration, and was soon seized with a relapse, which was aggravated by the disastrous tidings he was receiving from Sevastopol. He rapidly failed, and the empress, anxious as to the result, suggested that he should receive the sacrament of the Lord's Supper.

"No!" the emperor replied. "I can not approach so solemn a mystery undressed and in bed. It will be better when I can do it in a suitable manner."

The empress, endeavoring to conceal her tears, commenced the repetition of the Lord's prayer, in a low tone of voice. As she uttered the words "Thy will be done on earth as it is in heaven," he fervently added, "For ever, for ever, for ever." Observing that his wife was in tears he inquired, "Why do you weep? Am I in danger?" She, afraid to utter the truth, said, "No." He added, "You are greatly agitated and fatigued. You must retire and take some rest."

A few hours after three o'clock in the morning, Dr. Mandt entered. "Tell me candidly," said the emperor, "what my disease is. You know I have always forewarned you to inform me in time if I fell seriously ill, in order that I might not neglect the duties of a Christian."

"I can not conceal from your majesty," the physician replied, "that the disease is becoming serious. The right lung is attacked."

"Do you mean to say that it is threatened with paralysis?" enquired the emperor. The doctor replied, "If the disease do not yield to our efforts, such may indeed be the result; but we do not yet observe it, and we still have some hope of seeing you restored."

"Ah," said the emperor, "I now comprehend my state and know what I have to do." Dismissing his physician he summoned his eldest son, Alexander, who was to succeed him upon the throne; calmly informed him that he deemed his condition hopeless and that the hour of death was approaching. "Say nothing," he continued, "to your mother which may alarm her fears; but send immediately for my confessor."

The archpriest Bajanof soon entered, and commenced the prayers which precede confession. The prayers being finished, the emperor crossed himself and said, "Lord Jesus, receive me into thy bosom." He then partook of the sacrament of the Lord's Supper with the empress and his son Alexander. The remaining members of the imperial family were then summoned into the chamber. He announced with firmness his approaching end, and gave to each his particular blessing. The empress, overwhelmed with anguish, cried out, "Oh, God! can I not die with him?"

"You must live for our children," said the emperor; and then turning to his son Alexander, he added, "You know that all my anxiety, all my efforts had for their object the good of Russia. My desire was to labor until I could leave you the empire thoroughly organized, protected from all danger from without, and completely tranquil and happy. But you see at what a time and under what circumstances I die. Such, however, seems to be the will of God. Your burden will be heavy."

Alexander, weeping, replied, "If I am destined to lose you, I have the certainty that in heaven you will pray to God for Russia and for us all. And you will ask His aid that I may be able to sustain the burden which He will have imposed upon me."

"Yes," the emperor replied, "I have always prayed for Russia and for you all. There also will I pray for you." Then speaking to the whole assembled group, he added, "Remain always, as hitherto, closely united in family love."

Several of the important officers of the State were then introduced. The emperor thanked them for their faithful services and tried devotion, and recommended them to his son as worthy of all trust, gave them his benediction and bade them farewell. At his request his domestic servants were then brought into the room. To one, who was especially devoted to the empress, he said,

"I fear that I have not sufficiently thanked you for the care which you took of the empress when she was last ill. Be to her for the future what you have been in my life-time, and salute my beautiful Peterhoff, the first time you go there with her."

These interviews being closed, he addressed his son and Count d'Adelberg respecting his obsequies. He selected the room in which his remains were to be laid out, and the spot for his tomb in the cathedral of the Apostles Peter and Paul. "Let my funeral," said he, "be conducted with the least possible expense or display, as all the resources of the empire are now needed for the prosecution of the war." While conversing, news came that dispatches had arrived from Sevastopol. The emperor deeming that he had already abdicated, declined perusing them, saying, "I have nothing more to do with earth." Alexander sat for several hours at the bed side, receiving the last directions of his father.

On the 2d of March the emperor remained upon his bed, unable to articulate a word, and with difficulty drawing each breath. At noon he revived a little and requested his son, in his name, to thank the garrison at Sevastopol for their heroism. He then sent a message to the King of Prussia, whose sister he had married. "Say to Frederic that I trust he will remain the same friend of Russia he has ever been, and that he will never forget the dying words of our father."

The agony of death was now upon him, and he was speechless. His confessor repeated the prayers for the dying. At twenty minutes past twelve he expired, holding, till the last moment, the hand of the empress and of his son Alexander.

Alexander II., who now occupies the throne, was born the 29th of April, 1818. He is a young man of noble character and very thoroughly educated. At the age of sixteen, according to the laws of the empire, he was declared to be of age and took the oath of allegiance to the throne. From that time he lived by his father's side in the cabinet and in the court. His fare was frugal, his bed hard, and his duties arduous in the extreme. In April, 1841, he married the princess Maria, daughter of the Grand Duke of Darmstadt. She is reported to be a lady of many accomplishments and of the most sincere and unaffected piety. He is himself a man of deep religious feeling, and many who know him, esteem him to be a sincere and spiritual Christian. What character the temptations of the throne may develop, time only can determine. He is now struggling, against the opposition of the nobles, to emancipate the boors from the slavery of serfdom, being ambitious of elevating all his subjects to the highest manhood. The temporal welfare of perhaps ninety millions of men is placed in the hands of this one monarch. An indiscreet act may plunge all Russia into the horrors of a civil war, or kindle flames of strife through Europe which no power but that of God can quench. The eyes of Europe are fixed upon him, and the friends of the Redeemer, the world over, watch his movements with solicitude and with prayer.

INDEX.

www.ingramcontent.com/pod-product-compliance
Lightning Source LLC
LaVergne TN
LVHW021308110826
845150LV00003B/514

* 9 7 8 1 4 2 5 5 5 9 2 9 8 *